Accountability, Transparency and Democracy in the Functioning of Bretton Woods Institutions

Elena Sciso
Editor

Accountability, Transparency and Democracy in the Functioning of Bretton Woods Institutions

G. Giappichelli Editore

Springer

Editor
Elena Sciso
LUISS Guido Carli University
Rome, Italy

ISBN 978-3-319-57854-5 ISBN 978-3-319-57855-2 (eBook)
DOI 10.1007/978-3-319-57855-2

Library of Congress Control Number: 2017944359

Printed on acid-free paper

This Springer imprint is published by Springer Nature
The registered company is Springer International Publishing AG
The registered company address is: Gewerbestrasse 11, 6330 Cham, Switzerland

Preface

This volume is inspired by the results of a research carried out in the context of a project of national interest financed by the Italian Ministry of Education, Universities and Research on the observance of the principle of democracy by international economic organizations. Our research team has focused on the Bretton Woods Institutions. The results of this research have been the subject of a broader discussion with academics and experts in the field.

As is well known, the International Monetary Fund and the World Bank are financial institutions that came into existence towards the end of the Second World War, in 1944, about 1 year before the San Francisco Conference signed the creation of a new global organization, the United Nations. They were pillars of that same institutional framework, which aimed to guarantee a new global order based on the restriction of the use of force in the relations between States and on the observance of the fundamental rights of human beings. Until now, these institutions have undergone no significant changes to their original structure as far as their internal governance is concerned nor to their decision-making mechanisms, which still basically reflect the balance and principles of the period when they were created. This is so, despite the fundamental changes that have occurred within the international community, both in quantitative and qualitative terms and, consequently, within its internal balances.

Suffice it to recall that the reform that was finally ratified by the United States' Senate in December 2015 has only entered into force in the last few months. This reform, by eliminating the category of nominated Executive Directors, aims to overcome the disparity that has existed all these years between some Executive Directors, directly nominated by the five countries that in 1944 were the main economic and financial powers (to whom must be added the three Executive Directors nominated by the States whose currency had been most used in the transactions of the Fund during the 2 years preceding the election of the Executive Board, and today these are Russia, China and South Africa), and the remaining Executive Directors who on the other hand represented, based on elections, all the other member countries united in constituencies. Due to this substantial inequality of position among the members, which was prone to significantly influence the decision-making process and the overall governance of the Organization and also to condition the effective capacity of a Member State to have access to the Fund's resources, the credibility and legitimacy of these institutions has increasingly diminished over the years. This perception exists both in the public opinion in various countries and among governments especially in countries that are playing an increasingly important role on the global economic stage (such as China, India and several other Asian countries). It is no coincidence that these countries have, in the last few years, launched initiatives to create new organisms, which are, in fact, alternatives for the Bretton Woods Institutions, such as the Asian development banks and Funds, ranging from the Chiang Mai Initiative to the BRICS Bank and the *Asian Infrastructure Investment Bank*, which presents itself, even statutorily, as the main institution for the financing of investments in a large number of developing countries.

In the end, the above-mentioned reform has been much less substantial than expected: the five "powerful" States of the system continue to have their Executive Directors in the Board, although now they are no longer nominated but elected.

However, considering the "natural" relationship that subsists in the field of international organizations between legitimacy and efficacy, due to the fact that the organizations necessarily operate on the basis of consensus and with the support of their Member States, this general perception of scarce legitimacy has significantly affected the institutions' interventions. This is especially so for interventions of the International Monetary Fund but also, albeit to a lesser degree, for those of the World Bank, and this perception has clearly contributed to the emergence of a real identity crisis of the two institutions. The lack of trust in the behaviour of the Fund and the Bank has been further eroded by the fact that their interventions are coupled with the requirement of a rigorous respect of certain economic conditions, which not always, and not necessarily, have adequately taken account of the short- and medium-term repercussions that these reforms and/or the imposed structural adjustments can have on the socio-economic fabric of the countries concerned.

In recent years, from the last decade of the past century onwards, the World Bank and the International Monetary Fund have attempted to respond to calls for more transparency and "democracy" from the governments of many Member States and from global public opinion. To this end, they have launched some internal reforms while also promoting the adoption of internal control mechanisms for the interventions that are implemented and/or financed (such as the *Inspection Panel* of the World Bank or the *Independent Evaluation Office* in the IMF). However, some doubts could be cast on their efficacy, especially with regard to the nature and outcome of the new procedures. They are, in fact, purely internal mechanisms, which can sometimes also be activated at the initiative of private parties, citizens of the countries that have an interest in the implementation of a project financed by the institution, as is the case for the *Inspection Panel* of the World Bank. Moreover, both the initiation and the outcomes of the procedure are still subject to the exclusive control of the Organization and in particular of its restricted organ, the

Executive Board. Therefore, despite the novelty and the originality of this mechanism, the *Inspection Panel* cannot be included among the international procedures for the protection of human rights, even though it tends to take on the task of reorienting the Bank's actions towards a substantial observance of the fundamental social and economic rights of the populations concerned.

With a view to coping with the new needs created by the financial crisis that started to mature in that period, in 2009 the IMF launched some new and more flexible instruments for the access to resources, which the Fund makes available by way of precaution for "virtuous" Member States, which find themselves in a phase *before* actually manifesting a trade deficit.

In order to meet the demands for greater openness of the system to countries that are less represented or, in other words, to respond to demands for a more democratic internal governance of the institutions, in that same period, a revision of the system of calculation and allocation of quotas was launched. This revision has led to a significant transfer of voting power from the Western countries, especially the European ones, to developing countries and emerging economies. Also the decision to include the Chinese national currency, the yuan, among the reserve currencies that constitute the basket of the *Special Drawing Rights* (SDR), operative from October 2016, should be considered in the same perspective.

Even though these various initiatives differ in nature, on the whole they are all designed to foster a more equitable internal representation of the Member States within the organization, together with a better distribution of the voting powers and of the right to access to resources and consequently to greater democracy in the decision-making processes. These reforms were accompanied by a tendency, starting from the last years of the past century, to progressively overcome the rigid respect of rigorous standards of financial policy—known as the *Washington Consensus*—imposed on the Member States who intended to obtain the support of the IMF or the World Bank. This new approach is highlighted by the latest version of the *Guidelines on Conditionality*, adopted in 2002 by the Executive Board of the IMF, and even more so by the inclusion of some criteria which are not strictly economic—such as environmental protection, safeguarding the rights of workers, respect of the rights of indigenous peoples and others—among the *procedures* and *operational directives*, which constitute, for the staff responsible for their control, binding statutory guidance for the approval and implementation of projects financed by the World Bank. On the other hand, it could be underlined that a rigorous conditionality seems to have been successfully "exported" and adopted within the European economic governance, characterizing the interventions by the Troika in support of the countries in crisis of the Eurozone, with sometimes destabilizing effects for the socio-economic fabric of these countries.

In this context, it may be useful to recall that among the objectives of the IMF, stipulated in Article 1 of the *Articles of Agreement*, is also the duty to contribute "... to the promotion and maintenance of high levels of employment and real income and to the development of the productive resources..." within the Member States as primary objectives of economic policy, offering the Members the opportunity to correct any possible imbalances in their balance of payments "... without resorting to measures disruptive of national prosperity...". On the other hand, among the objectives for which the World Bank was created is the assistance to Member States "... in raising productivity, the standard of living and the conditions of labour in their territories" (Article I of the Articles of Agreement).

From the same perspective, it should also be taken into account that the IMF and the World Bank have, since 1947, been specialized agencies of the United Nations, based on an agreement concluded with the UN Economic and Social Council. Therefore, even though they are not formally parties to the Universal Covenants agreed among States, the Fund and the Bank are *de facto* held to promote the respect of the fundamental economic and social rights of the people who are affected by their interventions, in conformity with the relevant provisions of the universal instruments which apply in the field of their activities. Article 18 of the International Covenant on Economic, Social and Cultural Rights stipulates that the UN Economic and Social Council can make arrangements with the specialized Agencies in view of the presentation by the latter of periodic reports on the progress achieved in observing the provisions of the Covenant that fall within the scope of their activity. Various technical organizations, such as the ILO, UNESCO, the FAO and the WHO, have made use of this possibility, but not the Bretton Woods Institutions.

In response to the criticism that is often voiced about their behaviour with regard to the points considered above, both the Fund and the Bank have always relied on their extraneousness as third parties with respect to the obligations of the Covenant, stressing the fact that especially the Fund uses resources from the Member States for its interventions and that the Organization has specific responsibilities towards these members when using the relevant funds.

These considerations cannot exempt either the organizations or the Member States from their international responsibility for possible violations of the provisions of the universal Covenant, generated by or resulting from the respect, imposed to the debtor States, of loan conditions that can prejudice the enjoyment of the fundamental economic and social rights of their peoples. Indeed, it should be considered that, based on general international law, States have the obligation to promote respect and universal observance of human rights and that this obligation is reiterated in Article 2 of the Covenant on Economic, Social and Cultural Rights. It is also a general principle, recognized by the Draft Articles on the Responsibility of International Organizations (Article 61) and supported by international jurisprudence (recently, *cf.* ICJ, *Application of the Interim Accord of 13 September 1995, The Former Yugoslav Republic of Macedonia v. Greece*, 5 December 2011), that a Member State of an international organization incurs international responsibility if it acts within the competent organization with respect to one of its obligations, thereby circumventing this obligation. On the other hand, the State that knowingly forces another State to commit an illicit act must be held internationally responsible for this act according to Article 18 of the Draft Articles on the International Responsibility of States.

In this specific field, those general principles have been explicitly confirmed several times, in more or less incisive terms, by the Committee on Economic, Social and Cultural Rights—the monitoring body of the relevant Covenant of 1966—in several Comments concerning the provisions of the Covenant (*cf.* in particular *General Comment No. 2: International technical assistance measures* (Art. 22 of the Covenant), Fourth Session (1990), and *General Comment No. 19: The right to social security* (Art. 9 of the Covenant), Thirty-Ninth Session (2008)). Also some domestic courts of last instance, such as the Portuguese Constitutional Court in a judgement of 2013, and more recently the EU Court of Justice itself in a judgment of September 20th 2016 have considered whether the measures aiming at rebalancing public finances—that the international economic institutions, and in particular the so-called Troika, have imposed on the Eurozone countries in crisis—are coherent and proportional according to constitutionally guaranteed principles and rights as well as with reference to the basic principles of law recognized in Articles 2 and 6 of the EU Treaty, such as the respect for fundamental human rights.

Therefore, also based on these last considerations, it is doubtful whether the achievement of a higher degree of "internal" democracy within the Bretton Woods Institutions through the adjustments and reforms that were recently launched, based on a more equitable representation of the Member States and on a more balanced participation in the organization's governance, will automatically lead to greater "external" transparency and democracy of the interventions of these organizations. In particular, it is questionable whether it will lead to an appropriate respect of the obligations of transparency, information and control that characterize a democratic society, especially when the institutional context and the government policies of the Member State concerned do not reflect such characteristics.

Seventy years after their adoption, the statutory objectives of the Bretton Woods Institutions—to foster prosperity and to increase the level of income and occupation within the Member State in the context of a global market that is open to the free play of the economic factors—need to be reconsidered, in the light of new principles of international economic law, among which the principle of sustainable development has gained particular importance.

When implementing their interventions, the IMF and the WB should also be aware of the fact that the GDP is no longer universally recognized as the one and only indicator of countries' economic development. Other factors must be taken into account, such as the population's degree of alphabetization, environmental protection, the level of safeguarding public health, the respect of the rule of law, the fight against corruption and the presence of a "democratic" institutional fabric that may achieve good governance and respect of fundamental rights; all these elements contribute to providing a credible measure of the degree of well-being of a society.

The substantial failure of the traditional recipe of economic-financial rigour in the approach towards the Greek crisis, in which after 6 years no positive outcome can possibly be foreseen, with dramatic consequences for the population, provides the latest evidence of how economic development or economic reform cannot be pursued while at the same time sacrificing social development and equity.

Without indulging in ideal propositions, such as the one included in some international documents according to which happiness is a fundamental human objective, it cannot be ignored that, both with regard to an individual country and in a global perspective, the aim of achieving effective and stable economic growth in the medium to long term cannot be credibly pursued with only economic-financial instruments whose benefits are rather doubtful. Rather, a holistic approach is required, which puts the fundamental element of each society, even the universal one, at its centre: man and his needs.

This is the path that the Bretton Woods Institutions should take in order to regain their credibility and to give their activities renewed drive and direction.

This volume is part of a collection edited by Centro di Ricerca sulle Organizzazioni Internazionali ed Europee (Research Centre on International and European Organizations) of the LUISS Guido Carli University, under the responsibility of Professor Elena Sciso.

All contributions for the volume were delivered in October 2016.

Rome, Italy
October 2016

Elena Sciso

Contents

Contributors

M. Rodwan Abouharb University College London, London, UK

Pia Acconci University of Teramo, Teramo, Italy

Alessandro Aresu Italian Ministry of Economy and Finance, Rome, Italy

Foreign Affairs and International Cooperation, Rome, Italy

Antonio Bassanetti International Monetary Fund, Washington, DC, USA

Bank of Italy, Rome, Italy

David L. Cingranelli Department of Political Science, Binghamton University, Binghamton, NY, USA

Gianludovico de Martino Italian Interministerial Committee for Human Rights, Rome, Italy

Giuseppe Di Taranto Luiss Guido Carli University, Rome, Italy

Monica Frassoni European Green Party, Bruxelles, Belgium

European Center for Electoral Support (ECES), Bruxelles, Belgium

Alessandro Gili International Economic Law, Research Centre on International and European Organizations, Luiss Guido Carli University, Rome, Italy

Agostina Latino University of Camerino, Camerino, Italy

Dennis Leech Warwick University, Coventry, UK

London School of Economics, London, UK

Giada Lepore St. Thomas University School of Law, Miami, FL, USA

Alberto Monteverdi UBI Banca, Brescia, Italy

Giuseppe Parigi International Relations and Economics Directorate, Bank of Italy, Rome, Italy

Francesco Paternò International Financial Institutions Division, International Relations Directorate, Bank of Italy, Rome, Italy

Giulio Peroni State University of Milan, Milan, Italy

Elena Sciso Research Centre on International and European Organizations, Luiss Guido Carli University, Rome, Italy

Dimitri Van den Meerssche European University Institute (EUI), Fiesole, Italy

Maartje Van Putten Global Accountability BV Amsterdam, Member Panel Independent Complaints Mechanism, Dutch Development Bank FMO, Amsterdam, Netherlands

World Bank's Inspection Panel, Washington, DC, USA

Part I
The Governance and the Reforms in Progress

Transparency and Democracy in the Governance of the International Monetary Fund and Reforms in Progress: A Voting Power Analysis

Dennis Leech

Abstract The weighted voting system used by the International Monetary Fund in its board of governors and executive creates problems of democratic legitimacy because each member's influence over decisions taken by vote, that is its voting power, is not in general in proportion to its voting weight, that is, the number of votes it casts. This paper uses voting power analysis to analyse the distribution of voting power in the Board of Governors, showing that the voting rules enhance the voting power of the United States substantially at the expense of all other members. That is, the voting power of the United States is relatively much greater than its nominal voting power (its voting weight). Separate analyses are done for 2006 (before reform), 2008 (after increases to some emerging countries' quotas), 2016 (current situation) and the 2010 proposals. I find that the effects, apart from the large increase in the voting power of China, are somewhat disappointingly small. There is no analysis of the implications of the radical reforms of the Executive Board because the changes have not been introduced at the time of writing.

Contents

In November 2010 the Executive Board of the International Monetary Fund agreed a package of radical proposals to overhaul the governance of the organization aimed at strengthening its legitimacy and effectiveness. Managing Director Dominique

D. Leech (✉)
University of Warwick, Coventry, UK
e-mail: D.Leech@warwick.ac.uk

E. Sciso (ed.), *Accountability, Transparency and Democracy in the Functioning of Bretton Woods Institutions*, DOI 10.1007/978-3-319-57855-2_1

Strauss-Kahn welcomed it, saying: "This historic agreement is the most fundamental governance overhaul in the Fund's 65-year history and the biggest ever shift of influence in favor of emerging market and developing countries to recognize their growing role in the global economy." In this paper I investigate how far this ambitious claim can be substantiated, using the methodology of voting power analysis.

1 The Reforms

The reforms[1] consist of three elements:

1. increasing the financial resources available for dealing with crises by doubling the quotas contributed by all the member countries, known as the 14th General Review of Quotas, increasing quotas to approximately SDR 476.8 billion (about US$755.7 billion at current exchange rates);
2. making the voting system fairer by a major realignment of quota shares among members to reflect the changes that have taken place in the relative economic importance of countries, specifically a shift of more than 6% of quota shares to dynamic emerging market and developing countries, and more than 6% from over-represented to under-represented countries, while protecting the quota shares and voting power of the poorest members;
3. changing the composition of the Executive board to make it more representative and all-elected.

Mr. Strauss-Kahn said these changes "will enhance the credibility and effectiveness of the Fund's ongoing efforts towards greater global financial stability."[2] The first of the three elements obviously does that and requires little further comment, since it deals with ensuring that the IMF has the necessary fire-power in the form of monetary resources needed to deal with crises. But it is not immediately clear that the other two elements will do so; they are about governance, which is my concern here.

The process of improving the governance of the IMF has been slowly ongoing since the need for reform was accepted by all countries as part of the Monterrey Consensus agreed in 2002 and reiterated in Doha in 2008, after which interim changes to the distribution of quotas, hence voting power, among members, was agreed. But the full implementation of the agreed changes has depended on approval from the US Congress which was only granted in December 2015, following which the required amendments to the Articles were able to be agreed by the Executive Board in January 2016.

Central to the governance of the IMF is weighted voting, used in both its governing bodies: the Board of Governors and the Executive Board. All member countries have a voice in the Board of Governors but cast different numbers of votes

[1]IMF (2010).
[2]IMF (2010).

depending on their quotas. How many votes each country can cast is determined by a formula that gives it a number of so-called basic votes, the same for each country, plus a number proportional to its quota.[3] The membership of the Executive Board is restricted to 24 directors who are elected to represent the members; decisions are taken, and members elected, by weighted voting. Weighted voting in the IMF is somewhat problematic because it has resulted in a democratic imbalance with the distribution of voting power being massively biased against the developing and poor countries. This voting dominance by the industrialized countries has often been criticised by the developing countries as leading the organization to adopt policies that have taken insufficient notice of the concerns of those countries, especially the imposition of conditions on borrowers derived from the neo-liberal economics of the Washington Consensus.[4] On the other hand it has always been defended by spokesmen for the rich countries on the grounds that, as a general principle, the providers of capital are entitled to decide how it is used. However a consensus on the need to change distribution of voting power has been a major impulse for reform.

Changes that were agreed—aimed at giving greater voice to poor countries and emerging economies—are as follows. Quota changes which will mean four emerging market countries (Brazil, China, India, and Russia) will now be among the ten largest members of the IMF. (The other top 10 members include the United States, Japan, and the four largest European countries: France, Germany, Italy, and the United Kingdom). At the same time the quota shares and nominal voting powers of the IMF's poorest member countries will be protected.

The far reaching changes to the structure of the Executive Board mean that, for the first time, it will consist entirely of elected directors, ending the practice whereby the countries with the five largest quotas appointed their own directors while the rest were elected through a system of constituencies. There is to be further scope for appointing a second Alternate Executive Director in multi-country constituencies with seven or more members in order to enhance the constituency's representation in the Executive Board. This is specifically intended to benefit the two African constituencies in particular. Advanced European countries have committed to reduce their combined Board representation by two directors.

One major part of the reforms is the simplification of the formula by which quotas are in principle allocated.[5] Table 1 shows the byzantine system which formally this has been. It has been described as 'fiendishly complex', involving five different formulae and an algorithm for determining which formula would actually be used to give the answer. There is no need to discuss this further here, merely to note the minimal transparency in this formal stage in the process of allocating quotas before considering the even less transparent political negotiations. This has been replaced by a much simpler and much more transparent formula described in Table 2.

[3]One vote for every 100,000 special drawing rights of quota. Each country's quota is its financial stake in the IMF and meant to reflect its importance in the world economy.

[4]See eg. Buira (2003), Woods (2006).

[5]I say 'in principle' because the actual allocation has not, in the past, been simply a matter of automatically applying the official formula but rather a political matter involving negotiation.

2 Real and Apparent Voting Power

Besides this inequality in the voting arrangements that results from the use of weighted voting—inequality that has historically been intended as part of the design of a political institution on the principle that those who contribute most should have the most say—there exists a *further* source of inequality that is not at all transparent. The voting rules are designed to lead to inequality in power and influence but the design does not lead to the intended degree of inequality because of unintended, effects inherent in weighted voting itself. It is this that is the focus of the study reported in this paper.

The idea of using weighted voting is that each country's voting power should be set out in the rules of the organization to be proportional to its voting weight. However, a member's voting *power* is not the same as its *weight*: its *power* is its ability to be decisive whenever a vote is taken—in other words to make a difference to the outcome by voting one way rather than another—whereas its *weight* is just the number of votes it has been allocated. This distinction is a mathematical feature of weighted voting rules and it can only be revealed by detailed analysis that looks at outcomes, using the method of voting power indices. There is no general formula linking voting power to voting weight. Because the distinction between voting weight and voting power is often ignored in practice, designing constitutions that use weighted voting often leads to undesired and/or unexpected consequences.

Countries' voting weights are very unequal: the USA has more than two-and-a-half times as many votes as the country with the next-largest voting weight, Japan. That raises the interesting question of whether the influence over voting outcomes of the two countries are in the same or a different ratio. We use power indices to measure each member's voting power in order to address this. The USA turns out to have much more voting power than weight. This disproportionality is another argument for reforming the weights in a more radical direction than hitherto. More generally the lack of a direct link between power and weight adds to the case for decoupling the allocation of votes from both the provision of and access to finance.

Defenders of the present voting system claim it embodies democratic accountability if one accepts the principle that voting rights should be attached to the supply of capital. For example, when he was Managing Director Horst Köhler said: "I would also like to underline that still we are a financial institution, and a financial institution means you need also to have someone who provides capital and I think there is a healthy element in the fact that the provision of capital and voting rights is, in a way, combined, because this is also an element of efficiency, of accountability."[6] The distorting effect of weighted voting that we describe below makes this claim far from being true.

The method of voting power analysis requires us to analyse all the voting outcomes that can occur, and investigate the ability of every member to be decisive,

[6]House of Commons Treasury Select Committee, 4th July 2002.

in other words to be able to change the decision by changing the way it casts its vote. We will compute voting power indices to compare the powers of different members.

Our principal finding is that the voting power of the USA is far greater than its voting weight. That is, its *actual* power over decision-making far exceeds its *nominal* voting power. We also use the method for three important analyses: first the effect of the *ad hoc* increase in voting weight that occurred in 2008 for four emerging economies (China, Korea, Mexico and Turkey) that were previously badly unrepresented; second the more radical reforms agreed in 2010; third the actual voting weights as of 2016 after the reforms had begun to be implemented.

We begin with an outline of the principles of voting power analysis in the next section. Then in Sect. 3 the system of governance of the IMF is described, in Sects. 4 and 5 we present the analyses of the Board of Governors and the Executive.

3 Weighted Voting and Voting Power Analysis

A country's voting power is its potential to be decisive in a decision taken by vote, measured by the probability with which it can change what would otherwise be a losing vote to a winning one. In general this has a rather imprecise relation with its weight. In reality its power depends on all the other members' weights as well as the voting rule by which decisions are taken. A case that shows the issue starkly is that of the European Economic Community which also employed weighted voting in the council of ministers: the distribution of voting power among the six members was far from proportional to voting weight between 1958 and 1972. See Leech and Leech (2005b) for the details.

The approach is technically referred to as that of *a priori* voting power: each member's power index is its decisiveness as a fraction of the theoretically possible outcomes without regard for the likelihood of their occurring. The method can be thought of as an analysis of the implications for power of the voting rules, considered in the abstract, as giving what can be called constitutional power.[7] Probability theory is used as a tool for calculating the power indices. Technically the probability of a voter being decisive is the Penrose index (also known equivalently by various names including the Penrose measure, Penrose-Banzhaf index, absolute Banzhaf index). This is a measure of the a priori probability of the voter being decisive and is the simplest index for the purpose. Other power indices exist and could be used, but we take the view that the superiority of the Penrose-Banzhaf index is established on both theoretical and empirical grounds.[8] Since my purpose is

---

[7] No consideration is given here for the members' preferences, which would determine the likelihood of particular members voting in the same way as each other, which would produce an analysis of empirical voting power.

[8] See Felsenthal and Machover (1998), Leech (2002b) for a comparison with the other so-called 'classical' power indices.

to investigate changes in relative voting power among the member countries, I use the normalized version of the index, generally known as the Banzhaf index (or normalised Banzhaf index), that has the property that the indices for all the voters sum to one hundred percent, and therefore it provides a distribution of voting power. We will refer to values of this index as voting powers.[9]

4 Weighted Voting in the IMF Governors

All countries are members of the Board of Governors, and as such have direct representation at the highest level of formal decision-making, but the real day-to-day management is done by the Executive Directors (also known as the Executive Board).

In the Board of Governors and in the election of Executive Directors the voting weight of each country is made up of two components: a fixed component of so-called 'basic' votes which is the same for each country, and a variable component that depends on the country's quota. This formula for determining voting weight is intended as a compromise between two principles: the equal representation of member countries (via the basic votes), analogous to the UN General Assembly, and voting power based on contributions in the manner of a joint stock company. Over time the basic element had become severely eroded and the quota-based votes have become dominant. This is an important factor behind the disempowerment of the poor countries. The reforms provide for an immediate tripling of the basic votes and then maintaining them at the same level in relative terms thereafter.

There are currently 189 members, of whom the USA has[10] by far the largest voting weight, with 831,402 votes, 16.58% of the total, and the smallest is Nauro with 1480 votes, 0.03%. The second-highest voting weight is held by Japan with 6.17%, Germany 5.34%, France and UK with 4.05% each and so on.

A variety of decision rules are used for different types of decisions. Ordinary decisions are made by simple majority (50% of the votes cast plus one; the quorum for meetings of the Board of Governors being a majority of members having not less than two-thirds of the voting weight; that for the Executive Board being a majority of directors having not less than one-half of the total voting weight). A number of matters require decisions to be taken by a supermajority of at least 85%. This supermajority, taken in conjunction with the weight of the USA, means that the USA is the only member that possesses a veto, and that will continue under the reforms.

The American veto has always been an important feature built into the design of the governance of the Fund, the Articles having been amended to increase the supermajority threshold for special decisions from 80 to 85% in 1978 when the

[9]The indices are computed using an algorithm described in Leech (2003) and available to use via the internet on website Leech and Leech (n.d.) as software package *ipmmle*.
[10]In June 2016.

USA decided to reduce its quota. The existence of this veto power does not mean that the USA can be said to *control* the institution, however. Although it confers unilateral blocking power, at the same time it also limits that country's power because it equally ensures a collective veto for small or large groups of other countries. Any proposal by the United States can be blocked: in the terminology proposed by Coleman, while the 85% rule gives the United States complete *power to prevent action*, it also limits that country's *power to initiate action* (Coleman 1971). Therefore its voting power, which combines power to initiate and to prevent action, is limited so its power index is less than 100%. Because of this the 85% rule tends to equalize voting power. The use of a supermajority decision rule therefore tends to undermine the specific advantages of weighted voting. Taking the argument to its absolute limit, a unanimity rule would give every member a veto and equalise the power distribution. For these reasons the power analysis in this study considers only ordinary decisions that require a simple majority vote. Analysis of power in the IMF with supermajorities (before the reforms) was reported in Leech (2002a).

5 Impact of the Reforms on Voting Power Distribution

Table 3 shows four analyses which reveal the weighted voting effect and give a picture of the effects of the quota reforms:

1. for 2006 before the reforms;
2. for 2008 after the *ad hoc* adjustments to the quotas of four emerging economies, China, Korea, Mexico and Turkey, that were seriously out of line;
3. for 2016, after the partial implementation[11] of the reforms agreed in 2010; and
4. for the full implementation of the 2010 reforms.

The table shows, for each of the main countries, (1) its relative voting weight and (2) its normalized power index or vote share,[12] in each of the years. Significant changes in weights in the reforms are highlighted in bold. The table also shows the Gini coefficient of inequality over all member countries for both the voting weights and the voting power indices. Inequality is very high in 2006 and the reforms reduce it by very little. Inequality in voting power is slightly higher than it is for weight.

The table shows that the voting power of the United States is considerably out of line with its weight. In 2006 its voting weight of just over 17% gave it 24.49% of the voting power. Its weight went down slightly in 2008 and again in 2012 but it was still massively dominant giving it much greater voting power. All other members have less

[11]Quotas change when countries make the payments, which not all have done at the time of writing.

[12]These power indices have been calculated using the computer program *ipmmle* (accessible online at www.warwick.ac.uk/~ecaae) which implements the algorithm for computing power indices for voting bodies that are large both in having many members and where the voting weights are large numbers, described in Leech (2003). For an overview of computing power indices see Leech (2002b).

power than their weight. Thus we can say that the weighted voting system has a hidden tendency to enhance the power of the USA at the expense of all other countries.

The 2006 table also brings out a number of glaring anomalies pointing to the need for reform. Canada and China had the same number of votes, and voting power, despite the economy of China being much bigger than that of Canada. This bias against developing countries is seen, also, in the comparison of the voting weight of some rich countries like Belgium, Netherlands and Spain with large emerging economies especially India, Brazil and Mexico. A particularly glaring juxtaposition is that between Denmark and Korea,[13] the former having more voting weight than the latter despite its economy being much smaller than the latter.

The reforms have been in two stages: first the *ad hoc* increases for China, Korea, Mexico and Turkey implemented in 2008, then the changes resulting from the more radical reforms implemented in 2016. These were: (1) the introduction of a more transparent, simpler formula to replace the previous complicated fivefold system; (2) tying the quotas more closely to the formula; (3) tripling of basic votes for all members; (4) a second round of *ad hoc* increases for the four countries mentioned above. This second round was accompanied by an increase in general quotas. The main changes in relative voting weights were increases for China, Korea, India, Brazil, Mexico and some others at the expense of the USA, some European countries notably the UK and France, Saudi Arabia and Canada. None of the changes was greater than one percent of the total voting weight, so perhaps it is not surprising that the voting power effects are very small.

The effects are all small. They provide little support to the claim of the then IMF Managing Director, Dominique Strauss-Kahn that, "Taken together, it's a big shift in quotas and accordingly in voting power. It's a very important increase in the voice and representation of the emerging market and developing countries . . . it is a historical reform of the IMF."[14]

6 Gainers and Losers of Voting Power

Table 4 shows the biggest changes in voting power indices. China is the biggest gainer, increasing its share of voting power very substantially from 2.69 to 5.51%. No other country enjoys an increase in its power share of as much as 1%. The next largest gainer is Korea going from 0.7% in 2006 to 1.61 in 2016, then Brazil, India, Mexico, all emerging markets, with increases above 0.5%, followed by Spain. The biggest losers are USA and Saudi Arabia, losing more than one percent of voting power each. Then a group of industrial countries all suffer a relatively large loss of voting power, of more than 0.5%: UK, France, Belgium, Canada and Netherlands.

[13]Both are too small to be shown in the table which only shows the top 25 countries.

[14]Press Release: "IMF Board Approves Far-Reaching Governance Reforms", 5 November 2010, IMF Washington.

These changes are all moves in the right direction but only that for China could really be called radical, the others seeming to be more gradual. However it is interesting that although China has enjoyed a big increase in its voting power, that does not fully reflect its additional voting weight: its voting weight increased by 3.17% while its voting power increased by 2.83%.

7 Conclusions

I have used the method of voting power analysis and power indices to analyse the voting system by which the IMF is governed and the recent reforms that have been made to it or are in progress. I argue, and hopefully have demonstrated, that this approach provides valuable insights that help us better understand weighted voting systems.

My analysis has been confined to the distribution of voting power in the Board of Governors, where all member countries have a voice. It has not been possible to make an analysis of the Executive Board because the changes in it are structural and qualitative in nature, not just quantitative changes to the quotas and voting weights. An analysis of the distribution of voting power of members of the Executive Board requires much more information regarding the way in which members of the board are elected than we have because the move to an all-elected board in November 2016 will result in a fundamental reallocation of countries to constituencies and we cannot predict the voting weights controlled by the board members.

The principal finding is that the United States share of voting power is always substantially much more than its weight, while for all other members, their voting power shares are slightly lower than their weights. This is a pattern characteristic of many voting bodies where there is one dominant, though non-majority, member. Not only is the allocation of voting weight very unfair from the point of view of an ideal of "One person, One vote", with many large developing countries and emerging markets seriously under-represented, but this bias is compounded by the inequality in the distribution of weights and the voting rules.

The biggest gainer from the reforms is China, which gains a very large share of voting power. Other emerging markets, including Korea, Brazil, India and Mexico, also gain, but the effects are incremental rather than radical and relatively small: all are less than 1% of total voting power. These increases are mainly at the expense of the United States and Saudi Arabia, which suffer substantial falls of over 1%, and also some of the industrial countries including the UK, France, Canada, Belgium and the Netherlands. None of these effects are very great, which suggests that the reforms do not live up to some of the claims that have been made for them.

These results point to a serious limitation in the transparency and democratic legitimacy of the governance of the institution. And claims that the recent quota reforms are a major step towards improving the voice and representation of the poor countries and emerging economies are over statements.

Appendix

Table 1 The existing five quota formulae

Bretton Woods: $Q_1 = (0.01Y + 0.025R + 0.05P + 0.2276VC)\ (1 + C/Y)$;
Scheme III: $Q_2 = (0.0065Y + 0.0205125R + 0.078P + 0.4052VC)\ (1 + C/Y)$;
Scheme IV: $Q_3 = (0.0045Y + 0.03896768R + 0.07P + 0.76976VC)\ (1 + C/Y)$;
Scheme M4: $Q_4 = 0.005Y + 0.042280464R + 0.044\ (P + C) + 0.8352VC$;
Scheme M7: $Q_5 = 0.0045Y + 0.05281008R + 0.039\ (P + C) + 1.0432VC$;
where:
Q1, Q2, Q3, Q4, and Q5 = Calculated quotas for each formula;
Y = GDP at current market prices for a recent year;
R = 12-month average of gold, foreign exchange reserves, SDR holdings, and reserve positions in the IMF, for a recent year;
P = annual average of current payments (goods, services, income, and private transfers) for a recent 5-year period;
C = annual average of current receipts (goods, services, income, and private transfers) for a recent 5-year period; and
VC = variability of current receipts, defined as one standard deviation from the centered 5-year moving average, for a recent 13-year period.
For each of the four non-Bretton Woods formulas, quota calculations are multiplied by an adjustment factor so that the sum of the calculations across members equals that derived from the Bretton Woods formula. The calculated quota of a member is the higher of the Bretton Woods calculation and the average of the lowest two of the remaining four calculations (after adjustment).

Source: Quotas—updated calculations and data adjustments prepared by the finance department in consultation with the statistics and other departments, IMF, July 11, 2007

Table 2 The new quota formula

The proposed new quota formula includes four quota variables (GDP, openness, variability and reserves), expressed in shares of global totals, with the variables assigned weights totaling to 1.0. The formula also includes a compression factor that reduces dispersion in calculated quota shares.
The proposed new formula is:
$CQS = (0.5{*}Y + 0.3{*}O + 0.15{*}V + 0.05{*}R)^k$
Where CQS = calculated quota share;
Y = a blend of GDP converted at market rates and PPP exchange rates averaged over a 3 year period. The weights of market-based and PPP GDP are 0.60 and 0.40, respectively;
O = the annual average of the sum of current payments and current receipts (goods, services, income, and transfers) for a 5 year period;
V = variability of current receipts and net capital flows (measured as a standard deviation from the centered 3-year trend over a 13 year period);
R = 12 month average over a year of official reserves (foreign exchange, SDR holdings, reserve position in the Fund, and monetary gold); and k = a compression factor of 0.95. The compression factor is applied to the uncompressed calculated quota shares which are then rescaled to sum to 100.

Source: Reform of Quota and Voice in the International Monetary Fund—Report of the Executive Board to the Board of Governors, IMF, March 28, 2008

Table 3 Voting weights and voting powers in the Board of Governors (largest quota countries)

2006 (181 countries)			2008 (185 countries)			2016 (189 countries)			2010 Proposals (188 countries)		
	Weight	Power		Weight	Power		Weight	Power		Weight	Power
USA	17.09	24.49	USA	16.77	23.80	USA	16.58	23.39	USA	16.47	23.27
Japan	6.13	5.46	Japan	6.02	5.41	Japan	6.17	5.56	Japan	6.14	5.54
Germany	5.99	5.35	Germany	5.88	5.30	China	6.11	5.51	China	6.07	5.49
France	4.95	4.48	France	4.86	4.42	Germany	5.34	4.87	Germany	5.31	4.85
UK	4.95	4.48	UK	4.86	4.42	France	4.05	3.72	France	4.02	3.70
Italy	3.25	2.97	China	3.66	3.35	UK	4.05	3.72	UK	4.02	3.70
Saudi	3.22	2.94	Italy	3.19	2.93	Italy	3.03	2.79	Italy	3.02	2.78
China	2.94	2.69	Saudi	3.16	2.90	India	2.64	2.43	India	2.63	2.43
Canada	2.94	2.69	Canada	2.89	2.65	Russia	2.6	2.40	Russia	2.59	2.39
Russia	2.74	2.50	Russia	2.69	2.47	Brazil	2.23	2.06	Brazil	2.22	2.05
Nether.	2.38	2.18	Nether.	2.34	2.15	Canada	2.23	2.06	Canada	2.21	2.05
Belgium	2.13	1.95	Belgium	2.09	1.92	Saudi Ar.	2.02	1.86	Saudi	2.01	1.86
India	1.92	1.76	India	1.89	1.74	Spain	1.93	1.78	Spain	1.92	1.77
Switz.	1.60	1.46	Switz.	1.57	1.45	Mexico	1.81	1.67	Mexico	1.80	1.66
Australia	1.50	1.37	Australia	1.47	1.35	Nether	1.77	1.63	Nether.	1.76	1.63
Spain	1.41	1.29	Mexico	1.43	1.32	Korea	1.74	1.61	Korea	1.73	1.60
Brazil	1.41	1.29	Spain	1.39	1.28	Australia	1.34	1.24	Australia	1.33	1.23
Venezuela	1.23	1.13	Brazil	1.38	1.27	Belgium	1.31	1.21	Belgium	1.30	1.20
Mexico	1.20	1.10	Korea	1.33	1.23	Switz.	1.18	1.09	Switz.	1.17	1.09
Sweden	1.11	1.02	Venezuela	1.21	1.11	Indonesia	0.96	0.89	Turkey	0.95	0.88
Argentina	0.98	0.90	Sweden	1.09	1.01	Turkey	0.96	0.89	Indonesia	0.95	0.88
Indonesia	0.97	0.89	Argentina	0.97	0.89	Sweden	0.91	0.84	Sweden	0.91	0.84
Austria	0.87	0.80	Indonesia	0.95	0.87	Poland	0.85	0.78	Poland	0.84	0.78
S. Africa	0.87	0.80	Austria	0.86	0.79	Austria	0.81	0.75	Austria	0.81	0.75

(continued)

Table 3 (continued)

2006 (181 countries)			2008 (185 countries)			2016 (189 countries)			2010 Proposals (188 countries)		
	Weight	Power		Weight	Power		Weight	Power		Weight	Power
Nigeria	0.82	0.75	S. Africa	0.85	0.79	Singapore	0.81	0.75	Singapore	0.80	0.74
…	…	…	…	…	…	…	…	…	…	…	…
Total	100.00	100.00	Total	100.00	100.00	Total	100.00	100.00	Total	100	100
Gini	0.7780	0.7958	Gini	0.7819	0.7990	Gini	0.7665	0.7841	Gini	0.7729	0.7898

All power indices percentages. Power indices have been calculated using the program ipmmle available on the website www.warwick.ac.uk/~ecaae
Source: Author's elaboration

Table 4 Biggest gainers and losers in voting power in Board of Governors

Gainers				Losers			
	VP2016	VP2006	Change		VP2016	VP2006	Change
China	5.51	2.69	2.83	USA	23.39	24.49	−1.1
Korea	1.61	0.70	0.91	Saudi Arab	1.86	2.94	−1.1
Brazil	2.06	1.29	0.77	UK	3.72	4.48	−0.76
India	2.43	1.76	0.68	France	3.72	4.48	−0.76
Mexico	1.67	1.10	0.57	Belgium	1.21	1.95	−0.74
Spain	1.78	1.29	0.49	Canada	2.06	2.69	−0.63
Turkey	0.89	0.41	0.47	Netherlands	1.63	2.18	−0.54
Singapore	0.75	0.38	0.37	Argentina	0.42	0.90	−0.48
...	...	...	...	...	...	...	...

VP voting power. All figures percentages
Source: Author's elaboration

References

Buira A (2002) A New Voting Structure for the IMF, Washington: G24, www.g24.org/

Buira A (ed) (2003) Challenges to the World Bank and IMF: developing country perspectives. Anthem Press, London

Buira A (ed) (2005) The IMF and World Bank at sixty. Anthem Press, London

Buira A (ed) (2006) Reforming the Governance of the IMF and the World Bank. Anthem Press, London

Coleman JS (1971) Control of collectivities and the power of a collectivity to act. In: Lieberman B (ed) Social choice. Gordon and Breach, Amsterdam, pp 269–300

Felsenthal DS, Machover M (1998) The measurement of voting power. Edward Elgar, Cheltenham

IMF (2010) Press Release No. 10/418, November 5, 2010

IMF (2013) Quota Formula–Data update and further considerations, IMF Policy Paper

Leech D (2002a) Voting power in the governance of the IMF. Ann Oper Res 109:373–395

Leech D (2002b) An empirical comparison of the performance of classical power indices. Polit Stud 50(1):1–22

Leech D Computing power indices for large voting games. Manage Sci 2003, 49(6):831–838

Leech D (2013) A new analysis of a priori voting power in the IMF: recent quota reforms give little cause for celebration. In: Holler MJ, Nurmi H (eds) Power, voting, and voting power: 30 years after. Springer, Berlin, pp 389–410

Leech D, Leech R (n.d.) Website: "Computer Algorithms for Voting Power Indices". www.warwcik.ac.uk/~ecaae/

Leech D (2005a) Voting power implications of a Unified European representation at the International Monetary Fund. Warwick Economic Research Papers, Number 720, January 2005

Leech D (2005b) Voting power in the Bretton Woods Institutions. Homo Oeconomicus 22(4):1–23

Van Houtven L (2002) Governance of the IMF: decision making, institutional oversight, transparency and accountability. IMF Pamphlet Series No. 53. IMF, Washington

Woods N (2001) Making the IMF and the World Bank more accountable. Int Aff 77(1):83–100

Woods N (2006) The globalisers: the IMF, the World Bank and their borrowers, Cornell Studies in Money. Cornell University Press, New York

The Evolution of the International Monetary Fund in Response to the Global Financial Crisis

Giuseppe Parigi and Francesco Paternò

Abstract This short essay analyses the evolution of three key aspects of the International Monetary Fund in response to the Global Financial Crisis: (a) the adequacy of its own resources; (b) the shift of representation towards emerging and developing countries; (c) the review of the lending instruments. With respect to each of these topics, we describe the main policy choices which have characterised the past few years and provide our own assessment about them. Our main policy recommendations attain to: (a) the opportunity of preserving the overall size of the Global Financial Safety Net and in particular the role of the IMF; (b) the opportunity of dealing with the legitimacy problem arising from the strong underrepresentation of China at the IMF; (c) the opportunity of a very careful scrutiny for any new lending instrument.

Contents

1 Introduction

At the end of 2007 the use of the International Monetary Fund (IMF) credit allocated through the General Resource Account recorded an extremely low value, equal to just six billion Special Drawing Rights (SDR; equivalent to about

---

The views expressed in this study are those of the authors and do not involve the responsibility of the Bank of Italy. The authors would like to thank Marco Committeri for his comments. The authors are responsible for any error. This study was finalised on 21 September 2016.

G. Parigi • F. Paternò (✉)
Bank of Italy, Rome, Italy
e-mail: Giuseppe.Parigi@bancaditalia.it; francesco.paterno@bancaditalia.it

E. Sciso (ed.), *Accountability, Transparency and Democracy in the Functioning of Bretton Woods Institutions*, DOI 10.1007/978-3-319-57855-2_2

nine billion US dollars). This was the result of the successful repayments by Korea, Indonesia, Thailand and Russia of the loans made by the IMF to deal with the Asian Financial Crisis and the Russian crisis at the end of the nineties. It was also the consequence of a prolonged period of financial and macroeconomic stability. The decline of the IMF's outstanding loans and the strong accumulation of foreign exchange reserves, mainly by the Asian emerging and the oil-exporting countries, signalled a progressive loss of relevance of the IMF, which in the middle of the past decade started a downsizing process aimed at reducing its operational costs.

In September 2008 the Global Financial Crisis (GFC) changed dramatically this scenario. Two months later, amid a severe systemic crisis, with rapidly deteriorating economic conditions worldwide, the Leaders of the Group of Twenty (G20) met in Washington DC and agreed to "*stress the International Monetary Fund's (IMF) important role in crisis response, welcome its new short-term liquidity facility, and urge the ongoing review of its instruments and facilities to ensure flexibility*". In the action plan attached to the final declaration of the meeting, an entire section was devoted to the reforms of the International Financial Institutions (IFIs), with a few key recommendations such as: (a) "*We should review the adequacy of the resources of the IMF, the World Bank Group and other multilateral development banks and stand ready to increase them where necessary. The IFIs should also continue to review and adapt their lending instruments to adequately meet their members' need and revise their lending role in the light of the ongoing financial crisis*"; (b) "*We underscored that the Bretton Woods Institutions must be comprehensively reformed so that they can more adequately reflect changing economic weights in the world economy and be more responsive to future challenges. Emerging and developing economies should have a greater voice and representation in these institutions*".

These recommendations singled out three key issues:

(a) the adequacy of Fund's resources;
(b) the shift of representation within the Fund, towards the emerging and developing economies;
(c) the review of the lending instruments of the Fund.

Since then, the three issues have been largely debated; some key decisions—mainly the introduction of the Flexible Credit Line and the Precautionary and Liquidity Line, the 2010 Reforms, the 2012 Borrowing Agreements—have been taken; others, such as the XV General Review of Quotas (GRQ), are under discussion.

In this short essay we illustrate some of the policy choices which have been made and the open issues which are still debated; in so doing, we present our view about the achievement of the objectives defined in the G20 meeting of November 2008.

2 The Adequacy of Fund's Resources and the Role of Quotas

Once the systemic nature of the GFC was fully perceived, it was clear that the lending capacity of the Fund had to be enhanced. Three different sets of measures were adopted.

(1) In April 2009 the International Monetary and Financial Committee (IMFC), following an agreement reached by the G20 countries, decided to increase substantially the resources available to the IMF through the New Arrangements to Borrow (NAB) which in April 2010 were expanded to SDR 367.5 billion (IMF 2015a).
(2) In December 2010 the Board of Governors of the Fund approved a package of reforms (the so called 2010 Reforms), including the XIV GRQ featuring a doubling of IMF quotas (from SDR 238.5 billion to 477 billion) and a shift of quota shares towards emerging markets and developing economies (see Sect. 3 below).
(3) In April 2012 the IMFC and the G20 jointly called for further enhancement of the IMF resources through temporary bilateral loans and note purchase agreements; total pledges by 38 members amounted to about US$ 461 billion (IMF 2015a).

While (1) and (3) became effective in March 2011 and in the autumn of 2012,[1] respectively, (2) was completed only in January 2016, because of the delayed ratification by the US Congress of the 2010 Reforms. This sequence of events largely increased the overall amount of IMF's resources, assigning an unprecedented weight to their temporary components. This was partly reverted only in January 2016, when, following the entry into effect of the XIV GRQ, the NAB was rolled-back to about SDR 182 billion.

The size of the overall IMF resources is very important because it determines the positioning of the IMF in the Global Financial Safety Net (GFSN). Indeed, before the financial crisis the main components of the GFSN were the foreign reserves at country level and the IMF's overall (permanent and temporary) resources. After the crisis, new key components came to the fore, such as the Regional Financing Arrangements (RFAs) and the central bank swap lines (Fig. 1).

The development of a wide network of central bank swap lines is not expected to affect the role of the IMF as they are not a substitute for IMF lending to fill balance of payments needs; indeed, swap lines are mainly used by central banks, consistently with mandates typically focussed on domestic monetary and financial stability, to provide foreign currency liquidity to their domestic banking system. On the

[1]More precisely, in the last quarter of 2012, bilateral loan agreements for a total amount equivalent to about SDR 153 billion were signed by Italy, Japan, Saudi Arabia, Germany, Norway, Denmark, China, the Netherlands. Other 27 agreements were signed in 2013, 2014 and 2016 for a total amount equivalent to about SDR 130 billion.

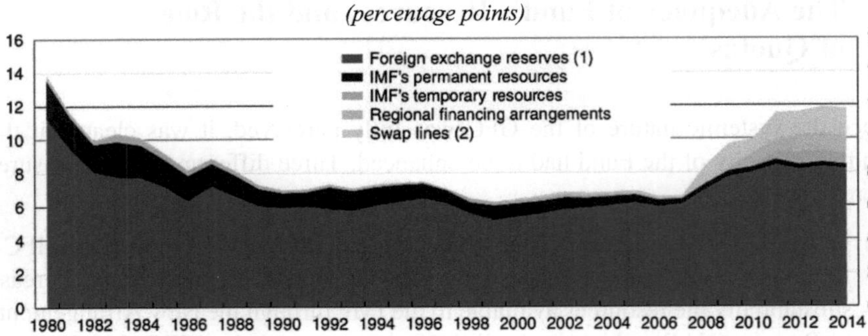

Fig. 1 Global financial safety net as percentage of international financial liabilities. *Source*: E. Denbee, C. Jung and F. Paternò, 'Stitching together the global financial safety net', Banca d'Italia, Questioni di Economia e Finanza (Occasional Papers), 322, 2016. (1) Does not include gold reserves. (2) The value of the resources provided through swap lines between central banks is estimated by (a) assigning the maximum value reached during the activation periods to the swap lines activated in the past, and (b) assigning an average of the values (in relation to GDP) assigned to the activated swap lines to those that have never been activated

contrary, the RFA could limit the role of the IMF in case of regional crises. However, in presence of a more systemic crisis, the RFA resources may quickly reveal to be insufficient. Indeed, there are at least two reasons justifying the simultaneous use of both IMF and RFA resources. First, in presence of a large shock RFA may not lead to the implementation of very large lending programmes, especially if callable capital plays a large role in the funding mechanism of the RFA. Second, the IMF has a know-how advantage in the design of adjustment programmes with respect to RFAs.

Because of these reasons, some of the most relevant RFAs make explicit the opportunity of a link with the IMF. In particular, the *Chiang Mai Initiative Multilateralization* (CMIM)[2] requires an IMF programme, and the conditionality which comes with that, whenever a country asks for a loan exceeding 30% of the country's total access. In the case of the *European Stability Mechanism* (ESM), the rules are less rigid, but the involvement of the IMF is still largely expected. Indeed, the ESM Treaty stipulates that "*The ESM will cooperate very closely with the IMF in providing stability support. The active participation of the IMF will be sought, both at technical and financial level. A euro area member state requesting financial*

[2]The CMIM is multilateral currency swap arrangement aimed to provide regional short term liquidity, to address balance of payments difficulties and supplementing existing international arrangements. Member countries are: Brunei, Cambodia, Hong Kong, Indonesia, Japan, Laos, Malaysia, Myanmar, the People's Republic of China, Philippines, Singapore, South Korea, Thailand, Vietnam. It is usually classified among the RFAs, not among the central bank bilateral swap arrangements.

assistance from the ESM is expected to address, whenever possible, a similar request to the IMF" (whereas nr. 8).[3]

The awareness of a carefully designed cooperation between the IMF and the RFAs is well documented by the debate at the G20 level, which in October 2011 led to the endorsement by Finance Ministers and Central Bank Governors of the G20 Principles for Cooperation between the IMF and the RFAs. These principles acknowledge that "*cooperation between RFAs and the IMF would be a step forward towards crisis prevention, more effective crisis resolution and would reduce moral hazard.*" However, their operational content is much limited. The G20 International Financial Architecture Working Group report, endorsed by Finance Ministers and Central Bank Governors in July 2016, deals with this problem by asking for more effective cooperation between the IMF and the RFAs and supporting explicitly a better exchange of information and experience.

In our view, the operational content of the G20 principles should go well beyond the exchange of information and experience and its enhancement should be a key objective to be pursued in the coming years. Given the need of taking into account the specific mandate and governance of each RFA, an ambitious target could be a set of differentiated agreements regulating the relationship between each RFA and the IMF and defining the key aspects of the framework of any potential joint programme aimed at supporting a country hit by a crisis.

Denbee et al. (2016) analyse how the resources of the IMF and the RFAs could be jointly used to deal with systemic crises. Resorting to a calibrated simulation exercise, they show that in response to a systemic sudden stop crisis affecting all emerging market economies (EME): (a) the overall (permanent and temporary) resources of the IMF coupled with the FX reserves and the support of the RFAs appear to be adequate; (b) RFAs are likely to play a minor role, also because their membership is limited to a subset of countries.

The composition of IMF's resources impacts on its governance (Woods 2010). In particular, a large share of quotas enhances the independence of the Fund potentially reducing the influence of member countries on its lending policy. Indeed, this is strongest when temporary resources are predominant (as long as their activation is subject to the approval of the creditor countries). This was made transparent by the US Congress, which in the law that ratified the 2010 Reforms introduced new requirements for the activation of the NAB, claiming specifically that the US Secretary of the Treasury is requested to document that: (a) "*the one year forward commitment capacity of the IMF (excluding borrowed resources) is expected to fall below SDR 100 billion during the period of the NAB activation*" and the (b) "*activation of the NAB is in the United States strategic economic interest*".

The main points briefly discussed in this section suggest that in the current environment a well-equipped GFSN is crucial for the correct functioning of the

[3]Balassone and Committeri (2015) argue that the interpretation of how binding is the request of an active financial involvement of the Fund is not fully clear; a renegotiation of the Treaty may be necessary to make clear this point.

world economy; in particular, the IMF resources, a sort of central core of the GFSN, should be kept unchanged in the medium term, either by a further substantial increase of quotas in the context of the XV GRQ or by maintaining the current level of temporary resources (i. e. NAB and bilateral loans). In the first case, the IMF independence would certainly be enhanced, which is in principle a positive result, even if it is still to be proved that this may effectively enhance the Fund's ability to achieve its objectives. However, some observers (Rajan 2005) have argued that this should be accompanied by a change of the governance aimed at increasing the independence of the Executive Board members, as well as at defining more rigorously the rules governing the Fund's policy decisions.

3 The Legitimacy Problem of the Fund and the Quota Shares

While the overall amount of quotas determines the positioning of the Fund in the context of the GFSN, the distribution of quota shares refers to the allocation of the decision power among countries. With the entry into force of the XIV GRQ the emerging and developing countries (EMDCs) saw their quota increase to 42.6%; that of the advanced economies declined correspondingly to 57.4%.

It is worth observing that a number of IMF's decisions require special majorities of 70% (to resolve financial and operational issues such as the rate of charge on the use of the IMF's resources and the rate of interest on SDR holdings) or 85% (for the admission of a new members, the increase in quotas, the allocation of SDR, and the amendments to the Articles of Agreement) of the total voting power. Given this voting structure, the United States, with a quota share of 17.4%, retains a veto power for all the most important decisions.[4]

The request for a shift of quota shares towards the EMDCs is motivated not only by the strong growth recorded by these economies in the past decades, but also by the Asian policymakers' frustration against the IMF at the time of the Asian Financial Crisis, carefully described by Ito (2007, 2012). Indeed, the deep disagreement between the Fund and the Asian policymakers in the selection of the most appropriate strategies to deal with that crisis was attributed to the predominance of advanced economies in the decision process at the IMF.

Even after the entry into force of the XIV GRQ many EMDCs still perceive as unfair the quota shares allocation and this originates a legitimacy problem for the IMF. Eichengreen and Woods (2016) argue that the Fund's legitimacy should be

[4]The share of voting power does not coincide perfectly with the quota share because of the presence of basic votes, which are the same for all members. The voting power of any country results from the sum of basic votes plus one additional vote for each 100,000 SDR in quotas. Basic votes, therefore, help strengthening the relative voting power of those members with the smallest quotas (IMF 2015a).

based on the input legitimacy, that is the legitimacy of the decision making process and the way the power is exercised. They also claim that "*a governance reform that gives appropriate voice and weight in decision making to all members is critical for enhancing the legitimacy and effectiveness of the institution.*"

The highly critical issue is how to calculate the "appropriate weight" of each country, an issue which is largely devoted to the procedure to compute the level of each country's quota share (the so called "quota formula"). According to the 2008 review of the quota formula, four principles should drive the design of the formula. More specifically, it should:

1. be simple and transparent;
2. be consistent with the multiple roles of quotas;
3. result in calculated quota shares that are broadly acceptable to the membership;
4. be based on timely, high quality, and widely available data.

Unfortunately, the number of quota formulas which satisfy these (very loose) four principles is very large, as witnessed by the several quota formulas proposed by the IMF staff in the past few years (IMF 2016a, 2015b, 2014a, 2013).

Without describing the results of the huge number of simulations which have been discussed in the past few years, we prefer to concentrate on: (a) the main features of the current quota formula adopted in 2008 and used in the context of the XIV GRQ; (b) the shift of quota shares from advanced to emerging market economies; (c) the reasons why a large number of countries ask for a revision of the quota formula.

The current quota formula is described by the following equation:

$$CQS = (0.50{*}GDPBlend + 0.30{*}Openness + 0.15{*}Variability + 0.05{*}Reserves)^{0.95}$$

where *CQS* is the calculated quota share, *GDPBlend* is a weighted average over the last 3 years of GDP at market (60%) and at purchasing power parity (40%) exchange rates; *Openness* of a country is the annual average of the sum of its current payments and current receipts (goods, services, income and transfers) over the last 5 years; *Variability* is the variability of current receipts and net capital flows (measured as standard deviation from the centered 3-year moving average over a recent 13-year period); *Reserves* is the 12-months average over a recent period of official reserves; and 0.95 is the so called "compression factor" (IMF 2015a).

This quota formula clearly assigns a higher quota share to the largest and more open economies (the compression factor is applied to mitigate this effect). As it includes the stock of official reserves, it plays largely against the countries issuing the main reserve currencies, which generally hold a comparatively small amount of official reserves.

According to this formula and the more updated information (up to 2014), the quota share of the EMDCs should be 49.3% (Fig. 2), well above the official quota share resulting from the XIV General Review of Quotas (42.4%). The difference between the two numbers may be considered as a sort of under-representation of the

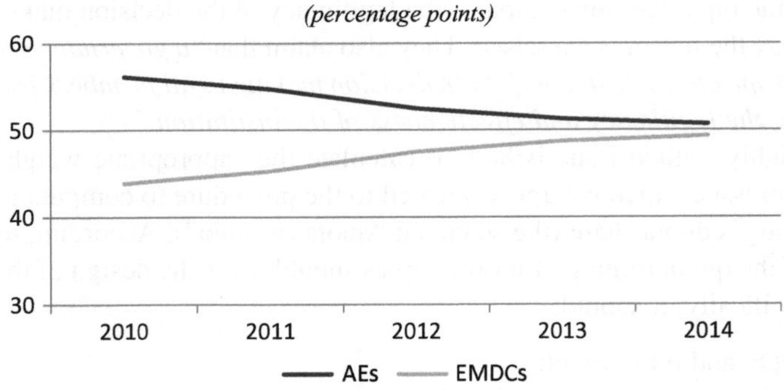

Fig. 2 Calculated quota share based on the current quota formula (1). *Source*: Authors' elaboration on IMF. (1) The year reported on the x-axis refers to the last year of the database used to compute the calculated quota share. For example, 2014 is the last year included in the most recent database, which was released by the Fund in August 2016

EMDCs as a group or the shift of quota shares from the advanced economies implied by the current quota formula. At a more granular exam, it emerges that only 63 of the EMDCs are underrepresented, while 100 of them are over-represented. The main country in the first group is China, whose calculated quota share is almost double the official one (12.0% against 6.4).

Note that the US calculated quota share is 14.3, below the level which allows them a veto power and this helps understand their strong support for a change of the quota formula. EMDCs also call for an increase of the weight assigned to *GDPBlend* and, above all, of the one assigned to GDP at purchasing power parity exchange rates because in this case the EMDCs share of World GDP is the highest, about 60%.

It is quite difficult at this stage to envisage a possible final outcome of the XV GRQ, which, according to the Board of Governors of the IMF, should be completed by the 2017 Annual Meetings of the IMF. A crucial point is to reduce the under-representation of China, which probably represents one of the main sources of the legitimacy problem of the Fund. This outcome could be achieved through an *ad hoc* allocation of quotas to China and a few other underrepresented countries,[5] without touching the veto power of the United States (this means that the overall amount of quota increases due to the *ad hoc* allocations should not exceed 10%).

[5] *Ad hoc* quota allocations, by allocating quota increases only to a small set of countries, may result into significant shift into quota shares even in a context where the overall increase of quotas is limited. By contrast, general review of quotas, which usually allocate most of the quota increases to all members in accordance with the quota formula, may result into a smaller shift in quota shares unless the overall increase of quotas is very large.

4 The Review of the Lending Instruments of the Fund

The review of the lending instruments of the Fund advocated by the G20 Leaders in November 2008 gave rise mainly to the introduction in 2009 of two precautionary instruments: the Flexible Credit Line (FCL) and the Precautionary and Liquidity Line (PLL).[6]

The FCL was designed to provide large upfront financing to countries with very strong fundamentals and policies; its main novel features are: (a) the introduction of a qualification framework, based on nine well defined criteria[7]; (b) the lack of any *ex-post* conditionality; (c) the lack of any access cap.

The PLL was thought to be a precautionary instruments useful to address the financial needs of countries with sound fundamentals and policies but which do not achieve the requirements of the FCL. The essential components of its design include: (a) a qualification framework based on five areas, with a strong performance in at least three of them[8]; (b) a focused *ex-post* conditionality based on six-monthly reviews; (c) an access cap, which in the case of PLL arrangements of 1–2 years equals 500% of the country quota upon approval and a cumulative limit of 1000% of the quota (IMF 2015a).

The setting up of lending instruments which could provide very large amounts of liquidity to countries with "very strong" or at least "sound" fundamentals can be interpreted as an answer to this Asian call. In effects, the FCL and PLL aim at providing a financing tool without the strong conditional requirements which characterize the traditional lending programs of the Fund. This largely responded to the perception by Asian policymakers that the Asian crisis was largely a liquidity crisis rather than a solvency one with fundamental structural problems (Ito 2007).

Since their inception, the Fund's experience with the FCL and the PLL has been marked by three features: (a) a very limited use (only Mexico, Poland and Colombia have so far requested (and have been assigned) a FCL); (b) a remarkably high amount of resources allocated to the FCL (at the end of August 2016, the IMF resources committed to these arrangements amounted to about SDR 83 billion); (c) a prolonged period of assignment (e.g., Mexico was originally assigned an FCL in April 2009 and since then the arrangement has been systematically renewed).

[6]More precisely, in 2009 the IMF created the Precautionary Credit Line (PCL) which evolved into the Precautionary and Liquidity Line (PLL) 2 years later. The main difference between the current PLL and the former PCL is that the PLL allows members with actual balance of payments needs to request an arrangement.

[7]The nine criteria are: a sustainable external position; a capital account position dominated by private flows; a track record of steady sovereign access to international capital markets at favourable terms; a good reserve position when the arrangement is requested on a precautionary basis; sound public finance, including a sustainable public debt position determined by a rigorous and systemic debt sustainability analysis; low and stable inflation; absence of bank solvency problems; effective financial sector supervision; data transparency and integrity (IMF 2014c).

[8]The five qualification areas are: external position and market access; fiscal policy; monetary policy; financial sector soundness and supervision; data adequacy.

An interpretation which is frequently proposed for the much limited use of precautionary instruments is the so called "stigma problem" deriving mainly from the political cost associated with negative perceptions about past experience with the IMF (Ito 2012). The most frequent interpretation about the repeated request by a few user countries of extension of FCL arrangement (the so called "exit problem") is that the loss of this highly relevant source of liquidity could potentially convey to the market a signal of weakness. If these interpretations are correct, this would reveal a flaw in the design of the precautionary facilities which calls for a review of them.

IMF is fully aware of the existence of potential flaws in the design of the FCL and PLL and is striving to elaborate proposals aimed to correct them. As far as the "stigma problem" is concerned, IMF (2014b) considered the hypothesis of prequalification, which essentially implies that the IMF takes care of periodically defining the countries satisfying the requirements of FCL or PLL. In this case, the need of a formal request would obviously be eliminated, thus reducing the stigma problem. However, the management of the information related to any prequalification mechanism is potentially very tricky. Should the prequalification list be made public to the market? Could any change of the list give rise to a disruptive market event?

As far as the "exit problem" is concerned, the Executive Board approved in July 2014 a proposal aimed to introduce and operationalize the use of an *external stress index*. This index, whose methodology was only sketched by the Fund (2014c),[9] could make the exit of a country easier, as a persistent decline of the index, as long as it is judged credible by the market, would convey the message that the country which had been assigned an FCL (PLL) not only maintains very strong (sound) fundamentals and policies but it is also less exposed to the risk of becoming an innocent crisis bystander.[10]

The precautionary lending tools may be an effective instrument to contain the systemic risk, especially for those countries which may perceive insufficient the coverage offered by the GFSN.[11] However, a much wider use of precautionary facilities should be framed in the more general analysis of systemic risk scenarios in two ways: first, by verifying that the assignment of the facilities does contribute to reduce the risk; second, by carefully considering the impact of a wider use of precautionary facilities on the forward commitment capacity of the Fund.

---

[9]The Fund (2014c) pointed to the employment of a structural Bayesian vector autoregression (BVAR) estimation to calculate the weights in the computation of the external stress index of a set of external variables which would signal the risk of balance of payments crisis. The external variables taken into account would be country-specific (e.g. exports to the United States and FDI from the United States in the case of Mexico).

[10]Recently, the IMF (2016b) made use of the external economic stress index in the process which led to the approval of a 2-year FCL for Mexico. The main message conveyed by this index was that external conditions could deteriorate rapidly if some risks (e.g. an U.S. growth rate 1.5 percentage points lower than projected) materialize. Furthermore, the comparison of the projections of the external economic stress index formulated in November 2014 with those formulated in April 2016 highlighted an increase of the vulnerability to external shocks.

[11]It is telling that the main user of FCL is Mexico, a medium-size economy which is not part of any large RFA.

5 Conclusions

The main points which we have tried to develop in this short essay may be summarized as follows.

First, after the last GFC, the ensuing crises and the sluggish recovery we are still experiencing at global level it appears to be of paramount importance to preserve the overall size of the Global Financial Safety Net and in particular the role of the IMF. This requires to maintain the overall size of the lending capacity of the Fund, either by keeping unchanged the current level of temporary resources or by achieving a substantial increase of quotas in the context of the XV General Review of Quotas. This point could be further analysed—once a sufficient experience would be accumulated on the effectiveness of the new financial regulation framework designed in the recent years and on the implementation of new macroprudential policy tools and capital flow management measures.

Second, the legitimacy problem can no longer be ignored. The under-representation of China, and other large emerging countries, should be significantly reduced. The difficulties of approving a change of the way quota shares are computed should not be used to delay this problem, as *ad hoc* allocation of quotas could help to achieve this target. The refinement of some existing financing tools process could play a complementary role to deal with the legitimacy problem of the Fund.

In our view, these policy recommendations are consistent with the achievement of the objectives defined in the G20 meeting of November 2008.

References

Balassone F, Committeri M (2015) Europe and the IMF: nec sine te, nec tecum ..., LUISS Guido Carli School of European Political Economy Working Paper 6/2015

Denbee E, Jung C, Paternò F (2016) Stitching together the global financial safety net, Banca d'Italia Occasional Paper No. 322

Eichengreen B, Woods N (2016) The IMF's unmet challenges. J Econ Perspect 30(1):29–52

IMF (2013) Quota formula - data update and further considerations. IMF, Washington

IMF (2014a) Quota formula – Data update and further considerations

IMF (2014b) Review of the Flexible credit line, the Precautionary and Liquidity Line, and the Rapid financing Instrument

IMF (2014c) Review of the Flexible credit line, the Precautionary and Liquidity Line, and the Rapid financing Instruments–Specific proposals

IMF (2015a) IMF Financial operations

IMF (2015b) Quota formula – Data update

IMF (2016a) Quotas–Data update and simulations

IMF (2016b) Mexico. Arrangements under the flexible credit line and cancellation of current arrangement – Press release and staff report

Ito T (2007) Asian currency crisis and the IMF, 10 years later. Asian Econ Policy Rev 2:16–49

Ito T (2012) Can Asia overcome the IMF stigma. Am Econ Rev 102(3):198–202

Rajan R (2005) Rules versus Discretion. Should the IMF have less of a free hand in resolving crises? Financ Dev 42(1):56–57

Woods N (2010) Global governance after the financial crisis: a new multilateralism or the last gasp of the great powers? Glob Policy 1(1):51–63

China and The IMF: A Troubled Relationship

Alessandro Gili

Abstract China is trying to find its place in the International Monetary System. In the last years there was an assumption that the Chinese development model could replace the traditional prescriptions of Washington Consensus and find followers in the emerging markets. The reality seems to be different: the China model is unique and it is hard to be replied abroad. Beijing is taking an active role in many regional financial institutions and mechanisms, such as in the Chiang Mai Initiative Multilateralization, but these efforts could not be necessarily inconsistent with the global framework provided by the IMF. The greater weight given to China in the IMF through the recent reforms and the inclusion of the renminbi in the SDR basket will probably inaugurate a new path of relationship between IMF and China, giving the country the role of a "responsible stakeholder" in the management of the world economy.

Contents

1 Introduction

The relationship between China and the main financial institutions has a troubled history. Since 1978, when the reforms of Deng Xiaoping wrote a new era in China's economic path, many progresses have been made. The main question arising nowadays from the involvement of China in international financial institutions is related to the role that Beijing is willing to pursue: a responsible actor struggling to

A. Gili (✉)
Research Centre on International and European Organizations, Luiss Guido Carli University, Rome, Italy
e-mail: croie@luiss.it

E. Sciso (ed.), *Accountability, Transparency and Democracy in the Functioning of Bretton Woods Institutions*, DOI 10.1007/978-3-319-57855-2_3

integrate itself in the existing framework or a main promoter of a different economic order, with the aim to rebalance and shift the global power from advanced western economies to the emerging ones?

Last year closed with important steps towards a comprehensive overhaul of International Monetary Fund's framework. The recent approval by US Congress in December 2015 of the governance reform will lead to a new pattern of relations within the IMF, through a significant rebalancing of voting powers in accordance with the current economic power of member States. In November, a second important step was taken in order to allow an enhanced representation of China inside the Fund: the inclusion of renminbi in the Special Drawing Rights (SDR) basket and, consequently, in the elite of world currencies. This last decision has largely been interpreted as a symbolic acknowledgment of yuan's relevance in the world economy. For the first time in the history of contemporary monetary system the renminbi has been recognized as a safe and liquid international asset, where foreign governments can park their wealth. Even though this interpretation is largely understandable, the way the decision was taken and the political and economic outcomes require a further analysis.

This paper, starting from the evaluation of the Beijing Consensus as a possible alternative model to the better known Washington Consensus, tries to identify the main elements that can lead to a judgement over the role of China in the main financial institutions and particularly in the IMF, evaluating also some regional arrangements such as the Chiang Mai Initiative Multilateralization which holds strong and interesting linkages with the financial framework provided by the International Monetary Fund.

2 The *Beijing Consensus*: A Successful Model?

The definition of "Beijing Consensus" originated through the work of Joshua Cooper Ramo, who in 2004 published an outstanding essay named "The Beijing Consensus: notes on the new physics of Chinese power".[1] The Beijing Consensus could be seen as an acknowledgment of China's success in the world economy and as a challenge to the traditional economic pattern linked to the Washington Consensus. Particularly, China refused the universal "one-size-fits-all" approach to development based on imitation of international best practises. There are five main elements that highlight the differences between the economic path pursued by China and the traditional prescriptions of Washington Consensus.[2]

- Incremental reform. Beijing is carrying on a program of vast reforms which are tested locally before being adopted nationwide.

[1] See Ramo Joshua (2004).

[2] Williamson (2012), pp. 6–7. See also Beeson and Iyanatul (2005).

- Innovation and experimentation. China claims the success of an economic model based on innovation-led development: the rise of overall productivity through innovation is one of the main reasons to explain the sustainability of Chinese growth and a useful tool to curb the huge internal imbalances.
- Export-led growth. China maintains a large current-account surplus as a primary vehicle of economic growth.
- State Capitalism. China has embraced the so called "socialism with Chinese characteristics". Even though Beijing has never formally abandoned the socialist doctrine, nowadays there are no longer any claims of central planning by government. Many companies remain State-owned enterprises (SOEs), but in the country new private-owned enterprises are finding their place. During the last global financial crisis (2008–2009) Beijing adopted an impressive plan of fiscal stimulus in order to overcome the world recession, reaffirming an enhanced role of the State in the economy.[3]
- Authoritarianism. This form of political pressure is supposed to have allowed higher growth rates, avoiding disturbances and demand of social rights.

Ramo adds two other central points. According to him, Beijing intends to carry on a sustainable and balanced growth, where the equitable distribution of wealth through policies has a central role. Furthermore, the Beijing Consensus would create a new core of emerging economies that refuse the liberal prescriptions of Washington Consensus and recognize to China a leading role in the elaboration and implementation of a new set of policies. These last two points are really controversial and not fully shareable. Indeed, China has taken some steps towards environment protection but the technical environment requirements for Chinese companies are far lower than the ones in the western countries. Concerning the second point, some evidences prove that Beijing complied with eight of ten main elements required by the Washington Consensus: China has been rigorous in terms of fiscal discipline and has maintained a competitive exchange rate, liberalizing trade and foreign direct investments. Increasing progresses have been made on four other points: spending review, tax compliance, easing barriers to market entry and strengthening property rights.[4]

In the last decades China has fostered growth and encouraged investment by suppressing wages, tolerating environment pollution and keeping the interest rates on loans artificially low; the central government has boosted exports by maintaining a weak currency. The main consequence is the huge current account surplus, where other countries have to run deficits. In recent years, China has become aware that the only choice relies on a new economic model because western economies are no longer able to import as much as before the global financial crisis, due to fiscal constraints and the need to reduce the high debt-to-GDP ratio; furthermore, an investment-driven growth is no more efficient, as witnessed by the housing bubble

---

[3]See Barboza (2008).

[4]Kennedy (2010), pp. 468–470.

which is bursting in many regions of China.[5] Prime Minister Wen Jiabao himself recognized that there were structural problems linked with the *China Model*, which caused "unsteady, unbalanced, uncoordinated and unsustainable growth".[6] Accordingly, the 12th 5 Year Plan pursued towards a transition from state-led investments to a more consumption-based economy. The World Bank in a working paper stressed the importance to orient the strategic direction of China's development towards these main issues:

- Completing the transition to a market economy
- Creating a positive environment for open innovation
- Turn the environmental troubles into green growth as a driver for development
- Modernizing and strengthening the domestic fiscal system
- Linking China's structural reforms to the challenging international economy.[7]

China's model of development is surely influenced by political factors and by the need for the ruling Chinese communist party to maintain a firmly control over the country. Since the government lacks legitimacy in the classic democratic sense, it tried to achieve an economic-based legitimacy instead, by steadily improving the living conditions of Chinese people. Nevertheless, China's astronomic growth in the past has left it in a precarious situation and the government tries to tackle popular uprisings and economic imbalances through "pain relievers", in order to lower regional disparities, to improve infrastructures, health care and education in rural areas and to contain the demand for higher wages.[8]

The China model and the Beijing Consensus are therefore going through hard times. The currency is experiencing an instable period, that triggered a capital flight towards safer markets. The sum of private and government debt raised from 160% of GDP in 2008 to 240% in 2016: this debt-to-GDP ratio is sustainable only if China will meet the growth forecasts—an average of 6.5% annually—for the next years. The problem is not only an economic one. The government and the communist party seem not to be capable to systematically tackle the imbalances and the challenges affecting China in the last years: in particular they are uncertain how to proceed in the complex reforms of the financial system, the currency policy and the management of state-owned enterprises. The Beijing Consensus and the China Model need a deep overhaul. The President Xi Jinping, during a meeting with the Central Committee, stressed the importance of market forces to be given a decisive role in the economy; therefore, structural reforms rather than huge state-led investment are the new path to ensure a sustainable growth for China, the so-called "China Model 2.0 Edition".[9]

---

[5]Peerenboom and Bugaric (2013), p. 6.

[6]Premier Wen Jiabao's Press Conference of 2007/03/17, Ministry of Foreign Affairs of the People's Republic of China, www.fmprc.gov.cn/enh/zxxx/t304313.htm.

[7]World Bank (2012), p. 11, available at: http://www.worldbank.org/en/news/2012/02/27/china-2030-executive-summary.

[8]Yang (2010).

[9]The Economist (2016a).

The Beijing Consensus is losing its leverage. Even though the Chinese development experience has some singular characteristics, they are not easy to be spread or replied abroad, because they are inherently correlated to China's distinctive political order. According to Edward Steinfeld, "China today is growing not by writing its own rules, but instead internationalizing the rules of the advanced industrial West."[10] The Beijing Consensus is ultimately a way to combine internal features with the unavoidable integration with the international financial system, without any claims to become a universal template for other developing countries.[11]

3 The Chiang Mai Initiative Multilateralization: The Seed of an Emerging Asian Monetary Fund

The Chiang Mai Initiative was established in 2000 by ASEAN+3 finance ministers, with the purpose to create a safety net of bilateral swap agreements and a liquidity facility within a financial framework of regional cooperation.[12] The members requiring financial assistance obtained the 10% of the needed liquidity immediately, whereas the remaining 90% should have paid off in accordance and within a program supervised by the IMF or through an emergency credit line. The linking between the grant of the liquidity and IMF conditionality has been seen as fundamental in order to ensure that such swap arrangements were not independent from IMF assistance and to guarantee the loan repayment and the fulfilment of the requested structural reforms. By the end of 2003, 2 years after the establishment of CMI, twelve bilateral swap agreements had been concluded, for an overall value of 39 billion dollars.[13] In 2005 the global amount increased sharply up to 90 billion dollars and the loan's share not subjected to IMF conditionality grew to 20% of the total loan.[14] In the Summit of Tokyo in 2007, the finance ministers reached an agreement to convert the bilateral scheme into a multilateral self-managed reserve pooling arrangement governed by a single contractual agreement (*Chiang Mai Initiative Multilateralization*).[15] Two years later, the twelfth Summit of ASEAN +3 in Bali triggered to important developments, identifying the shares of each member country, the loans requirements and an independent regional surveillance mechanism. The CMIM should have been able to meet two fundamental goals: tackling liquidity crises in the short-term and support the existing international agreements regarding financial cooperation.[16]

[10]Steinfeld (2010), p. 18.

[11]See Beeson and Li (2015), pp. 103–105.

[12]See ASEAN+3 (2000), par. 6.

[13]Kuroda and Kawai (2004), pp. 145–146.

[14]See ASEAN+3 (2005), par. 6 (IV).

[15]See ASEAN+3 (2007), parr. 6–7.

[16]See ASEAN+3 (2009), parr. 7–9.

In 2010 the Summit in Tashkent reached an agreement on the main AMRO's features: the surveillance mechanism would have been activated from 2011 with headquarter in Singapore, helping to promptly detect the major regional economic risks and the correlated corrective policies. The total size of CMIM's crisis resolution facility was decided to be around 120 billion dollars, with a contribution coming from China, Japan and South Korea of 80% and a remaining 20% from ASEAN countries. China and Japan have nowadays a share of 32% each, and the South Korea in a position of kingmaker with a share of 16%. China, Japan and South Korea represent the 72% of voting rights in CMIM, with representativeness concerns for the remaining ASEAN countries. The final agreement made the voting rights reliant on some quantitative elements, such as GDP at current prices, foreign reserves, and net contribution to CMIM. Fundamental issues (total size of CMIM, contribution of each CMIM party etc.) for the CMIM would be determined by a consensus approval at Ministerial Level Decision Making Body, which consists of ASEAN+3 Finance Ministers. Executive level issues (initial execution of drawing, renewal of drawing, events of default) would be determined by 2/3 majority at Executive Level Decision Making Body (ELDMB), which comprises the deputy-level representatives of ASEAN+3 Finance Ministries and Central Banks and Monetary Authority of Hong Kong, China.[17]

The member States of ASEAN+3 had to balance different and often opposite interests when considering the rules attached to credit lines: easing the liquidity could have undermined the fiscal discipline and triggered budgetary crises in neighbour countries. The agreement establishing the CMIM takes into account these concerns; therefore each member country is authorized to borrow a sum predetermined in advance and consistent with the contribution to CMIM's capital. For instance, ASEAN-5's economies are entitled to ask for loans equal to 2.5 times their financial contribution; smaller countries can receive up to 5 times their deposit in the CMIM. The member countries can apply for a loan to the countries that hold the rotating presidency (two chairs for China, Japan and South Korea and one chair for the remaining ASEAN countries). The lending countries have the possibility to escape a particular loan before the disbursement, if they are authorized by the fellow ASEAN+3 deputy finance ministers or in instance of force majeure or incompatibility with the internal legislation. If one or more countries deny the loan and it is notwithstanding approved, the remaining countries are called to cover the lacking liquidity.[18] This prevision ensures to the member States the right to take position against a disbursement when they have relevant implications for their internal situation. Nevertheless, the chance to opt out underlines some institutional weaknesses of CMIM and its lack of independence, highlighting the distance from more structured mechanisms, such as the IMF credit lines.[19]

[17]See ASEAN+3 (2010), Annex I, particularly par. 7.

[18]*Ivi*, par. 9.

[19]Ciorciari (2013), pp. 944–945.

In 2012, the CMIM was further enhanced. The total size of CMIM Stability Facility was doubled to 240 billion dollars, with unmodified contribution shares, purchasing multiples and voting shares. The IMF-delinked portion was raised from 20 to 30% of the total loan, with the possibility to be increased up to 40%. The maturity of IMF-linked portion was lengthened from 90 days to 1 year with two renewals, with a total supporting period of 3 years. The IMF-delinked portion was lengthened from 90 days to 6 months with three renewals, with a total supporting period up to 2 years.[20]

The main innovation came from the establishment of the CMIM-Precautionary Line. The introduction of this new credit line was a response to the concern that the CMIM was ineffective to prevent a currency crisis. The most important feature of the CMIM-Precautionary Line is the total independence from the IMF concerning its design. The country applying for a precautionary loan should fulfil five qualification criteria concerning external position and market access, fiscal policy, monetary policy, financial sector soundness and supervision, and data adequacy. The Executive Level Decision-Making Body (made by Deputies' Level Meeting) is responsible to decide on the grade of flexibility when assessing these criteria (ex-ante qualification criteria and ex-post conditionality), considering the economic reports by the requesting country and analyses by AMRO, Asian Development Bank and IMF as the basis for the decision. The CMIM-Precautionary Line can be replaced with the CMIM-Stability Facility if any recipient country is hit by a crisis and needs a strengthened support.[21]

The surveillance mechanism was designed to analyse and monitor the regional economies, with a central role in supporting the CMIM's decisional process. An effective CMIM needs therefore a credible surveillance tool, established with the *Macroeconomic Research Office* (AMRO) in 2010. Since the trade and financial sectors of ASEAN+3 economies are strictly interconnected, the AMRO's surveillance has to cover two main areas: (a) bilateral and multilateral surveillance and (b) macroeconomic and financial sector surveillance. AMRO's surveillance reports (*AMRO Regional Economic Monitoring* and individual economic surveillance reports) are submitted on a quarterly basis to the member countries' ministries of finance and central banks; twice a year, they are discussed during the meetings of vice ministers of Finance and deputy governors of the central banks of the ASEAN +3 economies.[22]

AMRO is not intended to duplicate the IMF's surveillance function; the new established surveillance mechanism is regarded as more efficient than the previous regional experiences in ensuring an economic surveillance in the region thanks to three fundamental features. First, it plays a central role in the surveillance of ASEAN+3 countries through the participation in the Economic Review and Policy Dialogue (ERPD). Secondly, the AMRO's design, made by economists and

[20]See ASEAN+3 (2012), par. III.

[21]*Ivi*, Annex I, par. 2.

[22]Siregar and Chabchitrchaidol (2013), pp. 18–19.

researchers with a thorough knowledge of economic strengths and weaknesses in the region, ensures a better comprehension about fiscal and financial imbalances and therefore on the member countries' economic outlooks. Finally, AMRO is an autonomous institution, with no dependence from existing organizations, even though a strict cooperation with IMF and Asian Development Bank is operating on an equal footing. AMRO's approach to regional surveillance is really different from the IMF. If the latter envisages a public pressure with a high degree of transparency, the former focuses on a peer review and a confidential relationship with the State. The reason has to be found in the instability of Asian economies, and in the consequent need to maintain an adequate level of confidentiality between the AMRO and the political and economic officers in the member States. The mechanism keeps open the possibility to share *early warnings* among all the member States, in case of no collaboration of the State under surveillance, that could trigger negative and systemic spillover effects on regional level.[23] One of the main critics about AMRO relies on the tendency to focus too narrowly on the domestic economy in the bilateral surveillance and less on external factors, such as other regional economies and global financial markets.[24]

In 2013 the Summit of ASEAN+3 held in New Delhi made a fundamental change, with the transformation of AMRO from a research office into an international organization, strengthening the legal basis and the ability to intervene. In order to make it possible AMRO reached an *Headquarter Agreement* with Singapore, granting a permanent institutional and administrative facility.[25] The AMRO as an institutional organization became effective and operative on 9 February 2016.[26]

There are several steps to further enhance the effectiveness of AMRO in the Asia region. To secure adequate financing for members in crisis within the IMF-delinked portion the total size of CMIM should be at least doubled. Second, purchasing multiples may be increased for ASEAN countries and reduced to China and Japan (unlikely to require CMIM assistance). Third, a further reduction of the CMIM's IMF link, ultimately to zero: the Summit of ASEAN+3 countries in 2016 confirmed the engagement to further reduce the IMF-linked portion by November.[27] Fourth, strengthen economic surveillance by moving beyond the information phase to a more binding peer review and pressure and, ultimately to a "due diligence" as in the European experience. If these steps are fulfilled, a new Asian Monetary Fund would emerge, capable of conducting effective surveillance and providing liquidity in case of crisis, with an independent conditionality policy. CMIM and AMRO need to work with the IMF in order to ensure a coordination framework and to boost complementarities and synergies.[28] Therefore, IMF and the CMIM should not be

[23]See Chabchitrchaidol (2012), p. 65.

[24]Siregar and Chabchitrchaidol (2013), p. 20.

[25]See ASEAN+3 (2013), parr. 7–13.

[26]See ASEAN+3 (2016), par. 13.

[27]See ASEAN+3 (2016), par. 7.

[28]Kawai (2015), pp. 27–28.

seen as competitive financial institutions in the Asia region, but the latter could serve as a complementary organization of the global financial architecture provided by the IMF, exchanging information on a routine basis, conducting joint analyses and financing together the member countries in the region if needed.

4 The Inclusion of Renminbi in the Basket of IMF Special Drawing Rights

The Special Drawing Rights (SDR) are an international reserve asset designed in 1969 by the International Monetary Fund as a supplement to foreign reserves of member countries and as a financial instrument for countries in balance of payment crisis. This facility cannot be defined as a currency, although it is linked to an interest rate and tradable with freely usable currencies. A national currency should meet two main quantitative requirements to be included in the Special Drawing Rights basket. First of all, the country has to be ranked among the top ten world exporters, with a share of at least 1% of the global trade. Secondly, the money should be freely usable, therefore widely used in international transactions and payments and traded in the fundamental exchange markets.[29] This second condition was introduced as a formal requirement only in 2000, and it is nowadays widely open to interpretation; in the context of IMF financing it aims at ensuring that the currency is liquid, convertible and used for the settlement of international transactions.

If China certainly fulfils the first qualification, being the first world exporter of goods and services, Yuan's leading position among the most traded currencies is a major controversial issue. According to some indicators on international money exchange, such as the utilization of renminbi in central banks' foreign reserves and in the debts international market, the Chinese currency seems to have less weight than Canadian or Australian dollar, even though these last two currencies are not included in the SDR basket. Popular Bank of China (PBoC) itself recognized that, during 2015, the value held by foreign central banks and denominated in renminbi was estimated at about 108 billion dollars, equal to 1% of total international foreign reserves. Nevertheless, central banks optioned 500 billion dollars in swap agreements in order to get yuan, more than any other currencies included US dollars. Since 2009, the Popular Bank of China focused in establishing bilateral swap agreements with foreign central banks in order to strengthen and expand the use of the renminbi in international trade and in the financial transactions. By September 2015, 34 central banks concluded swap agreements with the Chinese Central Bank for a total amount equivalent to roughly half a trillion dollars. These swap lines will surely enhance the renminbi's international use; the Central bank of Beijing is struggling to make a wider group of States ready to use renminbi-denominated instruments and financial facilities. Notwithstanding, IMF denied the possibility to identify swap agreements as an indicator on yuan's relevance in

[29] See IMF (2016b).

the world economy.[30] Despite the lack of convertibility, the renminbi has gained a modest but increasing role in some central banks' reserve portfolios. In September 2011, Nigeria announced its decision to diversify the external reserve holdings by including the renminbi in the existing currency mix.[31] Chile took a similar decision and other countries—such as Austria, Australia, Pakistan, South Africa, Switzerland, Tanzania, Russia and the United Kingdom—are checking the possibility to include renminbi-denominated assets to their reserve portfolios.[32]

The Fund has several times refused to admit political assessments in its decisions concerning governance framework and lending facilities, as clearly stated in the Articles of Agreement. Nevertheless, considering the last decisions, there could be an attempt to give more legitimacy to IMF's operations and governance by ensuring China a greater voice inside the Fund. The second reason—linked to the first one—is to be found in the IMF's willingness to contain Chinese efforts to create new financial and development institutions alternative to International Monetary Fund and World Bank, such as the Chiang Mai Initiative Multilateralization (CMIM), Asian Infrastructure Investment Bank (AIIB) and New Development Bank. Some policy makers—such as Edwin Truman, former US Secretary of Treasury and expert in Fund's affairs—convey the idea that IMF stressed the inclusion criteria in order to gain the support of a leading economic power. Therefore, Fund's decision would be an acknowledgment of China as a new economic superpower and a try to bind the country within a globally recognized framework and to comply with the rules of the international financial system.[33] Europe supported and had an important role in the raising from four to five currencies in the SDR basket: the economic ties between Beijing and the European Union are very strong, as witnessed by the swap agreement signed in October 2013, for a total amount of 45 billion euro.[34]

Christine Lagarde, managing director of IMF, stated that the decision to include renminbi in the SDR basket is a milestone on the way to integrate Chinese economy in the international financial system. Partially, the victory of China should be ascribed to the economic reforms pursued by the country in the recent years and to the efforts to liberalise the capital market, by making it compliant with international financial institutions' standards. The decision taken by IMF could strengthen reformers inside the government against the far conservatives and isolationists.[35]

In March 2009, the then President of the Popular Bank of China for the first time claimed the inclusion of the renminbi in the SDR basket[36] and proposed to enhance

[30]See Brasher (2015).

[31]See Central Bank of Nigeria (2011). The Renminbi was included among the US dollar, the Euro and the British pound sterling.

[32]Pradas (2016), pp. 80–81.

[33]Donnan and Anderlini (2015).

[34]Casarini and Fatiguso (2016).

[35]See IMF (2015a).

[36]See Xiaochuan (2009), in particular chapter IV.

the role of SDRs as a reserve currency. In 2010, the IMF applied strictly its criteria by recognizing that the yuan did not meet the requirements in order to be regarded as a freely usable currency and therefore to be included in the SDR basket.[37] In 2011, the G20 in Cannes shifted to a more flexible evaluation, recognizing that a broader SDR basket would be an important determinant of its attractiveness, and in turn influence its role as a global reserve asset.[38] In the same year the IMF issued a paper proposing core indicators in order to evaluate a currency's inclusion in the SDR basket: (a) volume of transactions in foreign exchange spot markets; (b) volume of transactions in foreign exchange derivatives markets and over-the-counter derivatives; (c) existence of an appropriate market-based interest rate instrument; (d) currency composition of official reserve holdings.[39] The 2015 review reported that the renminbi was not to be considered as freely usable at that time but, nevertheless, it was "exhibiting a significant degree of international use and trading".[40] The report concluded that the final assessment about the renminbi's inclusion in the SDR basket would have involved a significant element of judgment, due to the rapidly changing importance of the Chinese currency in the world trade and in the financial transactions.

As shown in Fig. 1, in 2015 the share of renminbi as a world payment currency is still modest (roughly 2.5% of global transactions) but it is quickly gaining some positions in the world ranking, passing from the 20th place in 2012 to the 5th place in 2015, just behind the US dollar, the euro, the pound sterling and the Japanese yen.[41]

The importance of the inclusion of renminbi in the SDR basket—which is effective from October 1st 2016—is to be found in some distinguishing elements. Since 1999, when Euro replaced German Mark and French franc in the reserve system, the basket was made by four main currencies: US dollars, Euro, Japanese Yen and British sterling. The admission of renminbi will change the relative weights in the club: from October onwards DSP basket will be 41.73% made up of US dollars, 30.93% of Euro, 10.92% of Chinese renminbi, 8.33% of Japanese Yen and 8.09% of British sterling.[42] It is important to highlight that the Yuan is the

[37]IMF (2010a).

[38]G20 (2011), Available at: https://www.oecd.org/g20/summits/cannes/Cannes%20Leaders%20Communiqu%C3%A9%204%20%20November%202011.pdf.

[39]IMF (2011).

[40]IMF (2015b).

[41]Pradas (2016), pp. 39–40.

[42]The inclusion of the renminbi in SDR Basket led also to a relative loss of the Euro compared to the US dollar. The US dollar decreased its share from 41.9 to 41.73% (−0.17%), meanwhile the quota of the Euro had a sharp reduction from 37.4 to 30.93% (−6.47%). In 2015, the Euro has tumbled 13% against the dollar, the most in a decade, and central banks have reduced the proportion of the currency in their reserves to the lowest since 2002. The Euro is getting the most impact from the inclusion of the renminbi in the SDR basket. In the years to come, this downgrade could lead to a diminished role of the Euro in the world transactions and as a reserve asset, being replaced by an enhanced renminbi.

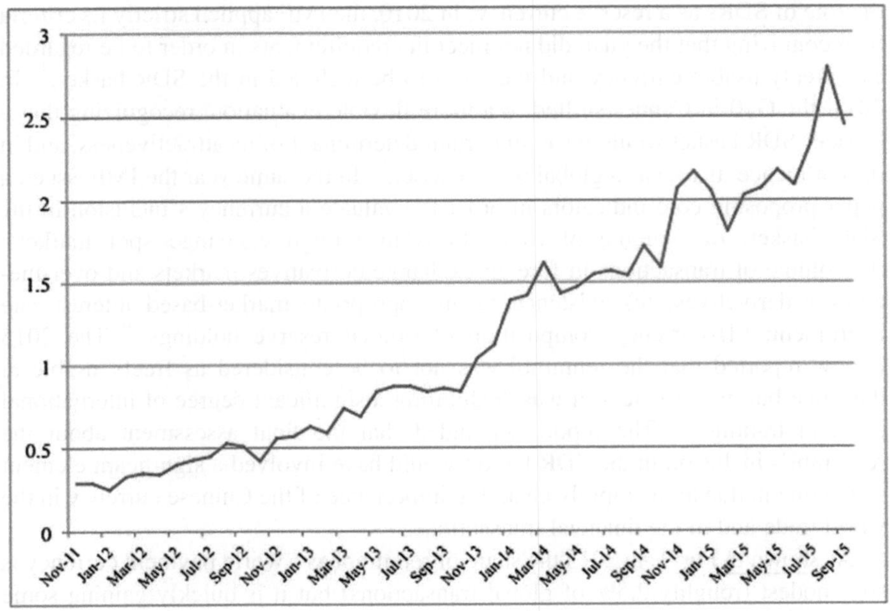

Fig. 1 Share of renminbi as a world payment currency. *Source*: Author's elaboration on SWIFT data

first currency to be admitted in the SDR belonging to a still formally emerging country, even though there are negotiations to grant China the status of market economy. Secondly, although Chinese GDP (PPP) is reaching the US GDP, per capita income is still a quarter compared to the other economies represented in the SDR basket. Finally, current members of the basket are all western democracies ruled according to principles of rule of law, with fully convertible currencies and open capital markets. China is different from many points of view: it is a non-democratic country run by a political system where the single party (Chinese Communist Party) has a central role and has tried to limit the yuan convertibility and foreign capitals.[43]

The inclusion of renminbi in the SDR basket will cause effects in the management of international economic affairs in the years to come. First, there will be a wider use of renminbi in commercial and financial transactions, ensuring China the role of global economic power. Secondly, the IMF decision could open the way to a depreciation of yuan: the Popular Bank of China (PBoC) will be stressed to handle with national currency in accordance with the path followed by central banks in the main advanced economies. Making the yuan more market-based will influence the ability of Chinese central bank in overseeing the renminbi performance. The supervision on exchange rate movements will be more difficult and more expensive but, at the same time, the liberalization will ensure more efficiency and accordance

[43]See Panda (2015).

with economic fundamentals. The Chinese government has already made the fluctuation band wider and it has linked the opening quote with the closure of the previous day; in recent times this value was determined discretionally by the central bank, considering political and geopolitical issues rather than monetary realities. China, in order to comply with Fund's requisites, was obliged to forego some of the tightest control tools on the currency, with effects on exchange rate that led to a sharp devaluation in August 2015. These changes have occurred in a time when China's economy is experimenting new imbalances—high domestic debt (particularly in the financial sector), market bubbles, and claims for higher salaries—while entering in a slowdown cycle.

The inclusion of the renminbi in the SDR basket will lead to some changes in IMF's financial operations. Single currencies in the SDR basket contribute to determining the interest rate attached to lending facilities. The entrance of China, that traditionally has higher interest rates than other western countries, will probably cause a rise in interest rates correlated to lending operations.

From a geopolitical perspective, the renminbi in the SDR basket is not supposed to threaten in the short and mid-term the supremacy of US dollar in the global monetary exchanges. The U.S. Treasury itself supported the renminbi inclusion in the SDR basket, provided that the currency meets the IMF's existing criteria.[44] Nevertheless, the rising importance of yuan in the world economy, triggered by the recent decisions of IMF, could weaken the ability of Western countries to impose financial sanctions on countries charged with human rights violations or considered to be a threat to international security, such as Sudan or North Korea. The acknowledgment of the China's yuan as one of the most important currencies in IMF operations could also weaken the resistance of western countries to grant the status of market economy to Beijing. The renminbi's inclusion in the SDR basket will probably erode the use of the dollar in the international financial transactions but, with the lack of an open capital account and free convertibility of the currency, it is unlikely that the yuan will become a prominent reserve currency.

5 The Representation of China Inside the Fund: Concluding Remarks

The representation of China has known a steady and increasing growth in the last ten years. In 2006, the ad-hoc adjustment rose the quota shares of China inside the Board of Governors to 2.94% (2.69% of the voting rights), far lower than the share of China's GDP in the world economy. In 2008, after the resolution 63-2, the country gained a further rise in its quota, which reached 3.19% (3.35% of voting

[44]U.S. Department of the Treasury (2015), *Readout from a Treasury Spokesperson of Secretary Lew's Meeting with Chinese Vice Premier Wang Yang and Finance Minister Lou Jiwei at the G20 Leaders Summit in Antalya.*

rights). The real news came from the decision of US Congress to ratify the 2010 reform, which meant almost a doubling of Chinese quota shares: the voting shares passed from 3.19 to 6.39% (from 3.81 to 6.07% of voting rights). It is clear that China is still underweighted inside the Board of Governors, if compared with 17.41% of quota shares for the United States.[45]

The increasing weight of China inside the IMF poses some challenges in the organization's internal governance. Some considerations could be drawn considering the Democratic Index developed by Economist's Intelligence Unit. The Democratic Index gives a picture of democratic situation in 165 independent countries, considering almost the whole world population and the States belonging to the international community. The index is based on five indicators: (1) pluralism and electoral process, (2) civil liberties, (3) process of government (4) participation in politics, (5) political culture. Up to the single scores (calculated in a scale from 0 to 10), each country is to be classified in one of the following categories of political system: (1) full democracy, (2) defecting democracies, (3) hybrid political system, (4) authoritarian system.

If the on-going reform process is surely positive, giving to underrepresented countries a greater voice in the internal decisional mechanisms and therefore ensuring a more effective representation of balance of power in the world economy, on the other side there should be an evaluation over the impact of the greater weight given to a non-democratic country. If we consider the States which have most gained from the reforms in the last years, some concerns about the overall democracy within the Fund arise. China, the main recipient of the reform process, takes 144° place in the Democratic Index, among the authoritarian political systems, with an overall score of 3 out of 10. In particular, China scores 0 in the category "pluralism and electoral process", 4.64 in "process of government", 3.33 in "participation in politics", 6.25 in "political culture" and 1.47 in "civil liberties".[46]

Therefore, if we consider the inner democracy in the IMF as a sum of citizens involvement in national politics and in the decisional process in their own State, the greater voice of China inside the Fund could hardly be greeted with enthusiasm in terms of IMF democratization. In China, the participation of citizens is almost void and therefore the Chinese representatives in the Fund are expression of the single ruling party rather than the result of a popular vote.

By stretching this argument and considering the inner democracy of IMF as a sum of countries' single performances, the outcome is a worse Democracy Index after the implementation of the 2010 reform: the overall score decreases from 7.03 to 6.90 (see Table 1). The fall has not been disruptive because the shift of voting rights and quota shares to emerging countries has been limited; a greater weight and voice to China, e.g. in line with its economic fundamentals, would have resulted in a sharp reduction of IMF's *Democracy Index*.

[45] IMF (2010b).

[46] See The Economist (2016b).

Table 1 IMF democracy index

Country	Voting rights 2006	Voting rights 2010	*Democracy Index* 2015
USA	17.023	16.471	8.05
Japan	6.108	6.135	7.96
Germany	5.968	5.306	8.64
France	4.929	4.022	7.92
United Kingdom	4.929	4.022	8.31
China	2.928	6.068	3.14
Italy	3.242	3.015	7.98
Saudi Arabia	3.21	2.009	1.93
Canada	2.928	2.213	9.08
Russia	2.734	2.586	3.31
India	1.916	2.627	7.74
Netherlands	2.375	1.76	8.92
Belgium	2.12	1.299	7.93
Brazil	1.402	2.217	6.96
Spain	1.408	1.918	8.3
Mexico	1.196	1.795	6.55
Switzerland	1.595	1.173	9.09
South Korea	0.76	1.73	8.06
Australia	1.494	1.331	9.01
Venezuela	1.229	0.767	5.00
Sweden	1.108	0.907	9.45
Argentina	0.981	0.661	7.02
Austria	0.869	0.808	8.54
Indonesia	0.964	0.95	7.03
Denmark	0.764	0.711	9.11
Norway	0.777	0.773	9.93
South Africa	0.867	0.634	7.56
Malaysia	0.692	0.749	6.43
Nigeria	0.814	0.516	4.62
Poland	0.638	0.841	7.09
Iran	0.697	0.736	2.16
Turkey	0.453	0.952	5.12
...	...	...	
Total	100	100	–
IMF Democracy Index	7.035	6.897	Average 5.579

Source & Note: IMF Democracy Index calculated by the authors (Gili et Monteverdi, "Democrazia e Trasparenza nelle Istituzioni di Bretton Woods", Research Project of Relevant National Interest, 2015) as a weighted average between the quota shares held by each country in the IMF and the Democracy Index attached to the same country. 162 countries have been taken into account; these countries represent roughly the 99% of the IMF quota shares

China during the last years called several times for enhancing its political influence and of the emerging market economies in the IMF and, consequently, for ensuring a greater decision-making power in the Executive Board. Beijing intends the IMF reforms as a unavoidable part of the overall shift towards a multipolar world economy. China is willing to use its position as one of the most prominent world powers in order to correct the imbalances on behalf of the other emerging economies.[47] The country, in occasion of the 2009 temporary emission of SDR-denominated securities, demonstrated its leading role among the BRICS when it purchased the largest share of IMF bonds (US $50 billion), while other BRICS economies subscribed US $10 billion each.[48] The BRICS represent the privileged and most important forum in order to push reforms in the IMF governance in favour of a more democratic representation inside the Fund: in occasion of the 2009 extraordinary emission of bonds, China and its allies decided to contribute in exchange of assurances of future transferring of votes and quota to developing economies.[49]

China lost its confidence in the IMF's framework during the 1997 Asian financial crisis due to the Fund's policies. Beijing claimed that the severe structural reforms and conditionality applied to the developing countries during the 1980s and the 1990s triggered a diminished legitimacy of this international organization. Chinese authorities have repeatedly questioned the dominant model of fiscal austerity backed by the IMF, preferring a less intrusive IMF, closer to a clearing-house for ideas on economic cooperation and on financial regulation, more pragmatic and open minded.[50] Beijing is pushing for an enhanced representation of Chinese and developing countries officers in the Fund and for a more "open, transparent and merit-based selection process of the IMF Managing Director.[51]

Summing up, China does not intend to destroy the current international economic order; on the contrary the country is taking the role of the "responsible stakeholder", using its leverage to gain a greater voice in the IMF not only for itself but also for the other emerging economies under-represented inside the Fund. The creation of new multilateral and regional financial organizations seems to be an attempt to affirm a leading role in the world economic affairs and it is not necessarily inconsistent with a support to the traditional Bretton Woods institutions. Beijing's actions aim to ensure the endurance of the international monetary system by reforming its governance, strengthening the legitimacy and granting fresh resources to the IMF's budget.

[47]See Momani (2013).

[48]IMF (2009).

[49]Glosny (2010), pp. 112–113.

[50]Momani (2015), pp. 269–270.

[51]China is represented in the IMF through a Deputy Managing Director. See IMF (2016a, c).

References

ASEAN+3 (2000) The Joint Ministerial Statement of the ASEAN+3 Finance Ministers' Meeting, Chiang Mai, Thailand

ASEAN+3 (2005) The Joint Ministerial Statement of the 8th ASEAN+3 Finance Ministers' Meeting Istanbul, Istanbul, Turkey

ASEAN+3 (2007) The Joint Ministerial Statement of the ASEAN+3 Finance Ministers' Meeting, Kyoto

ASEAN+3 (2009) The Joint Ministerial Statement of the ASEAN+3 Finance Ministers' Meeting, Bali

ASEAN+3 (2010) The Joint Ministerial Statement of the ASEAN+3 Finance Ministers' Meeting, Tashkent, Uzbekistan

ASEAN+3 (2012) The joint statement of the 15th ASEAN+3 Finance Ministers and Central Bank Governors' Meeting. Manila, The Philippines

ASEAN+3 (2013) The joint statement of the 16th ASEAN+3 Finance Ministers' and Central Bank Governors' Meeting. Delhi, India

ASEAN+3 (2016) The joint statement of the 19th ASEAN+3 Finance Ministers' and Central Bank Governors' Meeting. Frankfurt, Germany

Barboza (2008) China Unveils Sweeping Plan for Economy. New York Times

Beeson M, Iyanatul I (2005) Neo-liberalism and East Asia: resisting the Washington consensus. J Dev Stud 41(2):197–219

Beeson M, Li F (2015) What Consensus? Geopolitics and policy paradigms in China and the United States. Int Aff 91(1):93–109

Brasher K (2015) China's Renminbi Is Approved by I.M.F. as a Main World Currency. New York Times, 30 November 2015

Casarini N, Fatiguso R (2016) L'ascesa della finanza cinese e il ruolo Ue. Affari Internazionali. Available at: http://www.affarinternazionali.it/articolo.asp?ID=3586

Central Bank of Nigeria (2011) Nigeria Approves Inclusion of Chinese Renminbi in External Reserves. Central Bank of Nigeria Press Release

Chabchitrchaidol A (2012) AMRO's role in regional economic surveillance and promoting regional economic and financial stability. Financ Stab Emer Mark 65

Ciorciari J (2013) The Chiang Mai initiative multilateralization. Asia Surv 51(5):926–952

Donnan S, Anderlini J (2015) IMF poised to admit China's renminbi in elite currecy basket. Financial Times (November 29)

G20 (2011) Communiqué G20 Leaders Summit. Cannes

Glosny MA (2010) China and the BRICS: a real (but limited) partnership in a unipolar world. Polity 42(1):100–129

IMF (2009) Press Release: IMF Signs US$50 Billion Note Purchase Agreement with China. Press Release No.09/293, Washington

IMF (2010a) IMF Executive Board Completes the 2010 Review of SDR Valuation. IMF Public Information Notice 10/149, Washington

IMF (2010b) IMF Quota and governance reform – elements of an agreement. Approved by Andrew Tweedie, Sean Hagan, and Reza Moghadam, Washington

IMF (2011) IMF Executive Board Discusses Criteria for Broadening the SDR Currency Basket. IMF Public Information Notice 11/137, Washington

IMF (2015a) IMF's Executive Board Completes Review of SDR Basket, Includes Chinese Renminbi Press Release No. 15/540, Washington

IMF (2015b) Review of the method of the valuation of the SDR–initial considerations. IMF, Washington

IMF (2016a) Press Release: IMF Deputy Managing Director Min Zhu to Leave the Fund. Press Release No. 16/297, Washington

IMF (2016b) Special drawing rights factsheet. IMF, Washington. Available at: http://www.imf.org/external/np/exr/facts/sdr.htm

IMF (2016c) Statement by IMF Managing Director Christine Lagarde Proposes Appointment of Mr. Tao Zhang as Deputy Managing Director. Washington

Kawai M (2015) From the Chiang Mai Initiative to an Asian Monetary Fund. ADBI Working Paper No. 527

Kennedy S (2010) The Myth of the Beijing Consensus. J Contemp China 19(65):461–477

Kuroda H, Kawai M (2004) Strengthening regional financial cooperation. In: De Brouwer G, Wang Y (eds) Financial governance in East Asia. Policy dialogue, surveillance and cooperation. RoutledgeCurzon, New York, pp 170–185

Momani B (2013) China at the International Monetary Fund: continued engagement in its drive for membership and added voice at the IMF executive board. J Chin Econ 1(1)

Momani B (2015) China at the IMF. In: Lombardi D, Wang H (eds) Enter the Dragon: China in the International Financial System. Center for International Governance Innovation, Waterloo, pp 267–293

Panda A (2015) The Renminbi Joins the IMF's SDR Basket. Now What?. The Diplomat

Peerenboom R, Bugaric B (2013) The emerging post Washington, Post Beijing consensus: prospects and pitfalls. Paper presented at law and society conference, Boston

Pradas E (2016) China's Efforts to Expand the International Use of the Renminbi. Report prepared for the U.S.-China Economic and Security Review Commission

Premier Wen Jiabao's Press Conference of 2007/03/17, Ministry of Foreign Affairs of the People's Republic of China, www.fmprc.gov.cn/enh/zxxx/t304313.htm

Ramo Joshua C (2004) The Beijing Consensus: notes on the new physics of Chinese power. Foreign Policy Centre, London

Siregar R, Chabchitrchaidol A (2013) Enhancing the Effectiveness of CMIM and AMRO: Selected Immediate Challenges and Tasks. ADBI Working Paper Series No. 403

Steinfeld E (2010) Playing our game: why China's rise doesn't threaten the west. Oxford University Press, Oxford

The Economist (2016a) A Crisis of Faith

The Economist (2016b) Democracy Index 2015: Democracy in an age of anxiety. Economist Intelligence Unit

Williamson J (2012) Is the Beijing Consensus Now Dominant? Asia Policy 13(1):1–16

World Bank (2012) China 2030: building a modern, harmonious, and creative high-income society. Paper No. 11. Available at: http://www.worldbank.org/en/news/2012/02/27/china-2030-executive-summary

Xiaochuan Z (2009) Reform the international monetary system. BIS Review 41

Yang Y (2010) The End of Beijing Consensus. Can China's model of authoritarian growth survive? Foreign Affairs, Washington

The New Development Bank: Another BRICS in the Wall?

Agostina Latino

Abstract This article analyses the *New Development Bank* (NDB), the financial institution established through the inter-governmental agreements reached during the sixth Summit of BRICS countries held in Fortaleza, Brazil, on July 15th 2014, where the five main emerging economies were represented (Brazil, Russia, India, China, South Africa). These countries aim to become an alternative to the western Group of Seven (G7); indeed, the reasons underlying the creation of the NDB are strictly linked with the IMF's reforms and the lack of a strong acknowledgment of the rising importance of these economies in the Bretton Woods institutions. The NDB has the primary goal to finance infrastructural projects in the BRICS and in the developing countries and it can rely on a strategic fund of reserve capitals in order to cope with possible currency crises and with the short-term liquidity crises (*Contingent Currency Pool*), and to guarantee a prompt allocation, by BRICS Central Banks, of US denominated liquidity in cases of shortage. The Bank could be in the next years an important tool to foster investments on large development projects and to strengthen the economic and trade ties among the signatory countries. Notwithstanding, the governance framework of this new Bank seems to replicate some of the shortcomings still existing in the IMF and WB: time will tell if the NDB can assert itself as a real alternative to the Bretton Woods institutions, correcting the transparency and democratic deficit, or if it will replicate the same framework, beyond the different composition *ratione personarum* in the Bank management.

Contents

A. Latino (✉)
Department of Law, University of Camerino, Camerino, Italy
e-mail: agostina.latino@unicam.it

E. Sciso (ed.), *Accountability, Transparency and Democracy in the Functioning of Bretton Woods Institutions*, DOI 10.1007/978-3-319-57855-2_4

1 Introduction: The Missed Reform of International Monetary Fund as a Driving Force for BRICS Countries

As is well known, the acronym BRICS was coined by the then *Goldman Sachs Asset Management's* President Jim O'Neill in order to indicate Brazil, Russia, India, China[1] and South Africa,[2] representing the five main emerging world economies. These countries aim to become an alternative forum to the western Group of Seven (G7),[3] with the purpose to undermine the United States and European countries' leading role and to overcome the dollar currency dominance.[4] The New

[1]O'Neill (2001). The success of the acronym was endorsed by the formalization of the BRIC countries' group; following a first meeting of the Foreign Ministers on the margin of the 61th United Nations General Assembly in 2006, starting from 2009 and on a regular annual basis the leaders of these countries meet in order to discuss the economic and financial issues of joint concern.

[2]The acronym was modified to BRICS in 2010 with the inclusion of South Africa, a smaller economy if compared with the other four States, but with a leading role in the African Sub-Saharan region. The South Africa moving into the group caused some qualms, as witnessed by the doubts expressed by O'Neil. In an interview on *Mail & Guardian* he stated: "It's just wrong. South Africa doesn't belong in Brics (…) South Africa has too small an economy. There are not many similarities with the other four countries in terms of the numbers. In fact, South Africa's inclusion has somewhat weakened the group's power. (…) South Africa's case for legitimacy in this grouping is predicated on its geographic location and advantage on the continent. But, in fact, it has slightly diminished what was a strong political club with the four original countries", http://mg.co.za/article/2012-03-23-sa-presence-drags-down-brics. Afterwards, O'Neill published an article in which he argued objectively that South Africa could more than justify its presence in BRICS if it helped Africa to fulfill its remarkable potential by exploring cross-border expansion in trade and infrastructure, as well as improvements in domestic productivity: Jim O'Neill (2013). In doctrine see Petropoulos (2015), Soulé-Kohndou (2013), Martino (2016), Porteilla (2011).

[3]Actually the BRICS are neither a legal order, nor a simple economic block but a network and a knowledge producer which could trigger new parameters and new possible opportunities. These outcomes will be highly affected by the scale of values in each country and they will be able to legitimate or prevent constitutional changes—formal and informal—in the BRICS countries, through processes of constitutional borrowing and policy transfer: to this purpose see Carducci (2013). According to de' Robertis (2016), the acronym BRIC, created in 2001 to indicate an affinity in the dynamics of economic development of Brazil, Russia, India and China, in 2006 has taken, by the initiative of Russia, the significance of an association of States, a *format*, which compactly continue to highlight the need to adapt the cooperation mechanisms of the international system to the new economic and political realities of the twenty-first century through the reform, but not the abandonment of the principles and the sites of dialogue and decision-making created after World War II. Expanded with the inclusion of South Africa, the format has become BRICS and by the recurring rejection of recent military actions and sanctions of the West, it evokes the risk of a repetition of the dynamics that led to the formation of the Entente in the early twentieth century. See also Molinaro (2016), Carducci and Bruno (2014), Jiejin (2015).

[4]In the Putin's words: "In the modern world the factor of common borders does not play a defining role. On the contrary, global processes encourage us to join efforts as challenges and problems become shared. In the BRICS case we see a whole set of coinciding strategic interests. First of all, this is the common intention to reform the international monetary and financial system. In the present form it is unjust to the BRICS countries and to new economies in general. We should take a more active part in the International Monetary Fund and the World Bank's decision-making system. The international monetary system itself depends a lot on the US dollar, or, to be precise, on the monetary and financial policy of the US authorities. The BRICS countries want to change this": http://tass.ru/en/russia/740471.

Development Bank (NDB) is a financial institution established through the intergovernmental agreements reached by the BRICS during their sixth Summit held in Fortaleza on 15th July 2014.[5] The Bank, operating since 2016, is headquartered in Shanghai, whereas in Johannesburg a branch for the African area has been opened.[6] The decision regarding its creation took place during the fifth BRICS Conference held in Durban, South Africa, on 27th March 2013.[7] The creation of the NDB has drawn the world's attention and it is considered emblematic of the BRICS' rising strength and, at the same time, of the stagnation—or even the decline—in the traditional western economic power.[8]

As is well known, in fact, concerning the role played by the International Monetary Fund (IMF) three different stages can be identified: in the first one, between 1945 and the early Seventies, Bretton Woods' agreements were aimed at exchange parity among the signatory countries, in order to deprive the governmental policy in the single member States of the possibility to use frequent competitive devaluations and to avoid, therefore, the risk of a protectionist downward spiral like the one occurred between the war years. Since 1971, the main recipients in the Bretton Woods system (United States and the great western powers) established a new phase of free floating exchange rates among the currencies, where the dollar nevertheless remained the dominant one, to respond to the disproportionate pressures experienced by the currencies in an even more interconnected world, both in trade and in the financial field. In that context, the IMF undertook more and more an ex post stabilizing role of the periodic balance of payment crises in the emerging and developing countries, so that the system seemed to have achieved a duopoly equilibrium where the IMF intervened in the crises occurring in the "periphery of the world", meanwhile the great western democracies tried to "manage" the world

[5]In fact the establishment of the NDB had already been widely desired and predicted: Nicholas Stern, Joseph Stiglitz, Amar Bhattacharya, and Mattia Romani campaigned globally for the creation of a new BRICS-led bank. As the four economists pointed out in a 2013 op-ed "The infrastructure requirements in emerging-market economies and low-income countries are huge — 1.4-billion people still have no reliable electricity, 900-million lack access to clean water and 2.6-billion do not have adequate sanitation. About 2-billion people will move to cities in the next 25 years. Policy makers must ensure the investments are environmentally sustainable. To meet these and the other challenges, infrastructure spending will have to rise from about $800bn to at least $ 2-trillion a year in the coming decades or it will be impossible to achieve long-term poverty reduction and inclusive growth": *Proposed BRICS Bank Will Be Good for All of Us*, http://www.bdlive.co.za/opinion/2013/05/03/proposed-brics-bank-will-be-good-for-all-of-us. For a more detailed focus in the eve period before the NDB's creation see Griffith-Jones (2014).

[6]*BRICS Bank now Hiring in Johannesburg*, Times Live, 7th March, 2016 at: http://www.timeslive.co.za/local/2016/03/07/Brics-Bank-now-hiring-in-Johannesburg. This witnesses the attention paid by BRICS countries to the African continent, regarded as crucial for the Planet's future, but it can also be considered as an acknowledgement to South Africa for its refusal to join the embargo against Russia, in spite of strong pressures by western countries. See also the considerations of Martino (2016).

[7]http://www.ilsole24ore.com/art/notizie/2013-09-06/emergenti-attacco-072444.shtml?uuid=AbjLgpTI&fromSearch.

[8]See Lieber (2014), Choukroune (2014), Graham (2013).

economy through the coordination—in practice very weak—at the annual G5/G6/G7 Summits. Since the second 2000s, however, the Bretton Woods system entered a new phase of legitimacy crisis: this third stage arose in 2007 from the economic and financial crisis, which had relevant negative spillover effects for the Eurozone, already affected by huge macroeconomic imbalances. The crisis highlighted the fragility of the world areas unanimously considered as the strongest and most resilient, such as the United States and the European Monetary Union and, at the same time, it has become impossible to disregard the greater weight gained by some emerging countries. The economic growth rates of BRICS countries, in particular, had been for many years close or even higher to the double-digit, while the most relevant western economies were showing evidence of economic slowdown and, slightly later, they fell into the worst financial crisis since 1929 (Fig. 1).

In this "transitional" stage of the global economic and financial governance, the United States in 2008 pushed the first IMF reform since the end of the Cold War, making the G20 (the annual Summit of 20 countries which together represent roughly the 80% of the world economy) the main forum to cope jointly and in a coordinated way with the arising crises, re-writing the global economic and financial rules. The pressure to reform suffered a setback in 2011, when the United States—internally divided between a President favorable to the global governance reform and a Congress set against these proposals, according to the lame-duck paradigm—started to prevent the adoption of the second 2010 IMF reform which

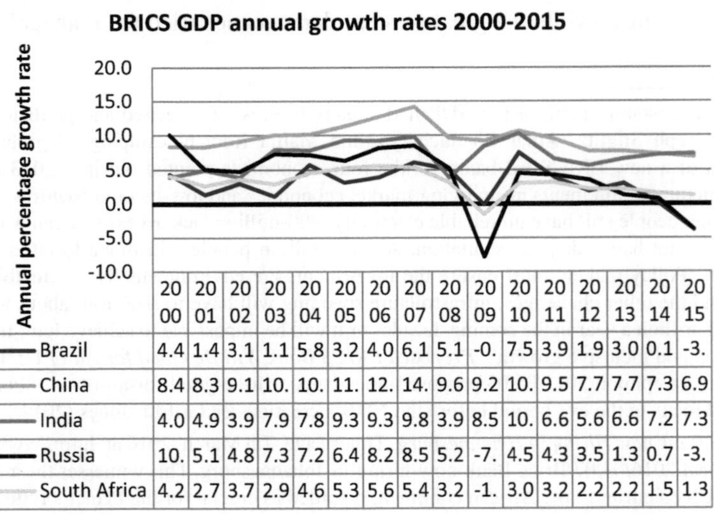

	2000	2001	2002	2003	2004	2005	2006	2007	2008	2009	2010	2011	2012	2013	2014	2015
Brazil	4.4	1.4	3.1	1.1	5.8	3.2	4.0	6.1	5.1	-0.	7.5	3.9	1.9	3.0	0.1	-3.
China	8.4	8.3	9.1	10.	10.	11.	12.	14.	9.6	9.2	10.	9.5	7.7	7.7	7.3	6.9
India	4.0	4.9	3.9	7.9	7.8	9.3	9.3	9.8	3.9	8.5	10.	6.6	5.6	6.6	7.2	7.3
Russia	10.	5.1	4.8	7.3	7.2	6.4	8.2	8.5	5.2	-7.	4.5	4.3	3.5	1.3	0.7	-3.
South Africa	4.2	2.7	3.7	2.9	4.6	5.3	5.6	5.4	3.2	-1.	3.0	3.2	2.2	2.2	1.5	1.3

Fig. 1 BRICS GDP annual growth rates 2000–2015. *Source*: Author's elaboration on IMF data

should have met the emerging countries' requests for an enhanced representation and a more decisive role in the global economic and financial governance.[9]

Consequently, the BRICS decided to promote an "alternative" reform of the global governance, with the purpose to shirk the American leadership, considered completely at odds with a deeply changed reality over the last 20 years (if in 1995 the BRICS held and produced less than 15% of the global GDP, in 2015 their share has more than doubled to 32%).[10] In other words, the US Congress' refusal to ratify the IMF reforms and to overcome the impasse pushed China and other rapidly emerging countries to look beyond IMF and World Bank (WB) and to build a new

[9]In fact, in 2010 China, Brazil and other rapidly developing countries agreed on an IMF reform, declaring they were open to double the financial resources granted to the Fund in return for a greater voting power, in accordance with their economic weight and with the performance of other developing countries which did not exist in 1944. The 2010 reform on IMF's voting rights stipulated that China should become the third most important country in the Fund, and that the other emerging economies (Brazil, China, India and Russia) should be included in the top-ten list of IMF's shareholders. This reform aimed to change the status quo where Washington held a *de facto* veto power, considering that United States' quota was about to 16.75% and that the major decisions require the 85% of total voting rights. Moreover, the geopolitical allies of Unites States (see Japan with the 6.23%, United Kingdom and France with 4.29% each and Germany with 5.81% of quotas) were able—with their voting package—to ensure that IMF policy was "friendly" to US national interests. The governance reform project aimed to align the Fund's framework to the quick evolution in the world economy in order to ensure that the governance remains consistent with the representation of its 188 member States. The reform relies on two main profiles. The first one focuses on the governance framework, the second considers the quotas. Considering the first profile, the 2010 reform triggered a relevant change in the Articles of Agreement in order to make the evolution towards a more representative Board of Directors easier, where all members will be elected (and not appointed). Regarding the second profile, the main changes focused on: (a) the doubling of quotas: from about 238.5 billion of Special Drawing Rights to 477 (equal to $ 669 billion at current exchange rate; (b) the shift of 6% quotas from overrepresented countries to underrepresented ones; (c) the shift of 6% quotas towards emerging and developing countries (*Emerging Market and Developing Countries*—EMDCs); (d) a significant realignment in quotas: as mentioned above, China would become the third most important country in the Fund and four EMDCs will be among the ten major IMF shareholders; (e) the protection of quotas and voting rights for the lowest-income countries, thus the States eligible to enter the *Poverty Reduction and Growth Trust*—PRGT: the countries whose per-capita income has sunk below 1.135 € in 2008 (the same threshold set by the International Association for Development) or the double of this amount for the smallest States. After 5 years of strong opposition by the US Congress, the stalemate ended on 18th November 2015. The 14th General Quota Review—which reforms the quota system—will be reality and will trigger a doubling in IMF's resources, up to 659.67 billion euro. China's voting rights rise from 3.8 to 6%, making this country the third most important power in the IMF only behind United States and Japan. Brazil gains four positions, meanwhile India and Russia enter the short-list of the ten most important countries represented in the Fund. On the contrary, Europe loses some power: apart from Spain—whose quota shifts from 1.68 to 2%—Germany, France, Italy and United Kingdom see their representation diminished. Notwithstanding, United States will keep their veto power: their voting rights is reducing only by 0.2%, from 16.7 to 16.5%. http://www.imf.org/external/np/sec/misc/consents.htm.

[10]See Biswas (2015), Bevir and Gaskarth (2015), Burns (2013), Cooper and Thakur (2013).

international financial framework.[11] Notwithstanding, the BRICS do not set up a cohesive and homogeneous block with shared and common targets[12]: in the practice they often disagree concerning the strategic and political issues.[13] The struggle for a greater voice in the existing multilateral Institutions overlaps with the turbulent

---

[11]They reaffirmed the role of BRICS countries as a multi-continental bloc whose activity is not soft-law or *ab-intra* oriented but, on the contrary, is supposed to give guidelines for an "imperative" *ab extra* action, consistent with the new Post Bretton Woods System's international governance, Panebianco and Verdecchia (2013).

[12]In particular, among the BRICS there are countries (see South Africa) that in the last years have been gradually losing their influence, two democracies which ask for more representativeness inside the United Nations Organization—Brazil and India—and two countries—Russia and China—really active on the world stage. Russia, in particular, tends to focus on the *pars dentruens*, blaming the Bretton Woods Institutions without proposing an alternative governance. Moscow seems to have a self-sustainable economy and financial system, even though the highly reliance on raw materials export is an important element of weakness. China, in its turn, has a current account surplus, elevated reserves of foreign currencies and a low degree of involvement in the financial markets, and it is now trying to gain greater weight in the international Institutions. Concerning the first profile—the internal pressure to reform the existing Bretton Woods institutions—the Chinese request to include the renminbi in the basket of Special Drawing Rights (SDRs) has been granted by IMF's Board on 30th November 2015 and it will become operational from October 2016. On the other side, considering the proposal outside the existing Institutions, China seeks to raise its financial leverage both through the powerful State banks (*China Development Bank*, *China Ex-Im Bank, Industrial and Commercial Bank of China Ltd., Bank of China*, ecc.), and through the promotion of plurilateral (as the mentioned New Development Bank) and unilateral initiatives (a new silk road "One Belt, One Road", the Asian Infrastructure Investment Bank (AIIB), the Bank of *Shanghai Cooperation Organization* and so on). These new initiatives are occurring in a time of important transitions in the Chinese economic system (from an export and investment-led growth to a consumption-led one) and after few months from the bursting of the first internal financial bubble (as is well known, between June and August 2015, the Shanghai Stock Exchange lost the 40% of its capitalization). It should be highlighted that, on the political and strategic side, a pressure is arising by some BRICS countries to turn their enhanced economic power into a greater weight in the defense and external action policies (like the increasing Russian involvement in Ukraine and Middle East and the Chinese focus on the South China sea, on Taiwan and on some land borders with India). According to Yu (2014a, b) "(...) the current framework of the BRICS mechanism is much like a platform for powerful emerging economies to seek the political discourse of power in the world rather than a real alliance for the trade".

[13]For a comprehensive analysis of the reasons why BRICS countries are at the same time an homogeneous and heterogeneous group see: Zani (2012). From an economic-structural point of view the BRICS countries share at least three characteristics: (a) low levels of debt which can further social and cohesion policies; (b) foreign-exchange reserves which can sustain a leading role on the world stage; (c) a population pyramid with over the 42% of the population able to foster consumption and private demand. In this regard see: Carducci (2013). Moreover, the BRICS countries are each other's main trade partners but also each other's competitors. This is very apparent in the number of trade disputes that pit BRICS countries against each other. About 70% of China's WTO disputes are with emerging powers. Brazil and other BRICS countries have introduced duties on China products, and by the end of 2012, India had no fewer than 149 anti-dumping cases against Chinese products. Brazil has lodged a complaint at the WTO against South Africa. India has complaints against Brazil and South Africa. Brazil and China have both been aggressively investing in Africa. China and India are both trying to gain regional preeminence in Asia: Rolland (2013).

launch of several initiatives—such as the New Development Bank—that are supposed to be alternative. In the medium and long term BRICS' heterogeneity could deeply undermine their ability to act in a proper and coordinated way, considering also the recent slowdown in many BRICS economies that underlines firstly the problems correlated with the classical "middle-income trap", which is the abrupt loss of competitiveness in the emerging countries when the salaries start raising due to economic growth and social pressures[14]; secondly, it highlights the even more immediate tension linked to capital flights triggered by the Federal Reserve's decision to increase the interest rates.[15]

In the last years important BRICS countries such as Russia and Brazil entered into recession, posing a threat to the rising importance of this economic group. Notwithstanding, according to the Statute, the bad economic performance of this two countries will not undermine the position of BRICS within the NDB: the governance framework resulting from the Articles of Agreement statues that each founding member "shall appoint 1 (one) Director and 1 (one) alternate".[16]

It is evident that the context is highly problematic. The figures suggest that three out of five countries are still growing, with dynamic rates—such as India and China—or more stagnant, as in the case of South Africa. The situation in Brazil and Russia, by contrast, has become far worse and for the first time after several years they knew a negative growth rate in 2015.

Nevertheless, we are discussing about economies that are deeply different from each other. In 2015, for example, Chinese GDP was about 11.181 billion dollars,[17] one and a half times higher than the three other BRICS combined. The chart demonstrates that the growth rates of China and India can more than compensate the recessions in smaller economies, like Russia and Brazil. Overall, BRICS countries grew in 2015 too.

---

[14]For example, see. Boni (2016). The Author was inspired by a lecture on the current foreign policy of Brazil held in Rome by ambassador Celso Amorin for CESPI, October 2015, to rebuild the great dynamism and design followed by Brazil in the Latin American continent as well as on the world stage especially over the years from the turn of the century to today. A dynamism that emerges as based on certain economic strength, strategic geographical position, wide availability of natural resources; but above all on a precise article of the Constitutional Law of 1988, passed after two decades of military dictatorship. This international projection of great importance finds nowadays serious obstacles in the heavy economic crisis, a real recession that hit Brazil in recent times. The analysis of this recession conducted by the Author allows to understand the nature of the structural deficiencies that still characterize the Brazilian economic and social system, in spite of the fast growth of the past decade, and their repercussions on the political order; deficiencies, the Author points out, that ultimately could weaken and even undermine the positive action that Brazil continues to play on the international stage, particularly in the BRICS coordination.

[15]In mid-December 2015 the FED raised the interest rates for the first time in 10 years, by a quarter of a point, from a 0–0.25% to a 0.25–0.50%.

[16]See Article 12(b) of the *Agreement on the New Development Bank*, Fortaleza, July 2015.

[17]See at the World Economic Outlook (WEO) database: https://www.imf.org/external/pubs/ft/weo/2016/02/weodata/index.aspx.

Broadly speaking, in the last years BRICS economies showed evidence of slowdown and none is growing at the rates of 5 years ago. Several economic analysts, indeed, are trying to explain the reasons underlying this slowdown[18] and the consequences for the world economy. The studies reveal that sentences like "China is not growing anymore" or "BRICS are not growing anymore" are incorrect and that despite a global economic slowdown, BRICS has been a main economic engine for the world economy.[19]

The aim of the present paper is to analyze the NDB as a challenge that BRICS countries pose to Bretton Woods Institutions. It can be regarded as a composite struggle that witnesses the heterogeneity of these great emerging countries, held together primarily by the frustration for the slowness (or, in many cases, for the inertia) in the global economic institutions' reforming process. Beyond the rhetoric, in fact, it is not clear how the NDB will be different from the existing development banks and how long it will take in order to become a large-scale Institution focused on sustainable development.[20] Concretely, the NDB's creation establishes a Bank with the core task of financing the cooperation among States representing a really significant share of the international community: the original four BRIC countries have a total population of more than three billion people, that is the 42% of the world population; they cover a quarter of the land area of the globe and they hold the 26% of global GDP.

2 The New Development Bank

The NBD has a starting capital of 50 billion dollars and will rely on a strategic Fund of reserve capitals (*Contingent Reserve Arrangement* establishing a *Contingent Currency Pool*—CCP), in order to cope with possible currency crises and with the short-term liquidity crises; the potential call-back liquidity is about 100 billion dollars.[21]

---

[18]Andrew Walker (2014), Davies (2015), Boumphrey (2015).

[19]Fact file: BRICS drive the global economy, October 15, 2016, http://thebricspost.com/fact-file-brics-drive-the-global-economy/#.WDq834WcHIU.

[20]For a specific analysis on the complex relationships with the main—and partially overlapped—emerging alliances see: Keukeleire and Hooijmaijers (2014).

[21]*BRICS establish $100bn bank and currency pool to cut out Western dominance, July 15, 2014* https://www.rt.com/business/173008-brics-bank-currency-pool/. *It was stated that "Though clearly funded in the private capital markets—with cofinancing from private and public lenders as well as private investors—the new development banks are owned and capitalised by national governments. They therefore provide a valuable instrument for helping implement and fund national, regional and global strategies. They can also help achieve policy aims, such as helping to achieve the Sustainable Development Goals": Griffith-Jones (*2015*).*

China will contribute to the Fund with 41 billion, Brazil, India and Russia with 18 billion each and South Africa with 5 billion.[22]

It should be highlighted that the Russian quota in the BRICS emergency fund is twice the size of the contribution in the IMF (before the reform)[23] and the Chinese is three times higher. It can be drawn a clear conclusion that these five emerging economies aim to have a greater voice in the management of the global financial portfolio, a position consistent with the current international economic landscape.

One of the most important issues has been focused on the outlook of the NDB and on the possibility for its members to operate with their own national currencies,[24] hypothesis not received in the Articles of Agreements.

The CCP—established with the agreement signed on 7th July 2015 by the BRICS central bank governors—has been created in order to allow the central banks to count on reciprocal resources to face possible shortages of dollar-denominated liquidity and budgetary deficits.[25]

---

[22]BRICS Development bank top on Agenda of 6th BRICS Summit, July 15, 2014 http://news.biharprabha.com/2014/07/brics-development-bank-top-on-agenda-of-6th-brics-summit/.

[23]See Riccieri (2016). The Author illustrates the Russian point of view on the BRICS's international initiative and reconstructs the set of the underlying reasons, the strategic goal as well as national interests that the Russian Federation intends to protect and deal with by the set-up, promotion and widening of the action's areas of the important coordination. The thesis presented in the article is that the main reasons of the Russian Federation are rather political than economic. Such thesis in supported by the analysis of two authoritative Russian contributions: one by the Director of the National Committee for the Research on BRICS, Georgy Toloraya, and another by the Russian Institute for Strategic Studies-RISS with the Report 1.2016; as well as through an in depth examination of the official documents of the seventh BRICS Summit held in Ufa, Russia, July 8th -9th, 2015, and of numerous initiatives implemented in the following period. The highlighted political element, in the Russian interpretation of the BRICS experience, finally leads the Author to connect the internal development model of the Russian system to the possibilities of success or failure of the external projection of such a system, precisely by means of BRICS coordination.

[24]http://it.rbth.com/mondo/2015/07/08/brics_e_sco_doppio_summit_a_ufa_36593.

[25]The text of the agreement is available on: http://brics.itamaraty.gov.br/media2/press-releases/220-treaty-for-the-establishment-of-a-brics-contingent-reserve-arrangement-fortaleza-july-15. See P. *Raimondi: "The CCP is a very important effort to cope with possible liquidity crises, heavy competitive devaluations, "driven" capital flights, destabilizing balance of payment crises and severe financial crises. All these events would put pressure on balance of payments. Indeed, emerging economies have been recently affected by several economic and currency devaluations due to the "yo-yo" policies enacted through the Federal Reserve's Quantitative Easing. Such destabilizations pushed many governments, starting with the Brazilian one, to denounce an on-going "currency war". Also the "driven falls" in the oil and gold prices are aimed at putting the BRICS in difficulty, particularly Russia and Iran."* Raimondi (2016). Working on official documentation produced by the BRICS summits and by the most important economic and political international organizations, the Author shows the global strategic importance of the BRICS coalition which goes much beyond its non-secondary relevance as a new economic and political block. In his opinion, 70 years after its creation, the Bretton Woods system, in which the dollar has been the only currency of reference in trade, in finance and in the monetary reserves, has concluded its historical cycle. Time has come to create a more transparent and balanced new economic order in which the emerging markets are the main motor of development. The BRICS alliance is

As stated by the Russian central bank governor, Elvira Nabiullina, the *Pool* is a "preventive tool": "This is the so-called preventive mechanism, when there is pressure on a [country's] balance of payments, to avoid a speculative attack on the national currency, (...) Or there is a short-term liquidity deficit which happens when a country sees a massive capital outflow[26] (...) the reserve was not created with sanctions specifically in mind, it could be used to provide additional financial flows should the West take further punitive action over Russia's actions in Ukraine".[27]

The Bank aims to contribute to development plans established nationally through projects that are socially, environmentally and economically sustainable. Taking this into account, the main objectives of the NDB can be summarized as follows: (1) Promote infrastructure and sustainable development projects with a significant development impact in member countries; (2) Establish an extensive network of global partnerships with other multilateral development institutions and national development banks; (3) Build a balanced project portfolio giving a proper respect to their geographic location, financing requirements and other factors.

According to art.3,[28] the NDB is governed by:

1. a Board of Governors,[29]
2. a Board of Directors,
3. a President.[30]

The Indian Kandapur Vaman Kamath has been appointed as first NDB President: he pledged to move the Bank "from best practices to next practices", adding

becoming the main instrument of such epochal change. The Author intends to demonstrate in the most concrete way how such a change, to be effective also in political terms, is going to be realized through new agreements in the monetary, trade and financial sectors. The analysis shows the different steps to create the preconditions for the new economic order: new credit development institutions like the BRICS NDB, the Contingent Reserve Arrangement, as a reserve fund to face possible monetary destabilizations, and the Asian Infrastructure Investment Bank; the growing use of national currencies in trade in the agreed currencies; the realization of large continental infrastructure development projects which should become the motor of a new global industrialization and technological modernization through which Eurasia would become the center of the planetary development and the alternative model to the bankrupted financialisation of the global economy and to the different "post-industrial ideologies"; the creation of a basket of important currencies which will lay the foundations of a multi-polar international monetary system.

[26]http://in.rbth.com/world/2014/07/17/brics_currency_fund_to_protect_members_from_volatility_russias_top_ba_36767.

[27]http://www.themoscowtimes.com/business/article/503571.html.

[28]The text of the Charter is available on: http://www.ndb.int/charter.php.

[29]As of June 2016, the members of NDB Board of Governors are as follows: Nelson Henrique Barbosa Filho, Brazil's Minister of Finance; Anton Siluanov, Russia's Minister of Finance—Chairman of the Board of Governors; Arun Jaitley, Minister of Finance, Corporate Affairs and Information & Broadcasting—Vice-Chairman of the Board of Governors; Lou Jiwei, China's Minister of Finance; Pravin Jamnadas Gordhan, South Africa's Minister of Finance.

[30]About the structure, see the following paragraph.

that traditional development lending was often "too rigid, inflexible, and slow".[31] Kundapur Vaman Kamath is supported by four vice-President coming from the other four BRICS countries.

Many observers see the Bank as proof that the BRICS have a revisionist agenda. Varun Sahni, for example, argues that the establishment of the NDB is "a strong example of revisionist power aggregation, insofar as it challenges the structures and legitimacy of the World Bank and the International Monetary Fund".[32] Others point out that the NDB is a natural reaction by emerging powers to an order that has been unwilling or unable to include them adequately.[33] NDB president Kamath insists that "our objective is not to challenge the existing system as it is but to improve and complement the system in our own way." Even though the Bank's website states the NDB is "operated (...) as an alternative to the existing U.S.-dominated World Bank and International Monetary Fund", calling the BRICS countries revisionist would be misguided. Quite to the contrary, the NDB's launch underlines the BRICS' willingness to help fix a system that no longer satisfies existing demands. Only those who regard US leadership, rather than the system's rules and functionality, as the decisive element of today's order will call the BRICS revisionist. As Daniel Chardell correctly writes, "(. . .) the NDB and CRA mark the BRICS' response to the widely acknowledged shortcomings of the existing global financial system. A common desire to reform global economic governance was the issue that drove the BRICS together and gave them legitimacy in the aftermath of the global financial crisis. For years, the BRICS have demanded an overhaul of the Bretton Woods institutions, where Western powers remain overrepresented at the expense of emerging economies. China, the world's second-largest economy, has just 3.81 percent of total votes in the International Monetary Fund (IMF). To put that in perspective, France and the United Kingdom each have 4.29 percent, yet their economies are three times smaller than China's, according to the latest IMF data. Clearly, some reshuffling is long overdue".[34]

[31] As stated to the *Financial Times* on 21st July 2015: https://next.ft.com/content/d8e26216-2f8d-11e5-8873-775ba7c2ea3d. Interestingly, Lou Jiwei, China's Foreign Minister, said at the signing ceremony of NDB that: "This bank will place greater emphasis on the needs of developing countries, have greater respect for developing countries' national situation, and more fully embody the values of developing countries. (. . .) Development is a dynamic process. There's really no such thing as so-called 'best practices'", *ib*.

[32] Sahni (2015).

[33] See Scridel (2016). The Author points out that the BRICS should be considered "emerged" better than "emerging" countries.

[34] Chardell (2015).

3 The NDB's Governance and the Impact on Membership

The NDB follows a governance model very similar to the one enacted by the WB and by the main Multilateral Development Banks—MDBs. This is a bit surprising considering the rhetoric about the building of a new type of MDB and of other governance structures which could have been chosen by NDB's founders.

In terms of estate and voting framework, the BRICS opted for a direct linkage between capital contribution and shareholders' voting rights.[35] The initial participation is absolutely equal among the BRICS, meanwhile the decisions about how to allocate the future shares among the existing or new members is not following any specific criteria; the definition of the criteria is delegated to the Board of Governors (upon which the BRICS countries will have a significant power and control, as following specified).[36] The only explicit criteria suggest that a non-BRICS country cannot have more than 7% of the overall voting rights and that non-debtor members cannot have more than 20% of the total voting rights.[37]

The decision taken by BRICS countries to conserve and block a 55% majority of shares for themselves—regardless of members or share allocation's changes—seems to be contrary to the critical approach of BRICS towards the IMF about the rewards of position of the (major) founding States.[38]

[35]Article 6—Voting "(a) The voting power of each member shall be equal to the number of its subscribed shares in the capital stock of the Bank. In the event of any member failing to pay any part of the amount due in respect of its obligations in relation to paid-in shares under Article 7 of this Agreement, such member shall be unable, for so long as such failure continues, to exercise that percentage of its voting power which corresponds to the percentage which the amount due but unpaid bears to the total amount of paid-in shares subscribed to by that member in the capital stock of the Bank; (b) Except as otherwise specifically provided for in this Agreement, all matters before the Bank shall be decided by a simple majority of the votes cast. Where provided for in this Agreement, a qualified majority shall be understood as an affirmative vote of two thirds of the total voting power of the members. Where provided for in this Agreement, a special majority shall be understood as an affirmative vote of four of the founding members concurrent with an affirmative vote of two thirds of the total voting power of the members; (c) In voting in the Board of Governors, each governor shall be entitled to cast the votes of the member country which he represents; (d) In voting in the Board of Directors each director shall be entitled to cast the number of votes that counted toward his election, which votes need not be cast as a unit."

[36]Article 8—Subscription of Shares "(a) Each member shall subscribe to shares of the capital stock of the Bank. The number of shares to be initially subscribed by the founding members shall be those set forth in Attachment 1 of this Agreement, which specifies the obligation of each member as to both paid-in and callable capital. The number of shares to be initially subscribed by other members shall be determined by the Board of Governors by special majority on the occasion of the acceptance of their accession".

[37]Art. 8—Subscription of Shares: "c) No increase in the subscription of any member to the capital stock shall become effective, and any right to subscribe thereto is hereby waived, which would have the effect of: (...) (ii) increasing the voting power of the non-borrowing member countries above 20 (twenty) per cent of the total voting power; (iii) increasing the voting power of a non-founding member country above 7 (seven) per cent of total voting power".

[38]Art. 8—Subscription of Shares: "(i) reducing the voting power of the founding members below 55 (fifty-five) per cent of the total voting power".

A sort of "granted participation" is not so unusual among the MDBs, but it is more common in regional MDBs as the African Development Bank or the Asian Development Bank (AsDB) in order to ensure the regional members' participation. In this case, a small group of countries want to secure an *a priori* voting majority in a Bank willing to widen its membership.[39] This provision gives BRICS countries the control over the main decisions—requiring the simple majority—taken by the Board of Governors and by the Board of Directors.[40]

Concerning some issues—as changes in the Articles of Agreements, modification in the capital framework, the admission of new members and the related capital subscriptions—it is necessary a two-thirds supermajority, that is the vote of (at least) four out to five BRICS countries.[41]

In these hypotheses there is room for non-BRICS members because the BRICS control is some way diminished. Notwithstanding, reaching the two-thirds of votes would require the 12% of voting rights to be casted with the BRICS countries' votes (considering that their total voting rights cannot be less than 55%, excluding their—unlikely- agreement to sink below this threshold), so that this disposition could trigger a veto power for BRICS countries, able to easily prevent any unwelcomed proposals.

Considering the structure, the Board of Governors will have ten seats, five of which will be reserved to BRICS[42]; it means that the other countries will be

[39] Article 5—Membership:"(. . .) b) Membership shall be open to members of the United Nations at such times and in accordance with such terms and conditions as the Bank shall determine by a special majority at the Board of Governors."

[40] Article 6—Voting "(. . .) b) Except as otherwise specifically provided for in this Agreement, all matters before the Bank shall be decided by a simple majority of the votes cast. Where provided for in this Agreement, a qualified majority shall be understood as an affirmative vote of two thirds of the total voting power of the members. Where provided for in this Agreement, a special majority shall be understood as an affirmative vote of four of the founding members concurrent with an affirmative vote of two thirds of the total voting power of the members."

[41] Article 7—Authorized and Subscribed Capital "(. . .) d) An increase of the authorized and subscribed capital stock of the Bank, as well as the proportion between the paid in shares and the callable shares may be decided by the Board of Governors at such time and under such terms and conditions as it may deem advisable, by a special majority of the Board of Governors. In such case, each member shall have a reasonable opportunity to subscribe, under the conditions established in Article 8 and under such other conditions as the Board of Governors shall decide. No member, however, shall be obligated to subscribe to any part of such increased capital."; Article 8—Subscription of Shares "(a) Each member shall subscribe to shares of the capital stock of the Bank. The number of shares to be initially subscribed by the founding members shall be those set forth in Attachment 1 of this Agreement, which specifies the obligation of each member as to both paid-in and callable capital. The number of shares to be initially subscribed by other members shall be determined by the Board of Governors by special majority on the occasion of the acceptance of their accession"; Article 44—Amendments "(a) This Agreement may be amended only by decision of the Board of Governors by special majority."

[42] Article 12—Board of Directors "(. . .) (b) Each of the founding members shall appoint 1 (one) Director and 1 (one) alternate. The Board of Governors shall establish by special majority the methodology by which additional Directors and alternates shall be elected, so that the total number of Directors shall be no more than 10 (ten)."

grouped together in one constituency which will be led in the Board by a country casting the votes of the whole constituency. This approach is one of the most critical aspects, confirming a democratic deficit already existing in Institutions such as the WB, where many countries believe that the electoral system used to allocate the seats in the Board of Governors is damaging their voting rights—in particular because many constituencies are ruled by non-debtor countries and the debtor countries—therefore—would not be able to exercise their voting right.

The NDB allows the votes in the plurinational seat to be "fragmented" according to the preferences of each constituency member[43]; this innovation represents a clear improvement from the WB, but the lack of a "direct" voice in the Board of Governors could become a serious concern for countries with no seat, further strengthening the weight of BRICS countries.[44]

Again, the Statute specifies that the NDB's President—who will conduct the ordinary business of the Bank[45] and that in case of equal division has the right to vote in the Board of Governors—has to be chosen by BRICS countries on a rotating basis.[46]

The NDB has at least four Vice-Presidents, considering that each BRICS country will nominate a Vice-President if not already represented through the President's office.[47] It should be highlighted that the NDB's Charter is the only one among the

[43] Article 6—Voting: "(. . .) d) In voting in the Board of Directors each director shall be entitled to cast the number of votes that counted toward his election, which votes need not be cast as a unit."

[44] *Contra* Zhu (2015): "The NDB reflects a principle of fairness. It boasts an innovative governance structure in that its stock rights are divided equally among the BRICS countries, thus delinking the division of stock rights from the proportion of BRICS countries' gross domestic product (GDP) in global GDP. This innovative attempt needs to be confirmed in practice. The BRICS countries share the view that fairness must be shown in the governance structure of the NDB. This is an attempt to democratise international relations in international finance, and its success depends on the BRICS countries maintaining this and promoting a co-operative spirit".

[45] Article 13—President and Staff "(. . .) b) The President shall be chief of the operating staff of the Bank and shall conduct, under the direction of the Directors, the ordinary business of the Bank, and in particular: (i) being, on this, accountable to the Directors, the President shall be responsible for the organization, appointment and dismissal of the officers and staff, and recommendation of admission and dismissal of Vice Presidents to the Board of Governors; (ii) the President shall head the credit and investment committee, composed also by the Vice-Presidents, that will be responsible for decisions on loans, guarantees, equity investments and technical assistance of no more than a limit amount to be established by the Board of Directors, provided that no objection is raised by any member of Board of Directors within 30 (thirty) days since such project is submitted to the Board."

[46] Art. 13a. Article 13—President and Staff "(a) The Board of Governors shall elect a President from one of the founding members on a rotational basis, who shall not be a Governor or a Director or an alternate for either. The President shall be a member of the Board of Directors, but shall have no vote except a deciding vote in case of an equal division. The President may participate in meetings of the Board of Governors, but shall not vote at such meetings."

[47] Article 13—President and Staff "(. . .) c) There shall be at least 1 (one) Vice-President from each founding member except the country represented by the President. Vice-Presidents shall be appointed by the Board of Governors on the recommendation of the President. Vice-Presidents shall exercise such authority and perform such functions in the administration of the Bank, as may be determined by the Board of Directors."

MDBs to explicitly mentioning the vice-presidency role in its organizational framework, thus suggesting a degree of political interest that could threaten the technical quality and horizontal democracy among the members of the Bank.

The importance of the Vice-Presidents is in fact witnessed by the establishment of an investment committee which is composed by the President and all the Vice-Presidents, with the power—delegated by the Board of the Governors—to decide on all the matters on loans and guarantees below a certain threshold.[48]

If this Committee is potentially useful from an organizational point of view as a tool to making voting decisions easier, on the other side it seems not to be consistent with the democratic principle among the non-BRICS members, due to the fundamental role played by vice-Presidents. It is essential that BRICS countries appoint Vice-Presidents with highly-recognized technical qualifications, which are extremely important in decisions concerning loans and investments; if "political" considerations prevailed, the reputation and legitimacy of the NDB would be deeply affected.

In general, many potential members could refrain from entering the NDB, due to the fact that the governance of the Bank is firmly controlled by BRICS members. In other words, from the non-BRICS countries' point of view, the NDB may simply appear as another MDB with a Bretton Woods background, but with BRICS countries instead of USA and G7 countries. The provisions on governance—combined with relatively high financial costs and shorter term loans compared with the main MDBs—could make the NDB less attractive for non-BRICS countries. In the first years of existence, the new members are likely to be small low-income countries which are less concerned about the governance and they need to get a loan on the very short term; these last countries are therefore more inclined to bind themselves with the BRICS countries due to political considerations. On the other side, the lack of large shareholders could allow the NDB to establish a more streamlined management, less bureaucratic than the existing development banks. Moreover, some countries could be willing to apply in order to allow the national companies to compete for NDB's contracts.

A partnership between BRICS and low-income countries could be an interesting outcome and a starting point for further developments in the NDB; however it has (at least) two disadvantages:

- financially, it could reduce the possible inflows of new capitals from the shareholders, considering the fact that low-income countries are supposed to contribute to a lesser degree in the capital paid due to budgetary constraints. At the same

[48]Art. 13b(ii). Article 13—President and Staff "(b) The President shall be chief of the operating staff of the Bank and shall conduct, under the direction of the Directors, the ordinary business of the Bank, and in particular: (. . .) (ii) the President shall head the credit and investment committee, composed also by the Vice-Presidents, that will be responsible for decisions on loans, guarantees, equity investments and technical assistance of no more than a limit amount to be established by the Board of Directors, provided that no objection is raised by any member of Board of Directors within 30 (thirty) days since such project is submitted to the Board."

time, NDB's loans portfolio would be less diversified, risky and on a small scale, so that it would have harder access to capital markets[49];

- the international legitimacy and the global impact of NDB would be undermined by a unbalanced structure and relationship between the BRICS and a group of more weakened countries.

In conclusion, not only the NDB follows existing models, but it establishes a high degree of control by BRICS countries, for some reasons a stronger one if compared with the MDBs blamed by its founding members. If it is partially understandable—the rise of BRICS economic power is the precondition to show their mightiness on the world stage—on the other side it could have negative "non-intentional" consequences for the NDB.

4 Outlook and Final Remarks

It should be underlined, as recognized by the Russian Foreign Minister Anton Siluanov speaking at the end of the Business Council Summit,[50] that the NDB has been established in order to finance infrastructural projects in BRICS and in the developing

[49]The reading of art. 19,d seems to prove an acknowledgement regarding this issue by BRICS countries: the article states that the NDB can loan to third countries under special circumstances. This should allow the NDB to build up a loans portfolio, notwithstanding an economic downturn in the new member States. Article 19—Methods of Operation "(. . .) d) The Board of Governors, by special majority, may approve a general policy under which the Bank is authorized to develop the operations described in the previous items of this article in relation to public or private projects in a non-member emerging economy or developing country, subject to the condition that it involves a material interest of a member, as defined by such policy. e) The Board of Directors, by special majority, may exceptionally approve a specific public or private project in a non-member emerging economy or developing country involving the operations described in the previous items of this article. Sovereign guaranteed operations in non-members will be priced in full consideration of the sovereign risks involved, given the risk mitigators offered, and any other conditions established as the Board of Directors may decide".

[50]Under the witness of the BRICS Heads of State, the BRICS Business Council was established during the BRICS Heads of State Summit of 26–27 March 2013 which was held in Durban, South Africa and in terms of the "Declaration on the establishment of the BRICS Business Council. The BRICS Business Council is composed of 25 prominent entrepreneurs from Brazil, Russia, India, China and South Africa, representing various industries and sectors in the BRICS nations. The BRICS Business Council has established five Industry/Sector Working Groups, which are: the Infrastructure Working Group which includes *transport, rail, road, ports, airlines*; the Manufacturing Working Group which includes p*harmaceuticals, healthcare and generic medicines, high technology, value added manufacturing, minerals beneficiation and value add, steel mills, agro-processing;* the Financial Services Working Group which includes *banking, insurance, investments, the BRICS Development Bank*; the Energy and the Green Economy Working Group which includes *electricity, renewable energy, solar power, natural gas, oil, hydropower*; and the Skills Development Working Group. The BRICS Business Council is one of the most important mechanisms for BRICS cooperation. As the "Declaration on the establishment of the BRICS Business Council" states, "The BRICS Business Council will constitute a

countries. In the next future new investments in foreign projects will be possible, but at the current stage priority will be given to investment projects in BRICS countries.[51]

The BRICS have been presenting several projects and the most effective will be selected by the NDB: there is a large number of proposed investments, some of them already accurately outlined. During the Summit of Brasilia in 2014, the Russian delegation unveiled 37 proposals, jointly drafted with the Commercial Chamber of Commerce of Russian Federation and with the Ministry of Economic Development. It is worth quoting, by way of example, the Rostekh project, a Federal State Agency 100% controlled by the Russian Customs Federal Agency, with the goal to build ready-made port facilities, which have been warmly appreciated by all BRICS countries. The Brazilian delegation proposed a transoceanic highway which should go through the territories of Brazil, Argentina, Paraguay and Chile.[52] Among the selected projects, in addition to the "One Belt, One Road" mentioned above, it could also be chosen the building of the high-speed railway Moscow-Kazan, designed as a section of the Moscow-Beijing line.[53]

Anyway, for the BRICS Business Council, the NDB should highlight regional infrastructures, energy and mineral resources, connectivity and skills development requirements in developing countries, and finance investment projects with medium

platform which will strengthen and promote economic, trade, business and investment ties among the Business communities of the five BRICS countries. The Business Council will ensure that there is regular dialogue between the Business communities of the BRICS nations and the Governments of the BRICS countries. The Business Council will also identify problems and bottlenecks to ensure greater economic, trade and investment ties among the BRICS countries and recommend solutions accordingly". As Putin has declared: "I will note that last year our countries' businesses established the BRICS Business Council. This institution is still to fully realize its potential, but we have already started work to identify and eliminate barriers that impede business interaction within of the association. It is clear that all the BRICS economies need serious infrastructure modernization. Our initiative to establish the Development Bank is aimed at expanding cooperation in this sphere. In the year since the Durban Summit, we have managed to achieve significant progress in this direction. In the near future, we expect to finalize all the remaining issues and we will be able to use this Bank's potential to realize major projects in our countries": http://tass.ru/en/russia/740471. See Mota Prado and Salles (2014), Scaffardi (2014).

[51]http://it.rbth.com/mondo/2015/07/08/brics_e_sco_doppio_summit_a_ufa_36593.

[52]http://iirsa.org/Page/Detail?menuItemId=101.

[53]The Russia-proposed idea of the Trans-Eurasian Belt Development and China's Belt and Road Initiative are economically complementary. The Russian initiative is an ambitious plan to build a grand transportation corridor across Russia, through the entirety of Siberia. And China's Belt and Road Initiative is a land-based economic development framework for integrating trade and investment in countries situated on the ancient Silk Road through Central Asia, West Asia, the Middle East and Europe. The two initiatives are aimed not only at the construction of railways, roads and energy infrastructure, but also at establishing large economic development zones. Investment in infrastructure construction is a way to counterbalance the influence of economic recession, and instead of resulting in inflation, it is a special driving force to bring the economy back to normal. Moreover, conjoining the Russian project with China's major economic development strategy will reduce Russia's dependence on the West, especially when the West has already imposed several rounds of sanctions on Russia due to the Ukraine crisis.

and long term loans. The NDB is suggested to play a positive role in the following areas:

(a) To strengthen the economic, trade and investment ties among BRICS countries;
(b) To promote trans-regional industrial cooperation and unleash the comparative advantages of BRICS countries;
(c) To push forward infrastructure construction for better connectivity among BRICS countries, as well as between BRICS countries and their surrounding regions;
(d) To optimize the allocation of financial resources among BRICS countries;
(e) To act as an assurance bank for the intra-BRICS commerce of manufactures;
(f) In the domain of skills development, to establish a "Skills Development Fund", designed to promote investments in the quality and access to technical, vocational education and training (TVET), taking as a starting point the concept note prepared by the Skills Development Working Group of the BBC. This funding mechanism would provide a platform for sharing of knowledge and lessons learned on improving systems and responses to evolving demands on TVET in BRICS and emerging/developing economies;
(g) To collaborate with commercial financial institutions, so as to reduce costs and risks. It should provide diversified financial products including loans, guarantees and consultation, the price of which need to be lower than that of commercial products. The current conditions of the developing countries need to be considered when devising relevant standards of the Bank;
(h) To enhance its risk prevention mechanism by establishing reserve funds, improving reserve structures, and creating effective guarantee model for project financing. It should also consider providing guarantees to large scale projects in BRICS and other developing countries;
(i) To serve as an information platform. An effective mechanism could be established through the NDB to share information on major projects among BRICS countries.[54]

Since it has been created after the AIIB and with the same amount of capital, it will be necessary to establish a sort of coordination between the two Institutions. In particular, with the contribution of both the Banks, it will be possible to carry on with remarkable and joint projects, which are involving several countries—such as Russia and China—interested in developing the Silk Road Economic Belt.[55] In the

[54]*Facing Challenges, Building Confidence*, BRICS Business Council Second Annual, Report 2014–2015, p. 10.

[55]In particular, in April 2015, the head of the Central Bank of Russia Elvira Nabiullina said that the BRICS New Development Bank and the AIIB will not compete, but rather complement each other: https://www.rt.com/business/250689-brics-aiib-imf-rival/. The NDB and the AIIB are sister institutions in many respects, said the NDB Vice President Leslie Maasdorp "These two banks have complimentary mandates and different geographic focuses, with the NDB being more focused on BRICS countries. At the same time, there is a certain overlapping between mandates of the NDB and the AIIB, as both of them are aimed at developing infrastructure and pay a special attention to sustainable development. However, due to the fact that current financing and investment patterns

agenda of the NDB management are mentioned extremely simplified procedures to take decisions: this decisional framework will have to be neither complex nor overly bureaucratic and it will have to focus on advanced standards of quality in order to compete with the mechanisms in place in other financial Institutions (see *supra*... But this at the expense of the horizontal democracy among the members).[56]

The logic behind the NDB seems to be unobjectionable. The BRICS, and in general the developing countries, have huge need for new infrastructures.[57] This problem does not involve China which, however, owns large building companies welcoming with excitement the possibility to have a key role on projects in other countries.[58] The targets of the future lenders are completely aligned with each other. Considering the contribution to development, the NDB should not be regarded as a "dangerous" competitor neither of the existing MDBs, nor of the WB, since the New Bank, with a 100 billion of subscribed capital, will not be able to compete to supply the demand of global infrastructures. Even though, actually, the insufficient capitalization can be improved in the longer term.[59]

Currently 20 MDBs are operating all over the world, among them the WB, several regional development banks and some specialized and sub-regional banks. The well-known MDBs include developing and industrial countries among their members—for instance, naturally besides the WB, it is important to quote the Asian

are inadequate in meeting investment needs, there is 'space for newcomers'": *5 Minutes with Leslie Maasdorp at the NDB,.Insigh* at http://insight.amcham-shanghai.org/5-minutes-with-leslie-maasdorp-of-the-new-development-bank/. See Snyder and Lu (2015).

[56]Wilkins and Papa (2013).

[57]In July 2014, Nobel Prize winning economist Joseph Stiglitz said the NDB marks a "fundamental change in global economic and political power". In his opinion, "The existing institutions just don't have enough resources": *Nobel Economist Stiglitz Hails New BRICS Bank Challenging U.S–Dominated World Bank & IMF, Democracy Now!* at http://www.democracynow.org/.

[58]See Zucca (2016), pp. 85–98. The Author illustrates the China contribution to the BRICS coordination and perform an in-depth analysis of the current, open problems in the development dynamism, both within the country and internationally. In particular, the Author analyzes the possible impact of the growing differences between the BRICS member States on the implementation of the common platform and the terms by which the specific national interests will be combined into a larger common interest, to internationally assert an incisive leadership of the BRICS. In particular, he raises the question how China will combine its position of global economic player, the inevitable reform choices of its internal development model and its contribution to BRICS coordination. The commitment in key strategic BRICS projects, as the NDB and the start-up of major infrastructure projects, as the Eurasian corridors, seem to indicate that China will continue with this experience. But the objectives and growing differences between China and the other member States are in fact creating uncertainty on the future role that it will play as a part of the BRICS.

[59]In March 2016, the NDB announced that it will do a bond issue in China to raise funding domestically on the Chinese market. According to media reports, the China's bond market is bigger than the ones in other BRICS countries and theoretically more accommodating for the bank because it obtained a triple-A credit rating in the country, which should allow it to borrow cheaply; Areddy (2016).

Development Bank, the African Development Bank and Interamerican Development Bank—meanwhile other less known Banks have different participatory models, like the Andean Development Corporation (CAF- Corporacion Andina de Fomento), the PTA Bank and the Islamic Development Bank (ISDB).

A different analysis should be reserved to the CCP, which aims to loosen the dependency of BRICS countries from the Federal Reserve and the dollar, considering that the five countries agreed to finance swap agreements—where all member countries can take financial resources—with a total amount of 100 billion dollars of foreign reserves.

In this case, the interest rates of future lenders and borrowers seem not to be consistent. Indeed, the next BRICS country hit by a crisis is likely to apply for lending money from the reserve fund; on the other side, the other members will probably be reluctant to grant a huge amount of liquidity, particularly if there are doubts about the country's solvency.[60] In other words, in contrast with development spending, in this case the potential incentives for lenders and borrowers are misaligned. This problem could be overcome by allowing the lenders to impose economic conditionality on borrowers, and with a regular surveillance on implementation and compliance. Notwithstanding, the prevision of conditionality on large, proud and different countries as the BRICS seems to be a remote hypothesis: it is hard to realize how Brazil, for instance, could accept to have a conditionality policy imposed by China.[61] 2016 will be a decisive year to understand the path BRICS countries will take as a group: it will be essential to see if China and India, the current "locomotives" of the five economies, will be able to find a shared

[60]For instance, Biswas (2015) points out that "The constraints on the foreign exchange reserves of both Russia and India have been tested by recent economic crises. India's economic crisis in 2013 triggered a protracted depreciation of the rupee that forced the Reserve Bank of India to intervene in currency markets over a period of months, and deplete its foreign exchange reserves, in order to smooth the depreciation. e Russian economic crisis that commenced in 2014 is still unfolding: capital fight in 2014 was estimated by the Central Bank of Russia at US$ 128 billion (The Moscow Times, November 10, 2014). The Central Bank is estimated to have used up US$ 80 billion of its foreign exchange reserves to intervene to stabilize the sharp depreciation of the rouble in 2014 (Reuters News, December 17, 2014). Total foreign exchange reserves are estimated to have declined from US$ 510 billion at the end of 2013 to US$ 416 billion by mid-December 2014. On the other hand, China's capacity to intervene to stabilize global crises could increase significantly if China manages to introduce full currency convertibility and establish the yuan as a global reserve currency. But this is still a long-term goal".

[61]Other efforts to create swap and credit lines, as the Chiang Mai Initiative Multilateralization, established after the Asian crisis, have been unsuccessful due to the same problem. The safety net provided by the Chiang Mai Initiative was even more wider than the one set up through the fund of BRICS countries, but divergent interests of loaners and borrowers made it useless, also in 2008, at the height of the global financial crisis. The authors of the Chiang Mai Initiative tried to break the log-jam by imposing to borrower countries using more than 30% of their swap to negotiate a financial arrangement with the IMF. The treaty establishing the BRICS reserve fund include the same clause, the article 12: this contradicts the opinion that this fund could be an alternative to the IMF. It is remarkable, as already highlighted, that the subscriptions of BRICS countries in the Fund are denominated in dollars. Therefore the NDB is supposed to have a sense and a future for BRICS countries, meanwhile the CCP seems rather to be a symbolic tool.

position and to defend it together or if the tendency to disaggregation and to a unipolarism of the five main regional actors will definitively prevail in the most important dossiers. As conclusive remark it is useful to quote the logo of the NDB.

The logo of the New Development Bank is represented by a Mobius strip that symbolizes the idea of continuous transformation. Its nature is not to unsettle but drive change in the existing system from within. The logo consists of a triangle in motion and, at the other end, a propeller, moving in the opposite direction, that represents speed and dynamism. These two entities are held together by a wireframe, the skeletal basic of infrastructure.

The logo is rendered in green that symbolizes sustainability. This constant motion symbolizes the values that the bank strives to live by—"agility, innovation and continuous transformation".[62]

Time will tell if the activity carried out by the NDB will be consistent with the meaning of the logo and if it will trigger a breakdown of the "wall" represented by the WB and the IMF, apparently impassable, or, on the contrary, it will mean a sort of "return to the past", doubling and drawing democracy and transparency deficiencies from the Bretton Woods Institutions.

References

Areddy JT (2016) BRICS development Bank pins hope on China bond sale. Wall Street J, March 10. http://www.wsj.com/articles/brics-development-bank-pins-hope-on-china-bond-sale-1457613691

Bevir M, Gaskarth J (2015) Global governance and the BRICs: ideas, actors and governance practices. In: Gaskarth J (ed) Rising powers, global governance, and global ethics. Routledge/ Taylor & Francis Group, London/New York, pp 74–96

Biswas R (2015) Reshaping the financial architecture for development finance: the new development Bank. London School of Economics and Political Science global South unit Working paper series, Working Paper No. 2

Boni S (2016) Il Brasile tra protagonismo internazionale e recessione economica. Rivista di Studi Politici Internazionali 83(1):99–109

Boumphrey S (2015) Divergent Growth: The Economic Outlook for BRIC in 2015. February 9. http://blog.euromonitor.com/2015/02/divergent-growth-the-economic-outlook-for-bric-in-2015.html

Burns M (2013) Shifting global power and shifting state power: DRIP, BRICs and CANZUS. In: Maguire R, Lewis B, Sampford C (eds) Shifting global powers and the international law: challenges and opportunities. Routledge/Taylor & Francis Group, London/New York, pp 154–170

Carducci M (2013) Il BRICS come "legal network" e le sue implicazioni costituzionali. In: Costituzione, Economia, Globalizzazione: Liber amicorum in onore di Carlo Amirante. Edizioni Scientifiche Italiane, Napoli, pp 1093–1105

Carducci M, Bruno AS (2014) The BRICS countries between justice and economy. Methodological challenges on constitutional comparison. Sociol Anthropol 2:46–58

[62] http://www.ndb.int/our-identity.php.

Chardell D (2015) The BRICS: beyond the hype. The National Interest, July 14. http://nationalinterest.org/feature/the-brics-beyond-the-hype-13322?page=show

Choukroune L (2014) Les BRICS et le droit international du commerce et de l'insestissement "entre autonomie et intégration". In: Les dérèglements économiques internationaux: crise du droit ou droit des crises?, sous la dir. d'Habib Ghérari. Editions Pedone, Paris, pp 203–227

Cooper AF, Thakur R (2014) The BRICS in the new global economic geography. In: Weiss TG, Wilkinson R (eds) International organization and global governance. Routledge/Taylor & Francis Group, London/New York, pp 265–278

Davies G (2015) Whatever happened to the Brics?, Financial Times, July 13. https://www.ft.com/content/42666123-2d48-3e0b-8993-ed4f023d9aad

De' Robertis A (2016) Genesi e sviluppo del fenomeno BRICS nel Sistema internazionale. Rivista di Studi Politici Internazionali 83(1):13–23

Griffith-Jones S (2014) A BRICS development Bank: a dream come true?, UNCTAD Discussion Paper No. 215

Griffith-Jones S (2015) Financing global development: the BRICS new development Bank, German Development Institute/Deutsches Institut für Entwicklungspoliti, Briefing Paper 13/2015

Graham T (2013) Russia, the BRICs, and the United States. Yale J Int Aff 8(1):23–29

Jiejin Z (2015) New South-South co-operation and the BRICS new development Bank, BRICS Insights Paper No 2

Keukeleire S, Hooijmaijers B (2014) The BRICS and other emerging power alliances and multilateral organizations in the Asia-Pacific and the global South: challenges for the European Union and its view on multilateralism. J Common Mark Stud 52(3):582–599

Lieber RJ (2014) The rise of the BRICS and American primacy. Int Polit 51(2):137–154

Martino A (2016) Una strategia BRICS chiamata Sudafrica. Rivista di Studi Politici Internazionali 83(1):123–135

Molinaro E (2016) Geopolitical trends: Statalist BRICS challenge Glocalist financial instability. Rivista di Studi Politici Internazionali 83(1):47–66

Mota Prado M, Salles FC (2014) The BRICS Bank's potential to challenge the field of development cooperation. Verfassung und Recht in Űbersee 47(2):147–197

O'Neill J (2001) Building better global economic BRICs. Global Economics Paper No: 66

O'Neill J (2013) South Africa's BRICS score: not all doom and gloom, the guardian, March 23

Panebianco M, Verdecchia A (2013) BRICS: gruppo internazionale di Stati. Diritto comunitario e degli scambi internazionali 52(1–2):1–30

Petropoulos S (2015) Opportunities, challenges and prospects of South Africa in the BRICS. In: Rewizorski M (ed) The European Union and the BRICS-complex relations in the era of global governance. Springer, London, pp 161–180

Porteilla R (2011) L'intégration de l'Afrique du Sud dans les BRIC: opportunités et risques. Recherches internationales 91:47–54

Raimondi P (2016) Il programma dei BRICS per la costruzione di un nuovo ordine mondiale. Rivista di Studi Politici Internazionali 83(1):27–46

Riccieri M (2016) I BRICS nell'interpretazione politica russa. Rivista di Studi Politici Internazionali 83(1):67–83

Rolland SE (2013) The BRICS' contributions to the architecture and norms of international economic law. Proc Annu Meet 107:164–170

Sahni V (2015) Brazil: fellow traveler on the long and winding road to Grandeza. In: Malone DM, Raja Mohan C, Raghavan S (eds) Oxford handbook of Indian foreign policy. Oxford University Press, Oxford, pp 524–538

Scaffardi L (2014) BRICS, a multi-centre legal network? Beijing Law Rev 5(2):141–148

Scridel E (2016) I BRICS e la nuova governance mondiale: il XXI secolo sarà il "secolo indiano"? Rivista di Studi Politici Internazionali 83(1):111–119

Snyder F, Lu Y (2015) The future of transnational law: EU, USA, China and the BRICS. In: Lu Y, Snyder F (eds) L'avenir du droit transnational: EU, USA Chine et les BRICS/The future of transnational law: EU, USA Chine and the BRICS International. Bruylant, Bruxelles, pp 1–22

Soulé-Kohndou F (2013) L'Afrique du Sud dans la relation BRICS-Afrique : Ambitions, défis et paradoxes. Afrique contemporaine: documents d'Afrique noire et de Madagascar 248 (4):31–43

Walker A (2014) Whatever Happened to the Brics Economies?, November 27. http://www.bbc.com/news/business-29960335

Wilkins D, Papa M (2013) The rise of the corporate legal elite in the BRICS: implications for global governance. Boston Coll Int Comp Law Rev 54(3):1149–1184

Yu S (2014a) A study on the cooperation in trade remedies among the BRICS countries. In: Jiaxiang H, Matthias V (eds) Regional cooperation and free trade agreements in Asia. Brill Nijhoff, Leiden/Boston, pp 301–328

Yu Y (2014b) Trade remedies: China in the BRICS. J World Trade Law Econ Public Policy 48 (6):1247–1277

Zani M (2012) Les BRICS et le nouvel ordre international. L'observateur des Nations Unies: revue de l'Association française pour les Nations Unies. Section Aix-en-Provence 33(2):7–14

Zucca F (2016) Luci e ombre del contributo della Cina ai BRICS. Rivista di Studi Politici Internazionali 83(1):85–98

Part II
The Constitutionalization of the "Washington Consensus" in the European Union

From Washington Consensus to Brussels Consensus

Alberto Monteverdi

Abstract The chapter argues that the neoliberal doctrine, which emerged in the 1980s as a response to the crisis of the Keynesian economics, has shaped both the IMF's conditionality policy and the European economic governance. The orthodox prescriptions known as the Washington Consensus have formed the "one-size-fits-all approach" applied for several decades all over the world by the IMF. The EU has given constitutional strength to the neoliberal principles through the Maastricht Treaty of 1992. However, this chapter also shows how the latest global financial crisis has represented a turning point for the IMF-EU consensus on macroeconomic policy. European policy makers have adopted a hyper-conservative approach by remaining devoted to the economic orthodoxy. The Fund has instead engaged itself in an open-minded discussion about the best policies to promote stability and growth which has led IMF researchers to challenge all the main neoliberal tenets.

Contents

1 Introduction

The term "Washington Consensus" was coined by the economist John Williamson in the background paper for the conference "Latin American Adjustment: How Much Has Happened?" held by the Institute for International Economics in 1989.[1]

---

[1] See Williamson (1990).

A. Monteverdi (✉)
UBI Banca, Brescia, Italy
e-mail: alberto.monteverdi@ubiss.it

E. Sciso (ed.), *Accountability, Transparency and Democracy in the Functioning of Bretton Woods Institutions*, DOI 10.1007/978-3-319-57855-2_5

Table 1 Policy prescriptions

Washington Consensus (Williamson)	"Augmented" Washington Consensus (Rodrik)
	The Williamson's list plus:
1. Fiscal discipline	11. Corporate governance
2. Reorientation of public expenditures	12. Anti-corruption
3. Tax reform	13. Flexible labor markets
4. Financial liberalization	14. WTO agreements
5. Unified and competitive exchange rates	15. Financial codes and standards
6. Trade liberalization	16. "Prudent" capital-account opening
7. Openness to foreign direct investment	17. Non-intermediate exchange rate regimes
8. Privatization	18. Independent central banks/inflation targeting
9. Deregulation	19. Social safety nets
10. Secure property rights	20. Targeted poverty reduction

Source: Author's elaboration on Rodrik (2002)

Williamson made a list of policy instruments which he claimed were "practically universally agreed in Washington to be desirable in most Latin American countries as of 1989".[2] For "Washington" he meant both the "political" Washington of the US Congress and the US Administration, and the "technocratic" Washington of the international financial institutions (IFIs), primarily the International Monetary Fund (IMF) and the World Bank, the economic agencies of the US government, the Federal Reserve Board and the think tanks. Williamson identified ten policy prescriptions that composed the Consensus: (1) fiscal discipline; (2) reordering public expenditure priorities (withdrawal of subsidies and increased spending in health and education); (3) tax reform (broadening tax bases and reducing marginal tax rates); (4) financial liberalization (market-determined interest rates); (5) a competitive exchange rate; (6) trade liberalization; (7) liberalization of inward foreign direct investment (FDI); (8) privatization of state enterprises; (9) deregulation of economic activities; (10) a solid guarantee of property rights.

These policies, initially addressed to one particular context, i.e. to Latin America during the 1980s, became over time the standard development recipe adopted by the IMF for more than two decades in very diverse contexts, such as Africa, East Asia, Brazil, Mexico, Argentina, Turkey and the former Soviet bloc. At the end of the 1990s, in response to the poor performance of the IMF financial assistance in developing countries, as well as the impressive success of many East Asian economies, which violated virtually all the rules of the Consensus, the Williamson's original list was expanded to include further ten policy prescriptions, the so-called "second-generation reforms". This new agenda for development, which Dani Rodrik called the "Augmented" Washington Consensus, preserved the core ideas of the original approach, while emphasized the importance of institutional and structural reforms, ranging from the design and mandate of the central bank to labour markets (Table 1).[3]

[2]Williamson (2004), p. 195.

[3]See Rodrik (2002).

Essentially, the Washington Consensus proposes a development model based on three main pillars: first, macroeconomic discipline (price stability, fiscal discipline, and exchange rate stability); second, a highly competitive market economy (privatization, liberalization, deregulation and other institutional/structural reforms); third, full integration with the world economy (openness to international trade and global capital flows).

The set of developing instruments described above continues nowadays to be associated with the Washington-based institutions, firstly the International Monetary Fund. The aim of this chapter is to show instead that today is the European Union (EU), not the IMF, the main supporter, and the purest example of application, of the policy prescriptions known as the Washington Consensus.

The chapter is structured as follows. Section 2 deals with the theoretical basis of the Washington Consensus. Section 3 is devoted to the European economic governance. Sections 4 and 5 describe the reactions of the EU and the IMF to the latest global financial crisis and show how the barycenter of the Consensus has recently moved from Washington to Brussels. Finally, Sect. 6 concludes.

2 The New Classicism

The Washington Consensus prescriptions reflect the neoliberal doctrine that prevailed in the 1980s, when the practice of an intrusive macroeconomic conditionality was attached to the IMF financial assistance programmes. In the previous decade, confidence in the Keynesian paradigm eroded as two oil price shocks had created an economic scenario in which most industrial economies experienced a combination of both rising unemployment and inflation that challenged the assumption of the "Phillips Curve".[4] This new phenomenon, the so-called "stagflation", was ignored by the demand-orientated Keynesian approach. The temporary confusion caused by the apparent inability to solve the new economic problems generated widespread dissatisfaction with Keynesian economics and resulted in a sudden surge of interest in alternative paradigms, notably the monetarism, the new classical macroeconomics, and the real business cycle theory.

The monetarism, started by Milton Friedman,[5] by incorporating in the Phillips Curve the "adaptive expectations" hypothesis, supported the idea of long-run neutrality of money. The new classical macroeconomics, led by Robert Lucas,[6] introduced the alternative hypothesis of "rational expectations",[7] shortening the transition period towards the equilibrium described by the monetarists, up to the

[4]See Phillips (1958).

[5]See Friedman (1968).

[6]See Lucas (1972).

[7]The rational expectations hypothesis was originally proposed by John Muth in the early 1960s, see Muth (1961).

point where it becomes an "instantaneous jump". The real business cycle theory, initiated by the seminal article of Kydland and Prescott,[8] pushed rational expectations to their limit and invoked technology and other supply-side shocks as the sole determinants of output fluctuations.

Between the 1970s and the 1980s these theoretical developments led to a "new classical revolution" which challenged the Keynesian paradigm and its reliance on active macroeconomic policies to ensure full employment.[9]

The Washington Consensus has its theoretical basis in this modern version of the neoclassical theory. Based upon the Walrasian tradition, the economy is perceived as being in continual short- and long-run equilibrium due to the interaction of fully rational agents and perfect price and wage flexibility. When combined with classical assumptions of perfect competition and continuous market clearing, this new classical approach dismisses the existence of involuntary unemployment. Markets, "if left free to operate without distortions, tend to converge spontaneously to "optimal" equilibria, characterized by full employment of resources and the maximization of a representative agent's welfare (the so-called Pareto efficiency). Price and wage flexibility, then, ensures that demand adapts to full employment supply (a principle known as Say's Law)".[10] In such a context, observed unemployment is voluntary, depending on preference of workers for leisure at the current real wage.

This model leaves very little space for macroeconomic policy. Since the absence of involuntary unemployment, there is no need for discretionary demand-side interventions. The economy operates at its natural equilibrium level (apart from random disturbances), both in the short- and long-term, so that any increase in government spending causes the "crowding out" of an equal amount of private expenditure, implying the absence of a role for fiscal policy. In addition, money is neutral, considered only a "veil" whose intrinsic utility is zero: an increase in money supply directly increases all prices and wages proportionately without changes on real variables, such as real output and employment. As a consequence, a monetary policy based on the objective of price stability is the best thing that a central bank can do to promote growth. The role of central banks is to keep the price level on a steady course (inflation targeting) in order to anchor private sector expectations and minimize deviations from the optimal path of the economy. In other words, by stabilizing inflation the central bank would also bring the output gap to zero, the so-called "divine coincidence".[11]

The new classical paradigm argues that real income and the level of employment in the economy are essentially determined by supply-side factors. These are technology, population growth, preferences of economic agents and all institutional aspects of the economy (i.e. regulations determining the flexibility and competition of labour and

[8]See Kydland and Prescott (1982).

[9]See Greenwald and Stiglitz (1987), Baimbridge and Whyman (2014).

[10]Saraceno (2015b), p. 4.

[11]The term "divine coincidence" was first coined by Blanchard and Galì, see Blanchard and Galì (2005).

product markets and incentives to supply labour and capital). The result is that the only effective economic policy relates supply-side measures that enhance the potential growth rate of the economy. Hence, the role of government is to implement "structural reforms" aimed at removing or minimizing those obstacles to free competition (i.e. informational asymmetries, externalities, excessive market powers, rigidities) that prevent markets from producing the best outcome in terms of resource allocation and growth. In general, the role of institutions, well emphasized in the "augmented" version of the Washington Consensus, is permitting the market economy to function effectively, by creating and maintaining a stable business-friendly environment.

In this theoretical framework there is no room for discretionary policies because they are considered ineffective to stabilize economic activity and distortionary for the free functioning of markets. Rules are to be preferred because they make policy predictable and therefore easier to embed in agent's expectations. The principle of money neutrality paves the way to a de-politicization of monetary policy and to a greater emphasis on the technical rather than political role of central banks, thereby influencing the nature of the relations between central banks and governments. Since the pressure to follow expansionary monetary policies typically comes from politicians pursuing short-term electoral gains, the central bank must be protected from this temptation by being an independent technocratic body and modeled on a strict mandate of price stability. As a strong anti-inflationary commitment increases credibility, divergences between central bank's policies and agent's expectations become smaller. Similarly, governments have no choice on fiscal policy but to comply with budgetary rules, which are adopted in order to avoid policy-induced uncertainty that could generate deviations from the optimal equilibrium.

3 The Maastricht Treaty: The Consensus in the Constitution

The European Union went very far in the internalization of the neoliberal doctrine, to the point that it was crystallized in the constitution. The Maastricht Treaty of 1992 defining the governance of the Economic and Monetary Union (EMU) codified what in the Washington Consensus were broad policy prescriptions.[12]

As regards the monetary policy, the Treaty gave the European Central Bank (ECB) two fundamental features. On the one hand, a hierarchy between price stability and the other economic objectives, on the other hand, a great independence of the central bank. This design is very consistent with the model of the Deutsche Bundesbank, a monetarist-inspired institution of which the ECB claims the heritage.

Article 127 TFEU states that "The primary objective of the European System of Central Banks (ESCB) shall be to maintain price stability", and only "Without prejudice to the objective of price stability the ESCB shall support the general

[12]See Fitoussi and Saraceno (2004, 2012).

economic policies in the Union". The Treaty does not give to the concept of price stability a precise content, and it is vague about the secondary objectives. Hence, the ECB is given a considerable autonomy in interpreting its mandate. The ECB's Governing Council has defined price stability as a year-on-year increase in the Harmonized Index of Consumer Prices (HICP) for the euro area of below, but close to, 2% over the medium term.[13] The ECB has instead remained silent on the secondary objective of supporting "the general economic policies in the Union". By doing so, the Governing Council has effectively restricted its area of responsibility to price stability. This represents a major difference with the US Federal Reserve (FED). The latter has a "dual mandate" of price stability and full employment, without hierarchy between the two objectives. The diverse approaches between the two central banks reflect the different intellectual environment in which they emerged. The Full Employment and Balanced Growth Act, which amended in the 1970s the Federal Reserve Act, was adopted in a period in which the Keynesian approach was still prevalent in the academic and policy debate. The ECB's focus on price stability is instead consistent with the new classical paradigm prevailing when its statute was being defined, according to which inflation targeting, by guiding agent's expectations, makes it possible for the central bank not only to stabilize inflation, but also to stabilize the economy around its natural level (the already mentioned "divine coincidence"). Coherently with its theoretical foundations, the ECB argues that the Eurozone's high unemployment originates mainly from structural rigidities on the supply-side of its member states' economies, and hence it denies responsibility for increasing aggregate demand to lower unemployment, since no scope exists to reduce unemployment without accelerating inflation.[14]

To protect the ECB's independence and the objective of price stability from political interference, the Treaty erects a "wall" around the central bank. Article 130 TFEU states that the ECB shall not "seek or take instructions" from Union or national institutions, while Article 123 TFEU introduces the principle of no public debt monetization. In spite of a high degree of independence, the Treaty requests to the ECB a relatively low degree of accountability. Formally, the ECB operates under the control of the European Parliament. However, when the President of the ECB appears before the European Parliament, he/she faces an institution that has no power to change the statute of the central bank. On the contrary, when the Chairman of the US Federal Reserve appears before the Congress, he/she faces an institution that can change its statute by a simple majority. In addition, except for extreme cases of serious misconduct, which included the intervention of the European Court of Justice, sanctions are not considered against the ECB's Executive Board members. This institutional setup makes the ECB one of the most independent and least accountable central banks in the world.[15]

[13]European Central Bank (2011), p. 9.

[14]See, for example, European Central Bank (1999, 2011).

[15]See De Grauwe (1999).

Turning to fiscal policy, the Eurozone is based on a unique arrangement whereby fiscal policies remain decentralized with regard to member states, but they are subjected to rules that restrict national autonomy and flexibility. This is provided by the Stability and Growth Pact (SGP), which complements and tightens the provisions laid down in the treaties.

Given the potential externalities and moral hazard risks arising from the ability of individual member states from borrowing in a monetary union, the founding fathers of the euro incorporated into the Maastricht Treaty several safeguards to prevent spillovers from national fiscal policies to the common monetary policy.[16] First, monetary financing of government borrowings by the ECB or national central banks is strictly forbidden (Article 123 TFEU). Second, under the so-called "no-bail-out clause" each member country is responsible for serving its debt. This implies that the bailing out of a member state in financial difficulty, either by the Union or by other member states, is excluded (Article 125 TFEU). Third, excessive fiscal deficits by member countries are prohibited. Where it is considered "excessive" an annual government deficit above 3% of GDP, unless the excess is close to the reference value and it is declining "substantially and continuously" or it is only "exceptional and temporary", and a government debt over 60% of GDP, "unless the ratio is sufficiently diminishing and approaching the reference value at a satisfactory pace" (Article 126 TFEU, and Protocol No. 12).

The SGP, on the legal basis of Articles 121 and 126 TFEU, enforced fiscal discipline as a permanent feature of the EMU by: (1) requiring member states to submit Stability (for euro area countries) or Convergence (for non-euro countries) Programmes with an annual frequency; (2) introducing a Medium-Term Objective (MTO) of a budgetary position, in structural terms, "close to balance or in surplus"; (3) specifying the conditions for the application of the Excessive Deficit Procedure (EDP) established by, but not elaborated in, the Treaty, including strict deadlines for the correction of excessive deficits; (4) imposing financial penalties on member states which do not promptly correct excessive deficits.[17]

The rationale behind the SGP is that the budget should be brought into surplus in good times in order to allow automatic stabilizers to operate in bad times without trespassing the 3% deficit ceiling. The SGP forces member states to rely solely on automatic stabilizers to cushion cyclical economic fluctuations (temporary country-specific shocks), thus ruling out any discretionary fiscal policy at national level. At the same time, no active macroeconomic stabilization role is conferred upon the EU budget that "shall be in balance" (Article 310 TFEU).

According to this "Washington-Brussels Consensus" the scope for macroeconomic stabilization policies is therefore limited, and only in the short-run. In the long-run, supply-side factors are considered to dominate in determining the level of economic activity. The main tools of economic policy are hence institutional and

[16]See González-Páramo (2005).

[17]See European Commission (2013).

structural reforms aimed at increasing integration and competition, and, in general, minimizing obstacles to the smooth working of market forces.

First, the treaties establish a European internal market as an area "without internal frontiers in which the free movement of goods, persons, services and capital is ensured" (Article 26 TFEU). Second, the EU imposes a severe discipline on national state aid, in order to reduce the distortionary presence of the state in economy, leaving the government the sole objective of dealing with the so-called "market failures", e.g. coping with externalities and providing public goods (Articles 106–108 TFEU). Third, a strict competition law promotes a high degree of competition within the Union by preventing excessive market powers, i.e. anti-competitive agreements, conducts and mergers (Articles 101–102 TFEU and EU merger regulation). Fourth, the Eurozone governance promotes deregulation of labour and product markets. The idea is that the high level of unemployment in the euro area is "structural in origin. It is caused mainly by the inflexibility of euro area labour and goods markets resulting, in part, from excessive or inappropriate regulation in these markets. Structural economic reforms aimed at reducing these inflexibilities are the appropriate policy response".[18] This ideological perspective is further exacerbated by the existence of a monetary union that is far from optimal.[19] In a context of low labour mobility, in fact, European policy makers advocate labour and product markets flexibility to enhance the adaptability of the EMU to asymmetric shocks.[20]

Initiatives to promote markets deregulation have been at the center of policy-making in the EU over the last two decades. This pressure over national governments comes from the European Commission, the ECB, as well as the governance framework of economic policy coordination in the EU, which includes the peer-reviews among member states within the ECOFIN and the Eurogroup. The "Lisbon Agenda" (today called "Europe 2020") is one of the clearest examples of such a pressure.[21] In the Lisbon Strategy framework various reports and guidelines are provided as a part of an annual coordination cycle. These include a set of Integrated Guidelines, formed by a package of the Broad Economic Policies Guidelines (Article 121 TFEU) and Employment Guidelines (Article 148 TFEU). Moreover, member states have to present National Reform Programmes on which the European Commission annually publishes assessments and country-specific recommendations. The Agenda puts particular emphasis on labour market reforms by endorsing the so-called "flexicurity".[22] Within this regulatory scheme over the last two decades member countries have implemented a series of structural reforms of their labour markets, which have reduced labour protection, tightened the conditions for receiving unemployment benefits and introduced highly flexible contracts (flexible working hours, temporary, part time, etc.).

[18]European Central Bank (1999), p. 41.

[19]See Mundell (1961).

[20]See, for example, Duisenberg (2002).

[21]See European Council (2000).

[22]See Commission of the European Communities (2007).

4 Global Death and European Resurgence of the Washington Consensus

On 9 August 2007 severe tensions emerged in interbank markets worldwide. Tensions reflected a lack of confidence among market participants and uncertainty about the financial health and liquidity of counterparties. This event made clear that the crisis would not be restricted to the US: in globalized and deregulated financial markets "toxic paper" had been distributed worldwide. Following the collapse of the US investment bank Lehman Brothers on 15 September 2008, the period of financial turmoil turned into a world financial crisis.[23]

The immediate repercussions of the global financial crisis seemed to spell the end for neoliberal policies and the revenge of the Keynesian economics. On 10 October 2008 the G-7 Finance Ministers Meeting agreed that: "the current situation calls for urgent and exceptional action. We commit to continue working together to stabilize financial markets and restore the flow of credit, to support global economic growth".[24] The major central banks in the world started to offer free or nearly free money to their financial systems by reducing interest rates and adopting unconventional measures. In November 2008, the IMF Managing Director Dominique Strauss-Kahn emphasized the need for a global fiscal stimulus to combat the crisis, a strategy immediately endorsed by the G-20 Washington Summit.[25] Discretionary fiscal policies were widely launched across the world in late 2008 and early 2009, which combined with the action of automatic stabilizers contributed to cushion the collapse in private spending and prevented the Great Recession from becoming a new Great Depression. In February 2009 the US President Barack Obama approved the "American Recovery and Reinvestment Act", a fiscal stimulus package of 787 billion dollars,[26] which followed the "Trouble Asset Relief Programme" of 700 billion dollars approved four months before by President George Bush.[27] In Europe, the European Commission launched a less ambitious "Economic Recovery Plan" of 200 billion euros.[28] At the G-20 London Summit of April 2009 the British Prime Minister Gordon Brown officially announced that the old Washington Consensus was declared dead.[29]

However, only few months later, the Consensus was resurrected in the EU with the emergence of the European sovereign debt crisis. When in October 2009 the socialist Prime Minister of Greece, George Papandreou, announced that the previous government had masked the size of the budget deficit, the European crisis

[23]See Wolf (2014).

[24]G-7 Finance Ministers Meeting (2008).

[25]See International Monetary Fund (2008).

[26]Public Law 111-5, 17 February 2009.

[27]Public Law 110-343, 3 October 2008.

[28]See European Commission (2008).

[29]See Kaufmann (2009).

suddenly became a story of unsound fiscal policies and excessive public debt. The solution identified by EU policy makers was in line with the prescriptions of the Washington Consensus: fiscal consolidations, tighter fiscal rules, and structural reforms.

According to this narrative, there was essentially nothing wrong with the architecture of the EMU. What had been wrong was the behavior of some member states. A view rooted in a sort of moralism that distinguished between "innocent" and "guilty" countries. While in the previous decade core nations had saved and implemented structural reforms, peripheral states had spent too much and taken on too much debt. Given that fiscal profligacy was at the roots of the crisis, the rebalancing would have to be on the shoulders of "fiscal sinners" alone. The latter must cut spending, reduce deficits and improve the functioning of their economies through supply-side measures. If they showed adequate courage and political resolve, markets would reward them with lower borrowing costs.[30]

In the course of 2010–2011, under the surveillance of the so-called "Troika" (European Commission, ECB, and IMF), Greece, Ireland and Portugal accepted a combination of deflationary fiscal and wage policies in order to obtain financial assistance by European partners and the IMF. Meanwhile, under the pressure of the German government, EU member states agreed to strengthen the rules contained in the SGP. The EU fiscal framework was amended through the adoption of the so-called "Six Pack" in 2011,[31] by the conclusion of an international treaty known as "Fiscal Compact" in 2012,[32] and through the so-called "Two Pack" in 2013.[33] These acts reinforced the Medium-Term Objective of a structural budgetary position "close to balance or in surplus". The "balanced budget rule" was to be incorporated into national legal systems, preferably at constitutional level. Deviations from the balanced budget rule were to trigger automatic correction mechanisms at national level. Moreover, it was agreed to reduce government debt exceeding the 60% of GDP threshold by 1/20 per year. All this translated into a huge policy reversal. Fiscal tightening was implemented not only by peripheral countries under financial distress, but also by core countries not suffering from the sovereign debt crisis. Thus, after 2010 the Eurozone's aggregate fiscal stance shifted away from countercyclical action towards contraction.[34]

Theoretical arguments for fiscal consolidation policies in the EU were provided by the feasibility of an "expansionary fiscal contraction". A neoclassical proposition first proposed by Giavazzi and Pagano in 1990[35] and relaunched by Alesina and Ardagna

[30]See Irwin (2013).

[31]Regulation (EU) No. 1173/2011, No. 1174/2011, No. 1175/2011, No. 1176/2011, No. 1177/2011, and Directive 2011/85/EU.

[32]Treaty on Stability, Coordination and Governance in the Economic and Monetary Union (TSCG).

[33]Regulation (EU) No. 472/2013 and Regulation (EU) No. 473/2013.

[34]See Baldwin and Giavazzi (2015), pp. 46–47.

[35]Giavazzi and Pagano (1990).

in 2009.[36] These Italian economists argued that significant and credible budget deficit reductions might have non-Keynesian effects, i.e. be associated with economic expansions rather than recessions in the short-run, particularly if achieved by cutting spending. According to this theory, fiscal consolidation perceived as permanent by agents may generate, via lower expected taxes, a positive wealth effect. Economic agents anticipate a permanent increase in their lifetime disposable income and this may induce an increase in current private expenditure. Moreover, fiscal consolidation, by increasing confidence in government solvency, may reduce interest rates and increase agents' financial wealth, which, in turn, boost private investment and consumption. The positive effects of fiscal consolidation on expectations of permanently lower taxes and interest rates may outweigh the depressing effects of reduced government deficit, resulting in higher growth.

While the reinforced fiscal framework and the "austerian ideology" pushed EU member states towards fiscal contraction, the narrow mandate on price stability delayed the ECB's policy response to the crisis. Whereas the FED put rapidly and aggressively in place all the conventional and unconventional instruments available, the ECB was much more timid. The European Central Bank, a supporter of the theory of "expansionary austerity",[37] accepted to act as a lender of last resort for governments only in summer 2012,[38] when the sovereign debt crisis was already close to destroy the Monetary Union, and it launched the "quantitative easing" (QE) in January 2015,[39] only when the Eurozone as a whole was in deflation and the "liquidity trap" already imposed limits on the ability of the monetary policy to boost the economy.[40]

5 The IMF *Mea Culpa*

There is ample evidence that in the course of the European financial turmoil the Washington Consensus was rehabilitated mainly by the EU rather than by the IMF. During the crisis, in fact, EU institutions promoted conditionality that was often tougher than what the Fund deemed sustainable. When the Latvian government asked the IMF and the EU for an emergency bailout, the IMF proposed to make the loan conditional to a devaluation of the national currency, breaking its peg with the euro, in order to render the adjustment program less harsh and economic recovery

[36]Alesina and Ardagna (2009).

[37]See, for example, European Central Bank (2004), pp. 47–49.

[38]The ECB started to act as a lender of last resort for governments in September 2012, when the Governing Council launched the Outright Monetary Transactions (OMTs) in secondary sovereign bond markets. For the technical features of the OMTs, see European Central Bank (2012), and Draghi (2012).

[39]For the technical features of the ECB's quantitative easing, officially called "Expanded Asset Purchase Programme (EAPP)", announced in January 2015, see European Central Bank (2015).

[40]On the ECB action during the crisis, see Saraceno (2015b), Tabellini (2015).

less painful. However, European policy makers were opposed to the IMF currency policy, because worried that a devaluation would have triggered contagion in non-euro member countries and postponed their adoption of the single currency.[41] In spring 2010, during the negotiation for the first Greek bailout, the EU, in particular the ECB and the German government, argued the need for a severe fiscal plan, whereas the IMF emphasized that the new generation of bailout programmes was much lighter on fiscal adjustment, reflecting the lessons of past mistakes.[42] Many at the IMF, at both staff and executive levels, were skeptical about the sustainability of the Greek programme without a drastic debt write-off. Emerging market members (and Switzerland) opposed the terms of the loan package for Greece, by protesting that it was intended to save the euro, not Greece. Eurozone members, instead, emphasized moral hazard arguments and spillover effects against a debt-restructuring agreement.[43]

Despite some profound disagreements in the course of negotiations, at the end, the IMF accepted the EU conditions and joined European bailouts. The IMF participation in the Troika-imposed austerity regime was, however, in open contradiction with the analyses by its own research department led by Olivier Blanchard. Since 2010, in fact, IMF researchers have engaged themselves in an open-minded discussion about the best policies to promote stability and growth, which has led to reassess the Fund's doctrine and increasingly challenge the orthodoxy behind European policy-making.[44]

First, the IMF staff disavowed the theory of "expansionary fiscal contraction". In 2010–2011 IMF officials studied 173 episodes of fiscal consolidation in advanced economies over the past 30 years, and they concluded that fiscal consolidations, even those focused on the spending side, had contractionary effects on output and raised both short-term and long-term unemployment.[45] In October 2012 the IMF disavowed its own previous estimates of the size of fiscal multipliers, and certified that austerity recently applied in the EU was self-defeating.[46] Multipliers were not 0.5 as estimated by the Troika at the time of EMU countries bailouts, but 1 point more. This meant that a fiscal consolidation of 1% of GDP was associated with a real GDP loss during 2010–2011 of about 1.5%. Fiscal multipliers were "larger than normal" because austerity measures in Europe were undertaken in a context where: (1) nominal interest rates were near the zero lower bound (a situation of "liquidity trap"), hence the ECB could not cut interest rates to offset the negative short-term effects of fiscal consolidation; (2) lower output and lower income, together with a poorly functioning financial system, implied that consumption and investment

[41] See Lütz and Kranke (2010).

[42] See Bastasin (2015), p. 161.

[43] See International Monetary Fund (2010a, 2013).

[44] See Saraceno (2015a).

[45] See International Monetary Fund (2010b), pp. 93–124, Guajardo et al. (2011), Ball et al. (2011).

[46] See International Monetary Fund (2012a), pp. 41–43.

depended more on current, rather than on future, income and profits; (3) the economy was already in recession.[47]

Second, in spring 2011 an IMF study broke another neoliberal taboo, by recognizing a relationship between income inequality and economic growth. IMF researchers argued that unequal societies tend to growth more slowly, thereby "attention to inequality can bring significant longer-run benefits for growth. Over longer horizons, reduced inequality and sustained growth may thus be two sides of the same coin".[48] In 2015 a new research showed that income distribution itself, not just the level of income inequality, matters for growth. "Specifically, if the income share of the top 20% (the rich) increases, then GDP growth actually declines over the medium term, suggesting that the benefits do not trickle down. In contrast, an increase in the income share of the bottom 20% (the poor) is associated with higher GDP growth".[49] Other IMF papers highlighted, instead, that fiscal consolidations, notably if expenditure-based, exacerbate the level of inequality, mainly because they increase the level of unemployment and affect wages more than profits and rents.[50]

Third, the Fund called into question one of the historical prescriptions of the Washington Consensus: capital flows liberalization. In November 2012 IMF researchers recognized that free capital movements may not generate only benefits but also be destabilizing. They argued that "liberalization needs to be well planned, timed, and sequenced in order to ensure that its benefits outweigh the costs" without presuming that "full liberalization is an appropriate goal for all countries at all times". When rapid and large inflows and outflows pose risks for macroeconomic and financial stability, "capital flow management measures" (i.e. restrictions to capital movements), in combination with macroeconomic policies, may be required.[51] Afterwards, in November 2015, IMF staff members pointed to an additional argument against financial openness: using panel data for 149 countries from 1970 to 2010, IMF researchers found that, on average, capital account liberalization reforms increase inequality and reduce the labour share of income.[52]

Fourth, in October 2014 another IMF work, by studying 181 countries over 1980–2011, found empirically robust results "strongly consistent" with the Milton Friedman's hypothesis according to which flexible exchange rates facilitate external adjustment. IMF analysts argued that "euro adoption has indeed significantly slowed down external adjustment among the Eurozone countries, increasing the half-life of bilateral trade balance adjustment by about 1 year". They concluded that these findings have serious implications for EMU countries trying to adjust under

[47]See Blanchard and Leigh (2013), pp. 3–4.

[48]Berg and Ostry (2011), p. 3.

[49]Dabla-Norris et al. (2015), p. 4.

[50]See Ball et al. (2011), Morsy (2011), Ball et al. (2013) and Woo et al. (2013).

[51]International Monetary Fund (2012b).

[52]See Furceri and Loungani (2015).

fixed exchange rate regime and point to "the formidable challenges facing them as they seek to regain competitiveness and restore external balance".[53]

Fifth, in autumn 2014 the Fund called for active fiscal policies. It argued that increased public investment raises output, both in the short-term, because of demand effects, and in the long-term, as a result of supply effects. "The time is right for an infrastructure push": borrowing costs are low and demand is weak, and there are infrastructure needs in many countries. Thus, "debt-financed projects could have large output effects without increasing the debt-to-GDP ratio".[54] IMF staff members challenged the neoclassical assumption according to which government spending displaces private investment. They asserted that in the current economic environment active fiscal policies would produce crowding in, not crowding out. The overall weakness in economic activity since the global financial crisis appears to be the primary restraint on private investment in advanced countries, hence additional public infrastructure investment may "spur demand in the short term, raise supply in the medium term, and thus "crowd in" private investment".[55]

Sixth, the IMF research department challenged another major tenet of the Washington Consensus: labour market deregulation. In the "World Economic Outlook" of April 2015, IMF researchers examined the impact of structural reforms on total factor productivity (i.e. on long-term growth). They found that the largest gains in total factor productivity levels were associated with product market deregulation, increasing R&D and ICT capital, and education reforms. In contrast, labor market regulation was not found to have statistically significant effects on productivity.[56] Other IMF works argued that higher employment protection for non-regular workers (i.e. temporary and/or part-time workers) would actually improve productivity.[57] In addition, the IMF staff found that more flexible labor market institutions, such as more lax hiring and firing regulations, a decline in unionization and lower minimum wages, were associated with higher inequality.[58] Finally, the IMF completed its "U-turn" on labour market by recommending to Japan structural reforms aimed at strengthening the bargaining power of workers and other bold measures to force profitable companies to raise wages, in order to generate wage-price dynamics that would lift the economy out of deflation.[59]

[53]See Ghosh et al. (2014).

[54]See International Monetary Fund (2014), pp. 75–114.

[55]See International Monetary Fund (2015a), pp. 111–143.

[56]See International Monetary Fund (2015a), pp. 104–107.

[57]See Aoyagi and Ganelli (2013).

[58]See Jaumotte and Osorio Buitron (2015), Dabla-Norris et al. (2015).

[59]See Everaert and Ganelli (2016).

6 Conclusion

The neoliberal doctrine emerged between the 1970s and 1980s as a response to the crisis of the Keynesian economics. This new version of the neoclassical theory shaped both the IMF conditionality policy and the Eurozone economic governance. The prescriptions of the Washington Consensus, as outlined by Williamson in 1989, and later "augmented" by Rodrik, formed the "one-size-fits-all approach" applied by the IMF for several decades to solve crisis in very different contexts. In the EU the institutionalization of the Consensus prescriptions went farther, by giving constitutional strength to the neoliberal principles through the Maastricht Treaty signed in 1992.

In short, the economic theory behind the Washington Consensus is based on a very optimistic view of the functioning of markets, while considers governments more part of the problem than the solution. Macroeconomic policies must be constrained, so that fiscal policy has to aim at a balanced budget and monetary policy has to deal only with inflation. The main policy recommendation is to pursue structural reforms that, by minimizing frictions to the smooth working of markets, allow to increase the potential growth rate of the economy. Short-term costs of these policy measures are not envisaged, and even if they emerge, they must be ignored because considered the necessary "pain" to improve economic performance in the long-run.

The global financial crisis seemed to spell the "death" of the Washington Consensus when the IMF and the G-20 called for stimulus policies at the world level. However, the neoliberal policy prescriptions were resurrected in the EU in 2009. During the European sovereign debt crisis, while the IMF placed itself on the lenient side of the austerity equation, EU policy makers advocated orthodox measures with unrivalled passion in return for their support. By relying on a fiscal interpretation of the crisis, rigid conditions were considered (by the European Commission, the ECB and EU core nations) necessary to avoid moral hazard by EMU periphery countries, thus the loans had to be accompanied by severe budgetary consolidations and a set of reforms aimed at eliminating structural weaknesses.

The participation to the Troika's austerity-based bailouts did not prevent, however, the IMF from casting aside ideological prejudices and engaging in a deep reflection on its own doctrine. Since 2010 the IMF research department has gradually challenged all the main tenets of the Washington Consensus: it has disavowed the benefits of fiscal consolidation and labour markets deregulation, highlighted the risks linked to capital flows liberalization and fixed exchange rates, recognized the importance of income inequality for economic performance, and acknowledged a role for fiscal policy both in smoothing cyclical fluctuations and in facilitating long-term growth.

The IMF seems to move definitely towards a "post-Washington Consensus era", in which the discussion about macroeconomic policies is less ideological.[60] The EU remains instead devoted to the neoliberal mantra, by invoking price stability, fiscal

[60]See, for example, International Monetary Fund (2015b) and Ostry et al. (2016).

discipline and markets deregulation as the only possible recipe for prosperity. What in late 1980s Williamson identified with "Washington Consensus" today does not exist anymore in Washington, but still lives in Brussels.

References

Alesina A, Ardagna S (2009) Large changes in fiscal policy: taxes versus spending. NBER Working Paper 15438, Cambridge MA

Aoyagi C, Ganelli G (2013) The path to higher growth: does revamping Japan's dual labor market matter? IMF Working Paper 13/202, Washington DC

Baimbridge M, Whyman PB (2014) Crisis in the Eurozone: causes, dilemmas and solutions. Palgrave MacMillan, London

Baldwin R, Giavazzi F (2015) Introduction. In: Baldwin R, Giavazzi F (eds) The Eurozone crisis: a consensus view of the causes and a few possible Solutions. CEPR Press, London, pp 18–61

Ball L, Leigh D, Loungani P (2011) Painful medicine. Finance Dev 48(3):20–23, Washington DC

Ball L, Furceri D, Leigh D, Loungani P (2013) The distributional effects of fiscal consolidation. IMF Working Paper 13/151, Washington DC

Bastasin C (2015) Saving Europe: anatomy of a dream. Brookings Institution Press, Washington

Berg AG, Ostry JD (2011) Inequality and unsustainable growth: two sides of the same coin? IMF Staff Discussion Note 11/08, Washington DC

Blanchard O, Galì J (2005) Real wage rigidities and the new Keynesian model. NBER Working Paper 11806, Cambridge MA

Blanchard O, Leigh D (2013) Growth forecast errors and fiscal multipliers. IMF Working Paper 13/1, Washington DC

Commission of the European Communities (2007) Towards common principles of Flexicurity: more and better jobs through flexibility and security. COM(2007) 359 final, Brussels

Dabla-Norris E, Kochhar K, Ricka F, Suphaphiphat N, Tsounta E (2015) Causes and consequences of income inequality: a global perspective. IMF Staff Discussion Note 15/13, Washington DC

De Grauwe P (1999) Independence and accountability of central banks. Paper prepared for the annual World Bank conference on governance, equity and global markets, Paris, 21–23 June 1999

Draghi M (2012) The monetary policy of the European Central Bank and its transmission in the euro area. Speech at Università Bocconi on the occasion of the opening of the academic year 2012–2013, ECB, Milan, 15 November 2012

Duisenberg W (2002) The euro as a catalyst for integration and competition in EMU. Speech on the occasion of the 30th economics conference on competition of regions and integration in EMU, ECB, Vienna, 13 June 2002

European Central Bank (1999) Monthly bulletin. Frankfurt, January

European Central Bank (2004) Monthly bulletin. Frankfurt, April.

European Central Bank (2011) The monetary policy of the ECB, Frankfurt

European Central Bank (2012) Technical features of outright monetary transactions. Press release, Frankfurt, 6 September 2012

European Central Bank (2015) ECB Announces Expanded Asset Purchase Programme. Press release, Frankfurt, 22 January 2015

European Commission (2008) A European economic recovery plan. COM(2008) 800 final, Brussels, 26 November 2008

European Commission (2013) Vade mecum on the stability and growth Pact. European Economy Occasional Paper 151, Brussels

European Council (2000) Presidency conclusions. Lisbon, 23–24 March 2000

Everaert L, Ganelli G (2016) Japan: time to load a Fourth arrow–wage increases. iMFdirect, Washington DC
Fitoussi J-P, Saraceno F (2004) The Brussels-Frankfurt-Washington consensus. Old and new tradeoffs in economics. OFCE document de Travail 2004/02, Paris
Fitoussi J-P, Saraceno F (2012) European economic governance: the Berlin-Washington consensus. OFCE Document de Travail 2012/20, Paris
Friedman M (1968) The role of monetary policy. Am Econ Rev 58(1):1–17
Furceri D, Loungani P (2015) Capital account liberalization and inequality. IMF Working Paper 15/243, Washington DC
G-7 Finance Ministers Meeting (2008) G-7 Finance Ministers and central Bank governors plan of action. Washington DC, 10 October 2008
Ghosh AR, Qureshi MS, Tsangarides CG (2014) Friedman Redux: external adjustment and exchange rate flexibility. IMF Working Paper 14/146, Washington DC
Giavazzi F, Pagano M (1990) Can severe fiscal contractions be expansionary? Tales of two small European countries. In: Blanchard OJ, Fischer S (eds) NBER macroeconomics annual 1990, vol 5. MIT Press, Cambridge, pp 75–122
González-Páramo JM (2005) The reform of the stability and growth Pact: an assessment. Speech at the Conference on New Perspectives on Fiscal Sustainability, ECB, Frankfurt, 13 October 2005
Greenwald B, Stiglitz JE (1987) Keynesian, new Keynesian and new classical economics. NBER Working Paper 2160, Cambridge MA
Guajardo J, Leigh D, Pescatori A (2011) Expansionary austerity: new international evidence. IMF Working Paper 11/158, Washington DC
International Monetary Fund (2008) World leaders launch action plan to combat financial crisis. IMF Survey Magazine, Washington DC, 15 November 2008
International Monetary Fund (2010a) Office Memorandum: Board Meeting on Greece's Request for an SBA – 9 May 2010. Washington DC, 10 May 2010
International Monetary Fund (2010b) World economic Outlook: recovery, Risk, and Rebalancing Washington DC, October 2010
International Monetary Fund (2012a) Word economic Outlook: coping with high debt and sluggish growth, Washington DC, October 2012
International Monetary Fund (2012b) Liberalization and Management of Capital Flows–An Institutional View IMF Policy Paper, Washington DC, November 2012
International Monetary Fund (2013) Greece: ex post evaluation of exceptional access under the 2010 stand-by arrangement. IMF Country Report 13/156, Washington DC, June 2013
International Monetary Fund (2014) World economic Outlook: legacies, Clouds, Uncertainties Washington DC, October 2014
International Monetary Fund (2015a) World Economic Outlook: uneven growth. Short- and Long-Term Factors Washington DC, April 2015
International Monetary Fund (2015b) Blanchard: looking forward, looking back. IMF Survey Magazine, Washington
Irwin N (2013) The alchemists: three central bankers and a world on fire. Penguin Press, New York
Jaumotte F, Osorio Buitron C (2015) Power from the people. Finance Dev 52(1), Washington DC
Kaufmann D (2009) The G-20 and the end of ideology: from Washington to London to New York. Brookings Institution, Washington
Kydland FE, Prescott EC (1982) Time to build and aggregate fluctuations. Econometrica 50 (6):1345–1370
Lucas RE (1972) Expectations and the neutrality of money. J Econ Theory 4(2):103–124
Lütz S, Kranke M (2010) The European Rescue of the Washington Consensus? EU and IMF lending to central and eastern European countries. LEQS Paper 22/2010, London
Morsy H (2011) Unemployed in Europe. Finance Dev 48(3):24, Washington DC
Mundell RA (1961) A theory of optimum currency areas. Am Econ Rev 51(4):657–665

Muth JF (1961) Rational expectations and the theory of price movements. Econometrica 29 (3):315–335
Ostry JD, Loungani P, Furceri D (2016) Neoliberalism: oversold? Finance Dev 53(2):38–41, Washington DC
Phillips AW (1958) The relation between unemployment and the rate of change of money wage rates in the United Kingdom, 1861–1957. Economica 25(100):283–299
Rodrik D (2002) After Neoliberalism, what? Remarks at the conference on alternatives to Neoliberalism, Washington DC, 23 May 2002
Saraceno F (2015a) The Blanchard touch. Sparse Thoughts of a Gloomy European Economist
Saraceno F (2015b) Challenges for the ECB in times of deflation. ILO employment Working Paper 183, Geneva
Tabellini G (2015) The main lessons to be drawn from the European financial crisis. In: Baldwin R, Giavazzi F (eds) The Eurozone crisis: a consensus view of the causes and a few possible solutions. CEPR Press, London, pp 170–175
Williamson J (1990) What Washington means by policy reform. In: Williamson J (ed) Latin American adjustment: how much has happened? Institute for International Economics, Washington, pp 5–20
Williamson J (2004) The strange history of the Washington consensus. J Post Keynesian Econ 27 (2):195–206
Wolf M (2014) The shifts and the shocks. What We'Ve learned – and have still to learn – from the financial crisis. Allen Lane, London
Woo J, Bova E, Kinda T, Zhang YS (2013) Consequences of fiscal consolidation and the role of fiscal policy: what do the data say? IMF Working Paper 13/95, Washington DC

The Constitutionalization of the *Washington Consensus* in the European Union: Giving up the Social Market Economy

Giulio Peroni

Abstract The expression *Washington Consensus*, coined in 1989 by the English economist John Williamson, is usually indicated by a set of ten economic policy prescriptions that constitute the "standard" reform package promoted by the International Monetary Fund (IMF), World Bank, and the US Treasury Department, all based in Washington D.C., for solving the economic crisis of developing countries. The paper, after describing the main characteristics of the *Washignton Consensus* economic model in the perspective of the international economic law, intends to underline the deep influence of this economic 'recipe' on the Maastricht Treaty and on the construction of the European Monetary Union (EMU) and its basic rules. In spite of the failure of this model, as showed by the current economic and financial crisis started in 2008, the European Institutions and the EU Member states still do not seem ready to change the primary provisions of the EU treaties devoted to the economic and monetary policy, with the real risk of increasing the disaffection of European citizens towards the European Union.

Contents

G. Peroni (✉)
Department of Italian and Supranational Public Law, University of Milan, Milan, Italy
e-mail: giulio.peroni@unimi.it

E. Sciso (ed.), *Accountability, Transparency and Democracy in the Functioning of Bretton Woods Institutions*, DOI 10.1007/978-3-319-57855-2_6

1 The *Washington Consensus* and Its Influence on Bretton Woods Institutions

The expression *Washington Consensus* was used for the first time by John Williamson[1] at the end of the 1980s during a conference convened by the Institute for International Economic on the Latin American debt crisis.[2] On that occasion, a group of economists and policy makers investigated the economic reforms in that area of the World and were in agreement with a common set of economic remedies. This favoured structural adjustments with the goal of substituting their traditional state economic system with a market based economic model.

Ten reforms were agreed on as a summary of what most economists in Washington thought Latin America ought to be undertaking: (1) Fiscal Discipline; (2) Reordering Public Expenditure Priorities; (3) Tax Reform; (4) Liberalizing Interest Rates; (5) A Competitive Exchange Rate; (6) Trade Liberalization; (7) Liberalization of Private Foreign Direct Investment; (8) Privatization; (9) Deregulation; (10) Protection of Property Rights.

In particular, for Williamson, the mentioned policies could be summed up "as prudent macroeconomic policies outward orientation and free market capitalism".[3] In other terms, a group of economic measures able to react to the 'development theories' that, for the 'founding father' of the *Washington Consensus*, were at the basis of the failed state economic policies.[4]

The *Washington Consensus* became rapidly the core of the Reagan and Thatcher political and economic Agenda, the conservative leaders of two of the most important economies in the World (USA and United Kingdom), influencing strongly their ultra-liberalist macroeconomic policies. In the same period, the *Washington Consensus* became an expression for the political, administrative and technocratic action of the International Monetary Fund (IMF), World Bank (WB), US Treasury Department, the Federal Reserve Board (FED) and the Inter America Development Bank (IADB).[5]

The described heterogeneous panorama of technocratic and political actors, geographically all based in the capital of the most world important country, underlines how the *Washington Consensus* was not only a species of ideological

---

[1]British economist (born June 7, 1937, Hereford) Senior Fellow at the Peterson Institute from 1981 to 2012. He was project director for the UN High-Level Panel on Financing for Development in 2001 and advisor to the International Monetary Fund (1972–1974) and economic consultant to the UK Treasury (1968–1970).

[2]The Conference in question took place in Barcelona (Spain), in 1989 and Willamson entitled it 'from the *Washington consensus* to Global governance'.

[3]See Williamson (1990), pp. 1–3.

[4]See Williamson (2009), pp. 7–26.

[5]The reference to 'consensus' wants in fact to mean that the ten points, mentioned in the text, were shared by power circles in Washington, including the US Congress and Administration, on the one hand, and international institutions such based in Washington International Monetary Fund and the World Bank, on the other, supported by a range of think tanks and influential economists.

and academic 'product' (inspired especially by Milton Friedman and Von Hajek, the 'founders' of modern monetarism[6] and neo-libelarism[7] respectively), but essentially a 'policy paradigm'. More precisely, this became "a powerful and enduring framework of related ideas and standards about policy—a model that specifies both the instruments that should be used in a policy area and the goals that the policy should be addressing".[8] In other words, the main aim of the *Washington Consensus* paradigm was to remove government intervention in socialist and developing countries and to set up a well functioning market system.[9] The undoubted economic success achieved by Thatcherism and Reaganomics (between 1980s and 1990s), was connected to the rapid economic growth registered in many regions of East Asia (the well known *Asian Tigers*).[10] It was also accompanied by the increase of trade and investments (favored by the introduction of the World Trade Organization -WTO in 1994) and gave a decisive impulse to the *Washington Consensus*'s expansion in world trade and economy.

Another decisive factor that determined the large recourse to *Washington Consensus* paradigm was the IMF's and WB's choice to base their macroeconomic conditionality mechanism on the 'Williamson List'. In particular, the *Washington Consensus* was implemented by the Bretton Woods Institutions through contract-like documents called *Letter of Intents* (in the case of IMF) or *Letter of Development policy* (in the case of the World Bank). In the above documents, the total amount of the loan granted to State in economic and financial difficulty with their

[6]In particular, Friedman argued that poor monetary policy by the Federal Reserve (FED) represented the main cause of the Great Depression in the 1930s. In his view, markets naturally move towards a stable center, an incorrectly set money supply can cause market's failure; in this way, the FED's failure to offset forces that were putting downward pressure on the money supply and for reducing the stock of money. These were the opposite of what should have been done. His position was criticized by 'Keynesians' for which the demand for goods and services is the key to economic output. Because the economy is subject to periodic instability and deep swings, it is dangerous to make the FED obliged to a preordained money target, they argued the FED should have some margin or 'discretion' in carry out monetary policy.

[7]An ideology and policy model that exalts the value of the free market competition and the minimal state presence in economic and social affairs. Since the 1970s, owing to the economic stagnation and increasing public debt some economists proposed a return to classical liberalism, which in its revived form became neoliberalism. In particular way, Von Hayek argued that government measures aimed at the redistribution of wealth lead inevitably to totalitarims. His point of view was enthusiastically embraced by the conservative political parties in Britain and the United States, which achieved power with the administrations of British Prime Minister Margaret Thatcher (1979–1990) and U.S. President Ronald Reagan (1981–1989).

[8]In these terms, see Hall (1993), pp. 275–296.

[9]It was also applied for more than two decades in other diverse contexts as Africa, and Asia, as well as in countries emerging from real socialism in Eastern Europe and Central Asia.

[10]A group of States (in particular, Hong Kong, Singapore, South Korea and Taiwan) characterized by high levels of economic growth, stimulated by exports and rapid industrialization, which enabled these economies to join the ranks of the world's richest nations. See Stiglitz (1996), pp. 151–177.

balance of payments were usually defined together with the repayment schedule and above all a series of economic policy commitments.

To avoid borrowers infringe in their commitments, the cited Letters establish payment tranches, along with scheduled reviews of the borrower's policies. In fact, in the case in which the beneficiary of the loan is found to be out of compliance, the IMF or the WB have the right to suspend their financial assistance. However, the compliance with loan conditions is not easy to implement because of the use by the Bretton Woods Institutions of the *cross conditionality* mechanism—a practice that consists of including World Bank-related program conditions in IMF programs and vice-versa.

Moreover, the IMF's and WB's conditionality is traditionally deeply influenced by the US government, who being the major shareholder of both Bretton Woods Institutions,[11] is able to exercise a real 'right of veto' on every crucial decision, especially on granting of loan to States in difficulty with their balance of payments. This aspect has inevitably favored an unequal use of the conditionality method[12] by the International Financial Institutions (IFI) and consequently a different level of compliance by borrowers, depending on their respective bargaining power within the international economic organizations.[13]

In this scenario, we have to realize that the IFI use the same type of economic intervention focusing essentially on macroeconomic stability and structural adjustment programs for every kind of beneficiary (without considering the specific peculiarities of each national economy).[14]

This approach was in line with the main aim of the *Washington Consensus* conditionality mechanism consisting in changing the economic structure of national economies according to the neo liberalist model. The consequence of this ambitious mandate was that IMF and WB, in contrast with their traditional aims,[15] were assigned with persuading governments to make politically difficult and raw structural reforms. This was done with 'the guarantee' that the social costs of said

[11]See https://www.imf.org/external/np/sec/memdir/members.aspx for IMF Member's Quotas and Voting Power, and IMF Board of Governors.

[12]Conditionality makes reference to the commitments contained within loan or grant contract that developing countries must adhere to if they are to receive all or part of the financial aid. In the case of IMF, it usually imposes two different types of macroeconomic conditions to countries that need its support: quantitative conditions and structural conditions. The first consist of imposing a set of economic targets influencing the level of fiscal deficit or public debt a government is allowed to go into. Structural conditions normally consist of adopting institutional and legislative reforms within countries and include trade reform, privatization and price liberalization.

[13]According to Stone Randall (2002), and Dreher and Jensen (2007), pp. 105–124, strategic allies of the US were noted to receive lighter punishments for non-compliance than less important borrowers.

[14]The nineties have seen a number of financial crisis among which include: September 1992 European Monetary System (strong devaluation of Italian Lira, British Pound and Spanish Peseta); December 1994 Mexico; June-November 1997 East Asia; July-August 1998 Russia; November 1998-Febraury 1999 Brasil; December 2001 Argentina.

[15]For IMF stabilizing currencies and for WB and regional development banks to lend money to finance recovery projects.

economic 'recipes' would be justified by an increase, in a short term, of their gross domestic production (GDP). This inevitably generated "the appearance of an unprecedented, global natural experiment of the effectiveness of liberal policies in developing countries".[16]

Indeed, the *Washington Consensus* paradigm has been strongly criticized, since the 1990s by a significant number of economists. Joseph Stiglitz, Chief Economist at the World Bank from 1997 to 2000, censured the policies recommended by the IMF in response to the financial crises which occurred in Russia and Asia at the end of the 1990s.[17] Particularly, Stiglitz and Naim[18] criticized such policies, arguing that they would lead to recession, because public budget cuts, higher taxes and interest rates would contribute towards the deepening of the economic and financial crisis.

In addition, other economists[19] underlined how the social costs imposed by IMF's and WB's economic 'recipes' were devastating for many countries above all those in the Sub-Saharan Africa. They outlined how the objective of the financial stability and market liberalization had a unequal impact on the poor, leading to greater poverty and unequal income distribution. Despite the negative impact, Bretton Woods Institutions displayed a certain degree of presumption in denying in any way the validity of the criticism leveled at them, limiting their reaction with compensatory programs.

Nevertheless, the massive and uncontrolled financial speculation, occurred since 2008, that has produced as it is well known, the worst global economic crisis since the Great Depression (1929),[20] has clearly showed a number of structural limits characterizing the *Washington Consensus* model. Particularly, we believe that the current global downturn has disclosed two significant aspects. Firstly, the supremacy of the financial sector over the real economy. This fact had, in particular, led to

[16]In these terms, see Babb (2013), p. 280.

[17]Cf. Stiglitz (2003).

[18]Cf. Naim (2010).

[19]Cf. Sahn et al. (1997).

[20]The current international economic and financial situation has been compared to another well-known event that shocked the World in the early decades of the twentieth century, the Crisis of 1929. Both phenomena would result from a lack of liquidity, suffered mainly by the US credit system, by an excessive liberalism, from a monetary policy too lax by the US Federal Reserve, by a heavy fall in the value of commodities and industrial production levels. However, the current crisis, unlike that of 1929 concentrated mainly in the US and Europe, has affected, though in different ways, all of the economic areas of the Globe. Moreover, it should be noted such as right on the basis of the mistakes made during the Crisis of 1929, in order to ensure liquidity to the market, it has seen in recent years a strong intervention by Central Banks (Federal Reserve, European Central Bank and Bank of England) to support the banking and credit system to boost the real economy, to allow greater circulation of money and facilitate access to credit by companies and individuals in general. For a comparison between the two crises, see Almunia et al. (2009), Krugman (2009), Sapelli (2008).

the creation of speculative 'bubbles',[21] and intensified vulnerability of populations, increasing unequal income distribution and the gap between rich and poor. Secondly, it showed the prevalence of 'neo liberal' economic model (in respect of Keynesian theories) that have been used as a basis for formulating and prescribing the macroeconomic policies, elaborated by Bretton-Woods Institutions at global level, with particular reference to their structural adjustment programs.

In truth, in the current crisis, there seems to be more awareness of the growing inequalities and the discriminatory concentration of income in the different layers of population. The dramatic rise of the percentage of poor people living longer not only in so-called emerging countries, but also in USA and Europe reveals how unequal income distribution represents the main question that Governments must deal with it in the years to come.[22] This scenario, apparently, should represent the basis for overcoming the *Washington Consensus* model, but, with specific reference to the issue of Eurocrisi's, we can observe how this economic paradigm with its distortions, is actually implemented by EU Institutions and European Member states.

2 The Treaty of Maastricht and Its Limits

The Treaty of Maastricht, or Treaty of the European Union (TEU),[23] constituted a turning point in the long and difficult European integration process. By modifying the previous European treaties the original economic objective of the European Economic Community (EEC), building a common market, was outdone and, for the first time, a strong wish of political union was claimed. In particular, Member States, after having transferred their sovereignty to the European Union in the field of trade and competition polices, agreed Monetary Union (EMU). Particularly, with the introduction of a unified economic and monetary zone Member states decided, particularly, to give up their *ius cudendae monetae*: in other words, the power of each country to exercise exclusive legal control over their own currency trough

[21]The subprime mortgage crisis, at the origins of the current worldwide financial crisis, started with the explosion of the american housing 'bubble' started in 2001 that reached its peak in 2007. A 'bubble' is usually characterized, how occurred in USA house market, by rapid increase in the valuations of real property until unsustainable levels are reached in relation to incomes and other indicators of affordability.

[22]Cf. Sumner (2010).

[23]It was signed on 7 February 1992 and entered in force on 1 November 1993. Its main purpose was to prepare for EMU and to introduce elements of political union like the European citizenship, common foreign and internal policy. Other significant changes were introduced, in particular, we have to remember the following: the establishment of the European Union and introduction of the co-decision procedure, giving Parliament more power in decision-making; new forms of cooperation between EU governments—for example on defence and justice and home affairs.

essentially the exercise of the exclusive authority to designate the legal tender forms of payment, and also the exclusive authority to control the issuance and retirement of their legal tenders.[24]

The main benefits of the EMU consisted of eliminating fluctuation risks and exchange rates between countries ensuring in this way stable prices for consumers and citizens. By contrast, the disadvantage is that Euro countries have lost their autonomy in taking currency decisions, with the effect that the Euro members are not longer allowed (as happened in the past, during the 'Monetary snake'-1972, and the 'European monetary system—EMS -1979),[25] to devalue their currency in order to balance their books and to give new *stimulus* to their economy. Monetary policy now became in the exclusive responsibility of the European Union (see art. 3 par. 1, lett. c TFEU).

More specifically, monetary policy is managed by European Central Bank (ECB) together with the European System of Central Banks (ESCB),[26] to which the European treaties, within a very strict mandate, give strong autonomy and independence in order to ensure a low rate of inflation as established by art. 127 TFEU: "the primary objective of the ESCB shall be to maintain price stability"

---

[24]It is in the judgment of the former Permanent Court of International Justice (PCJI) that for the first time we get the official recognition of monetary sovereignty in modern international law. As stated by the PCJI in 1929 in the Serbian loan case "it is indeed a generally accepted principle that a state is entitled to regulate its own currency". It is on this basis that the State's sovereignty over its own currency and by implication over both the internal and external aspects of its monetary and financial systems has traditionally been recognized by public international law. See the Case Concerning the *Payment of Various Serbians Loans Issued in France (France vs. Serbia)*. Judgment of 12 July 1929, PCJ Rep. Series A N. 20-21, p. 44.

[25]The 'Snake in the tunnel' was a mechanism, created by Member States in March 1972, for fluctuations of their currencies (the snake) inside narrow limits against the dollar (the tunnel). Owing to oil crises, policy monetary divergence between its members and dollar weakness (mainly due to Nixon's unilateral cancellation in 1971 of the direct convertibility of the United States dollar to gold) within two years the snake had lost many of its component parts. Its quick 'death' did not diminish the objective to realize in the European community an area of currency stability. A new proposal, took the form of the European Monetary System (EMS) in March 1979, with the participation of all Member States' currencies except the British pound, which joined later in 1990 but only stayed for 2 years. The EMS was built on the idea of stable but adjustable exchange rates determined in relation to the newly created European Currency Unit (ECU)—a currency basket based on a weighted average of EMS currencies. Within the EMS, currency fluctuations were kept within ±2.25% of the central rates, with the exception of the Italian lira, the Spanish peseta, the Portuguese escudo and the pound sterling, which were allowed to fluctuate by ±6%. See Victor (1990), Van Ypersele and Koeune (1985), Giavazzi et al. (1992).

[26]The *Maastricht* Treaty contains the institutional arrangements for the conduct of monetary policy in Economic and Monetary Union (EMU) in Europe. The Treaty, which entered into force in November 1993, provides the legal basis for the formation of the European System of Central Banks (ESCB), which includes the ECB and the National Central Banks (NCBs) of the 25 Member States of the European Union (EU). The term Eurosystem stands for a subset of the ESCB that comprises the ECB and the NCBs of those EU Member States that have adopted the Euro. The governing bodies of the Eurosystem are the Governing Council and the Executive Board.

and that "without prejudice to the objective of price stability" the ECB and the ESCB shall support the general economic policies of the European Union with a view to contributing to the achievement of the other objectives established in the European treaties. These aims are *inter alia* directed to ensure "a high level of employment [...], sustainable and non-inflationary growth, a high degree of competitiveness and convergence of economic performance". Thus, the primary rules of EU clearly establish a hierarchy of objectives for the ECB and assigns overriding importance to price stability.[27]

But, if the Treaty undoubtedly fixes the primary objective of the ECB, it does not give a precise quantitative definition of price stability. It is, on the contrary, a duty of the ECB's Governing Council to announce what the price stability is: "Price stability is defined as a year-on-year increase in the harmonized Index of Consumer Prices (HICP) for the euro area of below 2%.".[28]

On this specific point, it could be useful to remember that ECB's mandate to pursue price stability is limited in comparison with the task of the other monetary authorities; in particular, with the FED's multiple-objective mandate—one of the central banking institutions more involved in managing and solving the current crisis. The FED's statute clearly establishes that "the Board of Governors of the Federal Reserve System and the Federal Open Market Committee shall maintain long-run growth of the monetary and credit aggregates commensurate with the country's long-run potential to increase production, so as to promote effectively the goals of maximum employment, stable prices and moderate long-term interest rates".[29]

The mentioned limits characterizing the ECB's mandate have deeply reduced and influenced the Eurotower's action in front of the effects of the financial crisis and at the same time helped to explain the difficulties encountered till now by the European Union in resolving the dramatic economic scenario that we are living. In fact, the central monetary authorities are usually the only institutions that can,

[27]The importance of 'price stability' is also expressed in other provisions of the treaties especially in articles: 3 par. 2, TEU 119 parr. 2, 3 TFEU, 140, par. 1 TFEU, 141 par. 1 TFEU, 219 parr. 1,2,3 TFEU, 282 par. 2 TFEU.

[28]The target of 2% was established by ECB's Council in the January 1999 (see ECB *Bullettin*, January 1999, p. 39 ss.). See also article 12.1 of the Statute of ESBC for which "The Governing Council shall adopt the guidelines and take the decisions necessary to ensure the performance of the tasks entrusted to the ESCB under this Treaty and this Statute. The Governing Council shall formulate the monetary policy of the Community including, as appropriate, decisions relating to intermediate monetary objectives, key interest rates and the supply of reserves in the ESCB, and shall establish the necessary guidelines for their implementation. The Executive Board shall implement monetary policy in accordance with the guidelines and decisions laid down by the Governing Council. In doing so the Executive Board shall give the necessary instructions to national central banks. In addition the Executive Board may have certain powers delegated to it where the Governing Council so decides. To the extent deemed possible and appropriate and without prejudice to the provisions of this Article, the ECB shall have recourse to the national central banks to carry out operations which form part of the tasks of the ESCB.".

[29]Federal Reserve Act, Section 2A, 1913 and subsequent amendements.

assuming the role of lender of last resort, avoid the panic in financial markets and especially in sovereign bond markets. Central banks can buy governments bonds without any limit and in this way they can, first of all, prevent the State's default[30] and secondly, in the current scenario, characterized by strong deflationary tendencies, to give an important *stimulus* to economic recovery. But, the ECB could not take over the function of lender of last resort for the governments of Eurozone Member states, because that is expressly forbidden by the treaty provisions in particular by Article 123 TFEU.[31]

Nevertheless, the ECB's purchase of government bonds, from some Euro countries (namely: Portugal, Ireland, Italy, Greece and Spain, well known with the depreciatory term of PIGS), started with Security Market Program (SMP),[32] even if limited to the so called secondary market.[33]

The exclusion of the primary market is a consequence of the prohibition of mutualising the public debts among Member states (see art. 125 TFEU)[34] that is due to the fact that fiscal policy is firmly in the hands of national governments, even if strictly framed by the Stability Growth Pact (SGP): a set of fiscal rules designed to ensure that Eurozone countries pursue sound public finance and coordinate their economic policies.

The approach, here briefly, described, even if partially modified with the adoption of the instruments known as Outright Monetary Transactions (OMT), on September 2012[35] and above all with the Quantitative Easing (QE), on January

[30]See Frigo (2012), Tanzi (2012).

[31]According to the mentioned rule: 'Overdraft facilities or any other type of credit facility with the European Central Bank or with the central banks of the Member States (hereinafter referred to as 'national central banks') in favour of Union institutions, bodies, offices or agencies, central governments, regional, local or other public authorities, other bodies governed by public law, or public undertakings of Member States shall be prohibited, as shall the purchase directly from them by the European Central Bank or national central banks of debt instruments'.

[32]It consisted of a set of monetary interventions to restore a correct and normal monetary policy transmission mechanism, and thus the effective conduct of monetary policy oriented towards price stability in the medium term.

[33]The market place for the bonds that are already issued in the primary market and where the re-selling of government bonds is possible.

[34]For which 'The Union shall not be liable for or assume the commitments of central governments, regional, local or other public authorities, other bodies governed by public law, or public undertakings of any Member State, without prejudice to mutual financial guarantees for the joint execution of a specific project. A Member State shall not be liable for or assume the commitments of central governments, regional, local or other public authorities, other bodies governed by public law, or public undertakings of another Member State, without prejudice to mutual financial guarantees for the joint execution of a specific project.'

[35]See the ECB (2012), p. 7. Thanks to the OMT for the ECB is possible to purchase the sovereign bonds of specific euro area countries, always, on secondary markets with no set *ex ante* quantitative limits. The ECB Governing Council's aim in implementing this programme is to safeguard an appropriate monetary transmission process and the singleness of monetary policy. For the purchasing of the state bonds, the OMT programme establishes that the state in question complies with conditions specified in European Stability Mechanism, that establishes a permanent emergency fund which entered in force in September 2012.

2015 reflects the Bundesbank's philosophy, for which the single currency was built. The idea was to limit as far as possible the interference of EU Institutions in the field of economic policy. In other terms, *Maastricht* recognized the EMU as the only mechanism able to control the trend of inflation, as its restraint was considered, by its 'founding fathers', to be the *sine qua non* condition for Eurozone countries to ensure the *equilibrium* of their respective balance of payments[36] and at the same time the compliance with the macro economic criteria and parameters fixed in the articles 121, par. 1, 122, par. 2 e 123, par. 5 of *Maastricht* and successively transposed in the current article 140 of TFEU.

In synthesis, the EMU was built on the unbelievably naïve assumption that there would be no financial and macroeconomic turmoil able to put in crisis its structure, because for the 'founding fathers' of the *Maastricht* treaty it would have been sufficient to ensure at monetary level the price stability, and at fiscal level, the observance of the convergence criteria enshrined in art. 126 TFEU, and numerically expressed in the Protocol n. 12 on excessive deficit procedure.[37]

3 The *Washington Consensus* and Its Influence on the *Maastricht* Treaty

In the previous paragraphs, we have seen that the expression *Washington Consensus* was used to identify a set of economic policies essentially based on two fundamental characteristics: macroeconomic and financial stability, consisting in balanced budgets for ensuring price stability, and structural reforms directed to favor market's competition thanks a wide program of privatization, liberalization and deregulation.

We think that *Maastricht* and also the latest versions of European treaties (*Amsterdam, Nice* and *Lisbon*) have deeply embraced the *Washington Consensus* paradigm even if this economic and political model, as noted before, was strongly criticized and *de facto* put in crisis by different events.

But, there are various reasons that help to explain the robust influence exercised by the *Washington Consesus* especially on the *Maastricht* treaty, and consequently on the legal and economic structure of the EMU, created by that agreement. Firstly, we have to consider the 'time factor'. In fact, the Treaty of *Maastricht* was signed in 1990s in which the *Washington consensus* reached its *maximum* expansion and the most significant economic results, and moreover, in an intellectual and academic environment strongly inspired by the neoliberalism movement. Secondly, a crucial role was played by France and Germany, with the former ready to support, after the fall of the

[36]The balance of payments is functional to summary, for a specific time period, the economic transactions of an economy with the rest of the World. With reference to the conceptual framework of the balance of payments accounts and the international investment position and national accounts see IMF (2012), pp. 6–20.

[37]The ceilings of 3% of Gross Domestic Production (GDP) on budget deficits and of 60% of GDP on government debt: probably the best known elements of the EMU framework.

Berlin's wall (1989), the German reunification, but only within a European framework; and the second willing to accept losing his monetary sovereignty with the sacrifice of its 'deutsche Mark' in favor of the Euro under the condition of the *constitutionalization,* within the primary rules of the European treaties, of the principle of price stability, for prohibiting every kind of economic policy that could favor an uncontrolled rate of inflation. Thirdly, there was the need for the countries historically characterized by an high level of deficit and public debt, like Italy, to introduce an 'external constraint' capable of imposing economic policies and structural reforms that their weak political institutions were unable to implement.[38]

Starting from *Maastricht*, European policy makers progressively embedded the *Washington Consensus* prescriptions into the European economic policy, by limiting fiscal policy to automatic stabilization and monetary policy to inflation targeting. Inevitably, the continuous attempt to maintain a balanced budget has reduced public spending. This has progressively limited the presence of the State in the market and in the meantime favored a massive liberalization and privatization of many economic sectors (see *infra*) which were before, firmly in the hands and under the control of the national governments.

However, the legal framework on which the Euro is built has been criticized in many occasions, but most of the criticism were internal to the mainstream as only marginal corrections were requested.[39] As observed by Fitoussi and Saraceno "... paradoxically, the build up of public debt that followed the effort to save the financial sector and the economy from collapse in 2007-2009, led to a renewed emphasis on the need to constrain fiscal policy...' with the effect that '...Germany and EU institutions blamed the crisis on public finance excess, imposing austerity and the signature of the fiscal compact to introduce the balanced budget requirement in member countries constitutions.".[40]

4 No Changes in the European Approach to Monetary and Economic Policy Despite the Crisis

The sovereign debt Crisis of the PIGS States,[41] represented one of the most important effects of the economic and financial downturn, started in the USA in late August 2007.

---

[38]The EU's role as external constraint for Italian economy and policy is common among commentators and the public. There is the idea that Italy is unable to take care of itself without the help of the EU institutions. In particular way, many authors consider the pressure of EU on Italian government absolutely necessary in order to ensure the *equilibrium* of the public budget and in order to abandon dangerous expansionary economic policies. See Mittestainer (2014).

[39]See Wyplosz (2012), Buiter (2003), Buti et al. (2003).

[40]Cf. Fitoussi and Saraceno (2013).

[41]The Crisis can be divided in two different phases: a first stage corresponding to the burst of the financial downturn (2007–2008) and a second stage (2010–2012) that has specific characteristics to Euro zone and this has required many different actions of the European Union Institutions and

More precisely, the issue of sovereign debt is the climax of the economic and financial Crisis and it is the direct consequence of the incapacity of PIGS to comply with the macroeconomic rules established by the Maastricht provisions. This topic has not only shown the fragilities of the global financial system and, in particular, of the EMU[42] in front of speculative attacks,[43] but above all it helps to outline the lack of confidence of the financial operators in the economic stability of the Euro area and on the survival of its single currency: the Euro.[44] For many observers, it is not possible to exclude *ex ante* the possibility that one of the PIGS could leave the Euro zone in the future.[45] At the moment, this is an hypothesis not mentioned in any article of the European treaties.[46] If it were to happen, the economic effect on the Euro zone could be devastating. In fact, an exit from the Euro by one of its members would mean that country is no longer able to satisfy the EMU macroeconomic conditions and above all to repay its debts to its internal and foreign creditors.

In order to avoid this dramatic scenario, the European Union has, during the last 5 years, developed a policy package for solving the debt crisis and increase the lost competiveness and stimulate the growth of the Eurozone economy. In extreme synthesis, the mentioned economic approach consisted of: (1) Fiscal consolidation with the aim of restoring investor's confidence became paramount and various austerity measures were endorsed and imposed upon debtor-deficit countries; (2) Internal devaluation considered as the key point to recover competitiveness, including essentially nominal wage cuts; (3) Structural reform like liberalization, privatization and deregulation.

These objectives have been translated in particular, in so called 'Six pack', a set of European legislative measures directed to reform the Stability and Growth Pact and introduce greater macroeconomic surveillance which refers to all EU Member states and also in the Treaty on Stability, Coordination and Governance (TSCG) an international agreement, by which 26 EU (with the exception of United Kingdom and Czech Republic) members committed themselves to a lower limit for a structural budget deficit of 0.5% of GDP, in order to ensure the *equilibrium* of public counts.

---

above all of the European Central Bank. It is important to underline that until 2010 the interest rate spreads on sovereign bond issued by each of the State member of Euro zone did not represent for European Monetary Union a problem; in fact, for international investors Greek, Italian, Spanish and German bonds were considered the same.

[42]According to De Grauwe (2011), p. 1 "The reason is that national governments in a monetary union issue debt in a foreign currency, i.e. one over which they have no control. As a result, they cannot guarantee to the bond holders that they will always have the necessary liquidity to pay out the bond at maturity. This contrast with stand alone countries that issue sovereign bonds in their own currencies.".

[43]It should be noted that speculative attacks, justified or not by economic fundamentals, always start from small items (e.g. Grecian sovereign bonds) to arrive big ones. The former, because relatively cost less, is used as a test for verifying and implementing strategies against the latter, normally most expensive.

[44]See De Grauwe (2010), Hall and Peel (2010), Canale and Napolitano (2009).

[45]See Proctor (2006), Athanassiou (2009).

[46]See Peroni (2015), pp. 85–108.

A latere of these fiscal mechanisms, we have to mention the European Stability Mechanism (EMS) that establishes a permanent emergency fund for the Member states in financial difficulty. The EMS, through the instrument of the conditionality, submits every financial assistance from EU institutions and, particularly, by the ECB in respect of the strict budgetary discipline[47] expressed by the just mentioned 'Six pack' and the 'Fiscal compact'.

The conditionality required by EU institutions (in particular, Commission and ECB) and IMF, the well-known *Troika,* when supporting countries hit by the sovereign debt crisis (especially Greece, Ireland and Portugal) consisted of fiscal, financial and labor market reforms that assumed these following forms: -fiscal consolidation trough reduction cuts in unemployment benefits and family allowances a decrease in health spending and public investment; privatization (for example, of communication, energy, transport sectors together with a general reduction of state participation in industries); reforms of public administration with reductions in public employment and on increase in personal income tax.[48]

These measures, based on a clear austerity approach directed to limit in any way public spending, led progressively to a social unsustainable situation, with the effect that the EMU is evolving towards an inconsistent institutional setting. In truth, the EU, in the Article 3, par. 2 TEU, exalts the value of the 'social market economy', a system that aim at combining free initiative and social welfare on the basis of a competitive economy. In other words, a 'Third Way' which strongly differs from liberalism and socialist economic models, whose main objective is to support equal protection and opportunity of those that are unable to enter the free market labor force.

So, while in different countries of the World, especially in the USA, traditionally considered the land of neo liberalism, no particular weight is given to the social role of the State, whereas the EU recognizes importance to the social role of that governments play through the so called welfare state model. This is in line with the principle of solidarity that sharing both the advantages, prosperity, and the burdens equally and justly among Member states. A principle, expressed several times in the text of the European treaties,[49] as well as in the Chapter IV (articles 27–38) of the Charter of Fundamental Rights of the EU, just entitled 'Solidarity', but as concerns the area of economic and monetary policy[50] is invoked only in the

[47]These new treaties raise interesting questions with particular reference to their compatibility with the EU legal order. On this specific point see Peroni (2012), pp. 151–185; Peroni (2011), Tosato (2012), Bonvicini and Brugnoli (2012), De Witte (2011).

[48]See Hermann (2013), Vaughan (2014).

[49]See articles: 2 TEU, 3, par. 2 TEU, 21 TEU, 24, par, 2 TEU, 31 TEU, 67, par. 2 TFEU, 80 TFEU, 122 TFEU, 194 TFEU, 222 TFEU.

[50]See Article 122 TFEU: "1. Without prejudice to any other procedures provided for in the Treaties, the Council, on a proposal from the Commission, may decide, in a spirit of solidarity between Member States, upon the measures appropriate to the economic situation, in particular if severe difficulties arise in the supply of certain products, notably in the area of energy. 2. Where a Member State is in difficulties or is seriously threatened with severe difficulties caused by natural disasters or exceptional occurrences beyond its control, the Council, on a proposal from the Commission, may grant, under certain conditions, Union financial assistance to the Member State concerned. The President of the Council shall inform the European Parliament of the decision taken.".

case where a State member is struggling with sever difficulties "...in the supply of certain products, notably in the area of energy".

Owing to the solution adopted till now by EU Institutions for managing and solving the financial crisis, many authors[51] affirm that the Union is progressively transforming in an inconsistent framework dismantling its social insurance for satisfying the macroeconomic policies fixed by the EMU, in clear contrast with the value of solidarity before mentioned. This could lead in the medium term to extreme instability and dangerous social consequences, as occurred, above all, in the last years in Greece.[52] In other words, this policy based on the *Washington Consensus* paradigm seems clearly to betray the value of the cited social market economy.

5 Concluding Remarks

The experience of the European Monetary Union shows how the implementation of the monetary unification represents an objective directed not only to build an efficient and effective single market, but also an effective political union among European nations. However, as the EMU has lacked the typical 'leap forward' consisting of the transfer of economic policy from Member States to EU institutions: a step absolutely necessary according to Robert Mundell, the theorist of 'optimum economic areas',[53] and Werner Plan and the Delors' White Paper.[54] In other words, even before the signing of the *Maastricht* Treaty, it was clear to European policy makers that for realizing an efficient monetary area, there must be a full free movement of goods and capital, a system of fixed exchange rates and above all an economic fiscal policy not separated from monetary one. Not one of these elements has been fully realized by the European Union to date.[55]

For all these reasons, it is fundamental now more than ever to rethink not only the quantitative definition of the convergence criteria in order to increase the State's spending capacity (essentially, for favoring the investments), but above all the neoliberalist vision that inspire the most part of European primary rules devoted to the economic and monetary policy (in particular, Articles 119–144 TFEU). In fact, as long as the Member States continue to prefer the implementation of the target of price stability, as clearly established by Article 3 of the TEU and Articles 119 TFEU, 127 TFEU, to the construction of an effective social market economy, it will not be easy for European institutions to give up the *Washington Consensus* economic political model. In truth, the proposed change could represent a

[51] See Creel and Saraceno (2009).

[52] Cf. Peroni (2013).

[53] Cf. Mundell (1961).

[54] For an accurate reconstruction of the mentioned historical phases cf. Tedeschi (2013).

[55] With reference to the limits of the European internal market cf. Gronden (2006), Gareth (2003).

fundamental step for contributing to ensure that European Institutions are more responsible towards European citizens for the economic and political choices that the EU must adopt in order to solve the current crisis.

The different approach mentioned, connected also to the transfer of fiscal policy from each State to the European Union, will probably make a significant contribution in order to solve the Euro crisis. This is a longer term solution, but probably the most effective if we want to give a new value to the European integration process, not only in raw economic and monetary terms but also in social and political ones.

References

Almunia M, Bénétrix AS, Eichengreen B, O'Rourke KH, Rua G (2009) From great depression to great credit crisis: similarities, differences and lessons. National Bureau of Economic Research, Cambridge

Athanassiou P (2009) Withdrawal and Expulsion from The EU and EMU: Some Reflections, ECB Legal Working Paper Series No 10; December

Babb S (2013) The Washington consensus as transnational policy paradigm: its origins, trajectory and likely successor. Rev Int Polit Econ 20:268–297

Bonvicini G, Brugnoli F (eds) (2012) Il fiscal compact. Nuova cultura, Roma

Buiter WH (2003) Ten commandments for a fiscal rule in the EMU. Oxford Rev Econ Policy 19:84–99

Buti M, Eijffinger S, Franco D (2003) Revisiting Emu's stability pact: a pragmatic way forward. Oxford Rev Econ Policy 19:100–111

Canale R, Napolitano O (2009) The Recessive Attitude of EMU Policies: Reflections on the Italian Experience, 1999–2008. MPRA Paper No. 20207

Creel J, Saraceno J (2009) Automatic stabilization, discretionary policy and the stability pact. In: Creel J, Sawyer MC (eds) Current thinking on fiscal policy. Palgrave Macmillan, New York, pp 112–144

De Grauwe P (2010) Crisis in the Eurozone and How to Deal with it. CEPS Policy Brief No. 204

De Grauwe P (2011) Only a more active ECB can solve the euro crisis. CEPS Policy Brief No. 250

De Witte B (2011) The European Treaty Amendement for the Creation of a Financial Stabilitiy Mechanism. European Policy Analysis. http://www.eui.eu/Projects/EUDOInstitutions/

Dreher A, Jensen NM (2007) Independent actor or agent? An empirical analysis of the impact of US interests on international monetary fund conditions. J Laws Econ 50:105–124

Ecb (1999) Monthky Bullettin, January. Frankfurt.

Ecb (2012) Monthly Bullettin, September. Frankfurt

Fitoussi J, Saraceno F (2013) European governance: the Berlin Washington consensus. Camb J Econ 37:479–496

Frigo M (2012) Insolvenza delle imprese e insolvenza degli Stati: analogie ed elementi di differenziazione. Rivista di diritto internazionale privato e processuale 48:865–878

Gareth D (2003) Nationality discrimination in the European Internal Market. Kluwer, The Hague

Giavazzi F, Micossi S, Miller M (eds) (1992) Il sistema monetario europeo. Franco Angeli, Milano

Gronden JW (2006) The internal market, the state and public private arrangements in the light of European law. Leg Issues Econ Integr 33:105–137

Hall B, Peel Q (2010) Paris and Berlin at Odds over Default System. Financial Times, October 26

Hall PA (1993) Policy paradigms, social learning, and the state: the case of economic policymaking in Britain. Comp Polit 25:275–296

Hermann C (2013) Crisis structural reform and dismantling of the European social model. Institute for international political economy, Working paper 26

International Monetary Fund (2012) Balance of payments manual. International Monetary Fund, Washington, pp 6–20
Krugman P (2009) The return of depression economics and the crisis of 2008. Norton Pubblications, New York
Mittestainer A (2014) Italy between the EU and Berlusconi. Effects of external and internal factors on the Italian public debt. Anchor Academic Publishin, Hamburg
Mundell R (1961) A theory of optimum currency areas. Am Econ Rev 51:657–665
Naim M (2010) Fads and fashion in economic reforms: Washington consensus or Washington confusion? Third World Quart 21:505–528
Peers S, Hervey T, Kenenr J, Ward A (eds) (2014) The EU charter of fundamental rights. A commentary. Hart, Oxford, pp 749–1025
Peroni G (2011) Il Trattato di Lisbona e la crisi dell'Euro: considerazioni critiche. Il Diritto dell'Unione europea 4:971–998
Peroni G (2012) La Crisi dell'Euro: limiti e rimedi dell'Unione economica e monetaria. Giuffrè, Milano, pp 151–185
Peroni G (2013) L'azione dell'Unione europea in campo sociale e la crisi economica. In Milano GP, Daniele L, Malinconico C, Ciciriello MC (eds) Il Trattato di Lisbona due anni di applicazione. Atti della Giornata di studio in ricordo di Francesco Caruso (Roma, 7 ottobre 2011). Editoriale scientifica, Napoli, pp 409–424
Peroni G (2015) Il recesso dall'euro: una via percorribile, ma non auspicabile. Studi sull'integrazione europea 85–108
Proctor C (2006) The future of Euro. What happens if a member state leaves? Eur Bus Law Rev 17:909–937
Sahn DE, Dorosh PA, Younger SD (1997) Structural adjustment reconsidered: economic policy and poverty in Africa. Cambridge University Press, Cambridge
Sapelli G (2008) La crisi economica mondiale: dieci considerazioni Bollati Boringhieri, Torino
Stiglitz JE (1996) Some lessons from the East Asian miracle. World Bank Res Obs 11:151–177
Stiglitz JE (2003) Globalization and its discontents. W.W. Norton Company, New York
Stone Randall W (2002) Lending, credibility: the international monetary fund and the post-communist transition. Pricenton University Press, Princeton
Sumner A (2010) Global Poverty and The 'New Bottom Billion': What if Three-Quarters of the World's Poor Live in The Middle-Income Countries. IDS Research Summary of IDS Working paper 349, IDS, Brighton
Tanzi A (2012) Sull'insolvenza degli Stati nel diritto internazionale. Rivista di diritto internazionale 95:66–88
Tedeschi P (2013) Una moneta comune in Europa? Dal Piano Werner all'Euro: un'integrazione incompiuta e quindi pericolosa. Rivista di Storia Economica 29:319–341
Tosato GL (2012) L'integrazione europea ai tempi dell'euro. Rivista di diritto internazionale 95:681–703
Van Ypersele J, Koeune JC (1985) Il sistema monetario europeo: origini, funzionamento e prospettive Ufficio delle Pubblicazioni ufficiali delle Comunità europee. Lussemburgo.
Vaughan D (2014) The European social model in crisis: is Europe losing its soul? International Labour Organisation, Geneva
Victor JL (1990) Dal sistema monetario all'unione monetaria. Ufficio delle Pubblicazioni ufficiali delle Comunità europee, Lussemburgo
Williamson J (1990) Introduction. In: Williamson J (ed) Latin American adjustment: how much has happened? Institute for International Economics, Washington, pp 1–3
Williamson J (2009) A short history of the Washington consensus. Law Bus Rev Am 15:7–26
Wyplosz C (2012) Fiscal discipline in Emu: Rules or institutions', Paper prepared for the April 16, 2002 Meeting of the Group of Economic Analysis of the European Commission. http://ec.europa.eu/dgs/policy_advisers/archives/experts_groups/docs/wyplosz.pdf

Participatory Democracy Within the Revision of the European Economic Governance Due to the Euro-Zone Crisis

Pia Acconci

Abstract The EU rules on the economic governance have been revised to react to the euro-zone crisis. Under the perspective of the democratization of the European integration process and its law, the revision of the European economic governance can be assessed in light of a few relevant novelties brought about by the 2007 Lisbon Treaty, such as the inclusion in the Treaty on the European Union of relevant democratic principles. This contribution highlights that the responses to the euro-zone crisis have disregarded the need of 'democratic legitimacy' of the EU, by neglecting the novelties provided in the Lisbon Treaty in relation to the role of the European Parliament, as well as of the national parliaments of the EU Member States, and in relation to participatory democracy. As to the latter, this transpires, for instance, from the fact that the EU Commission has not resorted to any instrument of participatory democracy, such as on-line consultations, as to its proposals of the legislative acts included in the 'Six Pack' and in the 'Two Pack'.

Contents

1 Introductory Remarks

As a reaction to the euro-zone crisis the rules on the economic governance included in the Treaty on the Functioning of the European Union have been integrated through the adoption of seven Regulations, one Directive and the conclusion of two international agreements among a group of EU Member States. Five

---

P. Acconci (✉)
Department of Law, University of Teramo, Teramo, Italy
e-mail: pacconci@unite.it

E. Sciso (ed.), *Accountability, Transparency and Democracy in the Functioning of Bretton Woods Institutions*, DOI 10.1007/978-3-319-57855-2_7

Regulations, respectively the Regulations Nos. 1173/2011, 1174/2011, 1175/2011, 1176/2011, 1177/2011[1] and the Directive No. 2011/85/EU[2] are named the 'Six Pack', whereas the remaining Regulations Nos. 472[3] and 473[4] are named the 'Two Pack'.

The two international agreements were concluded outside the framework of the European Union law in order to establish the European Stability Mechanism and the so-called 'Fiscal Compact'. The first agreement was concluded among 19 Member States, except Bulgaria, the Czech Republic, Denmark, Hungary, Poland, Romania, Sweden and the United Kingdom, on 2 February 2012,[5] whereas the second was concluded among the EU Member States, except the Czech Republic and the United Kingdom, on 2 March 2012.

These new rules concern the co-ordination among the policies on economic matters of the EU Member States. Such a co-ordination focuses on the assessment of national budgets, the control of public debt and the common monetary policy that is based on the euro as the single currency administered by the European Central Bank and the European System of Central Banks, with the primary purpose of ensuring the stability of prices. In accordance with the conditions agreed at the EU level, the EU Member States are still entitled to establish their own policies on the job market, retirement programs and financial markets. The aim of the revision of the European economic governance has been to search for responses to the euro-zone crisis, through new mechanisms for a deeper coordination of the economies of the EU Member States in light of their strong interdependency, and to promote growth as well as job creation for the benefit of EU citizens as the EU Commission has stated many times.

---

[1]Regulation (EU) No. 1173/2011 of the European Parliament and of the Council of 16 November 2011 on the effective enforcement of budgetary surveillance in the euro area; Regulation No. 1174/2011 of the European Parliament and of the Council of 16 November 2011 on enforcement measures to correct excessive macroeconomic imbalances in the euro area; Regulation (EU) No. 1175/2011 of the European Parliament and of the Council of 16 November 2011 amending Council Regulation (EC) No.1466/97 on the strengthening of the surveillance of budgetary positions and the surveillance and coordination of economic policies; Regulation No. 1176/2011 of the European Parliament and of the Council of 16 November 2011 on the prevention and correction of macroeconomic imbalances; and Regulation (EU) No. 1177/2011 of 8 November 2011 amending Regulation (EC) No. 1467/97 on speeding up and clarifying the implementation of the excessive deficit procedure. All these Regulations are published in *EUOJ* L 306, 23 November 2011, 1 *et seq.*

[2]Council Directive No. 2011/85/EU of 8 November 2011 on requirements for budgetary frameworks of the Member States, *EUOJ* L 306, 23 November 2011, 41–47.

[3]Regulation (EU) No. 472/2013 of the European Parliament and of the Council of 21 May 2013 on the strengthening of economic and budgetary surveillance of Member States in the euro area experiencing or threatened with serious difficulties with respect to their financial stability, *EUOJ* L 140, 27 May 2013, 1–10.

[4]Regulation (EU) No. 473/2013 of the European Parliament and of the Council of 21 May 2013 on common provisions for monitoring and assessing draft budgetary plans and ensuring the correction of excessive deficit of the Member States in the euro area, *EUOJ* L 140, 27 May 2013, 11–23.

[5]For details about the functioning of the European Stability Mechanism, see www.esm.europa.eu.

Under the perspective of the democratization of the European integration process and its law, the revision of the European economic governance can be assessed in light of a few relevant novelties brought about by the 2007 Lisbon Treaty such as the new Title II of the Treaty on the European Union, that incorporates the basic democratic principles into the EU law as primary law, and Art. 2 of the Treaty on the European Union that refers to a number of values, like democracy, human dignity and solidarity, as the values of the European Union.

This contribution highlights that the responses to the euro-zone crisis have taken the 'democratic legitimacy' of the EU a step backward rather than forward because these responses have disregarded the novelties provided in the Lisbon Treaty, by neglecting in particular the reference to participatory democracy at Art. 11 of the Treaty on the European Union.

There has been a step backward in comparison with the empowerment process that started at the time of the negotiations of the Maastricht Treaty as to the European Parliament and at the time of the negotiations of the failed 'constitutional' Treaty as to the national parliaments of the EU Member States.

2 The Debate on the Weak Democratic Legitimacy of the Revised Governance

Several scholars have underlined the weakness of the revised European economic governance in terms of democratic legitimacy.[6]

Under the international law perspective of EU law, a number of scholars have focused on the institutional framework of such a revision in order to highlight the poor position attributed to the EU Parliament as the EU institution that is strictly connected to the safeguard of the interests of the EU citizens.

It is true that the EU Regulations included in the Six Pack and the Two Pack have been adopted in accordance with the 'legislative' procedure through which the EU Council and the EU Parliament share the decision-making power with binding effects. However, it is also true that, apart from this, the EU Parliament has been downsized because its role within the revised European economic governance is merely consultative.

The 'Six Pack' provides for the new working model named the 'European Semester'. During this 'Semester'—the first 6 months of each year—the EU Member States discuss, coordinate and synchronize their structural reforms, as well as budgetary and economic priorities, with particular regard to their need of

[6]See, among others, Ruffert (2011), especially 1801–1805; Editorial Comments (2012), p. 1833 *et seq.*; Baratta (2012), p. 645 *et seq.*; Roland Bieber, 'Democratic Governance of the Euro: Shortcomings and proposals for reform', EUI-R. Schuman Centre for Advanced Studies, Global Governance Programme, *The Democratic Governance of the Euro, RSCAS Policy Paper* (2012/08), 13–20; Allemand and Martucci (2014), p. 111 *et seq.*

growth and job creation in accordance with the 'Europe 2020' strategy.[7] In order to ensure transparency and, to some extent, accountability within the 'European Semester', the 'Six Pack' provides for the 'Economic Dialogue' among the EU institutions including the EU Parliament. In particular, the competent committee of the EU Parliament can invite the President or representatives of the Council, the Commission, the European Council or the Euro-group to discuss their respective decisions or present their activities in the context of the 'European Semester'.[8] In addition, the EU Parliament discusses the annual reports on the growth rate of each Member State, by giving opinions on its domestic job situation and by contributing to the preparation of the "Country Specific Recommendations" of a Member State.

Within the 'Reinforced Economic and Fiscal Surveillance' procedure established by the 'Two Pack', the competent committee of the EU Parliament can also invite representatives of the European Central Bank and/or the International Monetary Fund.[9] In the framework of the 'Economic Dialogue', the EU Parliament can further invite a Member State that is subject to a Council decision under the excessive deficit procedure or excessive imbalance procedure for an exchange of views.[10]

A few scholars have pointed out, this legal framework provides for a kind of "parliamentary involvement" that is not an inevitable and effective form of "parliamentary accountability" as no participation of the European Parliament in the exercise of the EU decision-making power is considered in the field of economic governance. This is the main reason of concern and criticism under the international law perspective of EU law, which focuses on the safeguard of the institutional balance among the EU institutions as it is provided in the EU Treaties.[11]

A similar criticism has arisen under the constitutional law perspective of EU law in relation to the unsatisfactory importance assigned to the Parliaments of the EU Member States. A number of scholars have underlined this other aspect of the democratic *deficit* of the revised European economic governance. This revised

---

[7]The first "European Semester" was in 2011. For a definition of this new working model, see EU Regulation No. 1175/2011, Art. 2-*a*.

[8]See, in particular, Art. 3 of the EU Regulation No. 1173/2011 and Art. 6 of the EU Regulation No. 1174/2011. In addition, see point 12 of the preamble of the Regulation No. 1176/2011; Arts. 14 of the EU Regulation No. 1176/2011; 2a (1) of the EU Regulation No. 1177/2011; 18 of the Regulation No. 472/2011; and 15 of the EU Regulation No. 473/2013.

[9]See, for example, para. 9 of Art. 3 of the Regulation No. 472/2011.

[10]See, for example, Art. 3 of the Regulation No. 472/2011, especially paras. 8 and 9.

[11]See, among others, Miguel Poiares Maduro, Bruno De Witte, Matthias Kumm, 'The Euro Crisis and the Democratic Governance of the Euro: Legal and Political Issues of a Fiscal Crisis', EUI-R. Schuman Centre for Advanced Studies, Global Governance Programme, *The Democratic Governance of the Euro*, *RSCAS Policy Paper* (2012/08), 3 *et seq.*; Roberto Baratta, 'Legal Issues' quoted at footnote 6, especially 672–673, 675, 677, 680–681, as to the involvement of the European Parliament in light of the 'Fiscal Compact'; Frédéric Allemand, Francesco Martucci, 'The Democratic Legitimacy' quoted at footnote 6, especially 115–118, as to the idea of establishing a special Parliament of participating States to the euro-zone in order to improve the democratic legitimacy of the European economic governance after the euro-zone crisis.

governance provides for a kind of "parliamentary involvement", rather than "parliamentary accountability", also from this perspective.[12] In any case, it is important to point out that, in light of Protocol No. 2 to the Lisbon Treaty, the national parliaments of the EU Member States had the power to control the conformity with the subsidiarity principle of the draft texts of the EU Regulations because these Regulations were adopted with the 'legislative' procedure. The same parliaments contributed to the entry into force of the two international agreements establishing respectively the 'Fiscal Compact' and the 'European Stability Mechanism'. These agreements were in effect ratified by the EU Member States, in accordance with their ordinary procedure that presupposes the approval of their Parliaments. In addition, the EU acts that are included in the 'Six Pack' and the 'Two Pack' provide for the involvement of such Parliaments within the framework of the 'Economic Dialogue'.

From both the international law and the constitutional law perspectives of EU law, it is relevant to highlight that, when the 'Fiscal Compact' will be incorporated in the EU Treaties, that is by 5 years of its entry into force,[13] the 'democratic legitimacy' of its provisions on the economic governance will be enhanced as the European Parliament and the national Parliaments of the EU Member States will be able to exercise their control over the implementation of such provisions. The 'Fiscal Compact' at Art. 13 provides for an inter-parliamentary cooperation among the European Parliament and the national Parliaments of the EU Member States.[14] This article aims to promote a certain 'democratic legitimacy' of its obligations, in relation to the "stability, coordination and governance" of the Single Monetary Union. However, Art. 13 does not say anything about the effective realization of such an inter-parliamentary cooperation. This will depend on the kind of implementation of the 'Fiscal Compact' carried out by each Contracting State within its domestic law.

[12]See, among others, Filippo Donati, 'Working Group on the Democratic Governance of the Euro. Proposals for Reform (In order to enhance the role of Parliaments in the governance of the Euro)', EUI-R (2012/08), pp. 23–26; Ioannidis (2014), especially 102.

[13]Art. 16 of the 'Fiscal Compact' runs as follows: "[w]ithin five years at most following the entry into force of this Treaty, on the basis of an assessment of the experience with its implementation, the necessary steps shall be taken, in compliance with the provisions of the Treaty on the European Union and the Treaty on the Functioning of the European Union, with the aim of incorporating the substance of this Treaty into the legal framework of the European Union". The 'Fiscal Compact' entered into force on 1 January 2013.

[14]Article 13 runs as follows: "[a]s foreseen in Title II of Protocol (No. 1) on the role of national Parliaments in the European Union annexed to the European Union Treaties, the European Parliament and the national Parliaments of the Contracting Parties will together determine the organization and promotion of a conference of representatives of the relevant committees of the national Parliaments and representatives of the relevant committees of the European Parliament in order to discuss budgetary policies and other issues covered by this Treaty.".

3 Democracy Under the Treaty on the European Union as Revised by the Lisbon Treaty

Articles 9–12 of the Treaty on the European Union highlight the absence of a single concept of democracy as a reference point in the EU law.

These articles refer to a plurality of concepts: the equalitarian democracy, the representative democracy and the participatory democracy. Such concepts have been discussed and taken into consideration as appropriate during the negotiations of the 2004 Treaty for an EU Constitution that did not enter into force.

The EU Member States have included different concepts in the Lisbon Treaty with the aim of recognizing that the democracy of the EU and its law needs to be based on elections, as well as on transparency, accountability, participation and deliberation. That is the main reason why Art. 11 refers to participatory democracy in order to widen the social consensus to the EU actions and to the exercise of conferred competences by its institutions.

This wide consensus can be seen as an implication of the heterogeneous society of the EU that is composed not only of the EU Member States but also of private parties, in particular of the citizens.

As a few scholars said, Art. 11 underlines that democracy is an objective by which the citizens should gain "a real say in/a real influence on government policy."[15] On the whole, the citizens of the EU Member States, however, appear unaware of the importance of the activity of the EU Parliament. In terms of the democratic legitimacy of the EU and its law, the fact that the EU Parliament is elected directly by such citizens is in reality less significant than that one may expect.[16] The EU citizens tend to vote in the elections for the said Parliament in light of the domestic affairs in their national Member States. The democratization of the EU decision-making power would enhance if a chain of responsibilities should be established through democracy at the EU level.[17]

At the time of the negotiations of the Treaty for an EU Constitution the introduction of a reference to participatory democracy appeared an appropriate answer to the criticism that had been brought by a few non-governmental organizations and representatives of the civil society against the EU and certain international economic organizations, such as the World Bank, the International Monetary Fund (IMF) and the World Trade Organization (WTO) during 2001.

The idea of according a direct, although non-binding, 'voice' to these categories of persons aimed not only at involving the citizens of the EU Member States,[18] but

---

[15]See, in particular, Hartley (2014), p. 45.

[16]See Weiler (2012), pp. 31–32.

[17]See, in particular, Lopez (2010), p. 124; Trevor Hartley, *The Foundations* quoted at footnote 15, p. 46.

[18]According to the 'White Paper on European governance' published by the Commission in 2001 "[t]he legitimacy of the EU now lies with the participation of its citizens." See Mendes (2011), p. 1849 *et seq.*, who points out that "participation [has become] an explicit principle of EU good

also at mitigating the criticism to the EU decision-making power of the civil society and the public opinion. The Commission had supported this idea even before the negotiations of the Treaty for an EU Constitution, in particular in its 2002 Communication on 'Towards a Reinforced Culture of Dialogue and Consultation',[19] in its 2001 'White Paper on European Governance'[20] and in its Communication on 'an Open and Structured Dialogue between the Commission and Special Interest Groups' which already referred to 'open administration' as a guiding principle of its activity.[21]

These acts show the attempts made by the Commission to establish a direct relationship with certain interest groups, in line with Protocol No. 7 to the Amsterdam Treaty related to 'the application of the principle of subsidiarity and proportionality' where it stated that "the Commission should [...] consult widely before proposing legislation and, wherever appropriate, publish consultation documents."[22] In particular, in its Communication on 'Towards a Reinforced Culture of Dialogue and Consultation' the Commission laid down a number of principles and standards in order to ensure the accountability, openness and transparency of consultations and therefore the enhancement of the same in the EU decision-making processes. To this end, such principles and standards also refer to the duties of "civil society organisations". "Civil society organisations" are seen as "facilitators of a broad policy dialogue".[23] In such acts, the Commission does not mention any specific interest group, but tends to refer to "civil society organisations" by using terminology such as "[...] the labour-market players", [...] "organisations representing social and economic players", [...] "non-governmental organisations" and "community-based organisations".[24] In the same Communication 'consultations' are defined as "the process through which the Commission wishes to trigger input from outside interested parties for the shaping of policy prior to a decision by the Commission.".[25]

---

governance and, as such, part of the Commission's strategy to enhance the social legitimacy of EU decision-making processes, i.e. an instrument to foster the societal acceptance of EU decisions" (1856).

[19]See Communication COM(2002) 704 final, 11 December 2002, that provides for 'General principles and minimum standards for consultation of interested parties by the Commission'.

[20]See Communication on 'European governance – A white paper', COM(2001) 428 final, *OJ* C287, 12 October 2001.

[21]See Communication 93/C 63/02, *OJEC* C63, 5 March 1993.

[22]See, in particular, the Communication COM(2002) 704 final, quoted at footnote 19, 4–5.

[23]See the Communication COM(2002) 704 final, quoted at footnote 19, 5.

[24]The Commission specifies that "'civil society organisations' are the principal structures of society outside of government and public administration, including economic operators not generally considered to be 'third sector' or NGOs. The term has the benefit of being inclusive and demonstrates that the concept of these organisations is deeply rooted in the democratic traditions of the Member States of the Union" (see the Communication COM(2002) 704 final, quoted at footnote 19, 6). For a general overview, see Armstrong (2002), p. 102 *et seq.*; de Schutter (2002), p. 198 *et seq.*; Quittkat and Kohler-Koch (2013), p. 41 *et seq.*

[25]See the Communication COM(2002) 704 final, quoted at footnote 19, 15–16.

4 Participatory Democracy Within the European Union and Within Named International Economic Organizations

The Treaty on the European Union refers to participatory democracy at Art. 11 of the Treaty on the European Union. This article recalls Art. I-46 of the Treaty establishing a Constitution for Europe, that was adopted by the European Convention on 13 June and 10 July 2003, and Art. I-47 of the final text of this Treaty that was signed on 31 October 2004, but did not enter into force.[26]

For the purposes of this essay, the following paragraphs of Art. 11 of the TEU are particularly important:

1. [t]he institutions shall, by appropriate means, give citizens and representative associations the opportunity to make known and publicly exchange their views in all areas of Union action.
2. The institutions shall maintain an open, transparent and regular dialogue with representative associations and civil society.
3. The European Commission shall carry out broad consultations with parties concerned in order to ensure that the Union's actions are coherent and transparent.

A few scholars have pointed out that the language of these provisions is "rethoric" and "leaves the impression of a 'shopping list' in which the participatory traits of current EU governance were included".[27] Others underline that the Treaty provisions on participatory democracy are to be read together with the principle of 'political equality', that is laid down in Art. 9 of the Treaty on the European Union, and, in any case, "[d]irect participation and political representation should be seen as complementary, strategies to democratize the EU".[28] Others wonder whether the implementation of Treaty provisions on participatory democracy would be more effective through the resort to binding legal instruments, rather than 'soft law'.[29]

The EU Commission tends to implement the provisions of Art. 11 through different instruments of 'civil dialogue', such as the accreditation of interest groups, associations and non-governmental organizations, informal public hearings, the establishment of special programs for active citizenship and/or 'participatory engineering' or 'interactive policy-making'. In particular, through digital technological

[26]As to the developments that have brought to the introduction of the reference to participatory democracy within the Treaties, see Lukšič and Bahor (2010), p. 85 *et seq.*

[27]See, in particular, Joana Mendes, 'Participation' quoted at footnote 18, 1851.

[28]See, in particular, Victor Cuesta Lopez, 'The Lisbon Treaty's Provisions' quoted at footnote 17, 131–132 and 138; von Bogdandy (2012), p. 330. Art. 9 of the Treaty on the European Union provides that "[i]n all its activities, the Union shall observe the principle of the equality of its citizens, who shall receive equal attention from its institutions, bodies, offices and agencies."

[29]See, in particular, Ferri (2012), especially 526–532.

means, the Commission carries out public consultations and/or on-line questionnaires and organizes forum and workshops.

Public consultations tend to be held on various aspects of the internal market, the protection of the environment or controversial aspects of the functioning of the EU, like the on-line consultation on investment protection and investor-to-State dispute settlement in the Transatlantic Trade and Investment Partnership Agreement (TTIP) under negotiation with the United States.[30]

It is relevant to highlight that, according to a few scholars, the instruments chosen by the EU Commission for the implementation of Art. 11 are unsatisfactory because the requirements and time-length of each of these instruments are determined by the EU Commission that enjoys wide discretionary powers in this regard.[31]

On the other hand, it is important to point out that, in comparison to the Council of Europe and other international organizations, the EU has institutionalized the recourse to participatory democracy at the level of the Treaties, that is the level of its primary law.[32]

From the website of the Council of Europe transpires that this organization is committed to the involvement of non-governmental organizations above all in the decision-making process in its Member States.

Other international organizations, such as the World Bank, the IMF and the WTO, on their official websites refer to the involvement of non-governmental organizations and civil society at large in order to enhance their accountability, moral integrity, openness and transparency, even if nothing in this regard is written in their primary sources of law, that is their establishing international treaties.

More specifically, the World Bank established different complaint mechanisms for local communities allegedly affected by a private investment involving the financial support by one of the organizations of the World Bank Group. The 'Inspection Panel' has been widely used for collective claims by peoples that have allegedly been affected by a private investment financed by the Bank or by the International Development Association (IDA). To the same end, peoples can activate the 'Grievance Redress Service' (GRS) and the World Bank Management. The World Bank also established the 'Compliance Advisory Ombudsman' for the alleged adversarial effects of the financing activities by the International Finance Corporation (IFC) and by the Multilateral Investment Guarantee Agency (MIGA); the 'Independent Evaluation Group' directed to promote the achievement of the Millennium Development Goals (MDGs), and today the post-2015 UN Development Agenda, through the activities of the Group of the World Bank; and the 'Integrity Vice Presidency', that is an independent Unit operating within the Group

[30]See the Commission Staff Working Document SWD(2015) 3 final, Brussels, 13 January 2015.

[31]See, among others, Joana Mendes, 'Participation' quoted at footnote 18, 1851–1854, as to a number of "interpretation problems" arising from the text of Art. 11; and Delia Ferri, 'Dal Libro Bianco sulla *Governance*' quoted at footnote 29, especially 514–526.

[32]Cf. Armin von Bogdandy, 'The European Lesson' quoted at footnote 331–334.

for the realization of inquiries and the determination of possible sanctions in case of corruption and/or fraud.

The IMF established a confidential telephone line (the 'IMF Integrity Hotline') at the disposal of whoever needs to report cases of lack of moral integrity by employees of the IMF. In addition, since 2011 an 'Independent Evaluation Office' has been operating within the Fund for evaluations of its activity. From the website it also transpires that the Fund follows the 'corporate social responsibility' model. This gives the impression that the Fund intends to mitigate economic and social interests within the framework of its lending and technical support activities.

The WTO organizes an annual 'Public Forum' and intermittently open consultations via its website.

In light of these trends, the 'accountability' of the decision-making power, through the promotion of the direct participation of people, rather than its 'democraticization', has been the target of international organizations. That is why a few scholars underline that [. . .] democracy remains the paramount concept when questions arise as to how international institutions can be linked to the values, interests, and convictions of the affected citizens and be responsible to them.[33]

5 Conclusion

The EU response to the euro-zone crisis has been designed in reaction to monetary and economic issues. More specifically, this response has focused on the functioning of the European System of Central Banks, the EU competence on monetary matters and on the co-ordination of the economic policies of the Member States.

A connection between the financial system and the real economy, that is between the financial and industrial crisis, has not been established. Social exclusion, due to the exclusion and marginalization of a large number of people from the production processes in several EU Member States have not been avoided, although, within the EU framework, sustainability is to be ensured both in economic and social terms, in light of Art. 3, para. 3, of the Treaty on the European Union,[34] and Art. 9 of the Treaty on the Functioning of the European Union.[35]

[33] See von Bogdandy (2014), p. 1003.

[34] According to Art. 3, para. 3, of the TEU, "[t]he Union shall establish an internal market. It shall work for the sustainable development of Europe based on balanced economic growth and price stability, a highly competitive social market economy, aiming at full employment and social progress, and a high level of protection and improvement of the quality of the environment. It shall promote scientific and technological advance. It shall combat social exclusion and discrimination, and shall promote social justice and protection, equality between women and men, solidarity between generations [. . .].".

[35] Art. 9 of the TFEU runs as follows: "[i]n defining and implementing its policies and activities, the Union shall take into account requirements linked to the promotion of a high level of

The protection of the stability of the euro currency and debt restitution have been the chief objectives of the EU answers to the crisis. This transpires from the pressure applied and the variety of restrictive economic and financial measures that the EU institutions have imposed on the most affected States, particularly Greece.[36] For the attainment of such a goal, the 'Two Pack' provides that the EU Commission can adopt rather strong and intrusive measures in relation to the choices of economic policy of the EU Member States through scrutiny of financial and economic activities. This scrutiny is based on conditionality and has a different intensity depending on the level of debt of the single Member State being taken into consideration.

The stability of price through the control of inflation ('inflation targeting'), the sustainability of the public finances of the participating States and the comprehensive financial stability of the euro-zone have eventually prevailed, as the reference values and objectives of the EU revised economic governance after the euro-zone crisis, over the values provided in Art. 2 of the Treaty on the European Union, such as democracy, human dignity and solidarity, and over the objectives mentioned in Art. 3 of the same Treaty, like social progress and the fight against social exclusion.[37]

In addition, as already pointed out, a loss of democratic legitimacy has occurred. The widening gap between the EU and the citizens of its Member States, rather than the erosion of the regulatory capacity on economic matters of these States, is one reason for this loss, although another contributory factor is the sort of blame shifting from the EU to the governments of its Member States and *viceversa* that has been occurring.[38]

The EU institutions that have revised the European economic governance have both disregarded 'democracy', as it has been included in the Treaty on the European Union by the Lisbon Treaty, and not paid much attention to the accountability and openness, through direct participation, of such a governance, notwithstanding Art. 11 of the Treaty on the European Union. From the EU website it transpires that the EU Commission has not referred to any instrument of participatory democracy, such as on-line consultations, in relation to the euro-zone crisis neither at the time of its culmination nor more recently. This gives the impression that the EU monetary policy and the co-ordination of the economic policies of the EU Member States tend to be kept out of the direct control of their citizens, that is from 'participatory

employment, the guarantee of adequate social protection, the fight against social exclusion, and a high level of education, training and protection of human health.".

[36]See, among others, Viterbo and Cisotta (2010), p. 961 *et seq.*

[37]According to a few scholars, the values provided in Art. 2 of the TEU are "the basic principles of public authority" of the EU law. See Armin von Bogdandy, 'Common Principles' quoted at footnote 33, 997.

[38]See, in particular, Michael Ioannidis, 'EU Financial Assistance' quoted at footnote 12, 104.

democracy'. A few provisions of the relevant EU legal instruments refer to their indirect control and involvement through the European Parliament.[39]

The implementation of both the 'Six Pack' and the 'Two Pack' does not provide for a special participation of the EU citizens that are those effectively hit by the effects of the economic and financial recovery programs brought about by the euro-zone crisis. The citizens of the indebted Member States are hit by the austerity programs recommended by the 'Troika'—the EU Commission, the EU Central Bank and the International Monetary Fund—that are mainly based on cuts of the public social expenditure and of wages, whereas the citizens of the other Member States are hit as tax payers. The 'Six Pack' and the 'Two Pack' do not establish any compliant mechanisms, whether binding or not, and do not refer to the 'new' provisions on participatory democracy included in the Treaty on the European Union by the Lisbon Treaty.

As the EU integration process intends to be based not only on the reduction and elimination of barriers ('negative integration'), but also on the establishment and development of common policies ('positive integration'), re-regulation, after de-regulation, might be grounded not only on financial and economic elements, but also on the assumption that, under the Treaty on the European Union, in particular under its Art. 3, para. 4, the Economic and Monetary Union is meant to be an instrument for the sustainability of economic growth, as well as for the solidarity among the EU Member States and among their citizens.[40]

References

Allemand F, Martucci F (2014) The democratic legitimacy of European economic governance. Revue de l'OFCE/Debated and Policies 134:111 et seq

Armstrong KA (2002) Rediscovering civil society: the European Union and the white paper on governance. Eur Law J 8:102 et seq

Baratta R (2012) Legal Issues of the "Fiscal Compact". Searching for a mature democratic governance of the Euro. In: Il Diritto dell'Unione Europea p 645 et seq

Cisotta R (2015) Disciplina fiscale, stabilità finanziaria e solidarietà nell'Unione europea ai tempi della crisi: alcuni spunti ricostruttivi. Il Diritto dell'Unione Europea 1:57 et seq

de Schutter O (2002) Europe in search of its civil society. Eur Law J 8:198 et seq

[39]For example, Art. 2-*a*, para. 4, of Regulation 1175 (2011) reads as follows: "[t]he European Parliament shall be duly involved in the European Semester in order to increase the transparency and ownership of, and the accountability for the decisions taken, in particular by means of the economic dialogue carried out pursuant to Article 2-*a* and *b* of this Regulation.".

[40]See Habermas (2012), p. 335 *et seq*., who refers to the need of expanding civic solidarity "… among the individual citizens of the EU" "… as a medium of political integration" (especially 339, 342). The author underlines that "[a] Europe-wide civic solidarity cannot emerge if social inequalities between the Member States become permanent structural features along the fault lines separating poor from rich nations. The Union must guarantee what the constitution of the German Federal Republic calls the 'uniformity of living standards'" (348). As to the relationship between the financial stability of the euro-zone and solidarity, cf. Cisotta (2015), p. 57 *et seq*.

Editorial Comments (2012) Debt and democracy: "United States then, Europe Now"? Common Mark Law Rev 49:1833 et seq

Ferri D (2012) Dal Libro Bianco sulla *Governance* al nuovo registro per la trasparenza: l'UE tra *Participatory Engineering* e democrazia partecipativa. Rivista Italiana di Diritto Pubblico Comunitario, especially 526–532

Habermas J (2012) The crisis of the European Union in the light of a constitutionalization of international law. Eur J Int Law 23:335 et seq

Hartley T (2014) The foundations of European Union Law. Oxford University Press, Oxford, p 45

Ioannidis M (2014) EU financial assistance conditionality after "Two Pack". Zeitschrift für ausländisches öffentliches Recht und Völkerrecht 74:102

Lopez VC (2010) The Lisbon treaty's provisions on democratic principles: a legal framework for participatory democracy. Eur Public Law 16:124

Lukšič AA, Bahor M (2010) Participatory democracy within the EU: a solution for democratic gap? J Comp Polit 3:85 et seq

Mendes J (2011) Participation and the role of law after lisbon: a legal view on Article 11 TEU. Common Mark Law Rev 48:1849 et seq

Quittkat C, Kohler-Koch B (2013) Involving civil society in EU governance. Kohler-Koch B, Quittkat C, Buth V, Altides C (eds) De-mystification of participatory democracy. Oxford University Press, Oxford, p 41 et seq

Ruffert M (2011) The European debt crisis and European Union Law. Common Mark Law Rev 48:1801–1805

von Bogdandy A (2012) The European lesson for international democracy: the significance of Articles 9–12 EU treaty for international organizations. Eur J Int Law 23:330

von Bogdandy A (2014) Common principles for a plurality of orders: a study on public authority in the European legal area. I-CON 12(4):1003

Viterbo A, Cisotta R (2010) La crisi della Grecia, l'attacco speculativo all'euro e le risposte dell'Unione europea. Il Diritto dell'Unione Europea 15:961 et seq

Weiler JHH (2012) Democracy and limits of EU competence. In: Challenges of multi-tier governance in the EU, Workshop 4th October 2012, pp 31–32

Brexit. Europe Betrayed?

Giuseppe Di Taranto

Abstract The result of the referendum between Brexit and Remain has confirmed the political inconsistency and economic inability of the EU. Great Britain has always been on the edge of the European Union, keeping itself as an "island" not only geographically, but also in its economic and political relations with continental Europe. After Brexit, there was much discussion about the domino effect which it could have on the calling for other similar referendums in other European nations. The many faults attributed to Brexit appear as alibis to cover the state of dissatisfaction that European citizens feel towards institutions that have made euro-bureaucracy prevail over euro-democracy. Neither Euro-scepticism nor Euro-optimism can be accepted in principle as dogma, without the participation of the peoples who, for better or worse, must live through, on a daily basis, the opportunities and constraints of a European Union which has betrayed itself.

Contents

1 The Island and Brussels

The result of the referendum between Brexit and Remain has been Great Britain's exit from the European Union. More particularly, however, it has confirmed the political inconsistency and economic inability of the EU, which had already yielded to all the demands of the United Kingdom should the "Yes" vote be victorious in the summit of 18th–19th February, 2016. Concerning economic governance, it was decided that the measures that aimed at a further deepening or widening of the economic and monetary Union will now be optional for the Member States whose

G. Di Taranto (✉)
Department of Business and Management, Luiss Guido Carli University, Rome, Italy
e-mail: gditaranto@luiss.it

E. Sciso (ed.), *Accountability, Transparency and Democracy in the Functioning of Bretton Woods Institutions*, DOI 10.1007/978-3-319-57855-2_8

currency is not the Euro, and that the institutions of the Union, together with the Member States, will facilitate the coexistence of different perspectives within the single institutional framework.

Furthermore, the European Council satisfied the demands of Great Britain for bureaucratic simplification concerning competitiveness. Indeed, it undertook to commit us to reducing the administrative burdens and costs of compliance for entrepreneurs, especially the small and medium-sized companies, at the same time continuing to ensure high standards as regards the protection of consumers, workers, health and the environment.

Regarding sovereignty, it was acknowledged that the United Kingdom, in the light of its special situation and in conformity with the treaties, is not bound to take part in any further political integration of the European Union. Substantive issues would be inserted in the treaties on the occasion of their next review, in accordance with the relevant provisions of the treaties themselves and the respective constitutional rules of the Member States, so as to make it clear that references to an ever closer-knit Union do not apply to the United Kingdom.

After all, from November 2015 the English prime minister Cameron had been formally requesting Tusk to obtain for Great Britain not only a derogation from the clause of the treaties that augurs a more cohesive and united Europe, but also a more independent role for national parliaments, the suspension of social welfare benefits for foreign citizens, the clear distinction between the eurozone and those EU countries outside the single currency. The European Council of 18th–19th February considered these demands "fully compatible with the treaties" and that they would take effect from when the British government of Prime Minister Cameron communicated its decision to remain in the EU[1]—subsequently contradicted by the result of the referendum.

The above explains why the remain campaign waged by Cameron—similar to that of Farage's for Brexit—was based largely on the propagation of figures and spurious data, in order to fomented misgiving, if not fear, that the citizens of the United Kingdom would pay for a "Yes" victory with higher social costs and a widespread decline in the standard of living. Research carried out by the by the British Treasury foresaw the GDP reduced by 3.6%, a loss of half a million jobs, and a 3% decrease in pay during the first year of Brexit. However, should there be a real, concrete shock rather than a predictable conjuncture, the result would be a GDP reduced by 6%, a loss of more than 800,000 jobs, and a wage decrease of 4%.[2]

[1]European Council, Secretary General of the Council (2016) Meeting of the European Council 18–19 February, Conclusions.

[2]On Brexit cfr. Among others, http://www.spiegel.de/international/europe/brexit-triggers-eu-power-struggle-between-merkel-and-juncker-a-1100852.html; https://keynesblog.com/2016/07/01/brexit-euro-europa-facciamo-chiarezza/?utm_source=dlvr.it&utm_medium=facebook; http://www.binghamton.edu/fbc/commentaries/index.html; http://www.politico.eu/article/a-very-british-betrayal-michael-gove-boris-johnson/; https://www.project-syndicate.org/commentary/brexit-future-referendum-by-christopher-granville-2016-06#comments; http://www.politico.eu/article/5-us-independence-movements-inspired-by-brexit/.

The so-called "politics of fear" is not new in the European Union since it actually goes back to the years preceding the Treaty of Maastricht. 1989, in fact, saw the publication of a report, requested by the Commission and signed by Paolo Cecchini, on the costs incurred by the failure to implement the European Monetary Union. The report quantified, in the short term, under both the micro—and the macro-economic profiles, the advantages which financial rigour—the so-called "austerity"—and the enlargement of the market would offer: an average GDP increase of 5.3%, prices reduced by 6.1%, an increase in employment of around two million a year, an improvement of the Community budget "by an average equivalent of 2.2% of the GDP, causing the balance of payments surplus to increase by about 1% of the GDP".[3] In the light of what happened after Maastricht, the Cecchini report should have pointed out the opportunities of the Monetary Union rather than the costs of failing to implement it. We hope that this does not happen to the studies prepared by the English treasury because Brexit represents, all told, the last stage of an economic policy of the United Kingdom which has always but ill sustained a Europe constructed on an institutional architecture inspired by France and Germany.

When looked at closely, Great Britain has always been on the edge of the European Union, keeping itself as an "island" not only geographically, but also in its economic and political relations with continental Europe. In June 1944 Winston Churchill declared to General De Gaulle: "every time we have to choose between Europe and the open sea, we shall always be for the open sea".[4] And it is no coincidence that Great Britain succeeded in entering the European Common Market only in 1972, after two attempts that failed due to the opposition by France and, in particular, Charles De Gaulle himself. From the historical perspective, as David Randall recently wrote, the anomalous relations between the Island and the Continent are not so much the result of Brexit "as of 44 years of unconvinced belonging to a united Europe".[5]

Cameron's decision to hold the referendum indicates that he had not foreseen the success of Nigel Farage's Ukip, nor the silence of both the Conservative and the Labour Parties on the phenomenon of immigration and, especially, the awareness of Europe's incapacity for an adequate solution. In fact, while not forgetting the UK's proverbial capacity to receive and integrate millions of immigrants coming from the Commonwealth countries and, historically, providing for the victims of political and religious persecution, the further five million arrivals from 1997 on are causing profound concern in terms of assimilation and its effect on social and health services. It is significant that "in the areas where the rate of immigration is highest, three out of four people voted to leave." Brexit, in the final analysis, "was the democratic revolt of 17 million people of the working and middle classes against a protected élite which did not represent them and which for too long continued to

[3]Cecchini (1988), pp. 142–189.

[4]Chavagneux (2016).

[5]Randall (2016).

ignore their concerns, considering them the fruit of ignorance and insisting on claiming to be the only one to know what was good for them".[6]

On the other hand, the separation of the *Island* from a united Europe is long-standing. On the signing of the Maastricht Treaty, the English Chancellor of the Exchequer was absent and, thanks to the opt-out clause, Great Britain rejected the single currency, the euro, did not become part of Schengen, nor did it adopt the Charter of Fundamental Rights on its territory.

A recent inquiry carried out by Eurobarometer has shown that the citizens of the United Kingdom are those who know least about the functioning and, indeed, the very geographical composition of the European Union.[7] The replies to certain particularly easy questions, such as whether or not Switzerland formed part of the Union, with 100 as the maximum score, the United Kingdom, with 57.3%, came last in the list against the EU's average of 66%, and beaten even by Latvia, Poland and Estonia. This explains why some hours after the result of the referendum a good number of the British had, via the internet, sought information about the EU.

After Brexit, there was much discussion about the domino effect which it could have on the calling for other similar referendums in other European nations. In this regard, one should remember that already in the recent past plebiscites have frequently rejected the process of unification or the treaties that were its foundation, at least initially. In 2001 Ireland opposed the ratification of the Treaty of Nice; in 2005, France and Holland blocked the European Constitution which then became the less ambitious Treaty of Lisbon against which, once more initially, Ireland voted no in June 2008, helping to confirm the reservations about the Treaty itself expressed by both the Polish President Lech Kaczynski and the President of the Czech Republic Vaclav Klaus.[8] In this context one must also remember not only the failed referendum proposed in Greece by George Papandreou in 2012, faced with a financial law untenable for the country's economic conditions but imposed by the austerity willed by Brussels, but also the opposition and the intrusion, always on the part of representatives of the EU institutions, in the internal politics of Greece at the time of the subsequent referendum called for and implemented by Tsipras in 2014.

When complying with Article 50 of the Treaty of Lisbon—which provides any EU country with the right to exit from the union on the basis of a choice made by its citizens, in the case of those countries where a referendum is allowed—one wonders if those same citizens might be subject to intimidation. This could take the form of fear mongering or outright threats as to what a vote against Europe could bring about. This would be in breach of the sovereignty of the various nation states, a breach in the application of the norms of direct democracy, as well as of the selfsame articles delineated in the treaties and willed by European institutions.

---

[6]Idem.

[7]Voxeurop (2016).

[8]Castronovo (2016), p. 57. The Treaty of Lisbon was then ratified by all the countries of the European Union in November 2009.

2 Creative Austerity

To better grasp the need for change, one need merely ask why, of the 200 or so countries that now make up our world, only the few that belong to the European Monetary Union are subject to such stringent budget constraints, and why the euro area is growing less than other regions, in particular the United States, the epicenter of the subprime mortgage crisis.

The chief current problems for Europe, apart from possible decisions bearing on the Schengen Treaty and its costs, concern compliance with the rules on the government budget deficit (3% of GDP) and the public debt (60%). The annual budget constraint is attenuated by the possibility of flexible application for individual members, while the debt limit is rendered harsher by the Fiscal Compact, which requires members to bring the ratio down to below the 60% threshold within 20 years.[9] It is worth recalling that if the Union's objectives for inflation and long-term interest rates have been practically attained, (owing in part to the recession caused by the sacrifices imposed by economic convergence), as regards the objective of fiscal sustainability four of the 12 original signatories of the Maastricht Treaty were running deficits larger than 3% in 1991 (Portugal and Belgium, 7.2%; Greece, 11%; and Italy, 11.4%), and at the end of that year five had debt ratios higher than 60% (Belgium, 127%; Greece, 82.2%; Ireland, 94.4%; Italy, 98.0%; and the Netherlands, 73.7%).

At the first of three scheduled monitoring exercises, at the end of 1993, the countries failing to comply with the deficit ratio were again Italy, whose deficit had come down to 10%, Belgium, where it was unchanged, Austria (which joined the European Union on 1 January 1995, together with Sweden and Finland) at 4.2%, and France, at 5.9%.

At the second assessment, as of 31 December 1996 nine members were above the 3% threshold and seven in violation of the 60% debt ratio limit. And despite improvements on the deficit front, at the final verification, 31 July 1998, the debt ratio was above the limit in seven countries and had risen in a good many others: by 20.1 percentage points in Germany, 22.3 in France, and 31.8 in Greece. After the three assessments, 11 of 12 countries were admitted to the single currency. Greece was admitted under derogation, soon to be terminated.

The acceptance of these members, which ignored their public finance problems, was possible thanks to an interpretation of Article 104C(b) of the Treaty that had been adopted in the earlier exercises as well; that is, greater importance was assigned to the deficit than to the debt ratio. As in December 1991, when the Treaty had been signed but not yet ratified, and five member states had debt ratios higher than 60%, it was posited that there was no definite limit to the volume of the public debt, and that accordingly it was sufficient for the debt to be coming down towards the desired value at a satisfactory pace, with no specific timetable for attaining it.[10]

[9] Di Taranto (2014), pp. 51–53.

[10] Guarino (2011), pp. 219–274; Guarino (2006), pp. 126–141. See also: Di Taranto (2012a), pp. 176–179; Di Taranto (2011), pp. 495–517; Di Taranto (2008), pp. 21–63.

This is the reading that has now brought about, instead, the Fiscal Compact, which lays down rigid time and quantity standards for lowering the debt ratio to 60%. Here, one of the linchpins of modern economic theory has been—willfully—ignored: namely, the Ricardian equivalence proposition, set forth in the second decade of the nineteenth century and refined by R. Barro in 1974, which postulates that the public debt can increase as long as the additional tax revenue deriving from greater economic growth produced by larger deficits is enough to cover the interest payments principal repayments on the debt.

As for the deficit ratio, the rules allowed for overshoots in temporary, exceptional circumstances. Hence, the deficit requirement turned out to be a necessary and sufficient condition for convergence on the standards of admission to the single currency.

Italy, with its very high public debt, in order to qualify quickly applied the Ricardian equivalence, enacting a burdensome "Eurotax" and not following the UK's lead in "opting out" under the Maastricht Treaty clause that allowed member countries not to adhere immediately, pending further consideration.[11]

These premises for the euro highlight the problems and constraints that would plague its proper implementation.

What, then, were the criteria behind the 3 and 60% limits? And what economists endorsed such limits in theory?

Before the advent of the euro, the 3% deficit parameter was ascribed to the so-called "golden rule of fiscal policy," namely that government should not borrow to finance current spending and that the deficit should therefore not exceed public investment expenditure, which was around that level in a good number of countries. Or else it referred to the benchmark applied by West Germany. Or, yet again, it was said to correspond to the deficit at which a public debt of 60% of GDP could be financed at an interest rate of 5%. This third criterion, however, implies a balanced budget net of interest payments and thus conflicts with the medium-term objectives of the Stability and Growth Pact.[12] Yet the Delors Report, upon which the Maastricht Treaty was based, only spoke of the need to "impose effective upper limits on budget deficits of individual member countries"; it did not quantify them.

Thanks to the French daily *Aujourd'hui*, we now know how the 3% deficit ratio originated and how it was adopted by the technocrats of Brussels. Its inventor was Guy Abeille, a budget department functionary at the French Finance Ministry during the presidency of François Mitterrand. The standard was set "with no theoretical reflection whatever," Abeille has said. "Mitterrand needed an easy rule to use in order to turn down ministers who came to ask for money. . . . We needed something simple." At the time, in the early '80s, France was running a deficit of around 2.6%, so "proposing 1 per cent would have been too hard, unfeasible," 2% would have "put the government under too much pressure"; the figure was therefore fixed at 3%. "3 per cent? It's a good number, a historic number,

[11]Savona (2012), p. 46.

[12]Magnifico (2008), p. 239.

calling the Trinity to mind." And in fact the former head of the Bundesbank, Hans Tietmeyer, acknowledged that the standard was "economically not easy to explain." The most striking thing, as *Aujourd'hui* emphasizes, is that the Brussels technocrats adopted the same method in their recent determination of "another seeming, and equally false, Cartesian rule: the structural deficit ceiling of 0.5%. Why not 1% or 2%? No one knows.".[13]

There has been no lack of proposals for modifying these postulates. The European Economic Advisory Group advocates modulating the budget constraints depending on the size of the country's debt. Other scholars hold that there is a need for some deficit flexibility in accordance with national economic growth rates. And the list could be extended.[14] So far, however, nothing has changed—least of all the obstinacy of the Eurocracy.

The theoretical underpinnings of the 60% debt ratio are traceable to what was called, in the '90s, "expansionary austerity," by now part of the mainstream neoclassical market model. Under the theory of expectations, the reduction of the sovereign debt thanks to fiscal consolidation through spending cuts will stimulate growth, because the cuts are perceived as the signal of future tax reductions and hence higher expected incomes. But the recent crisis has demonstrated that "expansionary" austerity was, instead, recessionary. The International Monetary Fund, at first the most vehement of the Troika's advocates of austerity, has now had to recognize that the fiscal multipliers were higher during the recession than before: 1.5 instead of 0.5, meaning that a fiscal contraction of €1.00 had a recessionary impact of €1.50 on the economy, and not of €0.50, as the theorists of expansionary austerity had estimated.[15]

The thesis of a negative correlation between debt and growth has been recently resumed and sustained by Carmen Reinhart and Kenneth Rogoff of Harvard. Based on empirical studies, they show that in the long run countries with high sovereign debt—over 90% of GDP, hence well above the more restrictive 60% parameter laid down by the European treaties and regulations—have lower growth. The study has been taken as the scientific justification for the adoption of austerity policies within the euro area and for the rule requiring reduction of the public debt to 60% of GDP by means of the Fiscal Compact and the incorporation of the balanced-budget principle in national constitutions.

But this empirical work on the correlation between debt and growth is flawed by spreadsheet errors, as was discovered by researchers at the University of Massachusetts and as Reinhart and Rogoff have admitted. What is more, it has been shown that there is in fact no "threshold effect," such as a ceiling of, say, 60%, and no direct causal nexus between debt and growth. Finally, the consequences vary from country to country, while empirical studies on the Reinhart-Rogoff model simply *postulate* that the relationship between debt and growth is the same

[13]Di Taranto (2012b), 16 November; Lops (2014), 29 January.

[14]Magnifico (2008), op cit, p. 241–243.

[15]Daniele (2013). For Italy, cfr: Pisauro (2012), pp. 53–61; IMF (2012), p. 53 ff.

independent of context. "The hypothesis could potentially produce misleading results, and studies using statistical techniques that *do not so postulate* cast doubt on the negative correlation between debt and growth in the advanced countries."[16]

3 Speculation: From Exchange Rates to Sovereign Debt

The advent of the single European currency has resulted in a switch in the focus of currency speculation, from exchange rates—which were flexible after 1978 both under the old monetary snake and also, albeit within a fixed fluctuation band, under the European Monetary System—to the rates of interest on the public debt of different countries. In other words, speculators switched from currencies as the representation of the conditions of a national economy to the market's confidence in a State's sovereign debt. While the spread between 10-year Italian Treasury bonds and German Bunds was 600 basis points in 1991 when Germany was reunified, rose to 700 basis points with the speculative attacks on Italy in 1992, and remained over 300 basis points until 1996, not a single analyst cited this as proof of Italy's economic weakness relative to Germany. The spread then declined and with the advent of the euro recorded negative values from 1997 to 2007, marking the first but in many respects also the last success for the single currency. As Jacques Sapir has noted, it went unobserved—or ignored—that this was the only sphere in which some effective unification was achieved at the time: "Product prices remained quite diverse across the various euro-area countries, and the prices of shares listed in the various stock exchanges absolutely failed to converge. Worse still, the differences in economic trends between the countries of the euro area continued to increase."[17]

The shortcomings of Europe's institutional architecture were then thrown into relief by the subprime mortgage crisis that broke out in the United States, the subsequent failure of major investment banks—first Bear Stearns, then Lehman Brothers—and Prime Minister Georgios Papandreou's declaration that Greece risked default. The resulting contraction of liquidity widened interest rate spreads vis-à-vis 10-year German bonds, spreads that hit their maximum during the summer of 2011 in Portugal, Ireland, Italy, Greece and Spain (the "PIIGS" countries) but also in Belgium. Actually, this constituted the realization of the conditions laid down by Germany for agreeing to Maastricht—the euro area had to arise as a community of financial stability, according to a decision of the German Constitutional Court, which consequently ruled out any form of mutualization of the sovereign debt of countries in difficulty. And given this line of thought, the European Central Bank, founded in 1998, could not act as lender of last resort,

---

[16]Panizza and Presbitero (2013), 20 April. Reinhart and Rogoff (2010), pp. 573–578. Herndon et al. (2013).

[17]Sapir (2012), pp. 24–39.

because its sole mandate was for monetary stability, interpreted narrowly as fighting inflation on the model of the Bundesbank.

Euro-area countries in difficulty, then, given the single currency, cannot mutualize their debt, or carry out competitive devaluations, or regulate interest rates. The sole instrument they can use to finance themselves is the free capital market—an instrument that even in 1999 Joseph Halevi had described as a boon to financial rents[18]—with a consequent increase in the public debt and the transformation of the liquidity crises into solvency crises. These in turn undermine investor confidence, threatening economic deterioration in the debtor states, insofar as the widening of spreads lowers the value of their government securities and means higher debt interest payments. It is no accident that the IMF has reconsidered its original position, admitted the damage done by the policies of austerity imposed through the Troika,[19] and, together with the OECD and the European Parliament, recognized the need for some control over capital movements.

The yield on sovereign debt instruments is correlated with the exchange rate, inflation, insolvency risk and, solvency being equal, their degree of liquidity. So a German Bund is more attractive in the international capital market than an Italian BTP, which in turn is more attractive than analogous bonds issued by Greece or Cyprus. Thanks to the soundness and reliability of the German economy, the Bund would appear to serve as a sort of safe haven. With the advent of the single currency, the first of these factors—the exchange rate—was eliminated and variations in inflation expectations were reduced enormously, to far less than 2 percentage points above the rates in the three most virtuous countries as established by the Maastricht Treaty. And in fact until 2007 the average spread with respect to German government bonds was only 27 basis points for Italy, 28 basis points for Greece, and a mere 9 basis points for Spain. This means either that the markets had unlimited confidence in the financial soundness of all the euro-area countries or else that they had failed to comprehend one of the constituent elements of Maastricht, namely the no-bail-out principle, which ensures the stability of the single currency and absolutely precludes any transfer of funds between member states.[20]

Jean-Paul Fitoussi has rightly observed that "the consequences of foreign exchange speculation, while serious, are infinitely less grave than those of speculation on the stability of States. The economic and social consequences of a currency devaluation are incomparably less severe than those of sovereign debt run."[21] In practice, the switch from speculation on exchange rates to speculation on sovereign interest rates coincided with the transfer of sovereignty from States to the supranational economy of finance. Whereas a national government can manage exchange rates by open market operations to regulate domestic liquidity through its

[18]Graziani (2001), p. 171.

[19]Sapir (2012), op cit, p. 12–16. For Italy, see: Growth and Financial Stability in Italy. Review of Economic Conditions in Italy 2001(1). In particular, Pisauro (2001), pp. 31–54.

[20]Sarrazin (2013), pp. 77–78.

[21]Fitoussi (2013), p. 122.

own central bank or by competitive devaluation—or revaluation, as envisaged by the EMS—it is impossible for any country, alone, to ward off speculative attacks on its stability, given the enormous volume of capital that liberalization has injected into the market with the financialization of the economy. This is because the euro-area countries' public debt is denominated in a supranational currency over which they no longer wield the monetary policy powers just mentioned. On the contrary, the crisis is deepened, as the danger of a State's default depresses its bonds, widens the spread, and depreciates the assets of the banks that hold them. Unless government intervenes, there is the danger of a bank run—as in Greece—and the flight of capital to States with sounder sovereign debt. Obviously this mechanism weakens the poorer countries, through speculation, and further enriches the affluent.

In this regard, Thilo Sarrazin has observed that "a bank that holds government securities denominated in euros takes on an extra risk with respect to the securities of a State whose central bank can issue money", and that this threatens to undermine its solvency.[22]

4 Brexit and the P Factor

Among the many faults attributed to Brexit—faults which appear as alibis to cover the state of dissatisfaction that European citizens feel towards institutions that have made euro-bureaucracy prevail over euro-democracy—there is also the consolidation of what I have defined elsewhere[23] as "The P Factor", namely populism. Concerning this term and its expanding interpretation—in part the consequence of the outcome of the British referendum—some clarification is due.

It has been rightly pointed out that the presence of populist parties, namely euro sceptics and euro critics, increased in the European Parliament from 2009 to 2014 (by 16.1 to 28.1%, as against a decrease in the traditional parties of centre, right and left, now around 70%) and that the clearest sign of the populist strength is attributable to two events following upon 2014: the Austrian presidential elections of last May, which will be repeated in October 2016 thanks to detected irregularities, and Great Britain's referendum on remaining in Europe.[24]

The author, having noted that populist movements are, however, present also in nations such as Norway and Switzerland, which have always been outside the European Union, attributes their growth and spread to the inequalities brought about by globalisation—both in Europe and in the United States—and to the so-called *political correctness* which has gone beyond the limits of common sense and "what ordinary people feel, who work hard to simply get by, and who

[22]Sarrazin (2013), op cit, pp. 24–41.

[23]Di Taranto (2014), op cit, pp. 59–68.

[24]Ricolfi (2016).

pay the receiving costs personally in the form of insecurity and competition in the labour market".[25]

The above should lead us to consider if accusing these movements of 'populism' reflects a democratic deficit, whereas they could be regarded as the affirmation of the will of the people.

Populism, in the etymological interpretation of Alfonso Berardinelli, relates back to the people, to their qualities and their primary rights, and not to the intellectual and political elite; "but the people today—he notes—are an unknown, because in their social composition there is now a myriad of frightened and quarrelsome groups. What unites them is the fear of impoverishment and downgrading".[26] By way of confirmation, it is sufficient to remember that in the European Union over 120 million citizens are in danger of poverty and social exclusion, and juxtaposed with a reduced political cohesion is an ever greater party-political fragmentation. And yet, in a book by Mario Monti and Sylvie Goulard, one reads: "Whatever the populists say of it, the task of government is not to blindly follow the urges of the people" because " the approach that consists in lashing out at the bureaucracy of Brussels is not simply wrong, since Brussels generally proves to be more useful and more thrifty than one tends to admit, but it is above all sterile, because it is incapable of developing proposals to meet the challenges of the moment at the same level".[27]

Not surprisingly, the ex-president of the Council of Ministers, Monti, together with the ex-president of the European Council, Van Rompuy, proposed in 2012 to hold a special summit on the subject in Rome, which relaunched the concerns of Chancellor Angela Merkel, because in a period in which she was hoping to complete integration, instead a dangerous opposing phenomenon was evolving. In this respect Jordi Vaquer, in an editorial in "El Pais" entitled *Euro-scepticism thanks the technocrats*, wrote that Monti embodied a new type of bureaucratic power, which pushes to the limit the political mechanisms of Member States intended to replace the elected representatives when they are no longer able to ensure the credibility of the government to "make reforms and cut expenses" in the times decided upon by the European Union, by the ECB and by Berlin.[28] This is exactly what happened in Greece in 2012.

After all, already in the aftermath of the afore-mentioned French and Dutch referendums that rejected the proposal for a European constitution, the "Financial Times", in an article entitled *Stop lying about the European Union*, saw in this result "the revolt of the people against too many years of lies about Europe told by those who govern it.[29] And in 1994 a fascinating document drawn up by Wolfgang

[25]Idem.

[26]In: Di Taranto (2013), 22 January.

[27]Goulard and Monti (2012), pp. 38–39.

[28]Published on 12 September 2012, in Voxeurop (http://www.presseurop.eu/it/content/article/2679361-l-euroscetticismo-ringrazia-i-tecnocrati).

[29]Padoa Schioppa (2006), p. 33.

Schäuble and Karl Lamers emphasised that the progressive enlargement of Europe would slow down integration, accentuate the divergence of interests, and stimulate a "regressive nationalism"[30] in many countries. And this is precisely what would happen, not only in the nations of the east which had accepted the Union but in the greater part of Europe, starting from the European Parliament elections of 2009,[31] a change from which the United Kingdom would not be exempt and which would be the origin of Brexit.

The point is that neither Euro-scepticism nor Euro-optimism can be accepted in principle as dogma, without the participation of the peoples who, for better or worse, must live through, on a daily basis, the opportunities and constraints of a European Union which has betrayed itself.

References

Castronovo V (2016) L'Europa e la rinascita dei nazionalismi. Laterza, Rome-Bari, p 57

Cecchini P (1988) La sfida del 1992. Una grande scommessa per l'Europa. Sperling & Kupfer, Milan, pp 142–189

Chavagneux C (2016) Quelle Europe après le Brexit? Alternatives économique, 27 Juin

Daniele V (2013) L'austerità espansiva e i numeri (sbagliati) di Reinhart e Rogoff. Economia e Politica, 20 June. http://www.economiaepolitica.it/index.php/primo-piano/lausterita-espansiva-e-i-numeri-sbagliati-di-reinhart-e-rogoff/

Di Taranto G (2008) L'Europa tradita. Dall'economia di mercato all'economia del profitto. In: Capriglione F (ed) La nuova disciplina della società europea. Cedam, Padua, pp 21–63

Di Taranto G (2011) The Internationalization Process in Southern Italy. Rev Econ Conditions Italy 2–3:495–517

Di Taranto G (2012a) Le basi problematiche della moneta unica. Aspenia 26:176–179

Di Taranto G (2012b) Ragioni liberali per criticare certi eccessi dell'austerity. Il Foglio, 16 November

Di Taranto G (2013) Le euro élite scioglierebbero il popolo per eleggerne un altro. Il Foglio, 22 January

Di Taranto G (2014) L'Europa tradita. Lezioni dalla moneta unica. LUISS University Press, Rome, pp 51–53

Editoriale (2011) Italia caput mundi. Limes La guerra dell'euro 6:17–19

Fitoussi JP (2013) Il teorema del lampione o come mettere fine alla sofferenza sociale. Einaudi, Turin, p 122

Goulard S, Monti M (2012) La democrazia in Europa. Guardare lontano. Rizzoli, Milano, pp 38–39

Graziani A (2001) Lo sviluppo dell'economia italiana. Dalla ricostruzione alla moneta unica europea. Bollati Boringhieri, Turin, p 171

Guarino G (2006) Eurosistema. Analisi e prospettive. Giuffrè, Milan, pp 126–141

Guarino G (2011) L'Europa imperfetta. Ue: problemi, analisi, prospettive. In: Guarino G (ed) Diritto ed economia. L'Italia, l'Europa, il mondo. I Quaderni di Economia italiana 8:219–274

[30] Editoriale (2011), pp. 17–19.

[31] Castronovo (2016), op. cit., pp. 80–90.

Herndon T, Ash M, Pollin R (2013) Does high public debt consistently stifle economic growth? A Critique of Reinhart and Rogoff. PERI (322). http://www.peri.umass.edu/fileadmin/pdf/working_papers/working_papers_301-350/WP322.pdf
IMF (2012) World Economic and Financial Surveys. Fiscal Monitor, October, p 53 ff
Lops V (2014) Parla l'inventore della formula del 3% sul deficit/pil: "Parametro deciso in meno di un'ora, senza basi teoriche". Il Sole 24 Ore, 29 January
Magnifico G (2008) Euro: squilibri finanziari e spiragli di soluzione. LUISS University Press, Rome, p 239
Padoa Schioppa T (2006) Europa in pazienza attiva. Malinconia e riscatto del vecchio continente. Rizzoli, Milan, p 33
Panizza U, Presbitero AF (2013) Quel nesso da dimostrare tra debito e crescita. lavoce.info, 20 April
Pisauro G (2001) The consolidation of the Italian economy, 31–54
Pisauro G (2012) Il risanamento dei conti pubblici. Economia italiana 1:53–61
Randall D (2016) Una rivolta democratica contro un'élite sorda e protetta. Internazionale, 5 July
Reinhart C, Rogoff K (2010) Growth in a time of debt. Am Econ Rev 2(100):573–578
Ricolfi L (2016) Il vento populista che soffia sul mondo. Il Sole 24 Ore, 16 August: 1–14
Sapir J (2012) Bisogna uscire dall'euro?. Ombre corte, Verona, pp 24–39
Sarrazin T (2013) L'Europa non ha bisogno dell'euro. Castelvecchi, Rome, pp 77–78
Savona P (2012) Eresie, esorcismi e scelte giuste per uscire dalla crisi. Il caso Italia. Rubettino, Soveria Mannelli, p 46
Voxeurop (2016) Quanto sono informati sull'Ue gli europei?. Voxeurop, 29 June

Part III
Accountability and Independent Complaint Mechanisms

Independent Accountability Mechanisms; How Multilateral Financial Institutions Can Be the Front Runners for Commercial Financial Institutions

M. Van Putten

Abstract Independent Accountability Mechanisms for Multilateral Financial Institutions (MFIs) already have existed since 1993 when the World Bank Independent Inspection Panel was established on the demand of the US Congress. The Congress expressed its dissatisfaction with severe impacts of World Bank financed projects on people in project areas: for the Narmada Dam in India 200,000 people had to be displaced while not even a resettlement plan existed. Most of the other MFIs followed the example and created their own mechanisms, while civil society—and in particular NGOs—started to use the opportunity to lodge complaints. The complaints mainly concerned severe environmental and social impacts. Most mechanisms have two functions: a mediation and a compliance/reporting function.

Contents

M. Van Putten (✉)
Global Accountability BV Amsterdam, Amsterdam, Netherlands
e-mail: mvanputten@globalaccountability.com

E. Sciso (ed.), *Accountability, Transparency and Democracy in the Functioning of Bretton Woods Institutions*, DOI 10.1007/978-3-319-57855-2_9

The mechanisms at first were welcomed and closely followed by the global political arena as a new phenomenon of transparency and openness which functioned to make the institutions often operating in secrecy accountable for their actions. Today, many mechanisms have a hard time remaining independent from the institutions they are tasked to hold accountable. The increasing control that management exercises over the mechanisms raises great concerns given the original emphasis on these mechanisms' independency and not making them the butchers that control their own meat. There is a need for revival of the original spirit: giving people a democratic voice over institutions that operate on the basis of public money.

The urgency for a revival of the accountability mechanisms of the MFIs is evident not only for the MFIs themselves to give them credibility for their actions, but also for the fact that a growing group of commercial financial institutions today are under pressure to establish accountability mechanisms, often named grievance mechanisms, for their investments and the large projects they finance. The strong demand is clearly laid down in the UN Guiding Principles on Business and Human Rights, and in the OECD Guidelines for Multinational Corporations, to name the most important recent instruments in this regard.

There is also pressure from governments. The Dutch government demands from different sectors that are at risk to not only adhere to the UN and OECD standards, but to also install an accountability mechanism. A small but increasing group of large EU based commercial banks closely follow the discussions taking place in Europe on the issue of the mechanisms and meet regular with experts of the MFIs mechanisms. A bottle neck is the fear for liability. Legal advice to overcome this fear, or misused excuse, is urgent. And finally, the mechanisms of the MFIs could play an important frontrunner role while preparing and implementing grievance mechanisms in the commercial financial sector.

1 Introduction

The creation of the so-called Independent Accountability Mechanisms for Multilateral Financial Institutions (MFIs) over the last two decades deserves more attention. The institutions work with public money and their financed projects could have impacts on the lives of many around the world. The somewhat semi-judicial mechanisms so far are the only access citizens have to be heard and lodge a complaint about negative impacts on their lives caused by the implementation of these projects. The group of mechanisms has steadily grown and created a group of specialists that today are used to deal with complex complaints arising by virtue of MFI financed projects.

This article describes the history, developments and challenges that the mechanisms are confronted with, such as the challenge to remain independent in order to be trusted by citizens that need access to the institutions. It finally describes how the mechanisms and their experts dealing with complaints concerning MFI financed projects could be advisors for the private financial sector and more specific those private financial institutions that today should consider to establish somewhat similar mechanisms for people harmed by their investments, as stated in the United Nations Guiding Principles for Business and Human Rights and the Guidelines for Multinational Enterprises 2011 of the Organization for Economic Corporation and Development (OECD).

2 History of Accountability Mechanisms

The creation of the World Bank Independent Inspection Panel (Inspection Panel n.d.) was the beginning[1] of a new era where MFIs, also known as development banks, opened their doors for citizens to lodge a complaint when they were harmed or could be harmed by a project financed by the institution. It was a forum set up by a joint resolution of both the International Bank for Reconstruction and Development (IBRD) and the International Development Association (IDA). The mandate and role given to the Panel was to determine whether the Bank is in violation with its own policies, rules and procedures. This type of action was new as MFIs working with public money had (and still have) immunity for legal actions against their operations in third countries.

For years, the World Bank Inspection Panel was the role model for other MFIs that followed suit by establishing their own Independent Accountability Mechanisms (IAMs), all of which are considered to be semi-judicial systems. As is the case with most[2] mechanisms, it is a Panel of three independent experts, appointed by the Board of the Bank; the President and Executive Directors. Each member has a non-renewable mandate of 5 years.

It was in the first place the US Congress (Van Putten 2008, p. 92) followed by the EU parliament (European Parliament Resolution 1991)[3] that insisted the World Bank create this open door for persons affected by projects it financed. Besides internal negative reporting about the quality of the Bank's loan portfolio (WB Wapenhans Report 1992) it was the Narmada dam in India that hit the Bank

[1]Some still argue that the Mechanism of the Inter-American Development Bank (IADB) was created just before the Inspection Panel of the World Bank. However, the Inspection Panel of the World Bank immediately had a more solid mandate with three members of the Panel dealing for at least 5 years with cases and with a permanent staff and office while the IADB worked with a roaster of experts and with more direct influence of management of the Bank.

[2]An exception is the mechanism of the European Bank for Reconstruction and Development (EBRD). The EBRD mechanism has a roster with seven independent experts. When a complaint arrives only one expert is selected to declare a case admissible. And if a complaint is admissible, it is another expert that will handle the case on its own.

[3]The resolution was adopted as a joint effort of several political groups in the EP.

the most in the outside world. As a result of the Narmada dam,[4] at least 200,000 indigenous people had to be resettled involuntary. The influence of the US Congress—and specifically Congressman Barney Frank (Democrat)—and a strong lobby of a group of advocacy groups and Non-Governmental Organisations (NGOs) in the US and in Europe insisted that the WB to establish a mechanism. The US Government was instrumental in pushing for the Inspection Panel's creation.

Under the leadership of World Bank President Wolfensohn, the process of implementation of the Resolution took place. At the time, Jim Wolfensohn benefited enormously from the legal guidance of Ibrahim Shihata, the general counsel of the Bank. Shihata's book, '*The World Bank Inspection Panel: In Practice*', has been an important source for many that tried to understand the far-reaching (judicial) implications of the introduction of the Inspection Panel at the World Bank. His work still forms the basis for describing and understanding the years of the resolution's implementation and the design both of the procedures and of the mutual relations between the panel, the board, and management (Van Putten 2008, p. 101). In those days, it was crystal clear for the outside world that independence[5] of the Panel was crucial and the only way to give the Panel credibility. However, a review of the Resolution establishing the Panel in 1993[6] noted that 'its members, during the inspection, must remain as faithful as possible to the role of the body to which they belong, being that of a fact-finding body on behalf of the Board' (Circi 2006, p. 10). The independence of the Panel is a constant issue in the debate about the functioning of the Panel.

The mechanisms of the other MFIs all have different mandates and procedures. One major difference existing between the Panel and the other mechanisms is that the Panel only has a compliance function (International Bank for Reconstruction and Development/International Development Association 1993). Its main task is to report to the Board of the World Bank, and finally the public, on whether the Bank is compliant with its own adopted policies and procedures. The other mechanisms have both a compliance function and a mediation or problem solving function. In this later group, there is even a difference between those that stick to the sequence: first try to solve problems with mediation, and only if that fails can the Panel experts then assess the process of the bank and determine to what extent the institution was in compliance. Others (mainly the European style) leave it open and are more

[4]The strong criticism of civil society on the by the World Bank financed Narmada Dam in India was one of the main reasons for the US Congress to organize a hearing in the Congress and to insist that the World bank created the Inspection Panel.

[5]The US Congress insisted that the contract with appointed Panel Members includes a clause that members of the Panel after their 5 year term is over never can work for the World Bank. The Congress wanted with that an assurance of Independence.

[6]See the website of the World Bank Inspection Panel: Review 1999.

flexible on the sequence; mediation could sometimes become an option during the investigation.[7]

All mechanisms have admissibility criteria. Some mechanisms accept complaints with a minimum of two or more affected people filing the complaint while at least six institutions[8] already accept a case of one individual. In practice it is overwhelmingly entire communities that sign complaints.

A difficult point is the relationship between the mechanisms. This emerges when a sensitive project is financed by more MFIs and a complaint arrives at the different mechanisms about the same project.

Moreover, MFIs all have their own policies. Without a doubt, it is the World Bank that has been standard-setting and that has had the longest experience with the issuing of the so-called safeguard policies. Many of those policies have often almost been copied by other MFIs. The 'lone wolf' is the European Investment Bank. As an official institution of the EU the Bank has to adhere to EU legislation and EU standards.

3 Limitations in the Mandates

In the case of the World Bank Inspection Panel, affected people are not allowed to file a complaint as soon as nineteen five percent (95%) of the budget for the project is spent. The Inspection Panel is the only mechanism with such a restricted limitation amongst its admissibility criteria. Other mechanisms allow people to file a complaint even after hundred percent (100%) of the project budget is disbursed. They draw a 'cut-off date' 2 years after the completion of the project or after the closing date of the loan, or after twenty four months of physical completion of the project or even do not have a 'çut-off date'. It has been pointed out critically on this World Bank restriction that projects could show negative (environmental) impacts only after full implementation of the project, as is often claimed with large infrastructural projects.

The building of a high way could disturb the watershed in such a manner that water sources important for farmers suddenly dry out or are polluted. The filling of a water reservoir during the construction of a hydropower dam could have unforeseen impacts on farmers that no longer can cross a river with their cattle. As long as the Environmental Impact Assessment (EIA) is done seriously and with a broad scope such effects cannot (or should not) be missed throughout the design of the project. This is simply a matter of due diligence. Yet, if the negative impacts

7 The EIB Complaints Mechanism and the Mechanism of FMO and DEG both are more flexible and do not per se stick to the sequence.

8 Black Sea Trade and Development Bank, European Bank for Reconstruction and Development (EBRD), European Investment Bank (EIB), International Finance Corporation (IFC), complaints mechanism of both the Dutch and German Development Bank FMO and DEG, and the mechanism of the United Nations Development Program (UNDP).

are missed it is exactly the function of the accountability mechanism to detect this omission or failure and bring the finding to the institution that could and should learn from this for future situations. How long after the project's initiation or completion complaints should be admissible is arbitrary. Should it be 2 years or as some NGOs argue, so long as the relations between the MFI and the project sponsor still exist? This is probably not a realistic demand. Can or should an institution that financed a project that already for years is operating in succession by a project sponsor still be held accountable for any negative impacts simply because the project sponsor or client of the bank is, *e.g.*, still paying interest rates?

4 The China Case

Without a doubt, the most difficult case in the history of the Inspection Panel concerned the Western Poverty Reduction project in China in 1999; 49,000 overwhelmingly Han Chinese had to be resettled at the Tibetan plateau due to population pressure and land erosion in the province of origin. The Board of the World Bank was about to take a decision and approve the project proposal when the media, mainly in the US,[9] started to publish very critical articles about the project that—according to the media and soon also the US congress—was to be considered as an act against the rights of the Tibetans. Ultimately the project became a highly sensitive project for the Bank. Due to these tensions, the Board did not want to approve the project and asked the Inspection Panel to investigate.[10] (According to the resolution establishing the independent Inspection Panel, the Board has a full right to ask the Panel to do an investigation). It took a year for the Panel to deliver its final report. Unfortunately, this was the only time the Board made use of the Inspection Panel in this manner. A year later the full Board discussed the findings of the Panel report with the Inspection Panel and management. The (sad[11]) outcome of an extensive debate was that the World Bank would no longer be involved in the project.

[9]Also in French papers.

[10]The author of this article was at the time one of the three independent members of the Inspection Panel dealing with this complex and highly political case and experienced that many and more in particular management of the World Bank overtime 'forgot' that it was the Board of the Bank asking the Panel to investigate the project, that before the approval of the board already was heavily criticized by the media and in particular members of the US Congress. The board instead of taking a decision asked the Panel to play its role.

[11]In the opinion of the author of this article this was a sad decision. The Panel reported about critical social and environmental impacts mainly for the people to be resettled and also for the herders that with their cattle make use of the Tibetan plateau. The Panel did not have any findings in their report concerning the predicted political consequences. The consequence of the World Bank leaving the project was that the substantial experience of the institution in such difficult circumstances (when large groups of people have to be resettled) was not used.

5 Influence of Non-Governmental Organizations

Criticasters inside MFIs sometimes say that the complaints are initiated by NGOs. And they are right. Without the work of NGOs definitely fewer complaints would arrive in the offices of IAMs. A group of international NGOs analysed all the complaints filed to all IAMs from their establishment until 30 June 2015. The group counted a total of 684 cases (Daniel et al. 2016, p. 25). According to the group 'more than half of the complaints were about infrastructure projects, and the most commonly raised concerns related to inadequate consultation and disclosure, insufficient due diligence and the environmental repercussions of projects.' (ibid.) In most, if not all, projects vulnerable people are the ones impacted. Without NGOs, many would not be able to lodge a complaint at one of IAMs. Regularly those people are not educated enough or lack sufficient means to run through the process of a complaint and in some cases it can be a risk to stand up and speak out against national or regional authorities that promote a project.

Besides, filing a complaint against an international institution is time consuming and costly. Time and money, *e.g.*, to travel to the capital to bring or defend their case at the right counter, is not what poor usually have. The role and support of international NGOs as watch dogs can be crucial for vulnerable people and without their support one can ask the question what level of access to justice is feasible. Finally, it is the duty of IAMs to thoroughly assess if outsiders, such as NGO representatives, represent affected people in the project area.

The 'clatter' inside the Bank was loud and today one can still hear the opinion that the final report of the Panel on the China project made middle income countries cautious to turn to the World Bank for loans. Those that use this argument 'forget' that loans at the commercial market are financially more beneficial than World Bank loans. The China case unquestionably was a turning point.

Nevertheless, the Inspection Panel was and still is considered to be *the only* opportunity people have to legitimately challenge the activities of the World Bank, an institution that continues to operate with public money as a closed bastion, just like most if not all of its sister organizations. Yet, soon criticism came up regarding the independence and limitations of the mandate.

6 The MFI Mechanisms on a Cross Road: Are They Independent?

While the Mechanisms first were welcomed and closely followed by the global political arena as a new phenomenon of transparency and openness in order to make these mainly in secrecy operating institutions accountable for their actions, many mechanisms today have a hard time remaining independent from the institutions they have to keep accountable. The increasing control that management exercises over the mechanisms raises great concerns given the original emphasis on these mechanisms' independency and not making them the 'butchers that control their own meat'.[12]

The resolution establishing the Inspection Panel in 1993 did not include a mediation role for the Panel, a function that most mechanisms in the other institutions have. In November 2013[13] the World Bank introduced a pilot project in what the Panel allows management first to take a position and solve problems in the project area by seeking early solutions, before the Panel itself takes up its role and presents its report with findings of compliance or non-compliance. It sounds like a congenial way to solve problems before they become part of a semi-judicial system that not necessarily ends with a solution. The Panel does not call it a mediation process. They consider it to be '[...] a facilitated opportunity to implement an agreed upon Action Plan between Bank Management and the Requesters' (Watanabe 2014, p. 2). However this will only work through a mediation process.

So instead of adding the 'mediation function' to the mandate of the Panel, management took on this role (see further below). According to the Panel in 2013 this approach is 'fully consistent with the Panel resolution'.[14] Still the Panel is in the lead as it is their discretion to decide if 'the case is well-suited for resolution under this approach'.[15] The Panel also needs the consent of the complainants[16] while considering the option for management to early address the concerns expressed in the complaint. Nevertheless, the question arises if the clear independence given to the Panel is principally undermined, since management is now involved in one way or another in the Panel's process despite the fact it is the Panel that decides if a complaint is suitable for the pilot approach. Can the Panel still make an impartial 'judgment' if the World Bank is in compliance with its own policies and procedures; for example, if the complainants that first accepted the transfer of their case back to management later on decide to go back to the Panel?

So far only two cases were selected for the pilot project; a project in Lagos and one in Paraguay. Unmistakable criticism soon arose about the project in Lagos and the role of both management and the Panel. On 27 August 2014, an international group of representatives of 21 NGOs write to the Panel and President Kim of the World Bank: 'The World Bank's accountability is undermined by the pilot, which provides an inadequate process for addressing the concerns of impoverished, project-affected people. [...] thousands of Nigerians who were forcibly evicted from their homes are still living in poverty, in precarious conditions or in danger of further forced evictions, [...] The pilot project only served to legitimize the Lagos

[12]As member of the World Bank Inspection Panel 1999–2004, as member of the Independent Review Mechanism of the African Development Bank 2007–2011, as independent senior advisor for the European Investment Bank mechanism 2009–2015, as reviewer of the mechanism of the Asian Development Bank 2010–2011, I have noted in all institutions the attempts to undermine the mechanisms.

[13]See on the website of the World Bank Inspection Panel: Document 82531, November 6, 2013.

[14]Idem, 1.

[15]Idem, 2.

[16]Complainants can also be called requesters.

State Government's 'take it or leave it' negotiations process, [. . .] the Pilot Program denies accountability for serious harm and interferes with the purpose and mandate of the Inspection Panel.'

A few days after the letter of the international group of NGOs, Amnesty International published a public statement on the Lagos case expressing their 'significant concerns', somewhat similar to those of the NGOs in the earlier letter. On the Panel's role they stated that it '[. . .] may have introduced the pilot with the intention of aiding swift resolution of complaints, the way the process has been implemented has left hundreds of people without an effective remedy' (Amnesty International 2014). No doubt the intentions of the Panel were focussed on improvement of the situation. The Chair of the Panel in her answer to the group of international NGOs refers to a payment by the Lagos authorities to over 9000 evictees, a precedent, she wrote, that never occurred before: the Lagos State Government providing compensation to evictees of a government-financed project. However, despite the good intentions, the Panel—as mentioned earlier—in a way has involved itself in the process of the Bank's activities. The case was not registered but submitted to management.[17]

Most of the other mechanisms today have also a hard time remaining independent. The executive directors of the World Bank and witnesses of the creation of the Inspection Panel in 1993 understood the importance of independence as described by their legal counsel. However, internal opposition has grown and later appointed executive directors not necessarily have knowledge about the history and philosophy of the authority the Panel was given: a semi-judicial entity that with its impartiality tries to find the truth between two conflicting parties; the project sponsors and its financers *in casu* management of the Bank and the people that are harmed by the project. A matter of impartial judgement for the Panel. A role the Panel received by the Board of the Bank and executed for the Board.

An international survey (Van Putten 2008, p. xxiv) in 2004, after 10 years of operations, focussed on the work and position of the Independent Inspection Panel, its mandate and procedures, procedures for the claimants, the inclusion of human rights in policies, its relation with executive directors and relations with management, the process for appointment of members of the Panel and its staff, and the importance of its independence. The 74 participants in the survey came from the small world of specialists who were familiar with MFI accountability mechanisms, either being members or former members of one of the mechanisms, staff of the MFIs and transnational corporations (TNCs, mainly private-sector financial institutions), representatives of civil society organizations, or recognized experts who have worked outside these entities (e.g., consultants and academics). They all were part of the same focus group and received the same questionnaire and were clear in their response to the importance of independence. They were asked to react to the

[17]According to public information about the pilot project, the pilot was supposed to end in 2015 and would be assessed by the end of that year. However, as of August 2016, there is no news whether the assessment has been executed by the Panel.

following statement: 'The level of an institution's accountability is related to the level of independence of its mechanism' (Van Putten 2008, p. 249).

Almost all the experts endorsed the importance of independence. Among private-sector experts only two individuals disagreed, while the majority agreed. Not surprisingly, the NGO experts overwhelmingly agreed, at 100%. Remarkable for members of the MFI group (management), the total was about the same: with one exception they all agreed. Among the independent experts, two had no opinion and the rest agreed. One respondent from the group of MFI experts noted *'In order to be objective you need to be independent'*, while another one wrote *'Conditio sine qua non'*. The respondents from management of the MFIs were those that worked with the mechanisms within their institutions and probably the best placed inside the institutions to defend the mechanisms.

As mentioned earlier, the average project manager fully occupied and convinced of the project he or she works on, receives the accountability mechanism sometimes as a hindrance, instead of a positive process of learning by doing for the Institution. It is a normal human reaction. However, things can go wrong during the implementation of major projects, and the institution should be proud it offers people an open door at least for the impacted to be heard. Nonetheless, and despite a growing resistance inside the MFIs against their own accountability mechanisms, still new mechanisms are created. At present, some regional and national finance and development institutions are creating their own mechanism.[18]

7 Urgency for Revival of the Mechanisms in a Changing Era

Since the creation of the Inspection Panel and the other IAMs, 23 years have passed. As the mechanisms were a creation to be understood in their own time period, the same is true for the MFIs themselves. 'From the 1950s to the 1990s, the international architecture consisted of only three pillars: the International Monetary Fund (IMF), and the Multilateral Development Banks represented the multilateral official pillar; the aid agencies of the industrial countries represented the bilateral official pillar; and the commercial banks and investors from industrial countries made up the private pillar' (Linn 2013).

This was still a well-organized world. The World Bank was praised for its lead in the development of strong safeguard policies and 'instituted the first of eight

[18]Examples are the mechanism of the Black Sea Trade and Development Bank based in Greece that some years ago created a mechanism. A unique complaints mechanism created in 2014 is one mechanism for two financial institutions: the Dutch Development Bank FMO (Financierings Maatschappij Ontwikkelingslanden) and the German Development Bank DEG (Deutsche Investitions-und Entwicklungsgesellschaft). In case of the Dutch, it was the Dutch parliament insisting that FMO also created an accountability mechanism. Other national development banks are at present willing to create a mechanism, such as the French Proparco. Both Japan with the Japan Bank for International Cooperation (JBIC) and the US with the Overseas Private Investment Corporation (OPIC) have already for years had accountability mechanisms.

safeguard policies designed to 'prevent or mitigate adverse impacts of its projects on people and the environment.' These policies formed the bedrock of a rules-based, 'do no harm' approach to development that 'improved significantly' the WBG's ability to mitigate social and environmental risks' (Bank Information Center 2016). It was at the end of that era that the Independent Accountability Mechanisms (IAMs) were created. Was it too late?

Soon after, the powers shifted. Today the World Bank no longer is the largest MFI lending to developing countries. 'The multilateral assistance architecture, previously dominated by the MDBs (Multilateral Development Banks or Multilateral Financial Institutions; both names are used), is now a maze of multilateral development agencies, with a slew of sub-regional development banks, some exceeding the traditional MDBs in size. For example, the European Investment Bank (EIB) lends more than the World Bank' (Bank Information Center 2016). On the initiative of the Chinese government, a new development bank came to light: the Asian Infrastructure Investment Bank (AIIB). The bank started operating after the agreement went into force in December 2015, with a capital of $ 100 billion.[19] The bank is operating on the same market as the World Bank, yet with its own rules and procedures, not as dominant, as some argue, as the strong 'Western' based policies of the World Bank with its Inspection Panel. Today already 57 countries, such as France, Italy, the UK, the Netherlands, South Korea and Australia, and recently also Canada, are member of this new development bank also called 'China's development Bank.' The bank is 'widely seen as an extension of China's growing economic and political heft and as counterweight to the World Bank and other institutions dominated by Western countries' (Perlez 2016, p. 15). On top of that there is also the initiative of the BRIC[20] countries and South Africa that recently created the New Development Bank (NDB), though not yet in operation.[21]

However, even the entire group of public development banks all together is no longer the major player at the world financial chessboard when looking at Foreign Direct Investments (FDI) of the private financial sector in third countries. In answer to these developments, the World Bank tried to maintain its position by reforming its role, accommodating its borrowers more and by reviewing its safeguard policies.[22] If these actions of the World Bank and those of the other MFIs—all trying to

[19]Half of de budget of the World Bank and 2/3 of the budget of the Asian Development Bank.

[20]BRIC countries: Brazil, Russia, India and China.

[21]Both, the Asian Infrastructure Investment Bank and the New Development Bank for the first time participated as observers in the Annual meeting of the Independent Accountability Mechanisms Network held in Manila in September 2016.

[22]The World Bank in 2012 took the initiative to update the safeguards. With a process of four years the public was able to comment on the new approach. In August 2016 the Board of the Bank approved the New Safeguards. In the new framework more emphasis is given to the borrowers' own frameworks. Nevertheless, the borrowers Responsibilities to implement high standards described in the new framework are mandatory for the borrowers and (!!!) subject to the Inspection Panel.

survive—will prevent their further marginalization on the international financial chessboard has to be seen.

In two decades, the governance structure of the global financial system has been transformed. The UN World Commission on the Social Dimension of Globalization (ILO 2004, p. 34) already in 2004 warned against the impacts of globalization and a world still functioning on the old Bretton Woods structure and national governance systems, while the information and communications technology (ICT) revolution and accelerating global connectivity facilitated sectors (ILO 2004, p. 76), such as the private financial sector, to operate on a global scale where borders are disappearing and governance structures not yet exist. Meanwhile, 'private financial flows have come to dwarf official flows, the role and influence of private actors such as banks, hedge funds, equity funds and rating agencies has increased substantially. As a result, these private financial agencies now exert tremendous power over the economic policies of developing countries, especially the emerging market economies. Rating agencies determine whether countries can have access to sovereign borrowing and, if so, the cost of this' (ILO 2004, p. 34). And those private sector financial institutions or commercial banks do not (yet) have an 'open door', or transparent and democratic systems, for people that are harmed or could be harmed by the projects they finance.

This could be an interesting new task for the World Bank and the other MFIs; their experience with the independent accountability mechanisms such as the Inspection Panel and the Ombudsman of the International Finance Corporation (IFC)[23] could be their niche or specialism that they sell to the private financial sector. It could perfectly fit into the New World Bank Framework in which greater emphasis on borrowers' capacity building is noted.[24] The same goes for the other Multilateral Financial Institutions, such as the mechanism of the Asian Development Bank, the European Investment Bank and those of the bilateral development banks.

The time is ripe. The UN in its report in 2004 about the impacts of globalization gives a lot of attention to the financial sector as one of the most changed sectors due to globalization. It notes the following: 'Another area which can potentially circumscribe policy space is the emerging framework for financial regulation in the global economy. New standards and codes are being promoted through the Review of Standards and Codes (ROSC) and Financial Sector Assessment (FSA) processes. While the objective of strengthening financial systems is laudable, there is a risk that these instruments, as currently formulated and promoted, will impose standards that are inappropriate for many developing countries. Many of them are still too institutionally underdeveloped to be able to embrace all these codes' (ILO 2004, p. 81). So for the MFIs that struggle to survive there is work to be done in this field.

[23]The International Finance Corporation is the member in the World bank group dealing with the private sector.

[24]See the website of the World Bank: www.worldbank.org search function. Fact Sheet, The World Bank's New Environmental and Social Framework, August 4, 2016.

The United Nations and the Organisation for Economic Co-operation and Development (OECD) both have stressed already for years that Multinational Corporations should establish grievance mechanisms. It speaks for itself that this also includes the financial sector. So what is it that they ask for?

8 Standards of the UN and the OECD Regarding Accountability Mechanisms[25]

In the UN Guiding Principles on Business and Human Rights adopted in 2011 a strong demand[26] is included that enterprises should establish non-judicial grievance mechanisms since business enterprises may cause or contribute to an adverse human rights impact.

Principle 28 reads as follows: 'States should consider ways to facilitate access to effective non-state-based grievance mechanisms dealing with business-related human rights harms'. And Principle 29 states: 'To make it possible for grievances to be addressed early and remediated directly, business enterprises should establish or participate in effective operational-level grievance mechanisms for individuals and communities who may be adversely impacted' (UN Guiding Principles 2011, p. 32). Principle 31 further notes the clear criteria for the non-judicial grievance mechanisms: They should be legitimate and enable trust from the stakeholders; be accessible and known to all stakeholder groups; be predictable with a clear procedure; be equitable and ensure that aggrieved parties have reasonable access to sources of information necessary to engage in a grievance process; be transparent and rights-compatible and a source of continuous learning.

In 2011, the same year of the adoption of the UN Guiding Principles, the OECD published the OECD Guidelines for Multinational Corporations. There must have been a lot of cooperation between the two institutions since there are clear similarities between the two adopted documents. The OECD Guidelines note in Chapter IV Human Rights:

> States have the duty to protect human rights. Enterprises should, within the framework of internationally recognized human rights, the international human rights obligations of the countries in which they operate as well as relevant domestic laws and regulations: 1. Respect human rights, which means they should avoid infringing on the human rights of others and should address adverse human rights impacts with which they are involved. 2. Within the context of their own activities, avoid causing or contributing to adverse human rights impacts and address such impacts when they occur. 3. Seek ways to prevent or mitigate adverse human rights impacts that are directly linked to their business operations, products or services by a business relationship, even if they do not contribute to those

---

[25] Accountability mechanisms are often also called grievance mechanisms.

[26] The UN Guiding Principles are not binding. However, a growing group of states insists that enterprises that are under their jurisdiction implement the Guidelines. Some states have implemented the Guidelines in national legislation.

impacts. 4. Have a policy commitment to respect human rights. OECD Guidelines for Multinational Corporations (2011), p. 31

And:

When enterprises identify through their human rights due diligence process or other means that they have caused or contributed to an adverse impact, the *Guidelines* recommend that enterprises have processes in place to enable remediation. Some situations require cooperation with judicial or State-based non-judicial mechanisms. In others, operational-level grievance mechanisms for those potentially impacted by enterprises' activities can be an effective means of providing for such processes when they meet the core criteria of: legitimacy, accessibility, predictability, equitability, compatibility with the *Guidelines* and transparency, and are based on dialogue and engagement with a view to seeking agreed solutions. Such mechanisms can be administered by an enterprise alone or in collaboration with other stakeholders and can be a source of continuous learning. OECD Guidelines for Multinational Corporations (2011) 34 (Art. 46)

9 The OECD Order of Expected Responsibilities

To understand the OECD Guidelines and in what way they 'impact' on financial institutions responsibilities one should also take into consideration the ranks of involvement identified by the OECD. These are in the following order with a somewhat declining responsibility: impacts caused by the corporation, impacts to what the corporation has contributed (OECD Guidelines for Multinational Corporations 2011, p. 20), or lastly, impacts directly linked to their operations. Although the last level by some is understood that it protects corporations fully from their duty to intervene since they did not cause or contribute to harm, this is not how it is perceived by the OECD.

According to paragraph 12 in part I, chapter II the General Policies of the OECD Guidelines enterprises should '[s]eek to prevent or mitigate an adverse impact where they have not contributed to that impact, when the impact is nevertheless directly linked to their operations, products or services by a business relationship. This is not intended to shift responsibility from the entity causing an adverse impact to the enterprise with which it has a business relationship' (OECD Guidelines for Multinational Corporations 2011, p. 20). And as noted above, this was repeated in the Chapter on Human Rights (OECD Guidelines for Multinational Corporations 2011, p. 31).

Paragraph 12 is probably for the moment the clearest text available and provides insight into what could be expected from enterprises and financial institutions: The legal responsibility remains with the party causing the problem. And it is them we should expect to take action, mitigate or compensate. However, if they do not take such actions or not good enough, the OECD and the international community expects that the linked enterprise or financial institution (in this theoretical case) take action towards their business partner by using their leverage what could be in many forms. And a positive act towards a business partner in the chain with the purpose to solve problems should never lead to the risk that the legal liability, if any is at stake, transfers from the party causing the problem to a linked business partner NOT causing the problem.

10 A Grievance Mechanism or Accountability Mechanism?

Following from the above, corporations are held accountable to protect human rights and therefore are encouraged by international institutions, as mentioned above, to create an effective (grievance) mechanism in addition to their due diligence process with proper and often extensive assessments to be made. In addition, there is a call from civil society and not the least, some governments. They ask the financial sector to show their willingness (in OECD terms 'using their leverage') to give a hand or show a flag and create an open door to their institutions to give a voice to people when their lives are impacted through projects (and other actions?) financed by these financial institutions. The question **how** enterprises and banks should take action is—aside from the basic and important criteria in Principle 31 of the UN Guiding Principles—not laid out in detail, neither by the OECD nor the UN. There is merely a demand for grievance mechanisms enunciated. The question arises which next steps should the financial sector take? And which commercial banks are ready to be a front runner in the sector?

11 Will European Commercial Banks be the First with an Accountability Mechanism?

The NGO community which has been tracking the conduct of private financial institutions has debated already for years the necessity and format of an accountability mechanism for commercial banks. NGOs such as BankTrack (Banktrack n.d.), an international umbrella organization uniting over thirty NGOs worldwide, express the opinion that commercial banks and at least those banks that have signed the so-called Equator Principles (Equator Principles (n.d.)) should establish an accountability mechanism just like MFIs did already many years ago. The financial sector bears a greater responsibility than other sectors, they argue, given that the commercial banks are the source for many other sectors, such as the oil and gas industry, the mining sector, the construction sector or the palm oil industry.

Since 2014, a small group of commercial banks, mainly banks with headquarters in the Netherlands and some other major commercial banks from other EU countries (France, Spain, Sweden) regularly meet on an informal[27] basis with experts of

[27] These are closed meetings and no information is public about the meetings. The author of this article is the chair of those meetings that in 2015 and 2016 took place in Amsterdam.

the mechanisms of some MFIs, given that they can provide insight into the functioning of such mechanisms in light of their year-long experience.

Those commercial banks at least are very interested in the work of the mechanisms and how they proceed. This should not be a surprise. To begin with, there are the above explained UN Guiding Principles on Business and Human Rights (the UNGPs), also known as the Ruggie Framework, and the OECD Guidelines for Multinational Corporations which both demand grievance mechanisms for international operating enterprises. And secondly, some European governments are insisting that the private sector—including the financial sector—adhere to the UN and OECD Guidelines (see below).

A bottle neck could be the fear for liability. There is a perception that if Banks intervene in projects they finance, or if they use their leverage, as is the wording in the OECD Guidelines, they become liable for the harm to people. Legal advice to overcome this fear, or misused excuse, is urgent. It cannot be that a Bank financing a project and delivering sufficiently on due diligence before the approval of the contract, assuring an (independent) impact assessments and action plans, as well as that proper compensation is delivered by either the project sponsor or authorities to those that are harmed, could later on be liable for the harm that nevertheless occurs.

12 Dutch Government Took Action

The Minister of Trade and Development and the Minister of Economic Affairs of the Netherlands together ordered a research to be conducted amongst the different important sectors in the economy of the Netherlands which could be at risk not to adhere to the UN and OECD standards. The research was carried out independently by KPMG for the government and indicated 13 different sectors (such as the oil and gas, food, agriculture, textile and clothing, metal and electronica, chemistry). This also included the financial sector. KPMG Advisory NV (2014) KPMG finalized its study in 2014.

Then both the Department Legislation and Juridical Affairs of the Ministry of Security and Justice and the Department Legal Affairs of the Ministry of Foreign Affairs asked the Utrecht Centre for Accountability and Liability Law of the Utrecht University to conduct a study: A comparative and empirical study on the status quo of Dutch law in the light of the UN Guiding Principles. The study 'Duties of care of Dutch business enterprises with respect to international corporate social responsibility' was published in December 2015.

The researchers note that the UN Guiding Principles having soft law nature 'do not establish any legal obligations for either States or business enterprises' and 'do not entail an obligation for States to transpose them into new national legislation or to implement them in existing national legislation' (Utrecht Centre for Accountability and Liability Law 2015, p. 4). Nevertheless they continue by underlining that the 'legal impact is much larger than their non-binding nature and limited scope might give reasons to believe.' The researchers argue that the influence of the UNGPs on other regulatory instruments was strong in the following statement:

> Since 2011 they have strongly influenced other ICSR-related regulatory instruments. Some of these are more comprehensive than the UNGPs themselves, e.g. the OECD-Directives that cover the broader range of ICSR subjects. In addition, some of these instruments entail stronger legal obligations than the UNGPs do, e.g. the EU Directive on Non-Financial Reporting, the English Modern Slavery Act, the Swiss federal law on private military and security companies and the proposed ICSR-related legal duties of care in France and Switzerland. The UNGPs also have an impact on existing domestic legal rules as they may influence the way in which certain open standards in fields such as company law and tort law are interpreted. Utrecht Centre for Accountability and Liability Law (2015), p. 4

The researchers also note that Dutch criminal law offers a 'range of possibilities to remedy violations of (I)CSR related standards, also where the violation has in whole or in part taken place abroad.' However little use has been made of the possibilities that the Dutch criminal law offers, they say. They continue by asking the question 'what is to be expected of Dutch internationally operating business enterprises that carry out activities (or have them carried out) in less developed host states, where the legal protection of people and planet related interests (is considerably) less strict?' The researchers carry on by expressing the need for an active prosecution policy and a more compelling legal framework (Utrecht Centre for Accountability and Liability Law 2015, p. 15), in order to provide the necessary means for the Dutch prosecutor's Office.

Finally, in the conclusions the researchers stress that the choice to observe due diligence 'with regard to people and planet in host states cannot be left to the discretion of business enterprises themselves' and 'cannot exclusively be left to Western society-based shareholders, investors and consumers'. Harmed people should have 'adequate access to remedy through tort law and criminal law mechanisms.'

With the outcome of the two studies, the government asked the Social Economic Council (SER)[28] to host with each sector separately closed meetings with civil society representatives, government officials and representatives of the unions, with the aim to develop a covenant for each sector. According to the government, the covenants should include the different provisions as mentioned in the OECD Guidelines for Multinational Corporations and the UN Guiding Principles for Business and Human Rights. As far as it is known, the debates also include the subject of grievance mechanisms especially in the group that discusses the covenant (agreement) for the financial sector. In the spring of 2016 the Dutch government sent a letter to the parliament with both studies as annexes and sketches its position about the duty of care of Dutch Companies. The roles for the different organizations regarding the implementation and supervision of compliance with the ICSR rules, such as the SER and the Dutch NCP, are mentioned, however not yet in-depth developed. A reference to the grievance mechanisms as mentioned in both the

[28]The Dutch Social Economic Council, the SER (Sociaal Economische Raad), is an independent Council that gives advice to the government on social economic issues.

UNGPs and the OECD Guidelines are not yet mentioned in the letter. Nevertheless, it is known that the demand for such mechanisms is on the table of the covenant negotiations.

On 28 October 2016 the "Dutch Banking Sector Agreement on International Responsible Business Conduct regarding Human Rights" was signed by all the major Dutch commercial banks, the Dutch Government (represented by the Minister of Finance and Minister of Trade and Development), Amnesty International, the Netherlands Trade Unions and the Dutch Banking Association. A milestone. After the agreement with the textile sector, the financial sector is the second sector reaching an agreement with the government. In paragraph 3 of the Agreement the parties jointly consider that:

> All Parties and banks adhering to this agreement (hereafter referred to as adhering banks) confirm the responsibility of corporations, including the banking sector, to respect human rights in conformity with the OECD Guidelines for Multinational Enterprises (hereafter referred to as the "OECD Guidelines") and the UNGPs;

Finally the demand of the public for an accountability mechanism or grievance mechanism is answered. In Chap. 7 ("Enabling remediation") it is noted:

> Within two years of signing the declaration of adherence the adhering banks will implement the following:
>
> a) With regard to project finance, the banks will require clients to establish or participate in a grievance mechanism through which grievances concerning the client's human rights performance can be raised by affected communities, in line with the UNGPs (principle 31) and international standards such as the IFC PS or the Equator Principles (principle 6);
> b) With regard to corporate loans the banks will, in the case of severe human rights violations known to the banks, actively promote their clients to establish, participate in or enable access to a grievance mechanism in line with the UNGPs [...]. (Sociaal-Economische Raad (SER) 2016)

The question remains what it could look like for financial Institutions that are ready to create a mechanism? What could they create at their headquarters and elsewhere? What modalities and procedures? Which criteria for admissibility of cases?[29] How could independence be guaranteed in order to protect the trust in the system created? And last but not least, what products of the banks can the mechanism accept. At the moment, it looks like most experts in the debate see the opportunities (only) for project finance while some argue that also trade in commodities and other bank products in the longer run should be taken into consideration for the mechanisms.

[29] Instead of a complaint it might be better to use the word 'cases' whereas people that complain will remain with the term complaint. The word case shows more neutrality for the financial institution.

13 Concluding

First of all, it is time that the political 'arena' refreshes its actions towards MFIs and guarantees that the institutions which operate mainly secretly and that work with public money give a strong and independent position to the accountability mechanisms they created in the last decades: including proper budgets, authority and proper methods for selection of the independent members of those semi-judicial mechanisms; a selection that should not be controlled by management itself, selecting its own controllers. The independence of the mechanism is crucial and only will deserve the trust of the public if the independence is guaranteed. And the international community should understand that such mechanisms are the only means the public still has to engage with MFIs and keep them accountable for the actions they execute.

And while some of those MFIs are already losing ground on the market of Foreign Direct Investment, they should today protect and even 'use' the accountability mechanisms as a niche they have in the market. Their experience and knowledge could be used for the commercial banks that currently are starting or are pressed by governments to adhere to the OECD and UN Guidelines and also install a grievance or accountability mechanism.

Finally, time has come for the private financial sector to open their doors and strongly use their leverage towards those clients that contribute or cause harm to people by their activities. If they do not take action themselves and create an accountability mechanism, they can wait for the public that will demand and governments that will regulate.

References

Amnesty International (2014) Public statement: World Bank—investigate Inspection Panel's pilot approach to early solutions and its application in Badia East, Lagos, Nigeria. AI Index: AFR 44/020/2014

Bank Information Center (2016) World Bank's new more flexible environmental and social framework must prioritize genuine citizen engagement. http://www.bankinformationcenter.org. Accessed 29 Sept 2016

Banktrack (n.d.) http://www.banktrack.org. Accessed 29 Sept 2016

Circi M (2006) The World Bank inspection panel: is it really effective? Global Jurist Advances 6 (3):1535–1661

Daniel C et al (eds) (2016) Glass half full? The state of accountability in development finance. SOMO, Amsterdam

Equator Principles (n.d.) http://www.equator-principles.com. Accessed 29 Sept 2016

European Parliament Resolution (1991) On the disastrous consequences of the Narmada project in India

Inspection Panel (n.d.) http://www.inspectionpanel.org. Accessed 29 Sept 2016

International Bank for Reconstruction and Development/International Development Association (1993) The World Bank Inspection Panel. Resolution No. IBRD 93-10 and Resolution No. IDA 93-6

International Labor Organization (ILO) (2004) A fair globalization. ILO, Geneva
KPMG Advisory NV (2014) Sustainability MVO sector risico analyse, aandachtspunten voor dialoog—a study on the request of the Ministry of Trade and Development and the Ministry of Economic Affairs of the Netherlands. KPMG.com/sustainability. Accessed 29 Sept 2016
Linn JF (2013) Realizing the potential of the multilateral development banks. Brookings Institution. http://www.brookings.edu. Accessed 29 Sept 2016
OECD Guidelines for Multinational Corporations (2011). https://www.oecd.org/corporate/mne/48004323.pdf. Accessed 29 Sept 2016
Perlez J (2016) Canada to join China-led bank, signaling readiness to bolster ties, International New York Times, Beijing (31 August 2016)
Sociaal-Economische Raad (SER) (2016) Dutch Banking Sector Agreement on international responsible business conduct regarding human rights. https://www.ser.nl/~/media/files/internet/publicaties/overige/2010_2019/2016/dutch-banking-sector-agreement.ashx. Accessed 6 Feb 2017
UN Guiding Principles (2011) Guiding Principles on Business and Human Rights, implementing the United Nations ‘Protect, Respect and Remedy’ Framework. New York, Geneva
Utrecht Centre for Accountability and Liability Law (2015) Duties of care of Dutch business enterprises with respect to international corporate social responsibility—English Executive summary of Study. Utrecht
Van Putten M (2008) Policing the banks—accountability mechanisms for the financial sector. McGill-Queens University Press, Montreal
Watanabe E (2014) Letter of the Chairperson of the Inspection Panel to Natalie Bridgeman Fields, accountability counsel, and colleagues. http://ewebapps.worldbank.org/apps/ip/Documents/Response%20to%20August%2027%20CSO%20letter.pdf. Accessed 29 Sept 2016
WB Wapenhans Report (1992) Effective implementation: key to development impact; the so-called Wapenhans Report 1992. World Bank
Website of the World Bank: http://www.worldbank.org. Accessed 29 Sept 2016

Accountability in International Organisations: Reviewing the World Bank's Environmental and Social Framework

Dimitri Van Den Meerssche

Abstract On August 4th, 2016, the Board of Executive Directors of the World Bank endorsed the new Environmental and Social Framework ('ESF'). The ESF is the latest of many steps that the Bank has undertaken to promote citizen-driven accountability regarding environmental and social damage, thereby seeking to rectify an accountability-gap that is omnipresent in international institutional law. The first contribution of this chapter is to provide an original typology of the four main innovations that the ESF brings to the safeguard mechanism in the World Bank. The chapter highlights how the topic-oriented safeguard standards, which were previously scattered in different independent operational policies (OPs), have now been integrated in a hierarchically organized, unified legal scheme (1). I further expose a shift from deontic reasoning to processes of qualitative managerial assessment in the environmental and social standards, which fundamentally alters their normative nature. This conclusion applies both to the increased focus on a specific methodological understanding of country ownership (2), and to the general substantive reformulation of the safeguard standards (3). Finally, the chapter sheds light on the new substantive areas of environmental and social protection in the ESF, such as labor and working conditions; climate change; non-discrimination; natural resource management; and—to a very minor extent—human rights (4).

Going beyond this descriptive and analytical typology, the chapter also critically assesses the changing nature of the safeguard model and situates the ESF in the broader context of international law. This section argues, first of all, that the ESF reflects the 'solipsism' of the World Bank: the safeguard standards are part of an endogenous legal structure and hierarchy, in which validity is produced without recourse to exogenous international legal sources. Secondly, I argue that the shift from deontic safeguard protection to risk-based managerialism risks to dilute the accountability of the Bank, both regarding its own responsibilities and regarding its supervision over the performance of borrowing countries. This dilution poses challenges for the Inspection Panel, which will need to draw clear normative lines in this maze of managerialism. The chapter identifies five techniques for the IP to achieve this, among which the systematic integration of external legal sources

---

D. Van Den Meerssche (✉)
European University Institute (EUI), Fiesole (FI), Italy
e-mail: Dimitri.vandenmeerssche@EUI.eu

E. Sciso (ed.), *Accountability, Transparency and Democracy in the Functioning of Bretton Woods Institutions*, DOI 10.1007/978-3-319-57855-2_10

and the recourse to teleological hermeneutics figure prominently. As a final point of caution and critique, I have pointed out that the ESF provides only limited coverage, excluding both Development Policy Lending and Programming-for-Results Lending in the World Bank. In conclusion, it is undisputable that the ESF can be seen as a new step in safeguarding the accountability of the Bank. This chapter provides an analytical framework to evaluate in which direction this step was made.

Contents

1 Introduction

The expansion of the normative powers and scope of operational activity of many international organizations (IOs) has cast a shadow of doubt on their formal status as mere vehicles of interstate cooperation (Alvarez 2005; Klabbers 2005, pp. 277–278; Von Bernstorff 2008). Not only have proliferating areas of practice within many IOs extended the constitutional boundaries of their mandate (Sinclair 2015), they have also put them in a direct operational, regulatory or disciplinary relationship with non-state actors—both individuals and collective groups, such as indigeneous peoples. As the Kadi cases before the CJEU, the World Bank Narmada Dam projects or the recent cholera outbreak in Haiti (on this case, see Klabbers 2015) illustrate, this relationship can be highly contentious, and its normative evaluation will vary significantly depending on one's legal vantage point.

Severe gaps render international (institutional) law unfit to holistically address the perils of this vertical relationship between IOs and non-state actors.[1] First of all, in the constitutive treaties of IOs, the question of accountability *vis-à-vis* non-state

[1]International Law is conceived here according the traditional doctrine of sources: Article 38 of the ICJ Statute.

actors is scarcely addressed. While concerns for citizens figure centrally in many—if not all—of these agreements, these citizens are rarely provided with legal tools or venues to vindicate any grievances that result from the acts or omissions by IOs (see Kingsbury 1999, p. 327).[2] Under the functionalist assumption that IOs are mere agents, resolving the collective action problems of their principles (the member states), the relationship with affected citizens is left out of the picture (Vaubel 2006; Von Bernstorff 2008; Klabbers 2015). This accountability issue is, secondly, only exacerbated by the fact that—motivated by concerns for independency and functional necessity (Klabbers 2001, p. 232; Reinisch 2016)—the assets and agents of almost every IO are endowed with privileges and immunities, which prohibit affected citizens from making claims before domestic courts.[3] Finally, while the ILC's recent Draft Articles on the Responsibility of International Organizations might seem to address exactly this issue of accountability, the initiative suffers from a plenitude of legal defects. While the Draft Articles have been criticized for their shallow grounding in the practice and primary sources of international law (Alvarez 2007)[4] and the absence of judicial venues for enforcement (Klabbers 2009, p. 292), their deficiency regarding the challenge set out in this chapter—*i.e.* an inquiry into the direct bridges of vertical accountability between IOs and non-state actors—is much more straightforward: following the traditional horizontal structure of international law, the Draft Articles provide only states (and other IOs) with the right to invoke the legal responsibility of IOs (ILC 2011, articles 43ff; Baimu and Panou 2012).

In short, the traditional structure of 'International Institutional Law' ('IIL') falls short in answering the call for citizen-driven accountability (for a traditional account of ILL, see Bowett 1982; Schermers and Blokker 1995). Bridging this abyss between the ever-increasing reach of IOs and the absence of formal legal accountability is a central aim of many contemporary meta-approach to international law and the law of global governance (see Kumm 2009; Von Bogdandy et al. 2010; Kingsbury 2012; Wouters et al. 2012).[5] In this chapter, I will provide an empirical account of the standards and quasi-judicial techniques that have been

---

[2]Obviously there are exceptions here, particularly in the European legal space. In general, however, diplomatic espousal is necessary for reasons further elaborated below (see Kingsbury 1999, p. 327).

[3]While the constituent charter of the ILO did not contain a provision on immunities, this was rectified by the 1946 amendment 15 UNTS 35. Regarding the UN, see Art. 105 (1) Charter of the United Nations, San Francisco, 26 June 1945: 'The Organization shall enjoy in the territory of each of its Members such privileges and immunities as necessary for the fulfilment of its purposes'), concretized in the Convention on the Privileges and Immunities of the United Nations, 13 February 1946, 1 UNTS 15. A more detailed provision is found in Article VII of the International Bank for Reconstruction and Development Articles of Agreement, Bretton Woods, 22 July 1944. Reiterating the functionalist logic, Section 1 states: 'To enable the Bank *to fulfill the functions* with which it is entrusted, the status, immunities and privileges set forth in this Article shall be accorded to the Bank in the territories of each member' (emphasis added).

[4]Alvarez (2007), p. 677: '[the Articles are] at best premature and at worst misguided'.

[5]Among the different approaches are the heuristic of International Public Authority (IPA—Von Bogdandy et al. 2010) originating in Heidelberg, the Global Administrative Law project (GAL—Kingsbury 2012) at NYU, the call for models of Global Constitutionalism (Kumm 2009), or the notion of Informal International Lawmaking (IN-LAW—Wouters et al. 2012). All have in common a quest for an increased accountability in contemporary global governance.

developed by the World Bank (the 'Bank')[6] with the aim of bridging this accountability-gap. The argument will process in three steps. First, I will focus on the creation of the World Bank Inspection Panel ('IP'), and contextualize this groundbreaking innovation in the provision of citizen-driven accountability, while also shedding light on the recent challenges the IP had to face (Part 2). Secondly, the chapter carefully unpacks the recently adopted Environmental and Social Framework ('ESF') and inquires into how this reform impacts the substantive nature of the Bank's environmental and social safeguard policies and the capacity of the IP to guarantee accountability (Part 3). After exploring and evaluating the innovative aspects of the updated accountability framework, I will address the shortcomings and perils of the reform and situate the Bank's safeguards policies in the broader context of global governance (Part 4). This final part extrapolates the empirical and descriptive parts of the chapter to general observations regarding the dynamics of endogenous accountability mechanisms in IOs and their nexus with exogenous sources of international law. This will allow for some broader conclusions regarding the decentralized path to increased accountability in IOs.

2 Filling the Void: Safeguard Standards and the World Bank Inspection Panel

2.1 The World Bank Inspection Panel and the Genesis of Citizen-Driven Accountability

'A stroke of genius!' This is how Werner Kiene, Chairman of the World Bank Inspection Panel ('IP') between 2004 and 2009, describes the creation of the IP in 1993, applauding the 'unique innovation in international governance' (World Bank 2009, p. ix). While the genesis of this accountability mechanism aligned with the increasing momentum of sustainable development in the late 1980s in the international community more broadly (Handl 1998; Clark 2002), the specific catalysts for change were two Bank-financed projects on the Narmada river in India. The scale of environmental damage and involuntary resettlement caused by the projects united local grassroots movements and international Civil Society Organization ('CSOs') in an unprecedented campaign for more accountability (Fox 1998). Enormous reputational risks ultimately urged the Bank's Board of Executive Directors (the 'Board') to commission an independent review on the Narmada projects (on the reputation of IOs and compliance with international law, see Johnstone 2011; Daugirdas 2014). The resulting report by Bradford Morse and Thomas Berger (Morse and Berger 1992)[7] inaugurated the practice of independent investigation of complaints, which would eventually crystalize in the 1993 Board Resolution on

[6]In this chapter, the World Bank (the Bank) refers to both the International Bank for Reconstruction and Development (IBRD) and the International Development Association (IDA).

[7]I will come back on this report, and its reliance on international law, in Sect. 4.1. below.

the creation of the IP (World Bank 1993, referred to below as 'Inspection Panel Resolution').

As this Resolution sets out, the IP has the power to investigate all claims from affected individuals or communities from whom '*rights or interests* have been or are likely to be directly affected by an *action or omission of the [Bank]* as a result of a failure of the Bank to follow *its operational policies and procedures* [...] provided in all cases that such failure has had, or threatens to have, a *material adverse effect*'.[8] In light of the shortcomings of general IIL in addressing citizen-driven demands for accountability, the importance of this institutional innovation can hardly be overstated (see, e.g. Bradlow 2005).[9] No longer do citizens or communities need to rely on diplomatic espousal; with the IP, the Bank has opened the path to vertical, citizen-driven accountability.[10]

As of August 10th 2016, 110 cases have been handled by the IP. Functioning as an investigative and advisory body, its goal has, first of all, been to produce concrete outcomes in specific cases. This ranged from providing remedial actions to affected people, over safeguarding rights of indigenous peoples, to the protection of cultural resources. IP procedures have resulted in the suspension of financing for projects, and led to significant changes in managerial project-design and implementation. Secondly, the IP process has generated a higher level of transparency in the Bank, and provided an incentive for institutional compliance with environmental and social safeguards. More broadly, the creation of the IP inspired changes in other International Financial Institutions (IFIs) and Multilateral Development Banks (MDBs) (Rigo Sureda 2005, p. 142).[11]

Since the creation of the IP in 1993, the development policy-landscape in which the Bank acts has undergone important shifts, ranging from changing borrower profiles, over diversification in the lending portfolio and competition among other development financers, to increased focus by Civil Society Organizations ('CSOs')

---

[8]Inspection Panel Resolution, par. 12 (emphasis added).

[9]Even authors who are critical of the IP's shortcomings appreciate the groundbreaking contribution of the Inspection Panel Resolution to the accountability of IOs; see Kingsbury (1999), p. 330.

[10]For a detailed overview of this procedure, see World Bank (2009), pp. 23–46. The notion of citizen-driven accountability needs to be nuanced, however. Even though the Inspection Panel, indeed responds to claims by private groups or citizens, it does not provide these citizens with direct legal remedies. Instead, the Inspection Panel reports its finding to the Board of Executive Directors, which, after considering the management's recommendations, decides on the course of action. As Sureda notes, 'the Panel was in effect established as a tool in the hands of the Executive Directors to reinforce the accountability of management towards them'. The end result of procedures before the IP is not a legally binding judicial decision, but a corrective 'action plan' at management level. Rather than a judicial venue, the Inspectional Panel should be seen as an intra-institutional mechanism of accountability. See Rigo Sureda (2005), p. 141; Kingsbury (1999), footnote 5.

[11]See (International Finance Corporation 2006; European Bank for Reconstruction and Development 2008; Asian Development Bank 2012; African Development Bank 2012).

on emerging fields of social and environmental concern. Below, I will briefly discuss these developments (Sect. 2.2), as an introduction to the new Environmental and Social Framework ('ESF') (Sect. 3),[12] which I will discuss in detail. Finally, in Sect. 4, I will set out what I consider to be the main limits and perils of the new ESF, and elaborate on the broader nexus between the Bank's ESF and international law.

2.2 *Adapting to a Changing Landscape*

The Bank's accountability mechanism consists of two dimensions: (1) the 'safeguards',[13] *i.e.* binding operational policies ('OPs') that set out environmental and social standards for all investment projects of the Bank (the 'substantive dimension'); and (2) the IP, which hears all complaints resulting from a potential violation of these safeguards (the 'procedural dimension'). Considering the substantive reliance of the IP on the safeguards, the former dimension clearly determines the latter. The IP, however, also has an interpretative influence on these standards (see Sects. 4.1 and 4.2 below), which renders the interaction between both dimensions essentially a 'two-way street'.

While groundbreaking in its inception (both from a substantive and a procedural perspective), by the turn of the millennium, this accountability mechanism was confronted with major challenges. In light of a shifting development landscape, changing profiles of borrowing countries, and variations in its lending portfolio, the Bank commissioned an Independent Evaluation Group ('IEG') to review its safeguard policies, and to formulate recommendations for progress (Independent Evaluation Group 2010, referred to as 'IEG Report'). This IEG Report inspired the recently concluded safeguards review in the Bank, which resulted in the updated ESF (see Sect. 3).

In reforming its safeguards policy, the Bank was confronted with two opposing pulls, each resulting from different grounds for adaptation. On the one hand, the prescriptive and compliance-based approach of the Bank's safeguards was considered as overly cumbersome; weakening its competitive position in a changing development landscape; and hampering country ownership and efficiency (NYU Clinic 2014).[14] With official development assistance accounting for an ever-decreasing part of development financing (mainly in favor of foreign direct investment), and in light of the proliferation of non-traditional donors[15] and the

[12]This Environmental and Social Framework ('ESF') was endorsed by the Bank's Board of Executive Directors on August 4th, 2016.

[13]Footnote 25 enumerates the old safeguards. They are also referred to as safeguard 'standards', 'policies' or mechanism'.

[14]See IEG Report, xiii: 'Implementation [...] has meant enforcing compliance with mandatory policies and procedures, which has not engendered strong client ownership'.

[15]Such as China, Brazil and India.

importance of other MDBs,[16] the detailed and prescriptive safeguard standards by the Bank were considered to form a competitive impediment.[17] In addition, the Bank saw itself increasingly confronted with a diversified group of borrowers, among which 'middle-income countries, with well-developed institutions and capacities' (World Bank 2012, referred to as 'Approach paper', par. 17). Considering this change, and in alignment with the 2005 Paris Declaration on Aid Effectiveness and with the 2008 Accra Agenda for Action (OECD 2005, 2008),[18] the Bank recognized the need for greater country ownership over development projects,[19] which implies a reliance on a country's own institutional framework instead of focusing on the Bank's detailed and prescriptive standards. Finally, for reasons of efficiency, the IEG noted that the Bank's prescriptive, deontic approach—resulting in a project's rigid *ex ante* assessment—should make place for a dynamic risk-and outcome-based approach to projects, which applies tools of assessment, monitoring and implementation support.[20] This managerial 'downstream' approach aligns with the shift in the Bank's portfolio to Programming for Results lending ('PfR'), as elaborated in Sects. 3.3 and 4.3 below.

On the other hand, the Bank was confronted with an opposite pull towards more concrete and more elaborate prescriptive standards. First of all, many experts and Civil Society Organizations ('CSOs') stressed the need for the multilevel protection of global commons and public goods, arguing that the Bank's current safeguards showed several *lacunae* in this regard, for example regarding the protection of biodiversity and the recognition of climate change as a primary concern.[21] Secondly, in line with the critiques of many CSOs, the IEG criticized the 'limited coverage of the social safeguards'[22] in the Bank, in comparison with the modern safeguards by the IFC. Several new social concerns were raised, among which labor conditions, gender, human rights and community health figured prominently.[23] Finally, many CSOs and UN special procedures mandate-holders urged the Bank to use this opportunity to align its safeguards with international law, by explicitly

---

[16]This year the Asian Infrastructure Investment Bank (2016) was created, with 37 founding members. It is noteworthy that this Bank does not include the United States and Japan as members.

[17]The IEG Report notes that 'the transaction costs of safeguards and rigidities in policy interpretation, particularly for the social safeguards, have led to risk aversion and, in some cases, to avoidance of projects or components that would benefit the poor', See IEG Report, 103.

[18]These declaration follow from the Second and Third High Level Forum on Aid Effectiveness, organized by the OECD with the aim of enhancing the impact of development aid.

[19]IEG Report, xiii; Approach Paper, par. 18: Calling for 'more emphasis' on 'aligning and harmonizing approaches to environmental and social sustainability [...] with borrower country systems'.

[20]IEG Report, xvii. This is applied in the IFC, which 'shifted the emphasis from prescriptive procedures to a more explicit focus on the client's social and environmental management systems (SEMS)', see *ibid.*, 4.

[21]This is recognized in Approach Paper, par. 19.

[22]IEG Report, xv.

[23]*Ibid.*, xxi; Approach Paper, par. 35.

connecting both (Office of the High Commissioner for Human Rights 2014, referred to as 'OHCHR Letter').

In sum, the Bank's management had to strike a balance between, on the one hand, the demand for country ownership, less prescriptive standards and the move to managerial approaches, and, on the other hand, the call for normative expansion and consolidation, and alignment with the prescriptive standards of relevant international law.[24] It is this sensitive balance that the new ESF needed to find.

3 Towards a New Environmental and Social Framework

On August 4th, 2016, after the most extensive consultation process ever conducted by the World Bank, the Board approved the new Environmental and Social Framework (World Bank 2016a, referred to as 'ESF'). This holistic framework of operational standards replaces, adapts and expands the environmental and social safeguards previously included in nine different Operational Policies and their respective Bank Procedures.[25] Below, I will set out what I consider to be the four major innovations of the ESF: the integration of the safeguards in a hierarchical normative framework (Sect. 3.1); the deepening of country ownership (Sect. 3.2); the managerial 'downstream approach' (Sect. 3.3); and the normative expansion of the safeguards (Sect. 3.4).

3.1 Hierarchy, Integration and the Division of Labor

The first important innovation of the ESF is the integration of separate and functionally independent operational safeguard policies and Bank procedures in one holistic normative framework. As noted by Dann and Von Bernstorff, this integrated approach to safeguards was first adopted by the IFC, and soon became the standard for other MDBs (Dann and Von Bernstorff 2013). The ESF consists of

---

[24]These two pulls echo two major normative meta-approaches to the study of IOs: functionalism and constitutionalism.

[25]These operational policies (or 'safeguards', see text with footnote 29) are mandatory norms adopted by the Board of Executive Directors that bind the staff in the design and implementation projects. They provide the substantive basis of the IP's investigation. The Environmental and Social Framework (ESF) replaces the following Operational Policies and Bank Procedures: OP/BP 4.00 (piloting the use of borrower systems to address environmental and social safeguard issues on Bank-supported projects); OP/BP 4.01 (environmental assessment); OP/BP 4.04 (natural habitats); OP/BP 4.09 (pest management); OP/BP 4.10 (indigenous peoples); OP/BP 4.11 (physical cultural resources); OP/BP 4.12 (involuntary resettlement); OP/BP 4.36 (forests) and OP/BP 4.37 (safety of dams). It does, however, not replace OP/BP 4.03 (Performance standards for private sector activities), OP/BP 7.50 (projects on international waterways) and OP/BP 7.60 (projects in disputed territories).

three integrated parts: (1) a Vision for sustainable development; (2) the World Bank Environmental and Social Policy (ESP), which sets out the mandatory requirements that apply to the Bank; and (3) the Environmental and Social Standards (ESSs), which set out the mandatory requirements that apply to the Borrowers and specific projects.

The vision statement sets out the general normative orientation of the ESF and the substantive goals it aims to achieve. It underlines the Bank's commitment to sustainable development, and introduces several new elements of the ESF: (1) the introduction of new substantive areas (e.g. climate change, biodiversity, non-discrimination, health and safety); (2) the move to country ownership; (3) the importance of stakeholder consultation[26]; (4) the shift from a 'do no harm' to a 'do good' approach[27]; and—importantly—(5) the careful mentioning of human rights.[28] With its references to open dialogue, public consultation, access to information and responsive grievance mechanism, the vision statement introduces the ESF as a perfect case for the paradigm of Global Administrative Law (GAL), which argues for the analogy between domestic administrative law and the contemporary normative schemes that are developed to contain the proliferation of global regulatory governance (see Krisch and Kingsbury 2006; Boisson de Chazournes 2009). It is important to underline, however, that this vision is only aspirational in nature and does not set out any concrete rights or obligations.[29] To the contrary, as elaborated in Sect. 3.1 below, by referring to the (contested[30]) limits of its mandate and by using vague, aspirational language,[31] the Bank is careful in not subjecting itself to any sources of international (human rights) law. The vision statement can nonetheless prove valuable in serving as a 'discursive reference point' for both staff and affected communities (Dann and Von Bernstorff 2013), and as an interpretative tool used by the IP to reduce the vagueness of the Bank's legal obligations or to bridge any remaining accountability gaps (NYU Clinic 2014).[32] In short, while the vision mainly contains vague aspirations, it can play a similar role as the preambles in international treaties: to guide teleological hermeneutics, and to serve as a focal point for the Bank's normative commitment around which local communities and CSOs can gather. The procedures and substantive responsibilities contained in the ESP and the ESSs are placed under the normative umbrella of this vision statement.

Apart from providing normative hierarchy under the umbrella principles of the vision statement, the ESF also contains a clear separation of rights and responsibilities between the Bank and the borrowing countries. The Bank's obligations,

---

[26]ESF, Vision, par. 8.

[27]This is parallel to the IFC Policy on Environmental and Social Sustainability, par. 9.

[28]ESF, Vision, par. 3. This will be discussed in detail in Sect. 4.1. below.

[29]ESF, Overview, par. 2.

[30]See, *inter alia*, OHCHR Letter.

[31]'The World Bank's activities *support* the realization of human rights' and 'the World Bank *seeks to avoid* adverse impacts [on human rights]'; in ESF, Vision, par. 3 (emphasis added).

[32]This is further elaborated in Sect. 4.1 below.

described in the ESP, are now determined in a general way, detached from any specific project or policy.[33] The mandatory requirements for the borrowing countries are set out generally (ESS 1, 'Assessment and management of environmental and social risks and impacts'), and with regards to specific topic-related risks and policies (ESSs 2–8[34]).

In conclusion, while the previous safeguard policies of the Bank were scattered across different topics without any overarching frame of reference,[35] the new ESF integrates these safeguards: it provides normative hierarchy under the principles of the vision statement; an integrated structure of general (ESP and ESS 1) and specific topic-bound (ESSs 2–8) obligations; and a division of powers and responsibilities between the Bank and its borrowing countries. This combination of legal *hierarchy* under overarching principles,[36] a clear *distribution of powers and binding responsibilities* between Bank and borrower,[37] and the provision of *grievance mechanisms*, is common to the safeguards frameworks of most MDBs[38] and hints at the incremental crystallization of rule of law-based constitutionalism in the sphere of development cooperation.[39]

3.2 Answering the Call of Country Ownership

The second general innovation of the ESF that I have identified is the desire of the Bank to 'renew its partnership with its borrowers', in line with the trends in the international development community to more country ownership, with the aim of 'enhanc[ing] development effectiveness'[40] and building institutional capacity in developing countries.[41] Instead of imposing the Bank's own prescriptive demands

[33] See ESF, ESP.

[34] These are: 'Labor and working conditions' (ESS2); 'Resource efficiency and Pollution Prevention and Management' (ESS3); 'Community health and safety' (ESS4); 'Land acquisition, Restrictions on Land Use and Involuntary Resettlement' (ESS5); 'Biodiversity conservation and Sustainable Management of Living Natural Resources' (ESS6); 'Indigenous Peoples/Sub-Saharan African Historically Underserved Traditional Local Communities' (ESS7); 'Cultural Heritage' (ESS8). The ESF also includes two additional safeguards regarding 'Financial Intermediaries' (ESS9) and 'Stakeholder Engagement and Information Disclosure' (ESS10).

[35] See footnote 25.

[36] As is well know, for Kelsen this pyramid-structure of legal hierarchy is the very precondition for the existence of any legal order, *i.e.* for 'law' itself (Kelsen 1967).

[37] 'The framework will clearly delineate the complementary but distinct roles and responsibilities of the Bank and the borrower', Approach Paper, par. 22.

[38] *Ibid.*

[39] The combination of hierarchy, legal organization and accountability, General Counsel Leroy argues, is essential to the internal rule of law in the Bank (Leroy 2011). This hypothesis will, however, be tested and contested in Sect. 4.2 below.

[40] Approach Paper, par. 24.

[41] IEG Report, 85.

and institutional blueprints, the aim of this innovation is to rely on the regulatory framework of developing countries in assessing, managing and monitoring social and environmental risks.

Already in 2005, responding to the Paris Declaration on Aid Effectiveness and the changing profile of its borrowing countries,[42] and with the aim of increasing cost-effectiveness of development projects and improving institutional capacity in developing countries, the Bank launched a pilot program to employ 'country systems' in enforcing and managing the environmental and social safeguards of investment projects. This resulted in a new operational policy (OP 4.00),[43] which defined country systems as 'a [borrowing] country's legal and institutional framework, consisting of its national, subnational, or sectoral implementing institutions and applicable laws, regulations, rules, and procedures'.[44] While this seemed to be a great leap forward, the initiative has experienced only very limited success as a result of several shortcomings in its design. According to this pilot program, in order for the Bank to rely on country systems, management had to determine for every single investment project[45] whether the borrowing country's environmental and social safeguards system is *equivalent* to the Bank's, and to confirm the '*acceptability* of [the borrowing country's] implementation practices, track record and capacity'.[46] The standard of *equivalence* is met only if the borrowing country's institutional framework is deemed fit 'to achieve the objectives and adhere to the applicable operational principles set out in Table A1'.[47] This annexed table provides a prescriptive and very detailed list of normative aims and institutional demands to which the borrowing country has to conform in order to be considered equivalent. For example, to satisfy the objectives regarding involuntary resettlement, the borrowing countries has to conform with 12 technically demanding procedures, such as 'through census and socio-economic surveys of the affected population, identify, assess, and address the potential economic and social impacts of the project that are caused by involuntary taking of land'.[48] The project-based focus, the rigidity and the overly prescriptive nature of the initiative, were mentioned by the IEG as sources for its very low success.[49]

[42]See, section 2.2 above.

[43]See footnote 25: OP 4.00 ('piloting the use of borrower systems to address environmental and social safeguard issues').

[44]OP. 4.00, par. 2, footnote 3.

[45]The IEG notes that 'the piecemeal approach, which focused on individual projects and policies in the UCS pilots, appears unworkable and needs a major redesign for it to be successfully scaled up', IEG Report, 87.

[46]*Ibid.*, par. 2 (emphasis added).

[47]*Ibid.*

[48]OP 4.00, Annexed Table 1.

[49]IEG Report, 85–86: 'Not a single pilot country was found equivalent to the World Bank on social safeguards in the first phase', 'staff members interviewed by IEG affirm that an underlying problem with the efforts to apply country systems, to date, is the highly process-oriented nature and rigidity of the Bank's own safe-guard policies'.

In order to address these shortcoming and to enhance country ownership, the new ESF introduced major changes. Primarily, the threshold for the use of a country's own institutional framework is substantially lowered: country systems can now be used whenever they are '*likely* to address the risks and impacts of the project and enable the project to achieve objectives *materially consistent* with the ESSs'.[50] This underlines the shift in the Bank from a deontic to a managerial approach of safeguard protection (see Sect. 3.2 below): instead of a prescriptive *ex ante* assessment, the current framework suggests an outcome-based approach, where lower thresholds are compensated with increased followup and capacity-building (World Bank 2016b).[51] The information note to the articles on country ownership clarifies that the 'ESF requires the consideration of *processes and outcomes*, but *not a test of legal equivalence*'.[52] Further, when the institutional framework of the borrowing country displays shortcomings, the Bank will address the regulatory gaps and agree with the borrowing country on suitable measures and actions,[53] which become legally binding. Importantly, this combination of assessment and capacity-building no longer has to stay limited to specific projects, but can be enacted through country-wide 'overview assessments'.[54] A final important change is that the use of country systems is no longer decided at the discretion of the Bank, but is now *agreed* between the latter and the borrowing country,[55] which further enhances inclusion.

In conclusion, the new ESF provides a model of country ownership that replaces the prescriptive, project-based pilot program on the use of country systems (OP 4.00), with an outcome-oriented approach grounded in risk-management, capacity building and mutual agreement. While this paradigm-shift answers the recommendations by the IEG, the move away from prescriptive standards to blurry qualitative assessment and downstream management threatens to hollow out the Bank's responsibilities and provides a focal point for critique, as elaborated in Sect. 4.2 below.

---

[50]ESF, ESP, par. 15 and ESS1, par. 19.

[51]The information note to the provisions on country ownership stipulates that: 'OP/BP 4.00 considers a Borrower's environmental and social safeguard system to be *equivalent* to the Bank's if the Borrower's system is designed to achieve the objectives and adhere to the applicable operational principles set out in Table A1 in OP 4.00, which are *very detailed and set a high threshold for equivalence*. In contrast, the ESF's approach to Borrower frameworks aims to enable the project to *achieve objectives materially consistent* with the ESSs. The term *'materially consistent'* is subject to qualitative interpretation, but in essence it means 'substantially' or 'considerably' similar to or 'agreeing/according' in substance with the ESS objectives', in World Bank (2016b).

[52]World Bank (2016b), p. 7, par. 34.

[53]ESF, ESP, par. 27.

[54]*Ibid.*, par. 29.

[55]This change from 'discretion' to 'agreement' was only part of the third and final draft of the ESF.

3.3 *The Downstream Approach: Assessment, Management and Implementation Support*

The paradigm-shift in safeguard protection from a deontic to a managerial approach is not only applicable in the context of country ownership, but figures centrally in the entire ESF.[56] Paragraph 6 of the ESP defines the current methodology of safeguard protection as a 'risk and outcome based approach'.[57] This shift, I want to argue, is part of a more general transformation of legal reasoning in the Bank. In a similar vein, regarding the constitutional interpretation of the Bank's mandate, former General Counsel Anne-Marie Leroy employed a managerial risk-based approach in legitimizing and shaping the Bank's operational involvement in the criminal justice sector (Leroy 2012). In a later essay, Leroy claimed that this opinion 'lays the groundwork for a possible paradigm for the future role of Bank lawyers in dealing with Articles' interpretation', and defines this paradigm as 'the shift from risk avoidance to informed risk-taking' and risk-management, 'with expert inputs as a key component to success' (Leroy 2013). In short, the methodology of safeguard protection sails on the bigger waves of the shift in constitutional and legal reasoning in the Bank: away from deontic *ex ante* categorization, to the expert-based assessment and management of risks and outcomes.

This approach to safeguard protection is noticeable throughout the lifecycle of a project. At the outset, rather than refraining from financing projects in potential violation of the ESSs, the Bank will support any project that is '*expected* to meet' the safeguard requirements 'in a *manner* and within a *timeframe* acceptable to the Bank'.[58] As indicated in the OHCHR Letter, this allows the Bank to finance project that are not *ex ante* in conformity with the ESSs and only aim for 'phased-in' compliance at some unspecified point during the project cycle.[59]

The focal point of this ongoing risk-management during the lifecycle of a project is the Environmental and Social Commitment Plan ('ESCP'), which sets out the actions to be undertaken for the project to meet the ESSs over a specific timeframe.[60] This ESCP is part of the legal agreement between the Bank and the borrower and integrates the *ex ante* assessments from both parties, and the results of stakeholder engagement.[61] Importantly, the plan sets out the management tools that will quantify the desires outcomes of the project, with 'targets and performance indicators that can be tracked over defined time periods'.[62] Hereby, the ESF answers the demand for sharper measurability and supervision, which is expressed

---

[56]Regarding the managerial, expert-based and output-driven 'anti-formalization' of politics and international governance more broadly, see Curtin (1997), Klabbers (2001).

[57]ESF, ESP, par. 6 and ESS1, par. 2.

[58]ESF, ESP, par. 7 (emphasis added).

[59]OHCHR Letter, 9.

[60]ESF, ESP, parr. 46–48 and ESS1, parr. 36–44.

[61]ESF, ESS1, par. 37.

[62]*Ibid.*, par. 42.

in both the Paris Declaration on Aid Effectiveness (OECD 2005) and the IEG Report, and which was considered as one of the core weaknesses of the old safeguard system (Dann and Von Bernstorff 2013, p. 24ff). This ESCP is not set in stone, but defines processes that allow for 'adaptive management', and the institutional response to any changes 'that are likely to cause an adverse change in the environmental or social risks' of the project.[63] A final important element is that the plan can integrate third party stakeholders (e.g. independent experts, local communities or NGOs) in project-monitoring and supervision.[64] In contrast to the previous safeguards—which focused on a prescriptive, *ex ante* assessment of projects—the gravity point of the new ESF is informed and ongoing risk-management.

This shift from rule-based *ex ante* evaluation of a project to the managerial 'long-term and phased approach'[65] of risk-management integrates the core concern of the IEG Report, but, I argue, also gives rise to two important points of criticism. First of all, it is clear that the shift from project preparation to life-time risk management will substantially increase the cost of the project (World Bank 2016c). Instead of connecting the cumbersome monitoring requirements to additional financing, however, the ESF stipulates that 'the borrower will ensure that adequate institutional arrangement, systems, resources and personnel are in place to carry out monitoring'.[66] In light of the development landscape sketched out in Sect. 2.2 above, this financial and operational burden might place the Bank at a competitive disadvantage. Secondly, as noted in the OHCHR Letter, several stakeholders are concerned that the shift from deontic to managerial reasoning holds the risk of diluting the Bank's accountability. This point of critique will be addressed thoroughly in Sect. 4.2 below.

3.4 Exploring New Terrain: Substantive Expansion of the Safeguard Standards

Aside from normative integration and increased ownership, one of the key features of the new ESF is its remarkable substantive expansion. As elaborated in the Approach Paper, this expansion results from an increased recognition in the Bank of the need to protect global commons and global public goods[67] and from growing pressure by NGOs to include emerging areas of environmental and social protec-

[63] *Ibid.*, par. 39 and 44.

[64] *Ibid.*, 45.

[65] *Ibid.*, 43.

[66] *Ibid.*, par. 35.

[67] For an enlightening exploration of these concepts and the challenges they pose, see Petersmann 2012.

tion.[68] In this section, I will highlight the areas of substantive expansion, and sharpen focus on the main controversies that arose during the three consultations rounds of safeguard review.

One of the most remarkable cases of substantive expansion in the ESF is the safeguard on 'Labor and Working Conditions' (ESS2). The latter contains prohibitions on child labor and forced labor,[69] obliges the borrowing country to apply measures aimed at occupational health and safety,[70] establishes the principle of non-discrimination regarding project workers,[71] and protects the rights to collective bargaining and freedom of association.[72] While this is undeniably a welcome extension to the safeguard system, I want to argue that two *caveats* are warranted. First of all, the support for the rights of collective bargaining and freedom of association is only offered in 'a manner consistent with [the] national law [of the borrowing country]'. The alignment of these rights with the modalities and potential restrictions inscribed in domestic legislation could imply a severe substantive downgrade compared to the related ILO standard (World Bank 2016c, p. 23). Secondly, and related to this, in defining this safeguard, ESS2 does not make any reference to international labor standards as protected under international law.[73] This underlines the solipsist nature of the ESF, as further discussed in Sect. 4.1. below.

In light of the concern for global commons and global public goods, a second normative expansion relates to climate change. Already in its second paragraph, the vision statement 'recognizes that climate change is affecting the nature and location of projects, and that World Bank-financed projects should reduce their impact on the climate by choosing alternatives with lower carbon emissions'.[74] The challenge is concretized in two specific standards. First of all, climate change is one of the environmental risks that need to be taken into account the Bank's due diligence and the borrowing country's risk-assessment.[75] Further, ESS3 ('Resource efficiency and Pollution Prevention and Management') stipulates that 'the Borrower will

[68]Approach Paper, par. 19 and par. 35: 'Some stakeholders have requested the Bank to consider in the review and update process a number of areas that are not addressed under the current set of safeguard policies. These include human rights, labor and occupational health and safety, gender, disability, the free, prior, and informed consent of Indigenous Peoples, land tenure and natural resources, and climate change'.

[69]ESF, ESS2, parr. 17–20.

[70]*Ibid.*, parr. 24–30.

[71]*Ibid.*, parr. 13–15. 'Projects workers' includes all workers who are involved in the project—both directly and indirectly. The notion encompasses direct workers, contracted workers, primary supply workers and community workers; See *ibid.*, parr. 3–7. The protection of the latter three categories was only added after the second round of consultations, as a result of outcry by several CSOs. See Human Rights Watch (2015b).

[72]*Ibid.*, par. 16.

[73]This was one of the main points of critique in Human Rights Watch (2015a).

[74]ESF, Vision, par. 2.

[75]ESF, ESP, par. 4 and ESS1, par. 28 and 35.

characterize and estimate sources of air pollution related to the project. This will include an estimate of gross GHG emissions resulting from the project'.[76] During the consultation round, several countries wanted to explicitly connect this provision regarding greenhouse gas (GHG) emissions to the methodology of the UN Framework Convention on Climate Change (UNFCCC), and the related Paris Agreement (World Bank 2016c, p. 24). Again, the Bank refused this explicit reference to external sources of international law, only requiring national methodologies to be in line with 'international agreements on climate change'.[77]

A third important expansion is the provision on non-discrimination. In the vision statement, the Bank sets out to ensure that 'there is no prejudice or discrimination toward project-affected individuals or communities', with specific attention to 'Indigenous Peoples, minority groups, and those disadvantaged or vulnerable'. This principle of non-discrimination is concretized in ESS1 ('Assessment and management of environmental and social risks and impacts') and ESS2 ('Labor and working conditions'), with regards to the risk-assessment of investment projects and specifically regarding labor relations. During the consultation rounds, the topic of non-discrimination was among the most contentious. While all stakeholders embraced the general principle of non-discrimination, the formulation and inclusion of a list of specific grounds of discrimination appeared overly cumbersome. A clear divide emerged between donor countries and NGOs on the one side, calling for the inclusion of specific protection for religious and ethnic minorities as well as LGBTI people, while several borrowing countries, on the other side, claimed that such provisions would contravene cultural values and national legislation (World Bank 2016c, p. 10). Ultimately, the Bank reached a deadlock: it decided to limit the ESF to a general provision on non-discrimination in the vision statement and to refrain from explicit listing of groups vulnerable to discrimination. A list will be drafted, however, by the Management of the Bank in a binding Directive.[78] In short, although the principle is broadly endorsed, non-discrimination is one of the few topics where the three consultation rounds did not result in a compromise and where the ultimate decision is postponed.

Additional safeguard protection was also added to already existing operational policies. Regarding the protection of indigenous peoples (ESS7, 'Indigenous Peoples/Sub-Saharan African Historically Underserved Traditional Local Communities'[79]), the Bank stipulated that every project which has adverse impact on the land and natural resources of indigenous peoples, causes relocation or affects cultural heritage, is prone to Free, Prior and Informed Consent (FPIC).[80] This provision was subject to severe discussion, with several countries 'vehemently

[76]ESF, ESS3, par. 13 and 16.

[77]ESF, ESS3, par. 16, footnote 13.

[78]ESF, Overview, par. 7.

[79]ESS7 on 'Indigenous Peoples/Sub-Saharan African Historically Underserved Traditional Local Communities' replaces OP/BP 4.10 on indigenous peoples.

[80]ESF, ESS7, par. 24 ff.

oppos[ing] the inclusion of the FPIC' (World Bank 2016c, p. 32). The Bank decided, nonetheless, to demand the *consent* of indigenous peoples, instead of the weaker requirement of *consultation*. Once again, however, the Bank refused to link this safeguard with external sources of international law—such as ILO Convention 169 (Art. 6) or UNDRIP (Art. 19)—despite explicit demands by several stakeholders.

Further, the ESF also sets out a much more comprehensive approach to 'Resource Efficiency and Pollution Prevention' (ESS3), compared to the previous policies which only concerned pest management (OP 4.09), and replaces OP 4.37 on the safety of dams by a general safeguard on 'Community Health and Safety' (ESS4). Similarly, OP 4.12 on involuntary resettlement was replaced by more comprehensive provisions on 'Land Acquisition and Restrictions on Land Use' (ESS5), while the protection of forests (OP 4.36) and natural habitats (OP 4.04) is replaced by a general environmental standard on 'Biodiversity Conservation and Sustainable Management of Living Natural Resources' (ESS 6). Finally, the protection of cultural heritage (OP 4.11) is also replaced by a broader safeguard, which also includes intangible cultural heritage (ESS8, 'Cultural Heritage').[81]

In sum, the ESF substantially extends the material reach of the environmental and social safeguard policies in the Bank. Thereby, also the mandate of the IP, which investigates the management's compliance with these policies,[82] expands. It is remarkable, however, that in delineating these new substantive fields, the ESF rejects making any reference to exogenous sources of international law. This act of legal solipsism, and the general normative nature of the new safeguard policies, will be discussed in Sect. 4 below.

4 The Environmental and Social Framework in the World Bank: Limits and Perils

After introducing the accountability mechanism in the Bank and setting out the major innovations of the new safeguard policy, in this part I will provide a typology of the latter's limits, and the perils of the recent reform. The ESF, I argue, broadly raises three issues that merit analytical inquiry: (1) first of all, I will inquire into the nexus between the current ESF and relevant sources of international law, which are kept exogenous; (2) secondly, I will set out the risks of the managerial turn in safeguards protection with regard to the functioning of the IP, paying specific attention to the changing nature of the Bank's role and responsibility; and (3) finally, I will briefly reiterate the limited applicability of the safeguards standards to the Bank's diversified lending portfolio.

[81]This includes 'practices, representations, expressions, knowledge, skills—as well as the instruments, objects, artifacts and cultural spaces associated therewith—that communities and groups *recognize* as part of their cultural heritage, as transmitted from generation to generation and constantly recreated by them in response to their environment their interaction with nature and their history'; in ESF, ESS8, par. 4.

[82]As explained in Sect. 2.2. above.

4.1 *The Nexus Between the Environmental and Social Framework and International Law*

The Morse-Berger report, which provided the groundwork of the citizen-driven accountability mechanism in the Bank,[83] evaluated the involvement of the Bank in the Narmada projects not merely in the light of its endogenous safeguard policies, but also integrated exogenous sources of international law (Morse and Berger 1992). The report made reference to ILO Convention 107 on indigenous or tribal peoples, and brought the Bank's policies and principles under the normative umbrella of general human rights law (Morse and Berger 1992; Kingsbury 1999, p. 330). The resolution that subsequently installed the IP, however, took a step back, stipulating that the IP can only hear claims arising 'as a result of a failure of the Bank to follow *its operational policies and procedures*'.[84] This reluctance to integrate international (human rights) law in the safeguards policies has given rise to fierce criticism (see UNGA 2015; for a broader critique on the relationship between the Bank and international human rights law, see, *inter alia,* Skogly 2001; Darrow 2003; McInerney-Lankford 2010). The Bank, however, claims that as an international financial institution with a specific technical and economic orientation,[85] it does not have a general human rights mandate, nor is it bound by the full corpus of international human rights law.[86] Not only is such a broad human rights mandate missing, it is argued, but to act accordingly would be in violation with the prohibition to interfere with political affairs, which is inscribed in the Bank's Articles of Agreement.[87] Critics rebut the Bank's recourse to the 'political prohibition clause' in avoiding responsibility and operational activity in line with international human rights law, claiming that the Articles of Agreement have to be read in light of the contemporary international legal order, and not the state of international law in 1944.[88] In the contemporary structure of international law, the critics' argument unfolds, the proliferation of human rights treaties and their impact on the formation of customary international law, have not only transformed the

---

[83]See Sect. 2.1 above.

[84]Inspection Panel Resolution, par. 12 (emphasis added).

[85]As stipulated by the 1947 Agreement between the IBRD and the UN.

[86]This is carefully argued in two legal opinions by former General Counsel Ibrahim Shihata in 1990 and 1995 (see Shihata 1991, 2000).

[87]This 'political prohibition clause' is inscribed in Articles 3(5) and 4(10) of the IBRD Articles of Agreement.

[88]This is argued, for example in the OHCHR Letter, 4–5 and Human Rights Watch (2015b). A focal point of this critique is the legal opinion on human rights by the Bank's former General Counsel Roberto Dañino in 2006, which referred to a wide range of human rights scholarship before concluding that the endorsement of human rights is in line with the Bank's mandate, including the restrictions of the political prohibition clause. This opinion, however, was never endorsed by the Bank's Board of Executive Directors and remains in the shadows of the aforementioned opinions by Shihata. See Dañino (2006).

nature of state sovereignty, but also limit the discretionary exercise of all international public authority by IOs.[89]

This debate essentially boils down to a question of general jurisprudence: what is the source of ultimate legal authority for the operational functioning, internal legal organization and accountability of the Bank (or any other IO)? This question can broadly be answered in two different ways, which echo, I want to argue, two distinct methodological approaches to international (constitutional) theory. On the one hand, it can be claimed that all acts of public authority—whether from a national state or an international organization—are subordinate to the procedural and substantive standards of a meta-normative framework, which is located outside the institutional reach of any specific venue of authority. While the doctrine of sources that informs this framework might differ—ranging from positivist human rights theory,[90] over interpretative theories of justice (see Kumm 2009), to natural rights theory—the essence is that the *Grundnorm* of every venue of public authority is exogenous. Legality, according to this line of reasoning, is determined by external criteria of a normative quality—e.g. the total *corpus* of international human rights law, cosmopolitan constitutional principles (Kumm 2009), or the moral notion of 'human dignity' (Schachter 1983)—and not by endogenous institutional sources and praxis. In this methodological frame, which I define as *cosmopolitan* constitutionalism, and which is broadly shared by those who aim to impose human rights standards on the Bank's policy and practice, neither sovereignty (for states), nor immunity and functional specialization (for IOs) provide legitimate ground for exoneration. Applying this cosmopolitan framework to the review of the Bank's safeguard policies, the inevitable critique is that 'it is imperative that the standards should be premised on a recognition of the central importance of respecting and promoting human rights'.[91] 'Human rights' in this sentence could, for the sake of this argument, just as well be replaced by 'human dignity' or by 'cosmopolitan constitutional principles'. The essence is that the *Grundnorm* of any IO is located outside the IO, in the sphere of global normativity.

On the opposite side of the spectrum, the different arguments can be summarized by the jurisprudential claim that ultimate legal authority is produced endogenously, *i.e.* within states or IOs. This is clearly reflected in the position by the Bank's former General Counsel Leroy, who argues that '[t]he Articles [of Agreement] represent the Bank's Grundnorm' (Leroy 2011, p. 54).[92] Accordingly, in this perspective, the

[89]Dañino's legal opinion explicitly refers to the work of Henkin on the relativization of sovereinty (Henkin 1999). This is also the core argument of the OHCHR Letter and Human Rights Watch (2015a, b).

[90]This is reflected in the OHCHR Letter, which traces the subordination of all public authority to human rights standards back to specific legal sources (*i.e.* the UN Charter, the Vienna Declaration and Program of Action, the ratification record of international human rights treaties, the Draft Articles on the Responsibility of International Organizations, etc.).

[91]See OHCHR Letter, 2.

[92]On another occasion, Leroy also argued that '[the Bank's] powers and responsibilities must be assessed primarily against the provisions of [its] constitutive instrument [...], its Articles of

social and environmental safeguards policy needs to be aligned with the Bank's internal constitutional sources, which determine the former's validity. The vector of constitutionalization in this methodological approach is reversed, *i.e.* turned inwards: legal formalization, the institutionalization of legal hierarchy and the path to accountability is defined in the specific language—and according to the specific limitations—of each venue of public authority. Legal authority is *produced* endogenously. This is the path of constitutionalization elaborated by Teubner, who argues—in line with Luhmann's system theory (Luhmann 1997; Teubner 2012, p. 84)[93]—that 'workable [constitutional] limitations can take effect only within the system's own logic' (Teubner 2012, p. 84). In this methodological frame, which I define (with Teubner) as *societal* constitutionalism—in opposition to its *cosmopolitan* competitor—'there can be no external political definition of transnational sectorial constitutions, but only indirect political impulses or constitutional irritations' (Teubner 2012, pp. 84–85). Put more abstractly, '[e]ndogenous growth imperatives can be combated only with endogenous growth inhibitors' (Teubner 202, p. 85). Instead of a globally integrated meta-constitutionalist framework, this societal approach, grounded in system theory, urges that '[i]n the sea of globality, only islands of the constitutional will emerge' (Teubner 2012, p. 52).

The new ESF in the Bank analytically fits the latter approach. Despite persistent demands by several donor countries, powerful CSOs and UN special procedures mandate-holders[94] to define the environmental and social safeguard standards in international legal terms (World Bank 2016c, p. 8), the references to general sources of international law in the ESF are scarce and weak. The ESF includes detailed provisions on labor and working conditions (ESS2), but without any reference to the eight core resolutions by the ILO.[95] It includes provisions on non-discrimination (Vision, ESS1 and ESS2), but without the specific listing of vulnerable groups, as defined in Article 2 of both the International Covenant on Economic, Social and Cultural Rights (ICESCR), and the International Covenant on Civil and Political Rights (ICCPR). The measures against climate change in the ESF do not once mention the United Nations Framework Convention on Climate Change (UNFCCC). And, finally, the most explicit and polemic aspect of the solipsistic attitude of the ESF towards international law is the provision regarding

---

Agreement'; in Leroy (2012) Response to Joint Allegation Letter of the U.N. Special Rapporteur on the right to food and the Independent Expert on the effects of foreign debt and other related international financial obligations of States. https://spdb.ohchr.org/hrdb/22nd/OTH_09.10.12_(7.2012).pdf (last consulted on August 10th, 2016).

[93]In a splintered landscape of global governance, consisiting of independent, functionally-oriented, 'autopoeietic' systems, Luhmann argues, '[e]very function system determines its own identity [. . .] elaborating semantics of selfinterpretation, reflection and autonomy. The mutual dependencies of the subsystems can no longer be formed in general. Indeed they can no longer be legitimized at all as a condition for order at the overall social level'.

[94]The OHCHR Letter stipulates that '[the Bank] must ensure that its ESSs reflect the full spectrum of relevant human rights protections and that individual ESSs fully comply with international human rights standards in their respective area'; OHCHR Letter, 13.

[95]See the critiques in Human Rights Watch (2015a), p. 9; OHCHR Letter, 14.

human rights. Paragraph 3 of the Vision statement provides that 'the World Bank's activities *support* the realization of human rights expressed in the Universal Declaration of Human Rights [...] *in a manner consistent with its Articles of Agreement*'.[96] Not only are human rights only mentioned in the aspirational vision section of the ESF,[97] which renders them void of any binding power, the provision also implicitly confirms that certain human rights policies would be in violation with the political prohibition clause in its Articles of Agreement, and thereby outside the Bank's mandate and legitimate practice.[98]

While cosmopolitan-and societal constitutionalism differ in their methodological approach towards the origins of legal authority in the international sphere, they do, however, not necessarily do so in terms of normative commitment. Specific content will be added to the new environmental and social safeguard standards (ESSs) in the Bank's future practice, management Directives and Guidelines, and IP reports. It remains to be seen if the substantive development of the standards will live up to the parameters of international law. What can be said at the outset, however, is that the source of their legal authority—and of the constitutionalization process in the Bank more generally—is produced endogenously, in line with the methodological blueprint of Teubner's societal constitutionalism.

Regarding the aforementioned substantive development of the safeguard standards, the IP surely has an important role to play. In the past, the IP has already developed the interpretative practice of clarifying gaps and vague provisions in the safeguards, and applying the Bank's operational policies (OPs), in light of existing sources of international law. In the *Chad-Cameroon pipeline case,* for example, the IP felt the need to examine 'whether human rights issues as violations of proper governance would impede the implementation of the project in a manner that was incompatible with Bank policies'.[99] Edward Ayensu, chairperson of the IP at the time of the *Chad-Cameroon case*, argued that certain 'human rights [are] implicitly embedded in various policies of the Bank'.[100] The aspirational provision on human rights in the vision statement of the ESF might serve as what Dann and Von Bernstorff call a 'discursive reference point' (Dann and Von Bernstorff 2013), and strengthen the IP's reliance on teleological hermeneutics grounded in exogenous sources of international law to fill potential gaps in the safeguard policies.[101] Again in line with Teubner's notion of societal constitutionalism, this

---

[96]ESF, Vision, par. 3.

[97]Apart from an independent provision regarding indigenous peoples in ESS7.

[98]ESF, Vision, par. 3.

[99]Inspection Panel, *Investigation Report—Chad-Cameroon Petroleum and Pipeline Project,* July 17th, 2002, http://ewebapps.worldbank.org/apps/ip/PanelCases/22-Investigation%20Report%20(English).pdf (last consulted on August 8th, 2016), par. 35.

[100]*Ibid.*; see also World Bank (2009), p. 50.

[101]This teleological hermeneutic has been displayed by the IP in several cases; see Inspection Panel, *China: Western Poverty Reduction Project – Investigation Report,* 2000, parr. 17–18 and Inspection Panel, *Pakistan: National Drainage Program Project – Investigation Report,* 2006, xxv. These cases are referred to in NYU Clinic 2014, 27–28.

demonstrates how external normative sources and developments are translated into system-specific processes of constitutionalization (Teubner 2012, p. 86).[102]

As the *Chad-Cameroon case* indicates, translation, rather than superimposition, seems to be the keyword in framing the nexus between the Bank's safeguard policies and international law.

4.2 *From Law to Management? On the Nature of Accountability*

In Sects. 3.2 and 3.3 above, I have underlined the 'managerial shift' in the current ESF framework. In this section, I will inquire into the impact of this shift on the nature of the Bank's accountability. This inquiry will focus on three elements: (1) the changing nature of the Bank's obligations under the ESF; (2) the delegation of responsibility from the Bank to the borrowing country; and (3) the role and nature of the IP in light of these changes.

4.2.1 Benchmarks of Compliance

As noted above, the IP investigates all claims resulting from a 'failure of the Bank to *follow its operational policies and procedures*'.[103] The obligations of the Bank, as set out in the ESP, broadly consist of two categories: (i) *ex ante* due diligence, and (ii) downstream monitoring and implementation support. Regarding the former (i), in assessing whether to provide support to proposed projects, the Bank needs to evaluate if these projects are '*expected to meet* the requirements of the ESSs in *manner* and within a *timeframe acceptable to the Bank*'.[104] Clearly, as a result of this risk-based approach, the non-compliance of a project with one or multiple ESS (s) does not on itself establish any responsibility on the part of the Bank. To hold the Bank accountable, the burden of proof is not merely to show that a specific ESS have been violated, but rather that the project should never have been 'expected to meet' the requirements of the ESS in an 'acceptable' manner and timeframe. The evaluation of this 'expectation' or institutional 'acceptability', however, is legally indeterminate, and prone to indefinite variations and interpretations of a managerial nature. The language is not only imprecise,[105] but more importantly, it dilutes the

[102]See Teubner (2012), p. 86: 'The application of external pressure means that the self-steering of politics, or law, or other subsystems, creates such irritations of the focal system, that ultimately the external and internal programmes play out together along the desired course'.

[103]Inspection Panel Resolution, par. 12 (emphasis added).

[104]ESF, ESP, par. 7 and par. 16 (emphasis added).

[105]This is argued in OHCHR Letter, 12: 'Due to the imprecise nature of the language used, it will be exceedingly difficult for requesters to argue that the Bank has committed a serious violation of this requirement'.

Bank's responsibility from safeguarding compliance with the ESSs to a responsibility of proficient qualitative assessment ('expected to meet'), which can be asserted even in the case of non-compliance. The latter is not only easier to establish, it also relies on an entirely different evaluative methodology: from deontic, requirements-based reasoning, to a qualitative evaluation of risk-assessment.[106] In the absence of clear legal standards, the risk is that the accountability procedure will devolve into a 'battle of experts', with each party arguing within epistemically diverging structures of managerial assessment, which cannot be traced back to, nor be resolved by, a legal apparatus of deontic reasoning.

Similar concerns hold with regard to the Bank's due diligence in using borrowing countries' regulatory frameworks. As elaborated in Sect. 2.2. above, in order to do so, the Bank needs to demonstrate that these frameworks are 'likely' to be 'materially consistent' with the goals of the ESF. Once again, these criteria are based on qualitative[107] and teleological interpretation (World Bank 2016b). The methodology of this interpretation—just as the assessment of whether projects are 'expected to meet' the ESSs—is unclear and does not provide any substantive criteria for *ex ante* assessment of the laws and institutions of the borrowing country. As argued in the OHCHR Letter, the provision 'clearly countenances the use of domestic frameworks that do not offer protection equivalent to the ESSs', as long as they were 'likely' to achieve similar results. In conclusion, both the Bank's general due diligence responsibility and its responsibilities regarding the assessment of borrowing countries' institutional framework, rely on an opaque set of purpose-driven criteria, which cannot be evaluated through deontic reasoning, but require qualitative managerial assessment. This clearly complicates the future task of the Bank's IP and holds the risk of dilution.[108]

The second category of Bank responsibilities—monitoring and implementation support (ii)—is to a large degree delegated to the borrowing country. I now turn to this problem of delegation.

---

[106]The Independent Evaluation of the Asian Development Bank's safeguards warns for the risks of such an approach: 'In essence, given the rising social risks and environmental threats, Independent Evaluation advocates the continued use of a requirements-based safeguards system as used by ADB, rather than a switch to an aspirational one of safeguards standards as is being proposed at the World Bank Group', see Independent Evaluation Asian Development Bank, 'News Release: ADB's Social and Environmental Safeguards, with Improvements, can be a Benchmark', November 11, 2014, http://www.adb.org/news/adb-s-social-and-environmental-safeguards-improvements-can-be-benchmark (last consulted on August 7th, 2016).

[107]'The term 'materially consistent' is subject to qualitative interpretation, but in essence it means 'substantially' or 'considerably' similar to or 'agreeing/according' in substance with the ESS objectives'; in World Bank (2016b), p. 9.

[108]The OHCHR Letter warns that 'language that sets out clearly and precisely the Bank's obligations and minimizes its discretion [...] is essential if the Inspection Panel and project-affected communities are to be able to hold the Bank to account for its actions and omissions'.

4.2.2 The Move to Ownership from the Perspective of Accountability

Apart from the benchmarks of compliance, another potential problem of the managerial turn in the ESF is the delegation of responsibilities from the Bank to its borrowing countries. As the Inspection Panel Resolution indicates, the IP cannot hear complaints 'with respect to actions which are the responsibility of other parties, *such as the borrower* [...] and which do not involve any action or omission on the part of the Bank'.[109] The specific environmental and social standards (ESS 1–8) of the ESF, however, aim their concrete policies and obligations solely at the borrowing country.[110] It is, therefore, pivotal to understand the nexus between the responsibilities of the borrower and those of the Bank, since only the latter are eligible to be evaluated by the IP, and only the former are concretely identified in the different ESSs (see also NYU Clinic 2016, Supplement 2).

This nexus is regulated in paragraphs 15 and 16 of the ESP, which state that '[t]he Bank will *require* Borrowers to conduct environmental and social assessment' and that '[t]he Bank will *require* the Borrower to prepare and implement projects so that they meet the requirements of the ESSs *in a manner and a timeframe acceptable to the Bank*'.[111] In other words, the obligation of the Bank regarding the substantive core of the ESF is to *require* the borrowing countries to comply with the ESSs in an *acceptable manner and timeframe*. As also noted by the IP in its comments to the draft of the ESF, this implies an important change in terminology from the Bank's obligation under the previous safeguard policies, according to which the Bank's responsibility was 'to "*ensure*" the consistency of Borrower's actions with applicable safeguard policies' (Inspection Panel 2015). This shift from *ensuring* to *requiring*[112] is significant: while the former expresses outcome-based responsibility, the latter merely signifies a commitment towards interaction.[113] In case the borrower falls short of safeguarding the environmental and social standards, the former clearly assigns responsibility to the Bank, which had to *ensure* compliance. If this is still the case under the new ESP is ambiguous.[114] Not only does the provision entail a semantic dilution (from *ensuring* to *requiring*), it also reiterates the managerial approach mentioned above, moving away from concrete requirements to the ambiguity of compliance in an *acceptable manner and timeframe*.

---

[109]Inspection Panel Resolution, par. 14 (emphasis added).

[110]As mentioned in Sect. 2.1 above, the specific ESSs (1–8) apply to the borrowing country, while only the general ESP sets out the responsibilities of the Bank.

[111]ESF, ESFP, parr. 15–16.

[112]The word 'require' is also used regarding the implementation of the ESCP (ESP par. 47), and the provision of grievance mechanism (ESP par. 60).

[113]Human Rights Watch regrets the change in terminology, claiming that '[t]he [B]ank has a responsibility separate from that of governments to *ensure* that communities and individuals [...] are not harmed by [B]ank projects', see Human Rights Watch (2015b).

[114]'Would the change in terminology also entail a change in the Bank's responsibilities and a potentional shift in accountability [...]?' in Inspection Panel 2015, 2.

The responsibilities of the Bank under the ESF for *monitoring* the environmental and social performance of a project and for providing *implementation support*,[115] *i.e.* 'downstream support', seemingly also lead back to the responsibility of the borrowing country. The core of both obligations departs from 'reviewing the Borrower's monitoring reports'.[116] In its comments on the ESF draft, the IP sharply concludes:

> [u]nder the draft Policy [which became the final policy], it seems that the supervision responsibilities of the Bank stem primarily from information provided by the Borrower with a more "hands-off" approach from the Bank, while there does not seem to be any framework or criteria to evaluate the quality of the information provided by the Borrower, or the methodology used in gathering it.[117]

In conclusion, regarding, on the one hand, the Bank's responsibility for the compliance of the borrowing country with the ESSs, and, on the other hand, its responsibility to provide implementation support to these borrowing countries, the requirement-based accountability of the previous safeguards has to make place for a stream of managerial assessments that are substantively indeterminate and almost invariably flow back to the borrowing country. In light of the growing recognition of the principle of country ownership and the ongoing operational delegation to borrowing countries, the dilution of the Bank's responsibilities both regarding the latter's compliance with the ESSs, and regarding its own supervision standards, will almost surely complicate the future task of the IP.

4.2.3 The Role of the Inspection Panel

In the previous sections, I have exposed the dilution of the Bank's safeguard standards, away from a deontic, requirement-based approach, to a managerial process of qualitative assessment on the basis of opaque standards.[118] The Bank's legal responsibility is expressed in standards such as 'expected to meet'; 'in a manner and within a timeframe acceptable to the Bank'; 'likely to be material consistent'; 'require the borrower' or 'reviewing the information'. Much of the success of the ESF and the recent reform in ensuring the vertical accountability of the Bank will, therefore, depend on the capacity and willingness of the IP to draw normative lines in the managerial maze. The aim of concretizing the vague and indirect responsibilities of the Bank can be achieved, I argue, through at least five different techniques, which have already been employed by the IP in previous cases[119]:

[115]ESF, ESP par. 3 (e) and parr. 56–59.

[116]ESF, ESP par. 32 and 57.

[117]Inspection Panel 2015, par.12.

[118]This is central to the critique of the Inspection Panel, the 28 UN special procedures mandate-holders and Human Rights Watch. See Inspection Panel 2015; OHCHR Letter; Human Rights Watch (2015a, b).

[119]This is in line with the conclusions regarding the role of the IP in Sect. 4.1. above.

1. Referring to the 'object and purpose' of the ESF to fill in gaps and resolve ambiguities. This teleological hermeneutic has already been employed by the IP in the past.[120] The vision statement of the ESF provides a fertile soil for this purpose-driven approach;
2. Reading the ESF in light of the relevant provisions of international law (*i.a.* human rights law, labor law, environmental law) and safeguard policies of other MDBs, along the lines of the 'systemic integration' technique of Article 31, 3 (c) VCLT;
3. Relying on (potentially external) expert-advice to concretize matters of qualitative interpretation;
4. Integrating also non-binding Guidelines and Best Practices in the interpretative practice, whenever they serve clarification (Kingsbury 1999, p. 331); and
5. Extending jurisprudential practice beyond an administrative case-by-case approach, by establishing and following normative precedents.

4.3 Development Policy Lending and Programming for Results

A final concern relates to the limited coverage of the new ESF regarding the Bank's lending portfolio. This portfolio consist of three lending mechanisms: (1) 'investment lending', which provides financing for specific projects (often related to infrastructure)[121]; (2) 'development policy lending' ('DPL'), which provides general budgetary support to governments conditional upon policy-and institutional reform[122]; and (3) the newest lending facility of 'programs-for-results financing' ('PfR'), which supports government programs in specific sectors and disburses funds upon the achievement of predetermined performance indicators.[123] While investment lending has historically always taken the lion's share of the Bank's financing, the IEG Report notes that '[d]evelopment policy lending for institutional and policy reforms [DPL], programmatic or sectorwide lending [PfR], and lending through financial intermediaries now comprise more than half the portfolio'.[124]

The environmental and social safeguards of the Bank, however, only apply to the first category of investment lending, and leave out the increasingly important DPL and PfR. The latter two lending facilities are subject to much weaker and more

[120] See Inspection Panel, *China: Western Poverty Reduction Project – Investigation Report,* 2000, parr. 17–18 and Inspection Panel, *Pakistan: National Drainage Program Project – Investigation Report,* 2006, xxv. Reference should be made here to NYU Clinic 2014, 27–28. This paper sets out the importance of teleological interpretation in the practice of the IP.

[121] See operational policy and bank procedure (OP/BP) 10.00.

[122] See OP/BP 8.60. This development policy lending is the successor of the Bank's 'Structural Adjustment Programs' (SAPs).

[123] This lending facility was created in 2012, see OP/BP 9.00.

[124] See IEG Report, xv-xvi.

indeterminate safeguards provisions.[125] Therefore, the IP urged the Bank to extend the coverage of the ESF to all its lending facilities, arguing that 'this review presents the opportunity to deliberate on the need to harmonize the safeguards coverage for instruments such as Development Policy Lending (DPL), and Programs for Results (P4R), which represent a considerable portion of the Bank's lending portfolio' (Inspection Panel 2015).[126] Also the OHCHR Letter argues that '[t]he ESSs should apply to all forms of Bank lending'.[127]

These demands fell on deaf ears, however, and the current ESF safeguards remain exclusively applicable to the Bank's investment lending. This is particularly problematic with regards to DPL programs, which have been considered by some as 'undermining, if not violating economic and social rights' (Hunter 1996; UNGA 2015). As the OHCHR Letter argues, 'these loans support policy and institutional reforms in areas that significantly affect the enjoyment of human rights', and '[p]ast experience has shown that the use of DPLs has resulted in critical gaps in environmental and social risk assessment and mitigation at the expense of the local communities and the environment'.[128] In conclusion, while the ESF covers extended substantive areas, its coverage of total lending steadily decreases, as DPL and PfR gain ground in the Bank.

5 Conclusion

On August 4th, 2016, the Board of Executive Directors of the World Bank (the 'Bank') endorsed the new Environmental and Social Framework ('ESF'), thereby rendering this policy legally binding. The ESF is the latest of many steps—with the elaboration of the original safeguard policies and the creation of the Inspection Panel ('IP') as earlier milestones—that the Bank has undertaken to promote citizen-driven accountability for environmental and social damage. As pointed out, the initiative thereby seeks to rectify an accountability-gap that is omnipresent in international institutional law. During the first two decades of the IP's existence, it gradually became apparent that the Bank's safeguard mechanism was in need of substantial revision. Section 2 sets out how a multitude of causes—*i.a.* a changing landscape of development policy; diversifying borrower's profilers; increasing competition between development banks; and growing pressures by NGOs for normative expansion—let the Bank to re-evaluate its safeguard policies. This

[125]See OP 8.60, parr. 9–10 and OP 9.00, parr. 8–9.

[126]Human Rights Watch echoed this demand, stating that '[t]he safeguards review [...] presents a rare opportunity for the World Bank to ensure consistency across its standards. [...] The Bank should remedy [the current inconsistency] by applying the policy to all World Bank activities, including direct policy loans (DPLs) and program for results lending (P4R)'.

[127]OHCHR Letter, 15–16.

[128]OHCHR Letter, 14–15.

re-evaluation, which drew on the biggest stakeholder consultation in the history of the Bank, eventually gave rise to the ESF.

Section 3 provides an original typology of the four main innovations that the ESF brings to the safeguard mechanism in the Bank. First of all, I demonstrate how the topic-oriented safeguard standards, which were previously scattered in different independent operational policies (OPs), have been integrated in a hierarchically organized, unified normative scheme. This principle-based integration, I argue, can play an important role in the process of teleological interpretation by the IP. Secondly, the chapter exposes a shift from deontic reasoning to processes of qualitative managerial assessment in the environmental and social standards, which fundamentally alters their normative structure. This conclusion applies both to the increased focus on country ownership (Sect. 3.2) and the general reformulation of safeguard standards (Sect. 3.3). Finally, I shed light on the new substantive areas of environmental and social protection in the ESF, such as labor and working conditions; climate change; non-discrimination; natural resource management; and—to a minor extent—human rights.

After providing a typology of innovations, Sect. 4 of the chapter critically assesses the changing nature of the safeguard model and situates the ESF in the broader context of international law. The first conclusion is that the accountability standards of the Bank are part of an endogenous legal structure and hierarchy, in which validity is produced without recourse to exogenous international legal sources. This process, I argue, follows the path of Teubner's *societal* constitutionalization, and should be contrasted with the *cosmopolitan* model of universally integrated legal authority. Secondly, I argue that the shift from deontic safeguard protection to risk-based managerialism risks to dilute the accountability of the Bank, both regarding its own specific responsibilities and regarding its supervision over the performance of borrowing countries. This dilution poses challenges for the IP, which will need to draw clear normative lines in this maze of managerialism. The chapter identifies five techniques for the IP to achieve this, among which the systematic integration of external legal sources and the recourse to teleological hermeneutics figure prominently. Finally, I have pointed out that the ESF provides only limited coverage, excluding both Development Policy Lending and Programming-for-Results Lending.

In conclusion, it is undisputable that the ESF can be seen as a new step in safeguarding the accountability of the Bank. This chapter helps one to evaluate in which direction this step was made.

References

African Development Bank (2012) African Development Bank's Integrated Safeguards System

Alvarez J (2005) International organizations as law-makers. Oxford University Press, Oxford

Alvarez J (2007) Book review of Dan Sarooshi, international organizations and their exercise of sovereign powers. Am J Int Law 101:674–679

Asian Development Bank (2012) Safeguard Policy Statement
Baimu E, Panou A (2012) Responsibility of international organizations and the World Bank inspection panel: parallel tracks unlikely to converge? In: Bradlow DD, Cisse H, Kingsbury B (eds) The World Bank legal review (vol. 3): international financial institutions and global legal governance. The World Bank, Washington
Boisson de Chazournes L (2009) Changing roles of international organizations: global administrative law and the interplay of legitimacies. Int Org Law Rev 6(2):655–666
Bowett DW (1982) The law of international institutions, 4th edn. Stevens & Sons, London
Bradlow D (2005) Private complainants and international organizations: a comparative study of the independent inspection mechanisms in international financial institutions. Georgetown J Int Law 36:403–491
Clark DL (2002) The World Bank and Human Rights: the need for greater accountability. Harv Hum Rights J 15:205
democracy. Kluwer, The Hague
Legal opinion on human rights and the work of the World Bank. The World
Washington
Dann P, von Bernstorff J (2013) Reforming the World Bank's safeguards: a comparative legal analysis. Deutsche Gesellschaft für Internationale Zusammenarbeit (GIZ)
Darrow M (2003) Between lights and shadow: the World Bank, the International Monetary Fund and international human rights law. Hart, Portland
Daugirdas K (2014) Reputation and the responsibility of international organizations. Eur J Int Law 25(4):991–1018
European Bank for Reconstruction and Development (2008) Environmental and Social Policy
Fox J (1998) When does reform policy influence practice? Lessons from the Bankwide resettlement review. In: Fox J, Brown LD (eds) The struggle for accountability: the World Bank, NGOs, and grassroots movements. MIT Press, Cambridge
Handl G (1998) The legal mandate of multilateral development banks as agents for change toward sustainable development. Am J Int Law 92(4):642–665
Henkin L (1999) That "S" word: sovereignty, and globalization and human rights, Et Cetera. Fordham Law Rev 68:1–14
Human Rights Watch (2015a) Human Rights Watch Submission: World Bank's Draft Environmental and Social Framework. https://www.hrw.org/news/2015/04/07/human-rightswatch-sub mission-world-banks-draft-environmental-and-social-framework#_ednref2 (last consulted on August 10th, 2016). Referred to as 'Human Rights Watch, April 2015'
Human Rights Watch (2015b) Human Rights Watch Submission: World Bank's Second Draft Environmental and Social Framework. https://www.hrw.org/news/2015/10/07/humanrights-watch-submission-world-banks-second-draft-environmental-and-social (last consulted on August 10th, 2016). Referred to as 'Human Rights Watch, October 2015'
Hunter D (1996) The role of the World Bank in strengthening governance, civil society, human rights. In: Bosshard P, Heredia C, Hunter D, Seymour F (eds) Lending credibility: new mandates and partnerships for the World Bank. Ciel et al, Washington
ILC (2011) Draft articles on the responsibility of international organizations, with commentaries. Yearb Int Law Commission 2(2)
Independent Evaluation Group (2010) Safeguards and Sustainability Policies in a Changing World: An Independent Evaluation of World Bank Group Experience. http://siteresources.worldbank.org/EXTSAFANDSUS/Resources/Safeguards_eval.pdf (last consulted on August 4th, 2016). Referred to as 'IEG Report'
Inspection Panel (2015) Comments on the Second Draft of the Proposed Environmental and Social Framework. https://consultations.worldbank.org/consultation/review-and-updateworld-bank-safeguard-policies (last consulted on Agust, 10th 2016). Referred to as 'Inspection Panel Comments on the Second Draft'
International Finance Corporation (2006) Policy on Environmental and Social Sustainability
Johnstone I (2011) Do international organizations have reputations? Int Org Law Rev 7:235–239
Kelsen H (1967) Pure theory of law (trans: Knight M). University of California Press, Berkeley

Kingsbury B (1999) Operational policies of international institutions as part of the lawmaking process: the World Bank and indigenous peoples. In: Goodwin-Gill G, Talmon S (eds) The reality of international law: essays in honour of Ian Brownlie. Clarendon Press, Oxford

Kingsbury B (2012) Introduction–global administrative law in the institutional practice of global regulatory governance. In: Bradlow DD, Cisse H, Kingsbury B (eds) The World Bank legal review (vol. 3): international financial institutions and global legal governance. The World Bank, Washington

Klabbers J (2001) The changing image of international organizations. In: Coicaud JM, Heiskanen V (eds) The legitimacy of international organizations. United Nations University Press, New York

Klabbers J (2005) Two concepts of international organization. Int Org Law Rev 2:277–293

Klabbers J (2009) An introduction to international institutional law. 2nd edn. Cambridge University Press, Cambridge

Klabbers J (2015) The EJIL foreword: the transformation of international org[illegible] Int Law 26:9–82

Krisch N, Kingsbury B (2006) Introduction: global governance and global administrative law in the international legal order. Eur J Int Law 17(1):1–13

Kumm M (2009) The cosmopolitan turn in constitutionalism. In: Dunoff JL, Trachtman JP (eds) Ruling the world. Cambridge University Press, Cambridge

Leroy AM (2011) Legal vice presidency annual report fy 2011-the World Bank and the rule of law. The World Bank, Washington

Leroy AM (2012) Legal note on Bank involvement in the criminal justice sector. The World Bank, Washington

Leroy AM (2013) The Bank's engagement in the criminal justice sector and the role of lawyers in the "Solutions Bank": an Essay. In: World Bank Legal Vice Presidency, Annual Report FY 2013: The World Bank's engagement in the criminal justice sector and the role of lawyers in the "Solutions Bank". The World Bank, Washington

Luhmann N (1997) Die gesellshaft der gesellshaft. Suhrkamp, Frankfurt am Main

Mcinerney-Lankford S (2010) International financial institutions and human rights: select perspectives on legal obligations. In: Bradlow DD, Hunter DB (eds) International financial institutions and international law. Kluwer Law International, Alphen aan den Rijn

Morse B, Berger TR (1992) Sardar Sarovar-report of the independent review. Resource Futures International, Ottawa

NYU Clinic (2014) The Changing Role of the World Bank Inspection panel: Responding to Contemporary Challenges at the World Bank. http://chrgj.org/wpcontent/uploads/2014/10/ChangingRoleoftheWorldBankIP_IOClinic.pdf (last consulted on August 4th, 2016)

NYU Clinic (2016) Empowering the Inspectional Panel: the Impact of the World Bank's Safeguards Review. http://ewebapps.worldbank.org/apps/ip/Documents/Empowering_the_Inspection_Panel_Web.pdf (last consulted on August 10th, 2016)

OECD (2005) The Paris Declaration on Aid Effectiveness. http://www.oecd.org/dac/effectiveness/parisdeclarationandaccraagendaforaction.htm (last consulted on August 8th, 2016)

OECD (2008) The Accra Agenda for Action. http://www.oecd.org/dac/effectiveness/parisdeclarationandaccraagendaforaction.htm (last consulted on August 8th, 2016)

Office of the High Commissioner for Human Rights (2014) Letter to the World Bank President Regarding the Review of the Environmental and Social Framework. http://www.ohchr.org/Documents/Issues/EPoverty/WorldBank.pdf (last consulted on August 7th, 2016). Referred to as 'OHCHR Letter'

Petersmann EU (ed) (2012) Multilevel Governance of Interdependent Public Goods Theories, Rules and Institutions for the Central Policy Challenge in the 21st Century. EUI Working Paper Series RSCAS 2012/23, Florence

Reinisch A (ed) (2016) The Convention on the privileges and immunities of the United Nations and its specialized agencies. Oxford University Press, Oxford

Rigo Sureda A (2005) The law applicable to the activities of international development banks-The Hague academy of international law. Martinus Nijhoff, Leiden

Schachter O (1983) Human dignity as a normative concept. Am J Int Law 77:848–854

Schermers HG, Blokker NM (1995) International institutional law, 3rd edn. Martinus Nijhoff, Dordrecht

Shihata I (1991) The World Bank and "Governance" issues in its borrowing members. In: Shihata I (ed) The World Bank in a changing world – selected essays I, Martinus Nijhoff Dordrecht

Shihata I (2000) Legal opinion on the prohibition of political activities in the Bank's Work. In: Shihata I (ed) The World Bank Legal Papers. Kluwer Law International, The Hague

Sinclair GF (2015) State formation, liberal reform, and the growth of international organizations. Eur J Int Law 26:445–469

Skogly S (2001) The human rights obligations of the World Bank and the International Monetary Fund. Cavendish, London

Teubner G (2012) Constitutional fragments: societal constitutionalism and globalization. Oxford University Press, Oxford

UNGA (2015) Report of the Special Rapporteur on Extreme Poverty and Human Rights. A/70/274

Vaubel R (2006) Principal-agent problems in international organizations. Rev Int Org 1:125–138

Von Bernstorff J (2008) Procedures of decision-making and the role of law in international organizations. German Law J 9(11):1939–1964

Bogdandy V et al (2010) The exercise of public authority by international institutions: advancing international institutional law. Springer, New York

World Bank (1993) Resolution of the Executive Directors Establishing the World Bank Inspection Panel, No. 93-10 (IBRD) and No. 93-6 (IDA). Referred to as 'Inspection Panel Resolution'

World Bank (2009) Accountability at the World Bank: the inspection panel at 15 years. The World Bank, Washington

World Bank (2012) The World Bank's Safeguard Policies Proposed Review and Update, Approach Paper. http://siteresources.worldbank.org/EXTSAFEPOL/Resources/584434130643139 0058/SafeguardsReviewApproachPaper.pdf (last consulted on August 8th, 2016). Referred to as 'Approach Paper'

World Bank (2016a) Environmental and social framework: setting environmental and social standards for investment project financing. The World Bank, Washington. Referred to as 'ESF'

World Bank (2016b) Information note assessing the Borrower's environmental and social framework. https://consultations.worldbank.org/consultation/review-and-update-worldbank-safeguard-policies (last consulted on August 9th, 2016). Referred to as 'Information Note on assessing Borrower ESF'

World Bank (2016c) Summary of Phase 3 Consultations and Bank Management Responses. https://consultations.worldbank.org/consultation/review-and-update-world-bank-safeguardpolicies (last consulted on Agust, 10th 2016). Referred to as 'Summary of Consultations and Responses'

Wouters J, Pauwelyn J, Wessel R (2012) Informal international law-making. Oxford University Press, Oxford

Part IV
Conditionality and Socio Economic Impact

IMF Conditionality and Socio-Economic Impact

Antonio Bassanetti

Abstract Conditionality in IMF-supported programs has two main objectives: ensuring that Fund's resources are used to solve member countries' balance of payment problems and, at the same time, safeguarding the temporary use of those resources. In this context, while macro-social conditionality has increased in recent years as a reflection of the greater emphasis that the Fund dedicates to social issues, it is important to note that IMF programs have traditionally managed to safeguard social protection, particularly in low-income countries. Notwithstanding, there is room for improvement and the Fund is regularly engaged in a self-evaluation process. The experience gathered in the aftermath of the global economic and financial crisis signals that in several circumstances the design of consolidation measures contained progressive elements that, despite the overall negative impact on the economy, contributed to prevent a worsening of inequalities. At the same time, addressing complex and intertwined macroeconomic imbalances might require more gradualism in the pace and calibration of the adjustment strategies.

Contents

This paper should not be reported as representing the views of the IMF or the Bank of Italy. The views expressed in this paper are those of the author and do not necessarily represent neither those of the IMF and IMF policy, nor those of the Bank of Italy. This paper reports the contents of a presentation that the author gave at the conference on *Transparency and Democracy in the Bretton Wood Institutions*, organized by the Research Center on International and European Organization of the LUISS University, held in Rome on January 28, 2016.

A. Bassanetti (✉)
IMF and Bank of Italy, Rome, Italy
e-mail: antonio.bassanetti@bancaditalia.it

E. Sciso (ed.), *Accountability, Transparency and Democracy in the Functioning of Bretton Woods Institutions*, DOI 10.1007/978-3-319-57855-2_11

1 Introduction and Main Considerations

Preserving the stability of the international economic and monetary system is at the core of the IMF's mandate. As such, over the course of decades the IMF has been called to intervene and provide temporary financial support to member countries facing balance of payment crises originated by some sort of macroeconomic imbalances—external and/or domestic. In order for these countries to return to a stable path of sustainable growth—and to avoid destabilizing spillovers to the broader international economy—financial assistance *per se* is clearly not enough and has to be accompanied by appropriate corrective measures targeted at the root causes of the crises. Conditionality in IMF-supported programs is intended precisely to ensure that the Fund's resources are used to help member countries solve their balance of payment problems. In addition, conditionality aims at safeguarding these very financial resources, which the IMF receives by its broader membership and is thus accountable for.

Of course, corrective measures—and program conditionality—are calibrated according to the gravity and complexity of the issues to be tackled. Undoubtedly, in severe circumstances—particularly when sizeable fiscal consolidations are unavoidable to ensure sustainability—they might entail significant social impacts. This paper makes the case that the IMF is fully aware of such important aspects. By learning from its own experience, and also because of the growing recognition that social stability is functional to macroeconomic stability and growth, over the course of time the Fund has progressively increased the emphasis and attention devoted to macro-social conditionality. However, this is not a process which can be completed once and for all, neither it is immune to slippages or mistakes. Rather, efforts to learn from past engagements—including the less successful ones—and better understand the social impact of policy measures, thereby improving their design and calibration, are continuous. Indeed, the Fund has increased these efforts in recent years.

To corroborate such point of view, this paper does not provide original results, rather it relies on a relatively small selection of the evidence contained in a number of recently published IMF documents or policy papers that are—in a way—a testament to the institution's regular engagement in a critical self-evaluation aimed at a better delivery on its mandate. The paper is organized as follows. In the second paragraph issues are put in context by recalling briefly both the rationale for having conditionality in IMF-supported programs, and the basic principles which inspire its design. Once the contours of the subject are defined, the third paragraph provides some trends and outcomes related to macro-social conditionality over the course of recent decades, arguing that IMF-supported programs have generally contributed to safeguarding social protection, particularly in low-income countries, as can be inferred by some evidence on public spending in health and education. In the final paragraph, the paper focuses on the experience gathered in the aftermath of the global economic and financial crisis, making the point that even in circumstances where sharp adjustments are unavoidable, policy design and calibration are essential to minimize the negative impact on the most vulnerable segments of the population. While there is evidence that the design of IMF-supported programs took into account such concerns, recent experience showed that a properly attuned pace of measures to tackle complex and intertwined macroeconomic imbalances is important.

2 Issues in Context: The Rationale for Conditionality in IMF Programs and Basic Principles for Its Design

As clarified by the Guidelines on Conditionality of the IMF (2002), '*conditions on the use of Fund resources are governed by the Fund's Articles of Agreement and implementing decisions of the Executive Board*'.[1] As it is well known, the Articles of Agreement represent the fundamental set of rules for the working of the institution.[2]

Against this legal background, conditionality in IMF-supported programs aims at two main objectives: (1) making sure that the Fund's financial resources are provided to member countries to help them solve their balance of payment problems, which is at the core of the IMF's mandate; (2) making sure, at the same time, that Fund's resources are adequately safeguarded for temporary use, which means ensuring that resources drawn ('purchased') by a member country in a financial assistance arrangement with the IMF are subsequently returned to the Fund ('repurchased') according to a well-determined repayment schedule.

It is important to recall, however, that in responding to a country's request for the use of Fund resources and in setting the relative conditionality, the IMF is guided by the principle that the primary responsibility for the selection, design, and implementation of economic and financial policies lies with the country itself. Of course, the Fund assists and provides advice, but the ultimate responsibility lies with the country. This is a crucial element because—on the basis of a long-standing experience—national ownership of policies and adequate administrative capacity have both proved to be essential ingredients for the successful implementation of IMF-supported programs. Moreover, the adoption of such a principle allows arrangements to be flexible, tailored to different member countries' circumstances, and adaptable to possibly changing macroeconomic conditions, both at the outset and during the program.

In this broad framework, when called to set and design program-related conditions, IMF staff follow the overarching criterion of *criticality*. Namely, conditions have to be of *critical* importance (i.e. neither unnecessary nor redundant) to achieve the objectives of the program or to monitor its implementation. In this respect, parsimony is an important characteristic for well-designed conditions, which means

[1]See IMF (2002). See also IMF (2014a).

[2]See IMF (2016).

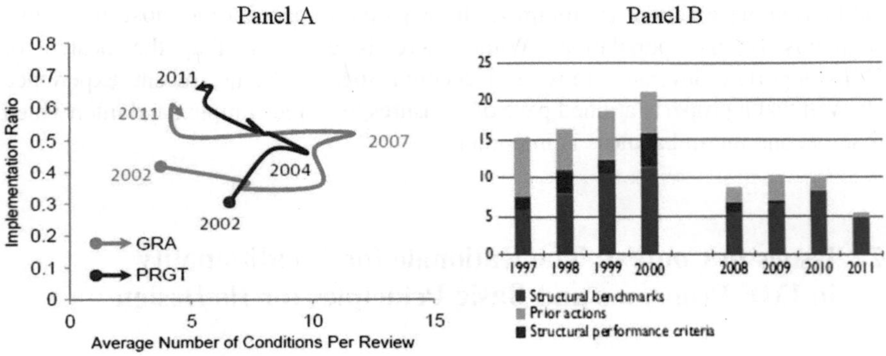

Fig. 1 Trends in conditionality. *Note*: Panel A is taken from the overview paper of the 2011 Review of Conditionality (IMF 2012); Panel B, which reports the number of conditions per program per year in Stand-By-Arrangements, is taken from the IEO evaluation of *IMF Response to Financial and Economic Crisis* (IEO 2014)

that they have to be streamlined and focused on achievable goals and key macroeconomic objectives, normally within the core areas of Fund's expertise.

On the basis of the latest available evidence—which was gathered for the 2011 Review of Conditionality—in recent periods structural conditionality of IMF programs has indeed followed a downward trend, it has been better tailored to country circumstances and preferences, and its implementation ratio has significantly improved (Fig. 1—Panel A).[3] Similar trends have been found also by the Independent Evaluation Office of the IMF (IEO 2014; Fig. 1—Panel B), which nonetheless observed that—as the recent global economic and financial crisis evolved—the number of structural conditions evolved somewhat and their focus extended increasingly beyond the IMF's core areas of competence.

One may wonder whether the broadly favorable outcomes reported in Fig. 1 apply to each single IMF program, and certainly they do not. Without entering into specifics, it can be said that, for example, the design of some of the recent high-debt crisis programs faced serious challenges and was characterized by much less parsimony (see par. 4). But the general trend is both encouraging and a testament to the growing attention to a streamlined and effective conditionality.

With this preliminary evidence as a background, and having sketched the general framework which regulates the design of IMF conditionality, the next paragraph will provide some further results which are more directly related to macro-social conditions.

[3]See IMF (2012) for the overview and background papers. The Review examined 159 programs from 2002 to September 2011, out of which 95 were created under the Poverty Reduction and Growth Trust (PRGT) and 64 under the General Resources Account (GRA).

3 Macro-Social Conditionality: Trends and Outcomes

The 2011 Review of Conditionality showed that, despite representing a small share of all structural conditions, macro-social conditionality has been rising toward the end of the review period. In particular, as can be seen from Fig. 2, programs created under the General Resources Account (GRA programs; Panel A) typically included civil service, pension and labor market reforms, while programs created under the Poverty Reduction and Growth Trust (PRGT programs; Panel B) focused mostly on civil service reforms.

According to the Review, this evidence reflects the increased emphasis that IMF programs dedicate to social aspects as a response to concerns about lack of employment opportunity and rising inequality. Furthermore, there is a growing recognition that social stability plays an important role in order to achieve macroeconomic stability and growth.

It has to be said, however, that the attention paid to inequality issues is not a new phenomenon at the IMF, having been traditionally a relevant component of all its three core institutional activities: lending to help member countries solve their balance of payment problems; macroeconomic surveillance; technical assistance and capacity building.

Actually, the attention to distributional issues within IMF-supported programs dates back a few decades. For example, in the late 1980s—particularly in programs related to developing countries and transition economies—there was a certain emphasis on the importance of using social safety nets to protect the most vulnerable groups of the population during structural and fiscal adjustments, thereby safeguarding their access to basic public services such as health and education.

The attention on social spending strengthened progressively during the 1990s, also as a reflection of the deepening of IMF's engagement on structural issues in

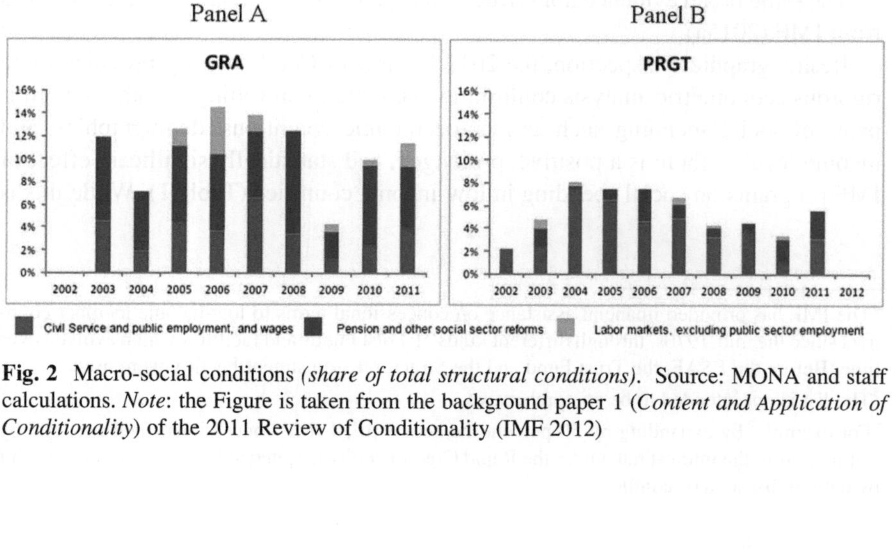

Fig. 2 Macro-social conditions *(share of total structural conditions)*. Source: MONA and staff calculations. *Note*: the Figure is taken from the background paper 1 (*Content and Application of Conditionality*) of the 2011 Review of Conditionality (IMF 2012)

low-income countries, particularly in the context of financial assistance provided on concessional terms through the Enhanced Structural Adjustment Facility (ESAF).[4] In the course of the 1990s and 2000s, a number of decisions and initiatives undertaken by the IMF further testify to the institution's growing involvement on social issues. Among such decisions and initiatives it is worthwhile recalling the following[5]:

- the Heavily Indebted Poor Countries (HIPC) initiative, which was launched in 1996 by the IMF and the World Bank, clarified that resources obtained from debt relief operations should be used to increase pro-poor spending;
- the creation of the Poverty Reduction and Growth Facility in 1999 (replacing the ESAF) allowed to enhance the focus on distributional issues, indicating poverty reduction and growth among the main objectives of IMF-supported programs for low-income countries;
- the adoption of the Multilateral Debt Relief Initiative (MDRI) for HIPCs in 2005 further reinforced this goals;
- the integration since 2009 of indicative social targets—specifically, floors on priority spending—in low-income country programs;
- the active engagement to help member countries achieving the Sustainable Development Goals set by the UN in 2015, including by providing—within the scope of the IMF's mandate—a wider safety net for developing countries,[6] capacity building, and policy advice (for example, besides inequality, pilot works are underway on gender and climate change issues).

Such initiatives have actually produced some important results. As can be seen from Fig. 3, during the period 1985–2009 spending in education and health increased more rapidly in countries with IMF programs than in non-program countries. While particularly striking for low-income countries, the evidence applies more broadly and indicates that IMF programs have generally safeguarded social protection.

The same broad evidence holds true also for more recent years, as can be inferred from IMF (2015a).

Beside graphical inspection, the 2011 Review of Conditionality provides some rigorous econometric analysis confirming that—after controlling for other determinants of social spending such as macroeconomic conditions, demographics, and income levels—there is a positive, prolonged, and statistically significant effect of IMF programs on social spending in low-income countries (Table 1). While this is

---

[4]The IMF has provided financial assistance on concessional terms to low-income member countries since the mid-1970s, through different kinds of Trust Funds and facilities which evolved over time. Before the ESAF, the Trust Fund and the Structural Adjustment Facility were used.

[5]The list is not intended to be comprehensive.

[6]For example, by expanding by 50 percent the access to all IMF concessional facilities, and by setting at zero the interest rate under the Rapid Credit Facility targeted at low-income countries hit by natural disasters or conflicts.

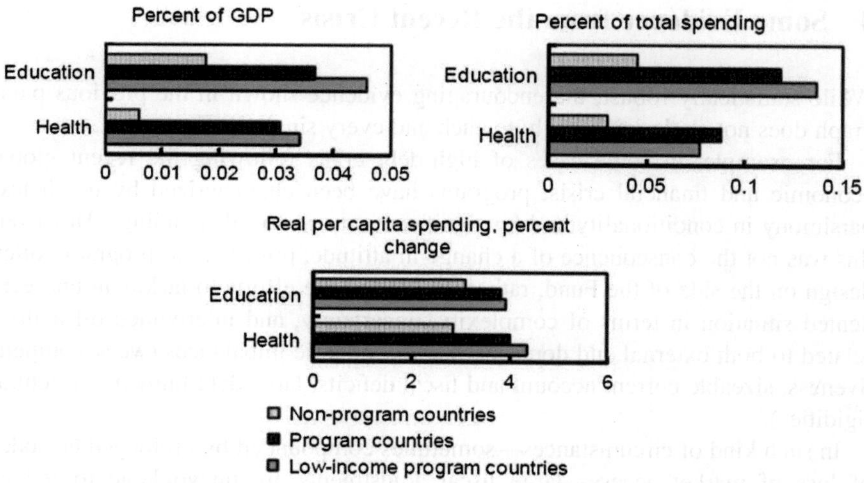

Fig. 3 Median annual change in social spending. Source: Fund staff calculation. *Note*: the Figure is taken from the background paper 3 (*Outcomes of Fund-Supported Programs*) of the 2011 Review of Conditionality (IMF 2012)

Table 1 Long-term effects of Fund-supported programs on social spending, 1985–2009[a]

	Year 1	Year 3	Year 5
	(in percent of GDP)		
Education spending	0.22	0.57	0.82
Health spending	0.27	0.69	0.98

Source: Fund staff calculations

Note: the Table is taken from the background paper 3 (*Outcomes of Fund-Supported Programs*) of the 2011 Review of Conditionality (IMF 2012)

[a]Indicated an increase in social spending (relative to the pre-program period) if a country has a consecutive period of Fund-supported programs

positive news, it has to be qualified that the effect does not seem to be significant for other group of countries.

To complete the picture, the 2011 Review of Conditionality provides another important result: higher spending in education and health is actually correlated with improvements in school enrollments rates and with lower child mortality. Altogether, this broad evidence can thus be taken as indicative that, indeed, IMF programs may have contributed positively to social outcomes.

A word of caution is certainly needed when interpreting these results; however, overall they are reassuring and supportive of further efforts to better include social issues into the IMF's policy advice (see par. 4).

4 Some Evidence from the Recent Crisis

While statistically robust, the encouraging evidence shown in the previous paragraph does not apply indistinctly to each and every single IMF program.

For example, in some cases of high-debt crisis following the recent global economic and financial crisis, programs have been characterized by much less parsimony in conditionality and by significant cuts in social spending.[7] However, this was not the consequence of a change in attitude, priorities, or program policy design on the side of the Fund, rather it reflected the efforts to tackle an unprecedented situation in terms of complexity, uncertainty, and intertwined difficulties related to both external and domestic macroeconomic imbalances (weak competitiveness, sizeable current account and fiscal deficits, large debt burdens, structural rigidities).

In such kind of circumstances—sometimes compounded by prolonged episodes of loss of market access—large fiscal adjustments are unavoidable to reduce imbalances and create the conditions for countries to return on a sustainable growth path. Undoubtedly, however, fiscal consolidations—while necessary—may have serious social impacts and foster inequalities. Policy makers are thus called—sometimes with the help of international institutions—to the complex task of designing well-paced and calibrated adjustments in order to minimize the impact on the most vulnerable segments of the population. It is a difficult but not insurmountable challenge. Recent work at the IMF provides interesting evidence on the matter.

According to a collection of contributions on Inequality and Fiscal Policy (IMF 2015a), the majority of fiscal consolidations undertaken between 2007 and 2013 by 27 European countries—not all of which engaged with IMF programs—were designed in a progressive way, thereby offsetting—at least in part—the worsening in inequality that otherwise would have been associated with the adjustment.

This result confirms previous evidence reported in an IMF policy paper on Fiscal Policy and Inequality (IMF 2014b). In particular, as can be seen from Fig. 4, the burden of the fiscal adjustments undertaken between 2008 and 2012 by a selected group of nine European countries was mostly borne by the households in the highest quantiles of the income distribution, which suffered from the largest income losses. The evidence on the progressive nature of the consolidation measures applies—among others—to some program countries such as Latvia and Portugal and, overall, it holds true also for Greece, although in this latter case the larger income loss was unfortunately incurred by the poorest decile of the population.

Moreover, according to the IMF policy paper, the redistributive design of the consolidation measures actually contributed to prevent a worsening of inequalities in seven out of the nine countries considered in the analysis, as indicated by the simulated changes in the Gini coefficients reported in Fig. 5.

---

[7]Entering into the specifics of the measures adopted in the various cases is beyond the scope of this paper. For additional information, the reader may be referred to IMF (2015a).

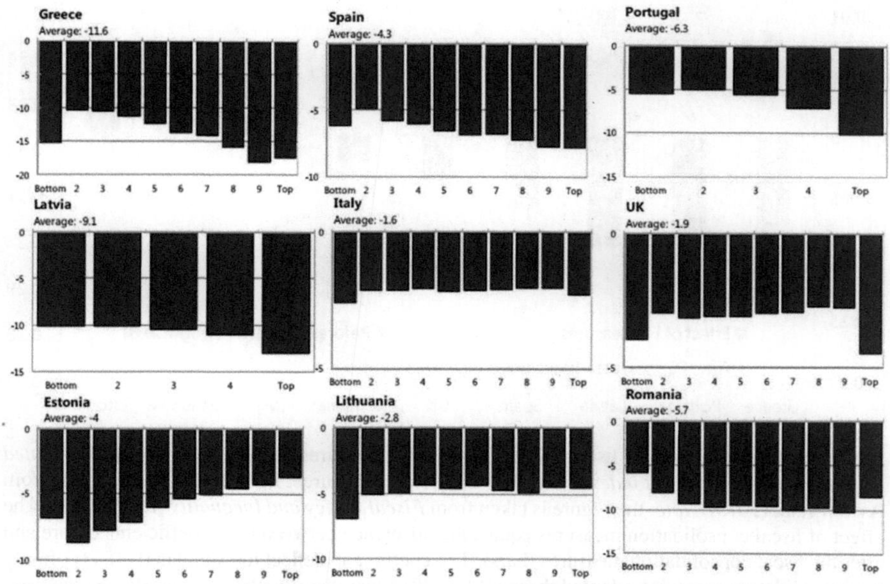

Fig. 4 Cumulative change in households disposable income due to simulated fiscal consolidation measures, 2008–2012 *(percentage of household disposable income)*. Source: Avram et al. (2013). *Note*: the Figure is taken from *Fiscal Policy and Inequality* (IMF 2014b). *Bars* refer to the impact of changes in cash payments, direct taxes, and VAT as a percent of each income quantile's total household disposable income

Focusing more specifically on IMF-supported programs, the recent Crisis Program Review—which gathers evidence over the period 2008–2015 (IMF 2015b)[8]—provides some interesting results on a number of fronts which are relevant for the purpose of this paper, including some data on the capacity to safeguard social spending. Furthermore, it offers broader interesting reflections on some of the adjustment strategies that were pursued to reduce the large macroeconomic imbalances and which had significant social impacts.

Starting with the evidence on social spending, the Review emphasizes that while it is true that euro area programs have been characterized by a decline in social spending-to-GDP ratios (Fig. 6, lower right chart), programs in other regions of the world were able to safeguard these very ratios and even to increase them compared to pre-program periods (it is the case for the Caribbean and Small States, in the upper left chart of Fig. 6, and—to a lesser extent—also for other Emerging Markets,

[8]The Crisis Program Review covers 32 arrangements financed from the IMF's GRA, approved during the period September 2008–June2013, and related to 27 countries from different regions of the world (euro area, European emerging markets, small open economies, Middle East and North Africa). The Review notes that '*As of early 2015, about half of the program countries had regained market access, and a third had reduced their reliance on official financing. Only 5 of the 27 program countries required successor arrangements*'.

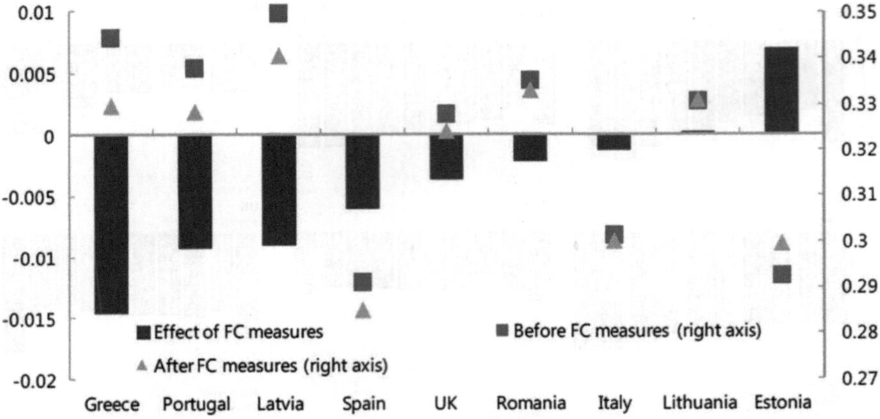

Fig. 5 Simulated impact of fiscal consolidation (FC) measures on Gini Index, 2012 *(simulated disposable Gini coefficient indexes and their differences)*. Source: Information upon request from Avram et al. (2013). *Note*: the Figure is taken from *Fiscal Policy and Inequality* (IMF 2014b). The effect of fiscal consolidation measures equals the difference between Gini coefficients before and after the fiscal consolidation measures (bars). The coefficients reflect the simulated effects of only the consolidation measures adopted during 2008–2012 that directly affect disposable income and were not reversed before mid-2012. Thus, the effects of these fiscal measures on market income (for example through their effects on economic activity and unemployment) are not captured

in the lower left chart). Moreover, based on income shares, the latter groups of countries also saw a partial redistribution of income from capital to labor, which bodes well in terms of a possible easing of inequalities (Fig. 6).

Overall, the broad results reported in this paragraph point to the fact that even when the severity of crises calls for harsh remedial interventions entailing cuts in social spending and decreases of household disposable income, policy design and calibration can play a crucial role in alleviating the negative impact on the most vulnerable. While the IMF is increasingly attentive to this kind of issues, there certainly remains room for improvement in future program design and conditionality.

In this respect, it is worthwhile recalling some of the considerations reported by the Crisis Program Review. As said, they relate to elements which—being important parts of the adjustment strategy pursued in recent IMF-supported programs—were the object of intense public debate in view of their potential impact on socio-economic conditions.

The first consideration regards the recessionary effects of fiscal consolidations. The Review acknowledges that—while some large adjustments were necessary—their negative short-term impact on output was underestimated, also on the back of larger than expected fiscal multipliers. The lesson to be learned is thus that the recessionary effects of fiscal consolidations should be better factored in and, when they are expected to be large, fiscal adjustments should be calibrated in a more gradual way. Of course, in the context of a program of financial assistance, a less

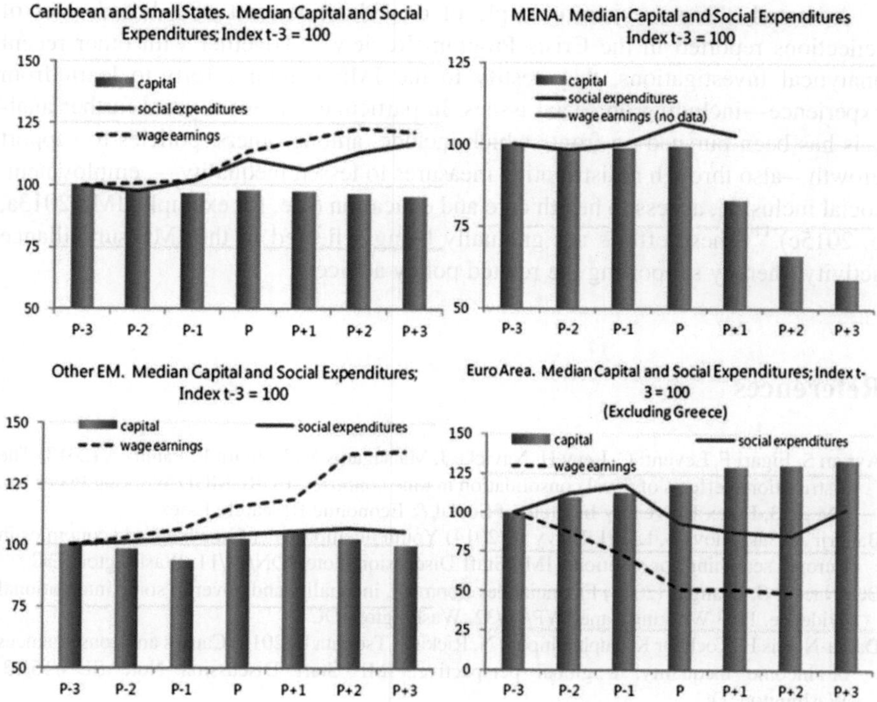

Fig. 6 Inequality and program social spending. Sources: WEO; WDI; ILO; and IMF staff calculation. *Note*: the Figure is taken from *Crisis Program Review* (IMF 2015b)

frontloaded fiscal consolidation would necessarily imply the need to seek for additional financing.

The second consideration relates to external adjustments, and in particular to the so-called 'internal-devaluation' strategy which was pursued to rebalance the external position of countries that could not rely on the more traditional nominal exchange rate devaluation (the case applies, for example, to members of currency unions). The Crisis Program Review recognizes that such strategy—which entails domestic price adjustments[9]—proved very difficult to be pursued, particularly when the broader international economy is characterized by low growth and low inflation. Furthermore, a strategy of internal devaluation may require structural adjustments which—though essential to enhance potential growth—can be achieved on a longer time span than originally expected and whose short-term growth dividend can be smaller than envisaged (i.e. their growth-enhancing effects may take some time to fully kick-in).

[9] In cases where real wages and productivity have diverged significantly over time, re-alignments are sometimes achieved also through wage corrections.

As noted, these are just a couple of considerations out of a broader set of reflections reported in the Crisis Program Review.[10] Together with other recent analytical investigations, they testify to the IMF regular efforts to learn from experience—including on social issues. In particular, in recent years further analysis has been pursued on fronts which include, among others, policies to support growth—also through redistributive measures to lessen inequality—, employment, social inclusion, access to health care and education (see, for example, IMF 2013a, b, 2015c).[11] These efforts are gradually being reflected in the IMF surveillance activity, thereby supporting the related policy advice.

References

Avram S, Figari F, Leventi C, Levy H, Navicke J, Matsaganis M, Militaru E, Paulus A (2013) The distributional effects of fiscal consolidation in nine countries. EUROMOD Working Paper No. EM 2/13, Essex University Institute of Social & Economic Research, Essex

Banerji A, Saksonovs S, Lin H, Blavy R (2014) Youth unemployment in advanced economies in Europe: searching for solutions. IMF Staff Discussion Note SDN/14/11, Washington, DC

Ben Naceur S, Shang R (2016) Financial development, inequality and poverty: some international evidence. IMF Working Paper WP/16/32, Washington, DC

Dabla-Norris E, Kochhar K, Suphaphiphat N, Ricka F, Tsounta E (2015) Causes and consequences of income inequality: a global perspective. IMF Staff Discussion Note SDN/15/13, Washington, DC

Decressin J, Espinoza R, Halikias I, Leigh D, Loungani P, Medas P, Mursula S, Schindler M, Splimbergo A, Teng Xu T (2015) Wage moderation in crises – policy considerations and applications to the Euro area. IMF Staff Discussion Note SDN/15/22, Washington, DC

Elborg-Woytek K, Newiak M, Kochhar K, Fabrizio S, Kpodar K, Wingender P, Clements B, Schwartz G, (2013) Women, work, and the economy: macroeconomic gains from gender equity. IMF Staff Discussion Note SDN/13/10, Washington, DC

Francese M, Mulas-Granados C (2015) Functional income distribution and its role in explaining inequality. IMF Working Paper WP/15/244, Washington, DC

Gonzales C, Chandra S-J, Kochhar K, Newiak M, Zeinullayec T (2015) Catalyst for change: empowering women and tackling income inequality. IMF Staff Discussion Note SDN/15/20, Washington, DC

[10]Others considerations pertain to: (1) the criticality of structural reforms and the need to better consider both the authorities' implementation capacity and the possibility that the reforms' short-term growth dividends may be contained; (2) policy priorities that might favor the clean-up of private sector balance sheets; (3) some early reflection on the cooperation between the Fund and Regional Financial Agreements.

[11]These efforts were done also in compliance with the recommendation of the 2011 Review of Conditionality about the necessity to strengthen the analysis of the social impact of policy measures envisaged in IMF programs. In addition, it should be recalled that individual IMF staff have also completed a number of Staff Discussion Notes and Working Papers on similar subjects, including on how to address the various dimensions of inequality. See, for example, Elborg-Woytek et al. (2013), Ostry et al. (2014), Banerji et al. (2014), Dabla-Norris et al. (2015), Jaumotte and Osorio Buitron (2015), Sahay et al. (2015), Gonzales et al. (2015), Decressin et al. (2015), Francese and Mulas-Granados (2015), Stotsky et al. (2016), and Ben Naceur and Shang (2016).

Independent Evaluation Office of the IMF (2014) IMF response to the financial and economic crisis. IMF Washington, DC. http://www.ieo-imf.org/ieo/pages/CompletedEvaluation227.aspx
International Monetary Fund (2002) Guidelines on conditionality. IMF, Washington, http://www.imf.org/external/np/pdr/cond/2002/eng/guid/092302.htm
International Monetary Fund (2012) 2011 review of conditionality. IMF, Washington, DC. http://www.imf.org/external/np/sec/pn/2012/pn12109.htm
International Monetary Fund (2013a) Jobs and growth – analytical and operational considerations for the fund. IMF, Washington, DC. http://www.imf.org/external/pp/longres.aspx?id=4750
International Monetary Fund (2013b) Guidance note on jobs and growth issues in surveillance and program work. IMF, Washington, DC. http://www.imf.org/external/pp/longres.aspx?id=4814
International Monetary Fund (2014a) Revised operational guidance to IMF staff on the 2002 conditionality guidelines. IMF Washington, DC. http://www.imf.org/external/pp/longres.aspx?id=4889
International Monetary Fund (2014b) Fiscal policy and inequality. IMF Washington, DC. http://www.imf.org/external/pp/longres.aspx?id=4849
International Monetary Fund (2015a) In: Clements B, de Mooij R, Gupta S, Keen M (eds) Inequality and fiscal policy. IMF, Washington, DC. http://www.elibrary.imf.org/view/IMF071/22448-9781513531625/22448-9781513531625/22448978151353l625.xml
International Monetary Fund (2015b) Crisis program review, Washington, DC. http://www.imf.org/external/pp/longres.aspx?id=5010
International Monetary Fund (2015c) Fiscal policy and long term growth. IMF, Washington, DC. http://www.imf.org/external/pp/longres.aspx?id=4964
International Monetary Fund (2016) Articles of agreement of the International Monetary Fund – 2016 Edition, Washington, DC. http://www.imf.org/external/pubs/ft/aa/
Jaumotte F, Osorio Buitron C (2015) Inequality and labor market institutions. IMF Staff Discussion Note SDN/15/14, Washington, DC
Ostry J, Berg A, Tsangarides CG (2014) Redistribution, inequality, and growth. IMF Staff Discussion Note SDN/14/02, Washington, DC
Sahay R, Čihák M, N'Diaye P, Barajas A, Mitra S, Kyobe A, Nian Mooi Y, Reza Yousefi S (2015) Financial inclusion: can it meet multiple macroeconomic goals. IMF Staff Discussion Note SDN/15/17, Washington, DC
Stotsky JG, Shibuya S, Kolovich L, Kebhaj S (2016) Trends in gender equality and women's advancement. IMF Working Paper WP/16/21, Washington, DC

The Human Rights Effects of Participation in Program Lending Versus the CESCR

M. Rodwan Abouharb and David L. Cingranelli

Abstract This is the first study to compare the competing effects of state participation in two international governmental regimes on government respect for human rights. Specifically, we compare the effects of participation in the international financial regime with participation in the international human rights regime on changes in government respect for economic and social rights in developing countries between 1981 and 2004. A longer period under World Bank or IMF program lending was found to be associated with lower life expectancy, a lower adult literacy rate, and a higher infant mortality rate. A longer period of participation in the International Covenant on Economic and Social Human Rights only was associated with an improved adult literacy rate. The use of a two-stage model ruled out the possibility that economic and social rights practices of governments would have changed in these ways even if governments had not participated or had participated only briefly in either regime.

Contents

M.R. Abouharb (✉)
Department of Political Science, University College London, London, UK
e-mail: m.abouharb@ucl.ac.uk

D.L. Cingranelli
Department of Political Science, Binghamton University, Binghamton, NY, USA
e-mail: davidc@binghamton.edu

E. Sciso (ed.), *Accountability, Transparency and Democracy in the Functioning of Bretton Woods Institutions*, DOI 10.1007/978-3-319-57855-2_12

Governments that choose to sign and ratify international human rights treaties and conventions are expected to change their domestic laws and policies to conform to treaty provisions. Changes in laws and policies, in turn, are expected to lead to improvements in their human rights practices.[1] These treaties and conventions and the United Nations committees that implement them constitute the international human rights regime. However, participation in many other international regimes may simultaneously affect the human rights practices of governments as well. Previous research on the human rights effects of structural adjustment programs (SAPs) found that program lending in less developed countries had worsened a variety of government human rights practices.[2] Here we compare the effects of participation in the human rights regime with participation in the international finance regime on government respect for economic and social human rights. This is the first large scale, selection-corrected research project exploring the economic and social rights impacts of participation in the human rights or international financial regimes.

The main purpose of this research project is to explore further the role of international governmental organizations (IGOs) and participation in the regimes they create as influence agents affecting the human rights practices of governments. While human rights scholars have begun to pay attention to the effects of international regimes to explain why some governments respect the human rights of their citizens while others do not, they have focused most of their attention on the effects of the human rights regime. This focus is understandable and justified as a first step, because the international community created that regime for the express purpose of ensuring government compliance with human rights norms as codified in UN conventions and treaties. Besides ensuring compliance, the human rights regime is designed to develop new human rights norms and to encourage acceptance of existing norms by states that have not joined. Scholars have paid less attention to the human rights effects of other international regimes such as the international finance regime. The international finance regime is the set of explicit or implicit principles, norms, rules, and decision making procedures prescribed by the International Monetary Fund (IMF) and the World Bank as conditions for the governments of developing countries who wish to receive World Bank and IMF loans. These conditions are contained in SAPs negotiated by the IMF or World Bank with the governments of loan recipient countries.

Another goal of this research project is to contribute to a theory that will explain why participation in some regimes has had a relatively strong influence on the behaviors of participating states, while participation in other regimes has had little effect. We argue that the international finance regime has three main advantages relative to the human rights regime as an influence agent. First the international finance regime has the ability to manipulate material sanctions and rewards whereas

[1]Hathaway (2002), Hafner-Burton (2005), Keith (1999), Landman (2005), and Neumayer (2005).

[2]Abouharb and Cingranelli (2006, 2007), Franklin (1997), Keith and Poe (2000), and Pion-Berlin (1984).

the human rights regime relies upon the much weaker mechanism of naming and shaming. Second, the norms of the international financial regime are endorsed strongly by the United States, arguably the most influential state in the international system, whereas the US government has not endorsed the affirmation of economic and social rights by the international human rights regime. Finally, the norms of the international financial regime are endorsed by the World Trade organization another regime with the ability to manipulate material rewards and sanctions. The only obvious potential advantage of the human rights regime as an influence agent is that its explicit mission is to change the human rights practices of participants.

We focus this research on government respect for economic and social rights, because several other international organizations besides the United Nations have poverty reduction goals, and poverty reduction is closely related to improvement in economic and social rights.[3] Since several international governmental regimes have missions related to poverty reduction, the linkages between compliance with the norms of other non-human rights international regimes and social and economic rights should lead to similar outcomes. Since the 1980s, the directors of the International Financial Institutions (IFIs) have promoted a shift in power from the state to the market.[4] The IFIs have promoted a variety of programs in developing and transition countries to achieve that goal. The commonality among these programs is the conditionality used to call upon recipient governments to liberalize and privatize economies in the context of strict budget discipline.[5] We collectively refer to these different arrangements as SAPs or program lending. Such measures were intended to jump start economic growth and free up resources for debt service. However, in most countries, public investment in critical areas (health care, education, and infrastructure) declined, growth rates were disappointing and debts mounted to unsustainable levels.[6] Many scholars have argued that worsened respect for economic and social human rights in some developing countries are, in part, the direct consequence of participation in Structural Adjustment Programs.[7]

---

[3]However, poverty reduction could be defined as improving the rate of growth of GDP per capita, whereas respect for economic and social rights implies benefits for the worst off in society or what some scholars refer to as equitable economic development (Abouharb and Cingranelli 2007).

[4]The IMF has four main types of agreements that involve policy conditions including The Stand-By Arrangement (SBA), the Extended Fund Facility (EFF), the Structural Adjustment Facility (SAF), and the Enhanced Structural Adjustment Facility (ESAF) (Vreeland 2003, p. 10). The ESAF was renamed to the Poverty Reduction and Growth Facility (PRGF) in 1999. The World Bank has used structural adjustment programs since 1980. In 1999 World Bank SAPs we renamed poverty reduction strategy programs (PRSP). See Blackmon (2008) for a good review of the differences in emphasis of the PRSPs compared to SAPs.

[5]Previous research has argued that the numbers and types of conditions associated with programs vary for a variety of political reasons (Dreher and Jensen 2007; Stone 2004), but all negotiated conditions in SAPs are consistent with the goal of shifting power from the state to the market.

[6]Pettifor (2001).

[7]Abouharb and Cingranelli (2007), Buchmann (1996), Chipeta (1993), Grusky (2001), Handa and King (1997), Lloyd and Weissman (2001), Munck (1994), Raja (2002), Sadasivam (1997), Sowa (1993), and Zack-Williams (2000).

This project incorporates several methodological refinements over most previous research on the human rights effects of participation in international regimes. Most important, the results we present are corrected for the effects of selection. Controlling for selection is necessary when evaluating the human rights impacts of any international regime, because it is possible that the governments choosing to participate were intrinsically different cases from those governments that chose not to participate at all or participated only briefly. Thus, in the case of program lending, poor human rights and economic outcomes might have occurred whether or not they were under SAPs. In the case of the International Covenant on Economic, Social, and Cultural Rights (ICESCR), perhaps only countries already having good records of economic and social rights performance joined the regime or joined early. Poor performers joined late or not at all. We needed to determine the counter-factual—namely, what would have happened in developing countries if they had never participated in program lending or if they had never ratified the International Covenant on Economic, Social and Cultural Rights.

The results of this study are consistent with the results of previous work on the human rights effects of participation in SAPs and in various human rights regimes. We found substantial evidence of negative impacts of program lending on government respect for human rights—in this case for economic and social rights—and no evidence of positive impacts.[8] The more years a developing country government spent under SAPs between 1981 and 2004, the lower was its score on the Physical Quality of Life Index (PQLI), the lower its literacy rate, and the higher its infant mortality rate. We found positive effects for participation in ICESCR on only one component of the PQLI index. The longer it had been since ratification of the ICESCR, the higher a country's literacy rate, but all other relationships with measures of economic and social rights achievement were statistically insignificant. Our model predictions indicated that the negative effects of SAPs on a country's literacy rate outweighed the positive effects of the International Covenant on Economic, Social and Cultural Rights.

1 What Are Economic and Social Rights?

Despite the recognition of economic and social rights in international human rights law, until recently international non-governmental human rights organizations such as Amnesty International and Human Rights Watch focused their reports and activities almost exclusively on identifying and remedying government violations of civil and political rights. Now there is a move towards an integrated human rights approach that reflects a belief in the complementarity, universality and indivisibility of all rights. The term economic and social rights refers to internationally

[8]But see Abouharb and Cingranelli's (2007) findings regarding the positive effects of SAPs on respect for civil rights and political liberties.

recognized human rights to a government that makes efforts to provide a minimal standard of living for its citizens. These rights were first recognized in the most basic of all international agreements, the United Nations Universal Declaration of Human Rights (UDHR), approved by the General Assembly in 1948. The UDHR recognizes the rights to an existence worthy of human dignity (Article 23), to a standard of living adequate to maintain health and well-being, to food, clothing, housing and medical care, to necessary social services (Article 25), to free elementary education, and to higher education on the basis of merit (Article 26). Similarly, the subsequent International Covenant on Economic, Social and Cultural Rights recognizes the right to a decent standard of living, to adequate food, clothing and housing, to continuous improvement of living conditions (Article 11), to medical care (Article 12), and to education (Articles 13 and 14).[9]

According to Article 2(1) of the ICESCR, each state party is obligated to take steps, ... to the maximum of its available resources, with a view to achieving progressively the full realization of the rights recognized ... including particularly the adoption of legislative measures. Thus, the international recognition of basic economic and social human rights does not guarantee every human being the full enjoyment of those rights no matter where he or she lives. However, Article 2 (1) does legally obligate all states parties to the ICESR to do the best they can, within their resource constraints, to satisfy those rights for their people. Clearly, there is great variance in the degree of efforts different governments are making towards these ends.

2 International Governmental Regimes Characteristics and Respect for Human Rights

While most human rights research has focused on state characteristics, or in the case of interstate war, on the relationships between states,[10] there has been more attention in recent years to the role of transnational processes such as the giving of foreign aid, trade, arms sales, foreign direct investment, and the activities of non-governmental organizations.[11] There also is increased attention to the effectiveness of transnational actors such as the theory of transnational human rights advocacy networks which predicts that international human rights regimes can

[9]The International Covenant of Economic, Social and Cultural Rights was concluded in 1966. Its purpose is to make legally binding the rights listed in the UDHR, as the UDHR is a non-binding resolution.

[10]See Poe (2004) for a review of the findings of global, comparative studies of human rights practices.

[11]Barratt (2007), Blanton (2000, 2005), Hafner-Burton (2005), Richards et al. (2001), and Welch (1995).

improve actual performance where such networks are strong[12] and international governmental regimes such as those that have been formed to regulate international trade, the availability of capital for development, labor standards, and human rights practices.[13]

Whether international regimes also affect the human rights practices of participants is an empirical question. A regime as defined by Young[14] is a set of rights and rules, decision-making procedures or programs that give rise to social practices, assign roles to the participants in these practices, and govern their interactions. Regimes structure the opportunities of actors interested in a given activity and they contain the expectation of compliance by their members.[15] Similarly, a regime is defined by Krasner as a set of explicit or implicit principles, norms, rules, and decision making procedures around which actor expectations converge in a given issue-area.[16]

Realists and liberal theorists disagree about the role of international regimes in changing the behavior of regime participants. Realists generally argue that regimes do not exert independent effects on state behavior. Instead, powerful states create regimes to serve their security and economic interests. Thus, regimes have no independent power over states, particularly great powers. They are simply intervening variables between the real independent variable (power) and the observed outcome (cooperation). According to this view, the post-Second World War international organizations such as the United Nations, World Bank and IMF are simply instruments of American grand strategy.[17] In contrast, liberals view regimes as independent actors in the international system. Participation in them increases the probability of cooperation by providing information about the behavior of others, monitoring the behavior of members, and reporting on compliance.[18] One goal of liberal regime theory should be to identify the attributes of regimes that are associated with greater or lesser impact on the behavior of participating states. Previous research on this point suggests several interesting hypotheses.[19] Four differences among the two regimes we examine deserve special attention: the degree of support they receive from powerful governments in the world, their relative ability to enforce compliance with their norms and rules; the degree to which their prescriptions are reinforced by other regimes, and whether changing the human rights practices of states is the avowed purpose of the regime.

[12]Keck and Sikkink (1998), Risse et al. (1999), and Ron et al. (2005).

[13]Abouharb and Cingranelli (2007), Hathaway (2002), Hafner-Burton (2005), Keith (1999), Landman (2005), and Neumayer (2005).

[14]Young (1992).

[15]Young (1980), pp. 333–342.

[16]Krasner (1983), p. 4.

[17]Strange (1988).

[18]Cortell and Davis, Jr. (1996), Keohane (1984), Keohane and Martin (1995), and Koremenos et al. (2001).

[19]Keith (1999), Legro (1997), Shannon (2000), Hathaway (2002), and Ratner (2004).

The powerful governments of the North, including the United States, are strong supporters of the international finance regime. Those governments along with the private international banks have assigned the IMF and the World Bank the responsibility for establishing the system of rules and decision-making procedures that determine which developing countries receive capital and under what conditions. When the IMF and World Bank declare that a government's economic reform program is off track, governments and banks usually withhold most financing from the government.[20] To emphasize the leadership role played by the US government, many observers have referred to the norms and principles of the international finance regime as representing the Washington consensus.[21] In contrast, the US government is not a strong supporter of the human rights regime. The record of the US government, as indicated by the willingness of its government to sign and ratify major international human rights agreements, is the weakest of any wealthy democratic state. This difference in regime support by the strongest state in the international system leads us to expect that the finance regime would exert a stronger influence on its participants than would the human rights regime.

Another important difference is that the finance regime has stronger mechanisms for encouraging compliance with regime norms and for punishing defections. The Bank and the Fund encourage compliance through their technical assistance programs, through rating the performance of governments according to the criteria in the Country Policy and Institutional Assessment and, more particularly, through the withdrawal of financing for governments that do not comply with their financing agreements. In contrast, governments that have ratified the ICESCR only have to file periodic reports to the UN documenting their degree of compliance with the provisions of the Covenant to the UN Committee on Economic, Social and Cultural Rights. Those governments that have not ratified the Covenant do not have to file any reports, and, other than naming and shaming, the UN Committee has no mechanisms at its disposal to punish defectors.[22] This difference in enforcement capability also leads us to expect that the finance regime would exert a stronger influence on its participants than would the human rights regime.

Regimes also vary in the degree to which other regimes support their norms, principles and rules and whether supporting regimes have strong or weak enforcement mechanisms. One could argue that other international regimes such as the international labor regime develop and enforce norms that reinforce those of the ICESCR, but none of those supporting regimes have strong enforcement mechanisms. However, the finance regime is supported by the norms required to participate in the world trade regime. The rules of the trade regime are developed by the World Trade Organization (WTO) with the enthusiastic support of the US government. The WTO has established adjudicatory procedures to handle cases of alleged noncompliance, and significant penalties, including the authorization of trade

20 Alexander (2006b).

21 E.g., Stiglitz (2002).

22 Hafner-Burton (2008).

boycotts, can result. Thus, the WTO has strong enforcement tools and some argue that participation in the WTO undermines respect for human rights.[23] This strong support from another regime with enthusiastic US participation and strong enforcement mechanisms also led us to expect that the finance regime would exert a stronger influence on its participants than would the human rights regime.

Finally, it is important to note that the avowed purpose of the human rights regime is to exert a positive influence on the human rights practices of all governments of the world, while, until recently, the World Bank did not acknowledge any responsibility for the promotion of human rights. By many accounts, the IMF still has not acknowledged its human rights responsibilities.[24] Some regimes openly acknowledge their efforts to change the behavior of states in a particular way, while other regimes potentially affecting the same behavior do not. It is likely that the effects of regimes on the behaviors of target states extend far beyond stated regime goals. Through what may be called mission creep, the roles of various international regimes overlap. In effect, human rights-related decisions made by the World Bank, the IMF, NATO, the EU, or the ILO become part of the larger international human rights regime as it operates on the government of any developing country.

3 The Negative Human Rights Effects of the International Finance Regime

So far, our discussion has focused on the expected magnitudes of effects exerted by different regimes. Now we turn our attention to explaining why participation in the program lending supervised by the IMF or World Bank would be expected to have negative effects on government respect for economic and social rights. Program lending by the IMF and World Bank typically caused governments to cut social programs to balance their budgets and pay the interest on existing loans. The lives of the poorest people often were affected in negative ways as social programs were cut.[25] Furthermore, SAPs are designed to weaken the role of the state and strengthen the role of the market in societies. A shift in power from the state to the market may cause worsened protection of economic and social human rights by governments, because a strong state and substantial government intervention in the market is essential for the protection of all human rights and especially economic and social rights.[26] The protection of economic and social rights, for example, requires government expenditures for health care, housing, education, and income support of the poor. As other examples, the protection of worker rights in general

[23] Aaronson (2007).

[24] Abouharb and Cingranelli (2007).

[25] Abouharb and Cingranelli (2007).

[26] Donnelly (2003).

and women's economic rights, in particular, requires that government actively regulate the relationship between workers and employers.[27]

However, previous research has demonstrated that many governments do not fully implement the provisions of their SAPs.[28] Even if the liberalization and privatization provisions of programs are not fully implemented, SAPs can cause greater government repression of their citizens by reducing the need for governments to raise revenue through taxes on their populations. The revenue argument begins with the contrast between governments that depend, largely or entirely, for revenue on *earned income* in the form of broad taxation and those that depend on *unearned income* from oil, gas and mineral exports, foreign grants or foreign loans.[29] In economies that are based on earned income and are less dependent on loans from international financial institutions, elites rely upon levying taxes across a broad base of their citizenry. In return citizens demand efficient and responsive government. This bargain establishes a legitimate political relationship between rulers and subjects. In states where the government depends on unearned income, elites are financially independent of citizen-taxpayers. This changes the political incentives that they face, and the ways they seek, use and retain power. The mutually beneficial relationship between rulers and subjects may not develop or, if developed already, may break down. More insidiously, those leaders who benefit from unearned income may perceive an effective and watchful civil service and civil society as a threat to the benefits they enjoy,[30] and they may take steps to thwart them. As a result, the economic and social needs of common citizens may be poorly served by their rulers.

There is a large body of mostly case study and small-n research suggesting that the balanced budget measures, economic deregulation, and privatization of public services promoted by SAPs all led to reduced social protections for the poor. There is research demonstrating that SAPs were used by loan recipient governments to justify cutting government spending for social programs.[31] Some studies have documented the disproportionate negative economic human rights consequences for women,[32] and for public sector employees and low-wage workers.[33] The poor and those in the public sector have seen their wages fall in real terms,[34] while at the same time they have faced increased living costs due to the removal of price controls and subsidies for essential commodities.[35] The implementation of SAPs

---

[27]SAPRIN (2004).

[28]E.g., Dollar and Svensson (2000), Killick (1996), and van de Walle (2001).

[29]Moore (1998, 2007).

[30]Alexander (2006a).

[31]Chipeta (1993), Fields (2003), Handa and King (1997), Sowa (1993), Meyer (1998), World Bank (1992), and Zack-Williams (2000).

[32]Buchmann (1996), Commonwealth Secretariat (1989), Elson (1990), and Sadasivam (1997).

[33]Daddieh (1995) and SAPRIN (2004).

[34]Daddieh (1995), Munck (1994), SAPRIN (2004), and Vreeland (2003).

[35]Zack-Williams (2000).

also has worsened the relative position of the poorest by increasing income inequality.[36] Moreover, efforts by developing countries to make their economies more business friendly have resulted in the adoption of policies hostile to worker rights.[37]

Examples illustrating how the common provisions in SAPs often lead to worsened respect for economic and social rights are numerous and compelling. Privatization of the provision of potable water is a particularly interesting case in point. Besides reducing the size of the state, it helps loan recipients balance their budgets, end subsidies, and is a step towards deregulation of the economy. Health professionals agree on the link between access to safe and affordable water and public health. According to one estimate, over two million children die each year of diarrhea, a disease related to the lack of access to clean water.[38] More than one billion people lack access to clean drinking water and approximately 2.5 billion have no sanitary means for disposing of human waste (Grusky 2001). Despite this knowledge and these conditions, in the 1990s, the World Bank and IMF adopted a policy of water privatization and full-cost water pricing. The concern expressed by the Bank and Fund was that the world is running out of fresh water sources at an alarming rate and that conflict over what remains is inevitable. Also, the Bank argued, governments of poor countries, which often subsidized the cost of providing potable water to their populations, had failed to deliver water to their populations efficiently.[39] Based on this logic, water privatization became a fairly common provision in SAPs negotiated by both the IMF and the Bank. A review of 40 randomly selected IMF loan agreements reached in 2000 revealed that the IMF included provisions for water privatization in 12 of them—Angola, Benin, Guinea Bissau, Honduras, Nicaragua, Niger, Panama, Rwanda, Sao Tome and Principe, Senegal, Tanzania, and Yemen.[40] The consequences for public health were usually disastrous. In most cases, water users were almost immediately hit with rate hikes of 100% or more. Those who were unable to pay higher prices turned to less safe sources of drinking water with serious negative public health consequences.

The privatization initiatives of the World Bank and IMF are reinforced by the rules of the World Trade Organization, another powerful international regime. Recently, in response to criticism concerning the takeover of water services by transnational corporations in some countries, the World Bank has encouraged public-private partnerships for water provision as a way to balance the efficiency norms of the finance regime while helping developing countries to better realize the human right to health. However, according to critics, the World Bank and IMF continue to contribute to governmental failure in the provision of potable water, because they have insisted that most cross-subsidies be stopped between profitable

[36]Daddieh (1995), Friedman (2000), and Handa and King (1997).

[37]Abouharb and Cingranelli (2007) and SAPRIN (2004).

[38]Grusky (2001).

[39]Alexander (2005).

[40]Grusky (2001).

sectors—telecommunications and electricity—and the unprofitable water sector. Cross-subsidies are illegal under World Trade Organization rules.[41]

There have been relatively few global, comparative studies of the human rights effects of participation in the finance regime. In general, the results of those studies have corroborated the conclusions of the case study literature concerning the negative effects of participation in the regime on government human rights practices of most types. Specifically, previous research of this type has found that governments undergoing structural adjustment for the longest periods of time have murdered, tortured, politically imprisoned, and disappeared, more of their citizens.[42] In addition, exposure to program lending has caused governments to allow more abuse of internationally recognized worker rights.[43]

Previous work has indicated that international financial institutions have preferences for entering into agreements with particular kinds of countries.[44] These selection biases should be accounted for when estimating the human rights effects of SAPs. Governments in economic difficulty tend to enter into structural adjustment programs.[45] Typically these economic difficulties manifest themselves in a number of ways. Countries that are poor, have over valued exchange rates, low levels of foreign currency reserves and little international trade are more likely to go under structural adjustment programs. A variety of political factors also affect the likelihood that countries will participate in program lending. Countries having military alliances with the United States or receiving relatively large amounts of US foreign aid are more likely to participate in program lending.[46] Likewise countries having a dependent relationship with other key backers of these IFIs—the UK, France, and Japan—were more likely to negotiate SAPs.[47] Considerable work has found that democracies are at a disadvantage in negotiating SAPs with these IFIs.[48] The end of the Cold War increased competition for limited IFI monies reducing the likelihood of SAP receipt.[49] Finally, domestic sovereignty arguments indicate that as the number of countries under an SAP in a particular year increases the perceived domestic sovereignty costs a government faces of going under IFI

[41]Alexander (2005).

[42]Abouharb and Cingranelli (2006, 2007, 2009), Franklin (1997), and Keith and Poe (2000).

[43]Abouharb and Cingranelli (2007) and Vreeland (2002, 2003).

[44]Abouharb and Cingranelli (2004a, 2005, 2006, 2007, 2009), Forsythe (1987), Joyce (1992), Przeworski and Vreeland (2000), Steinward and Stone (2008), Thacker (1999), Van De Laar (1980), and Vreeland (2003).

[45]Abouharb and Cingranelli (2004, 2005, 2006, 2007), Joyce (1992), Przeworski and Vreeland (2000), Steinward and Stone (2008), Stone (2004), Thacker (1999), and Vreeland (2003).

[46]Forsythe (1987) and Stone (2002).

[47]Frey and Schneider (1986).

[48]Pion-Berlin (1984), Przeworski and Vreeland (2000), Putnam (1988), and Vreeland (2003).

[49]Abouharb and Cingranelli (2004, 2005, 2006, 2007) and Williams (1994).

financial constraints declines, making it easier for additional governments to enter into these programs.[50]

4 Participation in the Human Rights Regime and Respect for Human Rights

In this section we review the logical arguments and empirical evidence linking participation in the ICESR to improved government respect for economic and social rights. The decision to participate in the human rights regime begins with a government signing a human rights covenant or treaty—in this case the ICESR—signifying the willingness of the executive branch to comply with its provisions. In many governments, full participation in the regime requires a two-step process. The second step is ratification, requiring the consent of the members of another government institution—usually the legislature. In the United States, for example, President Carter signed the ICESCR, but the Senate never ratified it. Thus, the United States is a signatory to the ICESCR, but is not bound to follow its provisions. Once the agreement is signed and ratified, there is a process supervised by the United Nations designed to promote compliance by the participating country. Full compliance exists when provisions in the constitution and statutory laws of the participating government are consistent with the provisions of the ICESCR and the behavior of government officials is consistent with its own constitution and statutes.

As noted, the provisions of the ICESCR obligate the ratifying government to make efforts to satisfy its citizen's economic and social claims affirmed in the Covenant's provisions. The state must develop institutions and procedures, must plan, and must mobilize resources as necessary to meet those claims. To comply with the ICESCR, governments must adjust taxing and spending plans and establish a network of agencies for social welfare. They must also provide some system of remedies to which individuals may resort to obtain the benefits to which they are entitled or be compensated for their loss.[51] Governments have considerable discretion in choosing how to achieve the objectives outlined in the ICESR, but government efforts should result in the progressive realization of good economic and social outcomes outlined in the Covenant such as higher literacy rates, longer life expectancy, and lower infant mortality rates.

The principal mechanism of supervision outlined in the ICESCR is a requirement that each ratifying party to the Covenant report periodically to a UN committee on its compliance with ICESCR provisions. The procedure involves the state party to the covenant providing a report on its progress towards meeting the economic and social rights of its citizens. The members of the relevant UN Committee may ask questions about the report. Representatives of the state party

[50] Vreeland (2003).

[51] Henkin et al. (1999).

are encouraged to attend Committee meetings and respond to questions. The state party representative may prefer to reflect, gather information, and then respond to some questions at a later time.[52] The Committee issues a preliminary report privately to the state party. The representative of the state party may respond. The Committee then issues a public final report including its principal concerns and recommendations. A negative report is the only sanction the regime can assess. A positive report is the only reward the regime has at its disposal. This method of insuring compliance to regime norms has been called naming and shaming.[53] It is a popular strategy to enforce international human rights norms. There is a debate over whether this weak mechanism for ensuring compliance has any positive effects on states parties such as faster progressive realization of the protection of their citizen's economic and social rights. Some research shows that governments put in the spotlight by being shamed do not subsequently improve their human rights practices.[54]

A number of multivariate studies have been conducted to determine whether participation in the human rights regime, itself, has led to later improvements in the human rights practices regulated by the regime's norms.[55] No previous study has estimated the economic and social human rights impacts of participation in the International Covenant on Economic, Social and Cultural Rights. However, concerning other human rights instruments, all previous studies have hypothesized that ratification would be associated with improvements in human rights practices. Those previous studies have controlled for alternative explanations of human rights performance and have discovered statistically insignificant or weak positive relationships with human rights outcomes. While international human rights treaties have been ratified by many nation-states, including those ruled by repressive governments, evidence from these studies suggests that participation in a human rights regime is most effective in improving human rights practices in stable or consolidating democracies or in states with strong civil society activism. Thus, treaty participation makes little difference in those states most in need of reform.[56]

Most studies have used a dichotomous measure of participation, assigning a government a score of 'one' if it had ratified the convention and a 'zero' if it had not.[57] Hafner-Burton and Tsutsui[58] measured participation as the number of years since ratification for each country in each year, suggesting that ratification had a cumulative effect over time, a measurement procedure we use in this research

[52]Ibid, pp. 515–519.

[53]Hafner-Burton (2008).

[54]Ibid.

[55]E.g., Hafner-Burton and Tsutsui (2005), Hathaway (2002), Keith (1999), Landman (2005), and Neumayer (2005).

[56]Hafner-Burton and Tsutsui (2005), Hathaway (2002), Keith (1999), Landman (2005), and Neumayer (2005).

[57]Hathaway (2002), Keith (1999), and Neumayer (2005).

[58]Hafner-Burton and Tsutsui (2005).

project as well. Landman[59] created a nine-point participation scale ranging from a score of zero if a country's UN representative had not even signed the agreement to eight if the government had ratified with no reservations. Governments that had ratified, but with reservations were coded between three and seven depending on the severity of the reservations recorded. Landman also controlled for the effects of selection when estimating the human rights impact of treaty ratification. Therefore, he has presented some evidence to counter the idea that some of the same factors that caused governments to participate in a human rights regime also caused them to improve or decline in human rights performance. We follow Landman's selection corrected examples in developing our estimate of the human rights effects of participation in the International Covenant on Economic, Social and Cultural Rights.

There is a continuing line of research exploring the question of why governments are willing to sign human rights agreements, and, therefore cede some of their sovereignty. Many governments ratify human rights instruments even though they have poor records of protection of the rights affirmed in the instrument. In fact, governments with poor human rights records ratify human rights agreements at rates similar to states with better levels of human rights protection.[60] The emerging consensus among scholars is that joining the international human rights regime creates opportunities for rights-violating governments to display legitimating commitments to world norms, leading them to ratify human rights treaties without the capacity or willingness to comply with the provisions.[61] Authoritarian governments are less constrained by domestic forces to follow through on their treaty commitments. Thus, they are more likely to ratify human rights treaties as a symbolic commitment.

Only Landman[62] (2005) has estimated a model explaining the decision by governments to join the ICESCR, and even he did not estimate the human rights impacts of participation in the ICESCR. He hypothesized that countries would be more likely to participate in the ICESCR if they were democratic, were wealthy, had joined a relatively large number of other IGOs, and had greater numbers of International Non-governmental Organizations (INGOs) present in their county. He expected that governments that were involved in domestic or international conflict would be less likely to ratify the ICESCR.[63] He found that democracies were more likely to ratify the ICESCR, while wealthy countries were less likely to ratify the covenant.[64] Landman explained that he did not estimate the human rights impacts

[59]Landman (2005).

[60]Hafner-Burton (2008), Hathaway (2008), and Vreeland (2008).

[61]Hathaway (2008), Hafner-Burton et al. (2008), and Vreeland (2008).

[62]Landman (2005).

[63]Landman (2005), pp. 28–31.

[64]Landman (2005), p. 80. Landman also included some regional controls which he did not have a hypothesized expectation about. The regional controls indicated that the East Asian and Pacific region, and the South Asian regions had lower levels of ICESCR ratification.

of participation in the ICESCR, mainly because of difficulties in measuring government economic, social and cultural human rights outcomes.[65]

5 Measuring Government Respect for Economic and Social Rights

Landman's concern was understandable, because there are no generally accepted measures of economic and social rights outcomes. The most widely used measure of the degree to which government policy results in satisfying basic human needs and rights to unpolluted air, water, food, education clothing, shelter, and healthcare guaranteed in the ICESCR is the Physical Quality of Life Index (PQLI).[66] In this research we use the PQLI index and its components as our measures of economic and social rights outcomes. Morris[67] developed the PQLI under the auspices of the Overseas Development Council. It is a composite of three indicators: infant mortality per thousand live births, life expectancy at age one, and the adult literacy rate. The ranges for the first two indicators are transformed to a zero to 100 scale, and then the index is computed by taking the unweighted arithmetic mean of all three indicators. The PQLI is a reasonable measure of the past attainment of the human rights to education and health. It is a better measure than, for example, the percentage of the population who live on less than the equivalent of one US dollar per day. Though societies with more total wealth as indicated by their GDP per capita, on average, also have higher PQLI scores, some societies use their wealth more effectively to provide the general population with better health, adequate shelter, and a longer life.[68]

The most common criticism of the PQLI is that there is no theoretical basis for assigning equal weights to the three components.[69] While this is true, Morris notes that there is no good theoretical basis for weighting the three components differently either, so equal weights are appropriate. Some scholars have analyzed each component separately to deal with this criticism,[70] a practice we follow in this research project. The Human Development Index developed by the United Nations Development Program is a well known alternative measure. It includes

[65]Landman (2005), p. 49.
[66]Milner and Callaway (2007).
[67]Morris (1979).
[68]Morris (1979) and Sen (1999).
[69]Bayless and Bayless (1982), Goldstein (1985), and Hicks and Streeten (1979).
[70]Milner et al. (2004).

two components of the PQLI, life expectancy at age one and adult literacy rate. It does not include the infant mortality rate, and it adds the combined gross enrolment ratio for primary, secondary and tertiary schools and GDP per capita. Thus, this measure indicates both the total wealth available in a society (as indicated by GDP per capita) and how it is used to help the poor.[71] We prefer the PQLI as a measure, because it does not include GDP per capita as part of the measure.

6 Hypotheses

Previous research provides the foundation for three hypotheses:

The longer a government's participation in structural adjustment program lending, the worse its respect for economic and social rights.

The longer a government's participation in the International Covenant on Economic, Social and Cultural Rights, the greater its level of respect for economic and social rights.

The negative impact of the participation in structural adjustment program lending on government respect for economic and social rights will be greater than the positive impact of participation in the International Covenant on Economic, Social and Cultural Rights.

A number of factors have been found in previous research to affect government respect for the economic and social rights of their citizens. It is also important to control for these factors, when trying to assess the impact of the ICESCR and Structural Adjustment Programs. The most widely reported findings in previous research is that the greater aggregate wealth of a country (as measured by its GNP or GDP per capita or the log of GDP per capita) and the more democratic a country, the greater the level of protection of economic and social rights of citizens as measured by the PQLI.[72] There is also some evidence that countries with higher PQLI scores have a higher population density and have had a British colonial experience.[73] The consequences of a British colonial past were to generate bureaucracies and civil servants that could more efficiently and effectively respond to the wishes of the government and the needs of the population as a whole. Surprisingly, previous research has found no relationship between whether a country is experiencing civil conflict or whether it is engaged in international war and its

[71] United Nations Development Program (2004).

[72] Callaway and Harrelson-Stephens (2004), Milner (2000), Moon (1991), Moon and Dixon (1985), Morris (1979), Park (1987), Milner et al. (2004), and Rosh (1986).

[73] Milner et al. (2004).

PQLI score (Milner et al. 2004). However, we include conflict measures as control variables in our analysis, because research has shown that domestic and international conflict tends to be associated with less respect for other types of human rights (Poe and Tate 1994; Poe et al. 1999), and evidence from many case studies suggests that conflict takes its toll on the social and economic conditions of the poor (Plumper and Neumayer 2006). Some studies have shown more liberalized economies are associated with higher PQLI scores,[74] while others have found them to be associated with lower PQLI scores.[75]

7 Research Design

Sample, Time Period, and Method of Estimation: To test these hypotheses, we examined the 131 developing economies that existed as independent states throughout the 1981–2004 period. Our sample excludes the OECD countries, because they were not eligible to participate in SAPs. We conduct two types of statistical analyses. First we estimate the model using pooled time series cross-sectional analysis, where the unit of analysis is the country year. Then, as a test of robustness, we estimate the same model using a cross-sectional analysis for 2004. For the pooled cross-sectional analysis, we estimated a two-stage model to account for selection effects. At the first stage, we estimated the likelihood of entering into a SAP with either the World Bank or IMF and then separately estimated the likelihood of ratifying the ICESCR. In order to account for these underlying 'selection effects' when trying to estimate the impact of the international financial and human rights regime we generated inverse mills ratios from each model. These inverse mills ratios were included as independent variables in the second stage model estimating the effects of the international financial and human rights regime on government respect for economic and social rights. We labeled these inverse mills ratios 'World Bank & IMF Inverse Mills Ratio' and 'Covenant on Economic and Social Rights Inverse Mills Ratio.' Their inclusion accounts for the potential selection issues we described earlier. Since we are linking these two models with predicted values it means that our standard errors in the models estimating human rights violations are not efficient because they violate the maximum likelihood estimation assumption of fixed co-variates. We rectify this problem through the use of bootstrapped standard errors.[76] We use 1000 replications to generate our second stage findings.

---

[74]Callaway and Harrelson-Stephens (2004) and Milner (2000).

[75]Milner (2000) and Moon (1991).

[76]Mooney and Duval (1993).

The Regime Participation Measures: The two independent variables of chief theoretical interest are the measures of participation in the human rights and international finance regimes. Following Hafner-Burton and Tsutsui, we measured participation in the human rights regime as the number of years since ratification of the ICESCR. Following Abouharb and Cingranelli,[77] each country's participation in the international finance regime was measured as the number of years each country spent under a World Bank or IMF-supervised SAP between 1981 and 2004. Most of the previous research by economists and political scientists on the effects of structural adjustment has focused on the IMF and its impacts, neglecting the role of the World Bank in promoting structural adjustment. Yet both are important actors. Over the period examined in this study, 1981–2004, the World Bank entered into 442 structural adjustment agreements, while the IMF made 431. It is easy to underestimate the effects of structural adjustment if one only examines the human rights impacts of IMF agreements without including the impacts of World Bank agreements with the same countries.

The Dependent Variable: The dependent variable was the PQLI index and its components, which are our measures of government respect for the economic and social rights. We updated and expanded the coverage of existing measures of PQLI, which had previously ended in 1996, to 2004. We also sought to fill-in missing values where possible with new data sources. Any remaining missing cases were interpolated. The component indicators do not fluctuate widely from year to year, so the straight-line interpolation method was used to estimate the values for missing years.[78]

Specification of the first-stage selection models and second-stage human rights impact models: It is important to control for the selection effects of both the international financial and international human rights regime. The factors that previous research has found to be important determinants of entering into agreements with the World Bank and IMF and ratifying the ICESCR along with indicators and data sources are described in Table 1. The factors that previous research has found to be important determinants of government respect for economic and social rights are described in Table 2.

[77] Abouharb and Cingranelli (2007).

[78] We wish to thank Rhonda Callaway and Wesley Milner who provided their data sets containing the component indicators for the PQLI and the calculated PQLI scores from 1976 through 1996. We filled in figures for years where the scores for one or more indicators were widely spaced over time and updated their data set through 2004. The same original sources were used wherever possible.

Table 1 Operationalization of World Bank & IMF selection and covenant on economic & social rights selection equations

Dependent variables	Indicator	Source
Entering into a World Bank or IMF SAP	Dichotomous 1 If SAP Received; 0 If Not	Correspondence with World Bank & Vreeland (2003), updated
Ratifying Covenant on Economic and Social Rights	Dichotomous 1 If covenant ratified; 0 If Not	Constructed from UN Sources
Independent variables		
Economic		
Debt as a Proportion of GNP	Total Debt Service as a Percentage of GNP	World Bank: World Development Indicators (2006) CD-Rom (WDI)
GDP Per Capita Change	Percentage Change in GDP Per Capita Current U.S. $ Purchasing Power Parity (PPP)	World Bank: WDI
Foreign Currency Reserves	Average Government Foreign Reserves to reflect Monthly Imports	World Bank: WDI
Exchange Rate Value	Average Annual Official Exchange Rate Local Currency Unit per US $	World Bank: WDI
GDP Per Capita	GDP Per Capita Current U.S. $ (PPP)	World Bank: WDI
International Trade	Trade as a Percentage of GDP	World Bank: WDI
Political		
Alliance With the United States	Correlates of War (COW) Alliance Measure	COW Alliance Dataset v3.03 (Gibler and Sarkees 2004)
Number of IGOs Joined	Annual count of IGOs joined by country	Pevehouese et al. (2003) and Wallace and Singer (1970)
Democracy	Democracy-Autocracy Measure	POLITY IVd Dataset (Marshall and Jaggers 2006)
Population Size	Logged Midyear Country Population	U.S. Census: International Data Base (2005)
Cold War	Dichotomous, 0 before 1991; 1 if 1991 or Later	Banks et al. (2003)
Conflict Proneness		
Interstate Conflict	0-3 Ordinal scale of interstate conflict	Gleditsch et al. (2002) and Strand et al. (2005)
Rebellion	0-3 Ordinal Scale of Civil Conflict	Gleditsch et al. (2002) and Strand et al. (2005)
Human Rights		
Respect for Human Rights	Mokken Scale: Killing, Disappearances, Torture, Imprisonment	Cingranelli and Richards (CIRI) (2004)
Respect for Workers Rights	0 = Not protected by Govt. 1 = Somewhat protected Govt. 2 = Protected by Govt.	CIRI (2004)
Temporal Dependence		
Cubic Splines	Beck et al. (1998) BTSCS Method	

Source: Author's elaboration

Table 2 Operationalization of economic and social rights practices (second stage) equation variables

Dependent variable	Indicator	Source
Physical Quality of Life Index	Ranges 0 low PQLI to100 high PQLI: composite index ranges of infant mortality rate, life expectancy at age one, and the adult literacy rate	Callaway (2001). Updated with UN Population Data & World Bank: WDI
Independent variables		
Implementation of Structural Adjustment Agreement (SAP)	Running Count of years a country has been implementing SAPs	Correspondence with World Bank & Vreeland (2003), updated
Control variables		
Economic		
GDP Per Capita	GDP Per Capita Current U.S. $ (PPP)	World Bank: World Development Indicators CD-Rom (WDI)
Increase GDP Per Capita	Percentage Increase in GDP Per Capita Current U.S. $ (PPP)	World Bank: WDI
Political		
Democracy	Democracy-Autocracy Measure	POLITY IVd Dataset (Marshall and Jaggers 2006)
Military Regime	Type of Regime: Civilian or Military	Banks (2003)
Population Size	Logged Midyear Country Population	U.S. Census: International Data Base (USIDB) (2005)
Population Change	Percentage Change in yearly Population (Constructed)	USIDB (2005)
UK Dependent/ Colonial Experience	The decision rule of the most recent possessor is used to identify the relationships under examination	Issues COW Colonial History Dataset v0.1 (Hensel 1999)
Conflict Proneness		
Interstate Conflict	0 = No Interstate Conflict 1 = 1000 Battle Deaths or More	Gleditsch et al. (2002) and Strand et al. (2005)
Rebellion	Ordinal Level of Civil Conflict	Gleditsch et al. (2002) and Strand et al. (2005)
Temporal dependence		
Cubic Splines	Beck et al. (1998) BTSCS Method	

Source: Author's elaboration

8 Results[79]

Table 3 shows the probability of entering into a structural adjustment program with either the World Bank or IMF during the period 1981–2004. The directions of the relationships are, in every case, consistent with the previous literature about the factors affecting the probability of entering into SAPs with either the IMF or World Bank. We found that countries were more likely to enter into these programs when they had lower levels of GDP per capita, and lower levels of foreign currency reserves, statistically significant at the .10 level of confidence. A number of political factors also affected the likelihood of entering into these programs. Larger countries, indicated here by the size of the population, governments with dependent or colonial relationships with the United States, and democratic countries were more

Table 3 Logit equation: which governments enter into structural adjustment programs 1981–2004, all developing countries[a]

Entering into a World Bank or IMF structural adjustment program	Coefficient	Robust standard error
Economic Factors		
GDP Per Capita	−.00004^	.00003
Exchange Rate Value	5.65e−06	.00004
Average Foreign Currency Reserves	−.043^	.028
Extent of International Trade	−.002	.002
International Political Factors		
Log of Population	.117*	.058
Cold War	.32**	.13
USA Dependent/Colonial Relationship	.47**	.178
UK Dependent/Colonial Relationship	−.224	.176
French Dependent/Colonial Relationship	.183	.152
Japanese Dependent/Colonial Relationship	.146	.21
Domestic Political Factors		
Level of Democracy	.031^	.02
International Financial Institution Factors		
Number of Countries Under an SAP that Year	.043***	.004
Constant	−3.472***	1.073
N		2105
Psuedo R2		.16

Source: Author's elaboration
P|z .1^ .05*, .01**, .001***
[a]Models are estimated with robust standard errors, with one-tailed significant tests. Cubic splines were used to control for temporal dependence

[79]A table of descriptive statistics of the variables used in the analyses is available as a web appendix.

Table 4 Logit equation: which governments ratify international convention on economic and social rights 1981–2004, all developing countries[a]

Ratifying international convention on economic and social rights	Coefficient	Robust standard error
Economic Factors		
GDP Per Capita	–.00001	.00002
International Political Factors		
Level of Regional ICESCR Ratification	.002***	.0004
Domestic Political Factors		
Level of Democracy	.294***	.063
Number of INGOs Present in Country	.0001	.0004
Number of IGOs Already Joined	–.008	.009
Log of Population	.04	.121
Constant	–3.876*	2.29
N		2335
Psuedo R2		.54

Source: Author's elaboration
P|z .1^ .05*, .01**, .001***
[a]Models are estimated with robust standard errors clustered on country, with one-tailed significant tests. Cubic splines were used to control for temporal dependence

likely to enter into these programs, statistically significant at the .10 level of confidence or higher. The end of the cold war increased competition for loans from newly independent countries, making access to capital from the IFIs more difficult. This increased competition, reduced the probability of receiving a loan in the post-cold war period, significant at the .01 level of confidence. Governments also were more likely to enter into SAPs when the sovereignty costs were lower, indicated here by larger numbers of other countries also under these programs in a particular year, significant at the .001 level of confidence. Given a recent review of the determinants of IMF lending[80] we initially estimated a more fully specified model that included measures of FDI flows, foreign aid flows from the United States, and a country's current account balance. The coefficients, while in the expected direction, were insignificant and led to the loss of just over 21% of our cases.[81] Therefore, these additional measures were dropped from our analysis.

Table 4 displays the probability of ratifying the ICESCR during the period 1981–2004. Like Landman, we also found that democratic regimes were more likely to ratify the covenant, significant at the .001 level of confidence. The results also indicate that countries whose regional neighbors had ratified the ICESCR were more likely to ratify the covenant, significant at the .001 level of confidence. This latter relationship was statistically insignificant in Landman's study. Landman also had found that wealthy countries were less likely to ratify the covenant, but we

[80]Steinward and Stone (2008).

[81]These results also are available from the authors upon request.

found no statistically significant relationship between the wealth of a country and its willingness to participate in the ICESCR. Like Landman, we found no statistically significant relationship between the likelihood of participation in the ICESCR and a country's population, the number of INGOs present in the country, or the number of IGOs the government already had joined.

Table 5 shows the progressive impacts of being under World Bank and IMF SAPs and participation in the ICESCR on government respect for economic and social rights. Longer periods under World Bank and IMF program lending reduced government respect for the economic and social welfare of their citizens on all of four indicators, significant at the .10 level of confidence or above. Countries that had been under World Bank and IMF structural adjustment for greater periods of time had lower scores on the PQLI, our main measure of government respect for economic and social rights and also had worse outcomes on each of the three components used in the PQLI measure. Life expectancy at age one and the literacy rates were both lower and the infant mortality rate was higher the longer a country has been exposed to program lending. These results supported our first hypothesis, that the longer a government's participation in structural adjustment program lending, the worse its respect for economic and social rights.

The effects of the control variables were inconsistent, but, generally exerted effects in the expected directions. Wealth, indicated by GDP per capita increased life expectancy at age one, and reduced the infant mortality rate, significant at the .10 level of confidence or higher. Economic growth, indicated by change in GDP per capita increased the literacy rate, significant at the .10 level of confidence. Trade had a significant positive impact on PQLI and the literacy rate, significant at the .10 level of confidence. Higher levels of democracy lowered the infant mortality rate, significant at the .05 level of confidence. Interstate conflict had a negative impact on the literacy rate, significant at the .10 level of confidence. Two results were against our expectation. The log of population has a positive impact on PQLI, life expectancy at age one, and the literacy rate, significant at the .10 level of confidence or higher. UK Colonial heritage had a negative effect on the PQLI index, significant at the .10 level of confidence.

Finally, controlling for the effects of selection mattered for the model predicting life expectancy at age one and the literacy rate, significant at the .10 level of confidence or higher. The results indicated that Bank and Fund tended to negotiate program lending agreements with the governments of countries that had lower life expectancies and higher literacy rates. Work which did not account for these selections effects would overemphasize the negative effects of World Bank and IMF SAPs on lowering life expectancy in developing countries. In comparison, work that did not account for these selection effects would underemphasize the negative effects of World Bank and IMF SAPs on worsening literacy rates in developing countries.

Robustness Tests and Predictions: Table 6 shows a cross sectional analysis to buttress our argument concerning the negative impact of participation in SAPs and the positive impact of participation in the ICESCR on government respect for economic and social rights. We took the factors that were found to have a

Table 5 Pooled time series: the impact of World Bank & IMF structural adjustment programs & ratification of international covenant on economic and social rights on government respect for economic and social rights: 1981–2004, all developing countries (OLS)[a]

Govt. respect for economic & social rights	PQLI	Life expectancy age one	Literacy rate	Infant mortality rate
Number of Years Under a World Bank or IMF SAP	−.02* (.01)	−.023* (.012)	−.022* (.012)	.064^ (.045)
Number of Years Under Convention on Economic & Social Rights	.011 (.009)	.011 (.01)	.023* (.014)	−.059 (.049)
Economic Factors				
GDP Per Capita	.00001 (.00001)	.00003** (.00001)	−8.48e−06 (.00002)	−.0001^ (.00006)
Change in GDP Per Capita	.00005 (.0001)	−.0001 (.0001)	.0002^ (.001)	−.0004 (.003)
Trade as a Proportion of GDP	.001^ (.001)	.001 (.001)	.005** (.002)	−.0002 (.005)
Log of Population	.045^ (.028)	.052* (.03)	.096* (.047)	−.081 (.117)
Domestic Political Factors				
Level of Democracy	−.002 (.013)	.008 (.014)	.002 (.037)	−.088^ (.057)
United Kingdom Colonial Heritage	−.117^ (.085)	−.039 (.105)	−.106 (.097)	.248 (.34)
Conflict Proneness Factors				
Interstate Conflict	.058 (.07)	.04 (.084)	−.113^ (.074)	−.292 (.439)
Rebellion	−.005 (.05)	.001 (.046)	.023 (.023)	.208 (.294)
World Bank & IMF Inverse Mills Ratio	.014 (.039)	−.054^ (.042)	.143** (.059)	.14 (.178)
ICESCR Inverse Mills Ratio	−.015 (.018)	−.018 (.023)	−.006 (.023)	−.087 (.081)
Lagged Dependent Variable	.985*** (.004)	.982*** (.007)	.978*** (.01)	.959*** (.016)
Constant	.796* (.47)	.437 (.572)	.16 (.781)	3.036 (3.061)
N (R-Squared)	1944 (.99)	1944 (.97)	1944 (.98)	1944 (.97)

Source: Author's elaboration

P|z .1^, .05*, .01**, .001***

[a]Models were estimated with bootstrapped errors and one-tailed significant tests. Longer participation in the ICESCR was found to be associated with improvements in a country's adult literacy rate, significant at the .05 level of confidence, but was not associated with improvement in (or worsening of) the PQLI or either of its other components. These results provided weak support for our second hypothesis, that the longer a government's participation in the International Covenant on Economic, Social and Cultural Rights, the greater its level of respect for economic and social rights. The difference in the consistency and magnitudes of participation in the two regimes provided strong support for our third hypothesis, that participation in program lending would have stronger and more consistent effects on government respect for economic and social rights than would participation in the ICESCR

Table 6 Cross sectional analyses: the impact of World Bank & IMF structural adjustment programs on government respect for economic and social rights: 2004, all developing countries (OLS)[a]

Govt. respect for economic & social rights	PQLI	Life expectancy age one	Literacy rate	Infant mortality rate
Number of Years Under a World Bank or IMF SAP	−.785*** (.198)	−.149 (.162)	−1.226*** (.236)	1.077* (.542)
Number of Years Under Convention on Economic & Social Rights	–	–	.741*** (.158)	–
Economic Factors				
GDP Per Capita	–	.002*** (.0003)	–	–[b]
Change in GDP Per Capita	–	–	1.742*** (.555)	−1.404^ (1.461)
Trade as a Proportion of GDP	.162** (.055)	–	.192*** (.056)	–
Log of Population	1.991* (.994)	.213 (.481)	3.827** (1.304)	–
Domestic Political Factors				
Level of Democracy	–	–	–	−5.794*** (.909)
United Kingdom Colonial Heritage	−2.299 (2.833)	–	–	–
Conflict Proneness Factors				
Interstate Conflict	–	–	−28.576** (10.323)	–
Rebellion				–
World Bank & IMF Inverse Mills Ratio	–	–[c]	–[d]	–
ICESCR Inverse Mills Ratio	–	–	–	–
Lagged Dependent Variable	–	–	–	–
Constant	40.803** (18.022)	54.816*** (7.688)	6.386 (22.75)	63.151*** (10.294)
N (R-Squared)	127 (.17)	116(.35)	118 (.30)	112 (.24)

Source: Author's elaboration
P|z .1^, .05*, .01**, .001***
[a]Models were estimated with bootstrapped errors and one-tailed significant tests
[b]GDP Per Capita dropped by STATA in the cross sectional analysis
[c]World Bank and IMF Inverse Mills ratio dropped by STATA in the cross-sectional analysis
[d]World Bank and IMF Inverse Mills ratio dropped by STATA in the cross-sectional analysis

significant impact in the pooled cross sectional time series regressions and used them to estimate a cross sectional analysis for 2004, the latest year for which we had data. We found that countries which had been under structural adjustment for longer periods of time between 1981 and 2004 scored lower on the physical quality of life index in 2004, had a lower literacy rate, and a higher infant mortality rate. These relationships were significant at the .05 level of confidence or higher. The

Table 7 Predictions: the impact of two international regimes on the level of government respect for economic and social rights: 1981–2004, all developing countries

Independent variable	PQLI	Literacy rate	Infant mortality rate
Never under Structural Adjustment Programs	83.19	92.05	42.32
Mean number of years under Structural Adjustment Programs (about 5 years)	79.34	86.03	47.61
One standard deviation above mean number of years under Structural Adjustment Programs (about 10.5 years)	74.93	79.15	53.66
Highest number of years under Structural Adjustment Programs (24 years)	64.36	62.63	68.18
Never under International Covenant on Economic and Social Cultural Rights	–	66.4	–
Mean number of years under International Covenant on Economic and Social Cultural Rights (just over 6 years)	–	70.94	–
One standard deviation above mean number of years under International Covenant on Economic and Social Cultural Rights (about 13.5 years)	–	76.4	–
Highest number of years under International Covenant on Economic and Social Cultural Rights (24 years)	–	84.19	–

Source: Author's elaboration

relationship between duration of participation in SAPs and life expectancy at age one was in the predicted direction, but statistically insignificant. In the cross-sectional model, participation in the ICESCR was still found to have a positive effect on the literacy rate, significant at the .001 level of confidence. In general, the cross-sectional results support the pooled, time series results presented earlier.

Table 7 displays the predicted levels of PQLI and its components given differing numbers of years of participation in SAPs or in the ICESCR. Each of these predictions was based on the cross sectional analysis displayed in Table 7. Examining the effect of structural adjustment on the PQLI index we see that countries that had never been under structural adjustment were predicted to have a PQLI of 83.19. This predicted PQLI score drops to 79.34 for countries that had been under SAPs for the average period of time, about 5 years in this study, and then drops again to 74.93 for countries that had been under SAPs for one standard deviation above the mean, about 10.5 years in this study. Finally, for those countries that had been under SAPs for the longest period in our study, twenty four years, the predicted PQLI score drops to 64.36.

When one examines the components of PQLI a similar story emerges. The literacy rate for those countries never under structural adjustment is predicted at 92.05%, dropping to 86.03% for those under SAPs for the mean number of years (about 5 years), and then falling to 79.15% for those under SAPs for one standard deviation above the mean (about 10.5 years). Finally, for those countries that had been under SAPs for the longest period in our study, twenty four years, the predicted literacy rate drops to 62.63%. Overall, the predicted literacy rate dropped a total of just under 32% when comparing countries that had never been under SAPs with those that had been under for 24 years.

The predicted literacy rate for those countries which never ratified the ICESCR was 66.4%, increasing to 70.94% for those under the ICESCR for the mean number of years (just over 6 years), and then increasing to 76.4% for those under the ICESCR for one standard deviation above the mean (about 13.5 years). Finally, for those countries that have been under ICESCR for the longest period in our study, twenty four years, the literacy rate increased to 84.19. Overall, the literacy rate increased a total of almost 26.8% comparing countries that have never been under the ICESCR for those that have been under the longest. In the case of the literacy rate both the international financial and international human rights regime had large and contradictory effects on the literacy rate in developing countries. In situations where a country had been under both regimes for the longest period the international financial regime would have had a *net negative effect* on the literacy rate reducing it by almost 5.2%.

Finally, structural adjustment worsens the infant mortality rate. The infant mortality rate for those countries never under structural adjustment is predicted at 42.32, increasing to 47.61 for those under SAPs for the mean number of years (about 5 years), and increasing again to 53.66 for those under SAPs for one standard deviation above the mean (about 10.5 years). Finally, for those countries that have been under SAPs for the longest period in our study, twenty four years, the infant mortality rate increases to 68.18. Overall, the infant mortality rate increases a total of just over 61% comparing countries that have never been under SAPs for those that have been under the longest.

9 Conclusions

The findings supported the three hypotheses of this study and, generally, the findings of earlier research on the human rights effects of participation in the human rights and international finance regimes. Though previous research had not estimated the human rights impacts of participation in the ICESCR, the relationships discovered for participation in other human rights regimes were statistically insignificant, weak, or conditional.[82] In this study, we found that governments that had a longer period since ratifying the ICESCR had slightly better respect for the economic and social rights of their citizens, providing weak support for our first hypothesis. Actually, of the four relationships with social and economic outcomes, only one—the adult literacy rate—had a statistically significant relationship with our measure of participation in the human rights regime. Still, the relationship we discovered between the length of participation in the regime and adult literacy rate was surprisingly strong and in the expected direction. Other things being equal,

[82]Hathaway (2002), Hafner-Burton (2005), Keith (1999), Landman (2005), and Neumayer (2005).

countries where the governments never ratified the ICESCR had a much lower predicted adult literacy rate (about 66%) than did countries that had ratified for 24 years or more (about 84%).

The findings also demonstrated that the longer a government's participation in structural adjustment program lending, the worse was its respect for economic and social rights as was previously demonstrated by Abouharb and Cingranelli.[83] However, participation in some non-human rights regimes may have positive effects on some human rights practices. For example, there is some evidence that long participation in SAPs has led to increased government respect for civil and political liberties in developing countries.[84]

One novel feature of our research design was that the effects of both regimes were estimated controlling for the effects of the other. Another was that estimates of both regime effects were corrected for the effects of selection by conducting a two-stage analysis, where the first stage equations identified the characteristics of countries whose governments were most likely to participate in each regime. These first-stage equations were important, because they identified characteristics of countries that made them good candidates for participation and predisposed them to better or worse human rights practices whether or not they participated. For example, the selection equation showed that democracies were significantly more likely to join the ICESCR. Democratic states have been shown in previous research to have relatively good human rights practices of all kinds. Thus, by controlling for selection, we can be sure that the positive human rights outcome we discovered for participation in the human rights regime was not spurious—that is, due to an overrepresentation of democratic states in the ratifying group. For participation in SAPs, the first-stage results showed that countries experiencing economic difficulties such as a low GDP per capita and countries with large populations were more likely to participate in SAPs. Previous research has demonstrated that poor countries and those with larger populations also are less likely to respect most human rights.

As we hypothesized, participation in program lending had negative effects on respect for economic and social rights, while participation in the human rights regime had positive effects. Also, as hypothesized, the negative effects of longer participation in the international finance regime were significantly stronger than were the positive effects of longer participation in the human rights regime. By identifying some important differences between these two regimes, we have taken a first step towards using empirical methods to identify the attributes of international governmental regimes that make them more effective influence agents over the behavior of member states. We speculated that the main advantage of the international finance regime as an influence agent was that the directors of the World Bank and IMF could manipulate material sanctions and rewards, while the UN committee that oversees the implementation of the ICESCR can only name and shame

[83] Abouharb and Cingranelli (2006, 2007).

[84] Abouharb and Cingranelli (2007).

defectors. Naming and shaming has been shown to be an ineffective tool to ensure compliance with human rights regime norms.[85] The international financial regime also has the strong backing of the U.S. government, but the economic and social human rights regime does not (as is indicated by the fact that the US government has signed but not ratified the ICESCR). Furthermore, the principals, norms and rules of the international finance regime are reinforced by the world trade regime. The main potential advantage of the human rights regime as an influence agent was that it has an explicit mission is to improve the human rights practices of participants.

The findings showing modest effectiveness of the human rights regime which provides some support for the liberal theory of regime influence—that regimes are independent actors in the international system. They are not simply tools of the US government in the international system. Despite lack of endorsement by the US government participation in the weak ICESCR regime increased the probability of cooperation with regime norms and rules.[86]

These findings indicate that research seeking to build theories of why governments respect human rights should give greater attention to the human rights effects of participation in intergovernmental regimes. However, this creates a problem for theory testing. What regimes should be included as potential influence agents in an analysis? Which ones should be left out? These questions should be answered by logic and by the results of previous research. Many international regimes besides the ones we examined in this project affect the human rights practices of governments around the world. Future work might consider participation in the labor regime supervised by the International Labor Organization or the world trade regime supervised by the WTO as factors affecting the economic and social human rights performance of participating states. Future work also should examine how a government's desire to join an international governmental regime with substantial human rights entry requirements such as the European Union affects that government's human rights practices.

References

Aaronson SA (2007) Seeping in slowly: how human rights concerns are penetrating the WTO. World Trade Rev 6(3):1–37

Abouharb MR, Cingranelli D (2004) Human rights and structural adjustment: the importance of selection. In: Carey SC, Poe SC (eds) Understanding human rights violations: new systematic studies. Ashgate Publishing, Aldershot, England

Abouharb MR, Cingranelli D (2005) When the World Bank says yes: determinants of structural adjustment lending. In: Rani G, Vreeland JR (eds) Impact of globalization on the nation-state from above: the International Monetary Fund and the World Bank. Routledge

85 Hafner-Burton (2008).

86 E.g., Cortell and Davis, Jr. (1996), Keohane and Martin (1995), and Koremenos et al. (2001).

Abouharb MR, Cingranelli D (2006) The human rights effects of World Bank structural adjustment, 1981–2000. Int Stud Q 45(2):219–239

Abouharb MR, Cingranelli D (2007) Human rights and structural adjustment. Cambridge University Press, Cambridge

Abouharb MR, Cingranelli D (2009) IMF programs and human rights, 1981–2003. Rev Int Organ 4(1):47–72

Alexander N (2005) The roles of the IMF, the World Bank, and the WTO in liberalization and privatization of the water services sector. Citizens' Network on Essential Services. Available from www.servicesforall.org. Accessed 3 Jan 2007

Alexander N (2006a) Decentralization and sovereignty: how policy space is eroded. Social Watch Report 2006: impossible architecture. The Third World Institute, Uruguay

Alexander N (2006b) Globalization and international institutions: the International Monetary Fund (IMF), the World Bank, and the World Trade Organization. Citizens' Network on Essential Services. www.servicesforall.org. Accessed 3 Jan 2007

Banks AS, Muller T, Overstreet WR (2003) Political handbook of the world 2000–2002. CSA Publications, Binghamton, New York

Barratt BA (2007) Human rights and foreign aid: for love or money? Routledge, New York

Bayless M, Bayless S (1982) Current quality of life indicators: some theoretical and methodological concerns. Am J Econ Sociol 43(1):185–198

Beck N, Katz JN, Tucker R (1998) Taking time seriously in binary time-series cross-section analysis. Am J Polit Sci 42(4):1260–1288

Blackmon P (2008) Rethinking poverty through the eyes of the International Monetary Fund and the World Bank. Int Stud Rev 10:179–202

Blanton SL (2000) Promoting human rights and democracy in the developing world: U.S. Rhetoric versus U.S. arms exports. Am J Polit Sci 44(1):123–131

Blanton SL (2005) Foreign policy in transition? Human rights, democracy, and US Arms exports. Int Stud Q 49(4):647–667

Buchmann C (1996) The debt crisis, structural adjustment and women's education: implication for status and social development. Int J Comp Sociol XXXVII:5–30

Callaway R (2001) Is the road to hell paved with good intentions? The effect of US foreign assistance and economic policy on human rights. PhD Dissertation, University of North Texas

Callaway RL, Harrelson-Stephens J (2004) The path from trade to human rights: the democracy and development detour. In: Carey S, Poe SC (eds) The systematic study of human rights. Ashgate, pp 87–109

Chipeta C (1993) Malawi. In: Adepoju A (ed) The impact of structural adjustment on the population of Africa. United Nations Population Fund. NH, Heinemann, pp 105–188

Cingranelli DL, Richards DL (2004) The Cingranelli-Richards (CIRI) Human Rights Database. Available from http:www.humanrightsdata.com. Accessed 1 Oct 2008

Commonwealth Secretariat (1989) Engendering adjustment for the 1990s: report of a commonwealth expert group on women and structural adjustment. Commonwealth Secretariat, London

Cortell AP, Davis JW Jr (1996) How do international institutions matter? The domestic impact of international rules and norms. Int Stud Q 40: (4) 451-478.

Daddieh C (1995) Structural adjustment programs and regional integration: compatible or mutually exclusive. In: Mengisteab K, Logan BI (eds) Beyond economic liberalization in Africa: structural adjustments and the alternatives. SAPES, Capetown, pp 243–271

Dollar D, Svensson J (2000) What explains the success or failure of structural adjustment programmes? Econ J 110(October):894–917

Donnelly J (2003) Universal human rights in theory and practice, 2nd edn. Cornell University Press, Ithaca

Dreher A, Jensen NM (2007) Independent actor or agent? An empirical analysis of the impact of US interests on IMF conditions. J Law Econ 50(1):105–124

Elson D (1990) Male bias in macro-economics: the case of structural adjustment. In: Elson D (ed) Male bias in the developmental process. Manchester University Press, Manchester, pp 1–28

Fields AB (2003) Rethinking human rights for the new millennium. Palgrave Macmillan, New York

Forsythe D (1987) Congress and human rights in U.S. foreign policy: the fate of general legislation. Hum Rights Q 9:391–411

Franklin J (1997) IMF conditionality, threat perception, and political repression: a cross-national analysis. Comp Polit Stud 30:576–606

Frey BS, Schneider F (1986) Competing models of international lending activity. J Dev Econ 20:225–245

Friedman TL (2000) The lexus and the olive tree. Anchor Books, New York

Gibler DM, Sarkees M (2004) Measuring alliances: the correlates of war formal interstate alliance data set, 1816–2000. J Peace Res 41:211–222

Gleditsch NP, Wallensteen P, Eriksson M, Sollenberg M, Strand H (2002) Armed conflict 1946–2001: a new dataset. J Peace Res 39(5):615–637

Goldstein J (1985) Basic human needs: the plateau curve. World Dev 13:595–609

Grusky S (2001) IMF forces water privatization on poor countries. Globalization Challenge Initiative. Available from www.ige.org. Accessed 13 Aug 2005

Hafner-Burton EM (2005) Trading human rights: how preferential trade agreements influence government repression. Int Organ 59(3):593–629

Hafner-Burton E (2008) Sticks and stones: naming and shaming the human rights enforcement problem. Int Organ 62(4):689–716

Hafner-Burton EM, Tsutsui K (2005) Human rights in a globalizing world: the paradox of empty promises. Am J Sociol 110(5):1373–1411

Hafner-Burton E, Tsutsui K, Meyer J (2008) International human rights law and the politics of legitimacy: repressive states and human rights treaties. Int Sociol 23(1):115–141

Handa S, King D (1997) Structural adjustment policies, income distribution and poverty: a review of the Jamaican experience. World Dev 25(6):915–930

Hathaway O (2002) Do human rights treaties make a difference? Yale Law J 111(8):1935

Hathaway O (2008) International delegation and domestic sovereignty. Law Contemp Probl (Winter): 115–150

Henkin L, Neuman GL, Orrentlicher DF, Leebron DW (1999) Human rights. Foundation Press, New York

Hensel P (1999) Issues COW colonial history dataset. Available from http://garnet.acns.fsu.edu/~phensel/icowdata.html#colonies. Accessed 1 Aug 2007

Hicks N, Streeten P (1979) Indicators of development: the search for a basic needs yardstick. World Dev 7:567–580

Joyce JP (1992) The economic characteristics of IMF program countries. Econ Lett 38:237–242

Keck M, Sikkink K (1998) Activists beyond borders: advocacy networks in international politics. Cornell University Press, Ithaca

Keith L (1999) The United Nations international covenant on civil and political rights: does it make a difference in human rights behavior? J Peace Res 36(1):95–118

Keith L, Poe SC (2000) The United States, the IMF, and human rights. In: Forsythe DF (ed) The United States and human rights. University of Nebraska Press, Lincoln, pp 273–299

Keohane RO (1984) After hegemony: cooperation and discord in the world political economy. Princeton University Press, Princeton

Keohane RO, Martin LL (1995) The promise of institutionalist theory. Int Secur 20(1):39–51

Killick T (1996) IMF programmes in developing countries: design and impact. Overseas Development Institute, London

Koremenos B, Lipson C, Snidal D (2001) The rational design of international institutions. Int Organ 55(4):761–800

Krasner SD (ed) (1983) International regimes. Cornell University Press, Ithaca

Landman T (2005) Protecting human rights: a global comparative study. Georgetown University Press

Legro J (1997) Which norms matter? Revisiting the 'Failure' of internationalism. Int Organ 51:31–63
Lloyd V, Weissman R (2001) Against the workers: how IMF and World Bank policies undermine labor power and rights. Multinational Monitor. (September). Available from www.globalpolicy.org. Accessed
Marshall MG, Jaggers K [2002] (2006) POLITY IV PROJECT political regime characteristics and transitions, 1800–2002. Dataset Users' Manual. http://www.systemicpeace.org/polity/polity4.htm. Accessed 15 Aug 2007
Meyer WH (1998) Human rights and international political economy in third world nations. Praeger, Westport
Milner WT (2000) Economic freedom, globalization and human rights: can we have it all? J Private Enterp 15(2):35–61
Milner WT, Leblang D, Poe SC, Smith K (2004) Providing subsistence rights: do states make a difference? In: Carey S, Poe SC (eds) The systematic study of human rights. Ashgate, pp 110–124
Milner WT, Callaway RL (2007) Using the physical quality of life Index to explore the level of subsistence rights. In: Callaway RL, Harrelson-Stephens J (eds) Exploring international human rights: essential readings. Lynne Rienner Publishers, Boulder, pp 59–68
Moon BE (1991) The political economy of basic human needs. Cornell University Press, Ithaca
Moon BE, Dixon WJ (1985) Politics, the state, and basic human needs: a cross-national study. Am J Polit Sci 29:661–694
Mooney CZ, Duvall RD (1993) Bootstrapping: a nonparametric approach to statistical inference. Sage, Newbury Park
Moore WH (1998) Repression and dissent: substitution, context and timing. Am J Polit Sci 42 (3):851–873
Morris MD (1979) Measuring the condition of the world's poor: the physical quality of life index. Pergamon, New York
Munck R (1994) Workers, structural adjustment, and concertacion-social in Latin-America. Latin Am Perspect 21(3):90–103
Neumayer E (2005) Do international human rights treaties improve respect for human rights? J Confl Resolut 49(6):925–953
Park HS (1987) Correlates of human rights: global tendencies. Hum Rights Q 9:405–413
Pettifor A (2001) Global economic justice: human rights for debtor nations. J Hum Dev 2(1):47–51
Pevehouese J, Nordstrom T, Warnke K (2003) Intergovernmental organizations, 1815–2000: a new correlates of war data set. Available from http://www.correlatesof war.org/COW2%20Data/IGOs/IGOv2-1.htm. Accessed 15 Aug 2008
Pion-Berlin D (1984) The political economy of state repression in Argentina. In: Stohl M, Lopez GA (eds) The state as terrorist: the dynamics of governmental violence and repression. Greenwood Press, Westport
Plumper T, Neumayer E (2006) The unequal burden of war: the effect of armed conflict on the gender gap in life expectancy. Int Organ 60(3):723–754
Poe SC (2004) The decision to repress: an integrative theoretical approach to the research on human rights and repression. In: Carey SC, Poe SC (eds) Understanding human rights violations. Ashgate Publishing, Aldershot, pp 16–42
Poe SC, Tate CN (1994) Repression of personal integrity in the 1980s: a global analysis. Am Polit Sci Rev 88(4):853–872
Poe SC, Tate CN, Keith LC (1999) Repression of the human right to personal integrity revisited: a global cross-national study covering the years 1976–1993. Int Stud Q. 43(2):291–313
Przeworski A, Vreeland JR (2000) The effects of IMF programs on economic growth. J Dev Econ 62:385–421
Putnam RD (1988) Diplomacy and domestic politics: the logic of two-level games. Int Organ 42 (3):427–460

Raja K (2002) New IMF loan conditions will raise water fees in Ghana. Third World Network. No. 276, March. Available from www.twinside.org. Accessed 13 Dec 2006
Ratner S (2004) Overcoming temptations to violate human dignity in times of crisis: on the possibilities for meaningful self-restraint. Theoretical Inquiries in Law 5:81–107
Richards D, Gelleny R, Sacko D (2001) Money with a mean streak? Foreign economic penetration and government respect for human rights in developing countries. Int Stud Q 45(2):219–239
Risse T, Ropp SC, Sikkink K (eds) (1999) The power of human rights: international norms and domestic change. Cambridge University Press, London
Ron J, Ramos H, Rodgers K (2005) Transnational information politics: NGO human rights reporting, 1986–2000. Int Stud Q 49(3):557–587
Rosh R (1986) The impact of third world defense burdens on basic human needs. Policy Stud J 15:135–146
Sadasivam B (1997) The impact of structural adjustment on women: a governance and human rights agenda. Hum Rights Q 19(3):630–655
Saprin (Structural Adjustment Participatory Review International Network) (2004) Structural adjustment: the SAPRIN report: the policy roots of economic crisis, poverty, and inequality. Zed Books, London
Sen A (1999) Development as freedom. Alfred Knopf, New York
Shannon VP (2000) Norms are what states make of them: the political psychology of norm violation. Int Stud Q 44:293–316
Sowa NK (1993) Ghana. In: Adepoju A (ed) The impact of structural adjustment on the population of Africa. Heinemann, Portsmouth, pp 7–24
Steinward M, Stone R (2008) The International Monetary Fund: a review of the recent evidence. Rev Int Organ 3:123–149
Stiglitz J (2002) Globalization and its discontents. W. W. Norton, New York
Stone RW (2002) Lending credibility: the international monetary fund and the post-communist transition. Princeton University Press, Princeton
Stone RW (2004) The political economy of IMF lending in Africa. Am Polit Sci Rev 98:577–591
Strand H, Wilhelmsen L, Gleditsch NP (2005) Armed conflict dataset codebook. Version 3. Available from http://www.prio.no/cwp/ArmedConflict/. Accessed 15 Aug 2008
Strange S (1988) States and markets. Blackwell, London
Thacker SC (1999) The high politics of IMF lending. World Polit 52:38–75
U.S. Census Bureau (2005) International database. Available from http://www.census.gov/ipc/www/idb/. Accessed 15 Aug 2008
United Nations Development Program (2004) Human development report 2004: cultural liberty in today's diverse world. UNDP, New York
Van De Laar AJM (1980) The World Bank and the poor. Nijhoff, Boston
Van de Walle N (2001) African economies and the politics of permanent crisis, 1979–1999. Cambridge University Press
Vreeland JR (2002) The effect of IMF programs on labor. World Dev 30(1):121–139
Vreeland JR (2003) The IMF and economic development. Cambridge University Press, Cambridge
Vreeland JR (2008) Political institutions and human rights: why dictatorships enter into the United Nations convention against torture. Int Organ 62(1):65–101
Wallace M, Singer JD (1970) International governmental organization in the global system, 1815–1964. Int Organ 24(2):239–287
Welch C (1995) Protecting human rights in Africa: roles and strategies of nongovernmental organizations. University of Pennsylvania Press, Philadelphia
Williams M (1994) International economic organizations and the third world. Harvester Wheatsheaf, Hemel Hempstead
World Bank (1992) The World Bank operational manual: operational directive adjustment lending policy, (OD 8.60). Available from http:wbln0018.worldbank.org/institutional/manuals/opmanual.nsf. Accessed 10 Mar 2005

World Bank (2006) World development indicators. World Bank, Washington

Young OR (1980) International regimes: problems of concept formation. World Polit 32 (3):331–356

Young OR (1992) The effectiveness of international institutions: hard cases and critical variables. In: Rosenau JN, Czempiel E (eds) Governance without governments: order and change in world politics. Cambridge University Press, pp 160–194

Zack-Williams AB (2000) Social consequences of structural adjustment. In: Mohan G, Brown BM, Zack-Williams AB (eds) Structural adjustment: theory, practice and impacts. Routledge, London, pp 59–74

Part V
The Impact of Bretton Woods Institutions on Civil Society

Bretton Woods: The Pursuit of Happiness?

Gianludovico de Martino and Giada Lepore

Abstract Bretton Woods set an unprecedented step in building a system of international financial and economic cooperation. It laid the foundations for post-war monetary and financial relations and reshaped the world economy in favour of a liberal multilateral system aimed at promoting economic development and better standards of living.

Contents

With the end of the system, the original architecture and its institutions have morphed into something different. The IMF and the WB have been evolving in the absence of a parallel construction of new economic governance: both retained their scope and original mandate, but had to adapt their activities to a changing world economy and to a globalized society where national states have lost their exclusive status of economy regulators in favour of a 'pluri-level and multi-actor' governance. Additionally, recent global challenges have shown that crises are interrelated, interdependent and with multiple effects (economic and financial, on political stability, on collective security and human rights).

G. de Martino (✉)
Interministerial Committee for Human Rights - Italian Ministry of Foreign Affairs and International Cooperation, Rome, Italy
e-mail: gianludovicodemartino@yahoo.it

G. Lepore
St. Thomas University School of Law, Miami, FL, USA
e-mail: giada.lepore9@gmail.com

E. Sciso (ed.), *Accountability, Transparency and Democracy in the Functioning of Bretton Woods Institutions*, DOI 10.1007/978-3-319-57855-2_13

How could the spirit of Bretton Woods be 'revived' to meet current challenges? And could its institutions play a decisive role in further promoting human rights together with economic progress?

Recognizing the role that states have in fostering market development domestically and the potential they could reach globally is pivotal. If it is true that human rights may flourish in economic prosperity, it also true that the promotion of political freedom, rule of law and human rights are the conditions for lasting social and economic development.

This contribution is aimed at assessing if the spirit and institutions of Bretton Woods might be means of human rights promotion and how, and to what extent, they could help meet current global challenges.

1 Human Rights, Democracy and Development

Political systems that are not democratic in nature—lacking accountability of the exercise of power—tend to curtail fundamental rights and freedoms, which are an essential feature of societies that have achieved high levels of growth and of "citizens' satisfaction". At the same time, developed and well-functioning economies, which are grounded on the principles of equality, rule of law and independency of judiciary, may play a crucial role in extending support for human rights and democracy.

It is not rocket science but somehow it is undeniable that, while many people perish trying to get West, there never was an eastward rush across the Iron Curtain; at present, the growing migratory pressure from sub Saharan Africa towards Europe (certainly not the other way round) shows how the welfare, freedom, rights and security enjoyed in Europe are themselves pull factors.

There is therefore an inextricable link between democracy, human rights and (economic and social) development. It could be argued that democracy itself is not a universally shared principle, nor are human rights as such: that both are products of 'Western' culture and politics, alien to other parts of the world. Yet this would be tantamount to denying the obvious: that mankind has gone and goes through a continuous process of evolution and adjustment of values. For example, in Europe slavery was common two thousand years ago and in various forms of servitude still in force well into the eighteenth century. The limitations of personal freedom went hand in hand with political economic systems such as feudalism, which in itself was an obstacle to economic improvement and growth and was finally discarded for that very reason.

The idea of democracy and human rights as we perceive them today in the West was as alien to the fifteenth or seventeenth century European mentality as it is today to societies still based on obeisance to the elder or exclusively male dominated or of theocratic nature and so on. Nor did the adjustments occur in the West harmoniously and all at the same time.

Human nature holds the innate aspiration to a better lot in life: at the core, freedom of choice and participation in decision making, the main connotations of democracy, appear to be regarded as a common feature of the latter.

The same attitude is mirrored in the way the functioning of the Bretton Woods Institutions can be perceived. They are certainly democratic in the same way their twin the United Nations are. But what has been their impact on democracy? Have those international financial institutions evolved in line with the progressive adjustment of global values? How can they ensure effective development while also giving meaningful support to human rights?

2 The Spirit of Bretton Woods

The global financial and economic framework finds its roots in the Bretton Woods system, created in 1944 after the Second World War to ensure macro economic stability by controlling the international monetary system and rebuilding European economies after the war, with the ultimate aim of achieving multilateral economic governance and stability.

The instruments designated by the Washington Consensus to carry out these goals were the International Monetary Fund, intended to ensure a stable exchange rate system and provide for emergency assistance to countries facing temporary crisis in their balance of payments regime; and the International Bank for Reconstruction and Development (later called the World Bank) to facilitate private investments and post war reconstruction in Europe, and later to assist the development of other countries.

Bretton Woods set an unprecedented step in building a system of international financial and economic cooperation: in order to prevent a recurrence of the effects of the Great Depression and nationalist protectionisms, and in the attempt to reconcile openness and trade expansion with the commitments of national governments to full employment and economic stabilisation, it laid the foundations for post-war monetary and financial relations and reshaped the world economy in favour of a liberal multilateral system.[1]

The liberal spirit of Bretton Woods was to promote economic development, to distribute its benefits, achieve full employment and better standards of living. As a matter of fact, at the centre of the Bretton Woods system was the idea that economic growth is the answer to fighting poverty, providing environmental security and strengthening social fabric, and that economic openness—erasing economic borders to allow free movement of goods and capitals—would represent the key to such growth. Parallel to this concept, in challenging the traditional economic belief of the "invisible hand", it has increased the awareness of the importance of state intervention in the economy (both at national and international level) and the need

[1] John Ikenberry (2007), pp. 155–198.

of fiscal and monetary policies to stimulate growth, reach employment and fix market problems.

This conception, known as "embedded liberalism", represents a compromise between free markets and social protection: it is a particular form of economic thought blending economic liberalism and domestic interventionism, providing tools to ensure domestic policy autonomy for social welfare targets within an open international economy.[2] This approach was also an essential plank in the overall philosophical architecture underpinning the countering of political ideologies such as communism.

The link between free market—economic growth—poverty alleviation and development for all was successful also thanks to the action of the two multilateral institutions, the International Monetary Fund (IMF) and the World Bank (WB), which respectively established a system of loans and assistance to the developing world and of economic assistance for countries facing emergency. Between 1950 and 1960 the macroeconomic growth and the expansion of international trade were higher than in the past, and economic prosperity was reached not just in western countries but also in smaller economies in East Asia, such as South Korea and Taiwan, and in Latin America, in Argentina and Brazil.[3]

The general improvement of material conditions in Western world went hand in hand with the affirmation of human rights and their positivisation within the United Nation (UN) system, peaking with the adoption of the two Covenants in 1966.[4] The economic cooperation promoted around Bretton Woods was indeed parallel to the "cultural" one growing around the development of human rights movements within the UN.

3 Challenges and Common Roots

With the end of the Bretton Woods system in 1973, the original system and its institutions have morphed into something different. While the financial and monetary policy collapsed, the general commitment to liberalism endured, as well as its two main instruments, the IMF and the WB. By then, the two multilateral institutions were however representing instruments of a system that was missing: their role has been evolving in the absence of a parallel construction of new economic

[2]Ruggie (1982), pp. 379–415.

[3]*See* World Bank Policy Research Report, *The East Asian Miracle*, Oxford University Press (1983).

[4]The International Covenant on Civil and Political Rights and the International Covenant for Economic, Social and Cultural Rights (1966). The former focuses on the recognition of the right to life and the fundamental freedoms, while the latter establishes principles such as the right to self-determination, the right to food and education, the right to work and to an equitable remuneration, etc. Together with the 1948 Universal Declaration of Human Rights, the two Covenants constitute the Bill of Rights.

governance. Both the IMF and the WB retained their scope and original mandate, but had to adapt their activities to a changing world economy.

Globalisation had a crucial role in this process: the rise of new actors such as multinational corporations and the integration of financial markets in global finance have determined a decrease in power, influence and capacity of states to cope with global problems. National states have lost their exclusive status of economy regulators in favour of a 'pluri-level and multi-actor' governance. Against this background, the IMF and the WB have filled the gap by expanding their power and original missions, with the result of acquire negative connotations in the perception of States and public opinion.[5]

This feeling has exacerbated by the increased social and economic impact these institutions have in carrying out their activities of financial assistance. Furthermore, recent global challenges have shown that crises are interrelated and interdependent, having effects on all aspects of global society (economic and financial, political stability, collective security and human rights protection). This imposes not only the resort to collective actions, but also the need of coherence between solutions proposed and their potential impacts.

In the West, the fear of negative growth and reduced incomes translates in the eyes of large sectors of public opinion into an infringement of human rights: less welfare, less health, less pensions, less employment and so on.

In several countries of the developing world, where often kleptocracies and economic monocultures have prevented growth of true democracies, the persistent uneven distribution of wealth and resources and social polarisation—enhanced by the disregard of basic human rights—are amongst the main causes of migratory flows from the "poor" south to the northern hemisphere.

One could argue that some of the challenges facing Europe are mainly self-induced and are linked to the introduction of the Euro. Likewise the repeal of the Glass Stegall Act has, according to many analysts, played a significant role in the global financial crisis starting in 2008. Rather than be blamed on a particular "global system" they could be regarded as the result widespread error of judgment. On the other hand, most challenges faced by developing world are due to the lack of a mechanism of enforcement of "common values", such as good governance, democracy and the rule of law.

---

[5]Stiglitz J.E., *Globalization and the logic of international collective actions: re-examining the Bretton Woods Institutions*, *available at* https://www0.gsb.columbia.edu/mygsb/faculty/research/pubfiles/1468/1468.pdf. Stiglitz describes how the changes of the role of IMF in terms of the leverage, power, lack of transparency and surveillance over states' economic policies have contributed to increase its negative connotation in the public opinion.

4 The Response of New Neoliberalism

Bretton Woods Institutions have faced many criticisms for their lack of commitments to human rights and environmental safeguarding in the implementation of their policies. The IMF has been much questioned for the strict conditions it attaches to the provision of financial assistance to countries in need. On several occasions, the interventions of the IMF have been perceived as too concerned on the rights of creditors focused on austerity and the rights of creditors and too little concerned with the welfare of the poor.

The World Bank has mainly been focusing (post World War II reconstruction) on poverty reduction and human development, on loans to developing countries, and has often been under scrutiny for failing to pay sufficient attention to the social and environmental consequences of the projects it funds.

A crucial role is playing by the Structural Adjustment Programs (SAPs), the programs of economic reform, whose implementation States are requested to undertake as a condition of financial assistance either from the IMF or the WB. They have often implied reshaping and overall restructuring of national economic priorities, with consequences also on the exercise of national economic and political sovereignty. Furthermore, the more severe the social and economic crisis, the stronger are the policy commitments requested.

The SAPs have usually included prescriptions on increase in labour flexibility, changes in taxation policy combined with cuts in social spending, privatisation of public sector enterprises, financial liberalisation. The negative impact of austerity programs and structural reforms has been well documented.[6] More recently, the measures established by the Troika in Greece have been defined as failing and destabilising in the IMF reports.[7]

5 The Role of Fundamental Rights as an Element of Economic Stability

Economic growth, measured by the Gross Domestic Product (GDP), has been considered for decades as the essential condition for economic development. GDP has indeed often represented the guiding parameter in the funding and lending policies of IMF and WB and also commonly used as an indicator of well-being.

More recently, this approach revealed to be insufficient and other indicators are being considered to measure economic and social progresses beyond mere economic and quantitative standards.

[6] *See* Türk (1992); *See also* Fischer-Lescano (2014).

[7] IMF, *Country Report: Greece. Ex Post Evaluation of Exceptional Access under the 2010 Stand-By Agreement* (13.06.2013), IMF Country Report No 13/156.

> [. . .] We ought to consider what is the end of government, before we determine which is the best form. Upon this point all speculative politicians will agree, that the happiness of society is the end of government, as all divines and moral philosophers will agree that the happiness of the individual is the end of man. From this principle it will follow, that the form of government which communicates ease, comfort, security, or, in one word, happiness, to the greatest number of persons, and in the greatest degree, is the best [. . .].[8]

Liberalism is based on the idea that every human being has natural rights such as liberty, life and the pursuit of happiness. The concept of happiness as a fundamental human goal is enshrined also in the 2012 UN General Assembly Resolution 65/309.[9] The Resolution affirms the inadequacy of indicators of economic performances such as national Gross Domestic Product (GDP) to measure the economic and social well-being and encourages governments to adopt a holistic approach to development that should also consider individual happiness.

In conducting their public economic and social policies, governments should therefore pursue personal and social well-being by taking into account additional factors such as values, education, wealth, community relations, health and environmental conditions. It is quite obvious that the promotion and the protection of fundamental human rights is an essential factor of the equation.

Is individual well-being achievable without economic growth and vice versa?

With regard to developing countries, the main question involves the potential true impact that liberalisation policies have had on democratic stability and social well-being. Especially with regard to African countries, liberalisation and free market economy were presented as winning strategies to fully exploit the benefits offered by the globalisation, in contrast with inefficient state controlled based economies. However, economic measures by themselves could not work in the absence of the rule of law or a strong political governance inspired by accountability and transparency.[10]

Looking at Europe, it is the place where the Nation-State rose during the seventeenth century and where it evolved into the Welfare State two centuries later. It is still, by far, the continent with the highest living standards and best system to protect social and economic rights in the world. In this context, the recession, which has affected many western economies since 2008, might well be a turning point of its history. Like the Great Depression of the 1920s, the current crisis is deeply influencing social habits, political opinions, and institutional frameworks. It is generating dangerous tensions among European states and within them. The crisis is also calling into question the implementation of fundamental rights.

Given the financial and public budget tensions that occurred during the crisis, and taking into account the austerity programs implemented by European institutions and the governments of member states (i.g. Greece), is the welfare state achieved in the developed West compatible with financial stability when it

---

[8]Adams (1776).

[9]UN General Assembly Resolution, A/RES/65/309, 2012.

[10]Ibhawoh (1999).

postulates budget cuts? Is there the risk of a "growing void" between provisions enshrined in legislation and their actual implementation?

The protection of human rights has become of utmost importance: the recent crisis in the Euro zone showed that welfare conditions which were taken for granted might be undermined by economic instability and stagnation; moreover, mass-scale migrations reveal that the goal of the attainment of happiness "for the greatest number of people" is strongly felt in developing countries and could be regarded as one of the pull factors of migration itself, whereas it is a fact that the greater the influx of migrants, the less European Union countries will be able to sustain the present welfare systems.

On the other hand, the cause of human rights—which we maintain cannot be separated from economic liberties and the growth of wealth—runs the risk of being thwarted by the ideology of "downsizing", meaning the cult of "happy decline" and populist economic theories, where the abstract rights of groups prevail over the concrete rights of individuals: tools of a new totalitarianism which aims at introducing through social engineering enforced equality, in the guise of a push to the bottom.

6 Conclusions: Bretton Woods and the Pursuit of Happiness?

The Bretton Woods system ended in 1973 and what survive are its institutions, the IMF and the WB. These institutions have adapted to new roles and gradually changed their functions but it is not very clear what their policies should concretely consist of and if (and to what extent) they could bring about significant improvements in the economic and social development.

On one hand, Bretton Woods Institutions have meet their goals in terms of open market and free barriers economy; on the other, they appeared to have missed their ultimate purposes, namely the poverty reduction and promotion of economic prosperity for all.

How could the spirit of Bretton Woods be 'revived' to meet current challenges? And could its institutions play a decisive role in further promoting human rights together with economic progress?

The idea according to which globalisation and open market economy would have spread democracy around the world is not consistent with reality: in fact promoting economic growth has not always been an effective way to promoting democracy.[11] Economic priorities should indeed be guided by a broader vision of

[11]"[...] economic growth stabilizes regimes rather than undermines them. China, therefore, is best viewed not as the exception to the rule that growth produces liberalization, but as emblematic of the fact that it usually does not [...]".

B.B. de Mesquita and G.W. Downs, *Development and Democracy in Foreign Affairs*, available at https://www.foreignaffairs.com/articles/2005-09-01/development-and-democracy.

changes and reforms that envisage the promotion of political freedom, rule of law, transparent and accountable governance, and human rights: these are the conditions that can guarantee (especially in developing countries) the instruments and the capacities to create social and economic development in a long-term period.

After the fall of Communism, transitioning to free market economy did not automatically imply access to the benefits that Western nations have enjoyed for decades and this because economic development must go hand in hand with political and social development. This was an unrealistic expectation and the same paradigm could be applied to the developing world.

The spirit of Bretton Woods can be revived by recognising the crucial role that states have in fostering market development domestically and the potential they could reach globally. On the first level, by giving centrality to welfare and on the second one, by creating a new system of international cooperation to spur socio-economic improvements in developing countries. If it is true that human rights may flourish in economic prosperity, it also true that economic development and prosperity cannot last in absence of the essential political and governmental structure.

The latest world financial crisis, which has hit the richest countries hardest, has renewed calls for a new global framework of financial regulation, but it has also shown that "financial rectitude should be a mean to an end, not an end in itself". Economic and financial concerns cannot prevail over the ideas and values that Europe has been spreading all over the world since its origins. But the current reality makes this task more complex than then, because of emergence of economic multipolarisms, with no country in a dominant position.

No country is an island and multilateral political cooperation is fundamental to shift the focus of adjustment reforms from state macroeconomics to the primary social well-being of the individual.

References

Adams J (1776) Thoughts on government. April 1776, 4:86–93

Fischer-Lescano A (2014) Human rights in terms of austerity policies. The EU institutions and the conclusion of memoranda of understanding. Centre of European Law and Politics, University of Bremen

Ibhawoh B (1999) Structural adjustment, authoritarianism and human rights in Africa. Comp Stud S Asia Af Middle East XIX(1)

John Ikenberry G (2007) The political origins of Bretton Woods. In: Bordo MD, Eichegreen B (eds) A retrospective on the Bretton Woods system: lessons for international monetary reform. University of Chicago Press, pp 155–198

Ruggie JG (1982) International regimes, transactions, and change: embedded liberalism in post war economic order. Int Organ 36(2):379–415

Türk D (1992) The realization of economic, social and cultural rights. Final Report of the Special Rapporteur, Sub-Commission on Prevention of Discrimination and Protection of Minorities, UN DOC para 40 (3 July 1992)

Accountability and Transparency in Bretton Woods Institution. Two Concrete Experiences

Monica Frassoni

Abstract The Bretton Woods Institutions hold persistent questions about accountability and transparency. The former is undermined by the lack of clear mechanisms overseeing the implementation of policies and programs; the latter has not met a real interest of decision-makers yet. The experience in the parliamentary network of the World Bank (PNOWB) reinforced my conviction that the importance of an effective public control over international financial institutions is not fully recognized among MPs and MEPs. The Greek crisis highlighted the European resistance in establishing common means of debt mutualization, which has triggered the intervention of the IMF in a strictly EU crisis. The austerity measures implemented were clearly unfit to solve the country's imbalances, and the only result has been the suffering of the Greek population, as acknowledged by the IMF itself.

"Accountability" is the obligation or willingness to accept responsibility or to account for one's actions. Transparency is the quality of "being easily seen through" and, in governance, is when actions of an organization are "scrupulous enough to bear public scrutiny."[1]

Is it at all possible to rate "accountability" and "transparency" in the Bretton Woods institutions? And accountability and transparency in relation to whom? Governments and public opinion of course. Here is where problems start. Apart from the fact that (unfortunately) we do not have a "global" representation of public opinion, some governments are more influential than others on the way the WB and the IMF enforce their tasks and determine the priorities of their actions. For example, as a commentator put it, even if the recent reform of the IMF and WB is symbolically important, in reality it made China and not the Global South emerge and the system was reorganized according to a "US perspective."[2]

[1] http://whatis.techtarget.com/definition/transparency.

[2] http://www.brettonwoodsproject.org/2016/04/what-is-left-of-the-rise-of-the-south-sceptical-prospects-for-multipolarity/.

M. Frassoni (✉)
European Green Party, Bruxelles, Belgium
e-mail: monica.frassoni@europeangreens.eu

E. Sciso (ed.), *Accountability, Transparency and Democracy in the Functioning of Bretton Woods Institutions*, DOI 10.1007/978-3-319-57855-2_14

Furthermore, over many years the Bretton Woods institutions, along with their most influential members, have come to develop "ideological bias" that is incredibly resilient to facts; for the IMF, a sort of "populism of budget discipline," as once Mario Monti appropriately called this obsession of seeking to curb indiscriminately public spending and wages as the main conditions to get any assistance. And for the WB, the preference for huge projects, notably in the energy field, without a careful analysis of their impacts on environment and populations, was combined—at least till a few years ago, when things started to change—with little attention given to governance or corruption issues.

Both these elements strongly undermine the possibility of being really accountable toward the international community at large and toward those exposed to those "actions," also because there is no procedure to determine that mistakes were made and that therefore sanctions or remedies should be applied.

So a fundamental element of "accountability"—to bear the consequences of one's actions—is structurally impossible to realize, as nobody really pays for the mistakes done. As for transparency, over the years a lot of efforts were done by many international institutions, including WB and partly IMF, to become more open, thanks also to the tireless work of activists and campaigners, who often acted despite governments. But there is still a very long way to go, also because many decision-makers do not seem to have a real interest in more transparency and are not convinced that being more open brings much to the efficiency and the credibility of these institutions anyway, maybe because most of the people involved are bankers and economists. This is a pity, a lost occasion of improving their impact and legitimacy; it reminds me of the European Commission, desperate to be loved by European citizens and spending millions in PR campaigns and then incapable to invest and use better and more visibly those competences it already has and which could bring it closer to their heart and minds, like environment, youth, jobs, civic rights or consumers and food issues.

Having said that, I would like to share a few personal experiences and thoughts on some aspects of accountability and transparency in the Bretton Woods institutions.

Let us start with the World Bank.

From 1999 to 2009, I was a Member of the European Parliament and I was asked to join the newly founded parliamentary network on the World Bank (PNOWB). The platform was set up in 2000 by the WB Pan-European dialogue Manager Jean-Christophe Bas and the then MP and current Foreign Minister of the Netherlands Bert Koenders, with the strong support of Jean-François Rischard, then WB Vice President for Europe, and of James Wolfensohn, WB President; its goal was to answer to the increasing pressure to make the Bank more transparent and accountable, by involving a selected number of MPs and MEPs and having them do the work of "checking" the allocations of aid by the Bank and "fostering the oversight role of Parliaments and civil society."[3] Over my years of activity in PNOWB, I had

[3]http://www.parlnet.org/about/mission.

the chance to meet with really outstanding personalities and to understand better the immense amount of work and effort behind development policies, but I also understood that not everybody, even among Members of Parliament, shares the same ideas about the importance of ensuring a proper public control of international financial institutions. Just to make an example, at the end of a very interesting mission in Vietnam, we were only a tiny minority in the MP delegation to consider that issues of governance and democracy should also be a part of WB's agenda and that it was not really normal that we were not allowed to come in contact with some opposition activists in that country or that we were only confronted with the positive sides of the cooperation with the WB.

On the other hand, I noticed that there is a real added value even in the simple exchange between MPs from donors and recipient countries; WB programs are negotiated only with the governments, and it is very difficult for lawmakers to have a real overview and control of measures taken. Still, I also realized that our organization did not have the resources and even the legitimacy for a real "scrutiny" since we were all there on our personal capacity and not in representation of our Assemblies; also, Members had quite different perspectives about what the platform should do; we did have problems of ensuring sufficient financing, and it was difficult for many WB staff to understand exactly what they could share or not share with us on specific programs and projects. It took PNOWB years to be invited to the annual meetings; I understand that the current organization, which now also works with the IMF,[4] is still more of a platform for sharing knowledge among MPs than a real "scrutiny" tool. It is therefore a valuable initiative, but its potential to ensure more "accountability" needs to be further enhanced and combined with other civil society initiatives, if we are to avoid the risk that it becomes a simple PR exercise.

As for the IMF, at the beginning of the Greek drama I was very saddened by the real reason underlying the decision to bring in the IMF: unreadiness to establish common means of debt mutualization and rush to save German and French banks by transforming private debt into public one. In a word, it is total lack of solidarity among Europeans, who "dragged" a reluctant IMF in the management of a strictly European crisis.

I was surprised also because the IMF had proven catastrophic records in the management of restructuring of sovereign debt in several countries, and I could not believe that, instead of facing quickly and together what was a problem of insolvency of a small country, the EU and its member states chose to deliberately push Greece toward the abyss and all of us into a profound uncertainty about virtually everything, from the currency we carry in our pocket to the chances for survival of the whole EU project. After six years, the situation is far from stabilized: Greece is still exposed to the same crazy "austerity" policies, and its debt is rising; the ideological obsession with budget balance and indiscriminate budget cuts as the punitive answer to ill governance is still producing a tragic vicious cycle of more debt, more cuts, more misery, only partially balanced by the vague promise of a

[4] http://www.parlnet.org/.

debt relief in a faraway future; the stubborn refusal to any mutualization of the debt and Germany's broken promises on the realization of a true banking union are undermining the timid attempts to relaunch an investment and a job-creation-oriented economic policy at EU level and to apply a relative flexibility to the outdated Maastricht criteria; the persisting unwillingness of Germany to abide by the rules that forbid both an excessive deficit and excessive budget surpluses[5] is prolonging unhealthy unbalances. Worse, in certain moments, the negative effects of the divergent choices of each creditor were multiplied in a never-ending spiral, with the IMF being opposed to stopping the pressure on pension and wages, the Commission and the Eurogroup refusing any discussion on debt reduction, and the ECB excluding Greece from the quantitative easing.

In a report adopted at the EP, it is recognized that there is a real issue with accountability and democratic legitimacy of the actions of the Troika, the group composed by representatives of IMF, ECB and Commission, which managed concretely the "support" initiatives in Greece, Spain, Ireland and Portugal; the recognition that the Eurogroup (also a non-official organ without any kind of parliamentary control or transparency obligation) was simply approving the proposals of the Troika without much discussion, along with a long list of examples of lack of transparency and sheer errors of evaluation, led the EP to ask for the IMF to be only an "option" in the management of the Eurozone crisis and to the Eurogroup, Commission, and the ECB to change radically their ways, precisely in terms of accountability and transparency.[6] To date, there were only some "cosmetic" changes, after Tsipras' election in Greece. But the key procedures remain pretty much the same, whereas the disagreements among creditors are on the rise.

The IMF thus shares with the Commission, the most important members of the Eurozone (notably Germany and France), and the ECB the full responsibility of this avoidable disaster, which imposes so much human suffering on so many people and is still nowhere near the end.

The interesting thing is that it was the first—and to date the only — institution to officially recognize it.

Already in 2013, the IMF recognized the terrible mistake done when assessing the effects of extremely harsh austerity measures and unrealistic GDP improvements in Greece.[7] It went on with a recent article by Poul Thomsen,[8] pointing to the need of debt relief and the negative effects of unrealistic assumption of debt repayment; it is worth noting of course that Thomsen does not say that he personally was in the IMF driving seat when exactly those mistakes were made.

---

[5]Germany violates systematically EU budget rules which impose member states to running current account surpluses to 6% of GDP. The current account is set to hit 8.5% this year, compared to 8.8% in 2015, according to the European Commission.

[6]http://www.europarl.europa.eu/sides/getDoc.do?pubRef=-//EP//TEXT+REPORT+A7-2014-0149+0+DOC+XML+V0//EN.

https://europeansting.com/2013/06/06/imf-sorry-greece-it-was-a-mistake-of-11-of-your-gdp/.

[7]https://www.theguardian.com/business/2013/jun/05/imf-admit-mistakes-greek-crisis-austerity.

[8]https://blog-imfdirect.imf.org/2016/02/11/greece-toward-a-workable-program/.

Finally, in its recent "Debt sustainability analysis,"[9] the IMF insists that only with massive debt relief that it will be possible to actually come to terms with the Greek drama. The IMF is well aware that if Germany and the Eurozone do not stop this crazy pressure on Greece, we may have to give up on any kind of hope of economic recovery and dangers of another violent crisis cannot be excluded. It is certainly against this backdrop that, just before the recent Debt Sustainability Analysis was released, it appeared that the IMF was considering to go very far in making its point: in a very embarrassing conversation revealed by Wikileaks between the IMF envoy in Greece Delia Velculescu (or Draculescu as the Greek press calls her) and the very same Poul Thomsen, the two were discussing the idea of bringing Greece close to almost bankruptcy again in order to convince its partners to change their ways.[10] In the end it did not happen, and another quite unsatisfactory agreement delaying real decisions was reached last May.[11] But the fact that this conversation ever took place shows clearly the level of almost despair caused by the incapability of all actors involved, including the IMF, to accept accountability for their past tragic mistakes and by their refusal to change direction. We do not know how the story will end. What we know, however, is that we are still a very long way from a system of accountable international institutions, able and willing to take responsibility and to fix their mistakes.

[9] http://www.imf.org/external/pubs/ft/scr/2016/cr16130.pdf.

[10] https://wikileaks.org/imf-internal-20160319/transcript/IMF%20Anticipates%20Greek%20Disaster.pdf.

[11] https://next.ft.com/content/0f432c22-2223-11e6-9d4d-c11776a5124d.

Negotiating the EU's Future: An Italian Perspective

Alessandro Aresu

Abstract This essay offers an Italian perspective on the future of the European Monetary Union amid the severe crisis of the integration project.

The current crisis of integration takes place in an age of unprecedented political volatility in postwar Western politics, while we experience an ambiguous return of the State in global geopolitics.

Since 2010, the European Monetary Union has managed to survive through a process of continuous negotiation between Member States and between the European Commission and Member States. This has led so far to a fragile settlement, where national policies increasingly take account of the negotiation process.

However, our age of negotiation and political volatility can avoid chaos only if we have a frank assessment of how national sovereignty changes and if we acknowledge the double nature (both national and European) of crucial policies. An open and transparent debate on national-European strategic policies, such as the one advanced by the Italian Government in 2015–2016, could offer "confidence building measures" to face the crisis of confidence we still live in.

We live in interesting times for international financial institutions and for the governance of globalization, and the LUISS research on "Transparency and Democracy in the Bretton Woods institutions" rightly focuses our attention on a number of key challenges. I will give my contribution mainly on the EU (particularly the euro area), on the long age of the European crisis, and on Italy's perspective.

First of all, let us consider the length of our crisis. Living through a long crisis, we are forced to rename it "the new normal" and we often find ourselves repeating our analyses. We find ourselves (analysts, scholars, policymakers) trapped in the 1993 movie "Groundhog Day", where Bill Murray lives in a time loop. This is a side effect of the politics of muddling through. For instance, we point at the "end of the tunnel" and then we wake up 2 or 3 years after that, and we are still waiting for

His views are strictly personal and do not reflect the opinion of the aforementioned institutions.

A. Aresu (✉)
Italian Ministry of Economics and Finance, Rome, Italy
e-mail: alessandro.aresu@tesoro.it

E. Sciso (ed.), *Accountability, Transparency and Democracy in the Functioning of Bretton Woods Institutions*, DOI 10.1007/978-3-319-57855-2_15

the end of the tunnel, while the crisis has transformed itself into a social crisis and Schengen is at stake.

In 2014, Loukas Tsoukalis wrote: *"Everybody talks about the crisis in Europe, a crisis that manifests itself in different ways. And now, some are beginning to see the light at the end of the tunnel, grasping with anticipation at the first signs of economic recovery. Others are, however, less sanguine: they fear that recovery looks modest and fragile at best, that it is uneven, and that big problems remain unresolved, reminding us that the crisis runs very deep. It is not just the economy, stupid"*.[1] After 2 years, this could be a comment on today's Europe. 2016 seems to be a daunting year for Europe, if we look at the development of the migration crisis, the risk of dismantling Schengen, but also at recent turmoil in international markets and at the slowdown in international trade. The combination of Mediterranean turmoil and of what we can call a "tradeless recovery" is particularly worrying for Italy and for Europe. Institutionally, Europe seems to be in waiting. Waiting for what? Waiting for 2017, widely considered an electoral year in major countries. We will certainly have elections in France and Germany in 2017, but terrorist attacks within Europe, the impact of an escalating migrant crisis, the anticipation to 2016 of the British referendum on EU membership, after German regional elections, could force the EU and Member States to wait less than expected. While we wait, two points are worth reminding:

a) We live in an age of political volatility, where extreme and radical scenarios are likely, where mainstream parties can actually get to single digits or even die, and new competitors within the political market can emerge, trying to forge a new consensus. However, political volatility applies also to them[2];
b) We live in the age of the ambiguous "return of the State".[3] Reality did not follow many prescriptions and forecasts of the 1990s, which imagined the end of the nation-State and the triumph of international governance, embodied by international organizations, international corporations and NGOs. No more than a brief glance at European politics is needed to concur with the economist Dani Rodrik: *"The nation-state refuses to wither away. It has proved remarkably resilient, and remains the main factor in the global distribution of income, the primary locus of market-supporting institutions, and the chief repository of personal attachments and affiliations"*.[4]

In this context, in order to have an honest debate about the present and the future of European Monetary Union, we should consider ends and means.

[1]Tsoukalis (2014), p. 17 (at http://www.policy-network.net/publications/4602/The-Unhappy-State-of-the-Union).

[2]For previous definitions of political volatility, see Aresu (2012), http://www.limesonline.com/volatile-ma-pianificata-il-paradosso-della-politica-europea/35576 at; Id., "The growth of Euroscepticism, the recovery of nationalism and the risk of fragmentation of the Member States", N&K – *Rapporto Nomisma 2013-2014 sulle prospettive economico-strategiche*, Nomisma, 2014.

[3]See Grewal (2010), pp. 38–43.

[4]Rodrik (2012).

First, ends: what is the goal of EMU? According to the so-called Five Presidents' Report, *"a complete EMU is not an end in itself. It is a means to create a better and fairer life for all citizens, to prepare the Union for future global challenges and to enable each of its members to prosper"*. Well, to be honest, this has not been the EMU's goal during the last years. The EMU's immediate goal was rather: *responding to crises*. We thought in a crisis mode, we worked in a crisis mode, we told ourselves "never waste a crisis" or "crises are opportunities", but these sentences are often pointless compared to gloomy realities, particularly compared to youth unemployment in a number of Member States. Therefore, we need both more humility and more honesty. Our ultimate end has been survival: the survival of EMU, the survival of the euro (of course, *"whatever it takes"*).

Second, let us consider means. How did we manage to survive? The key feature of both the EMU and the EU has been one word, "negotiating". The modus vivendi of the EU, in its intergovernmental incarnation, with the key role of both the European Council and the Eurogroup, has been a continuous negotiation. Of course, this applies to a wide range of policy issues within the EU (just consider fiscal policy and state aid), but we should also take politics into account. According to Evangelos Venizelos, Greece's former Deputy Prime Minister and Minister of Foreign Affairs (and a victim of what I called "political volatility"), *"the EU, both as a function (that is, as a day-to-day state of affairs), and as an integration project (namely as a strategic dynamic) is a continuous negotiation. It is not a negotiation based on the deontology of the founding treaties, but a harshly trans-national (intergovernmental) negotiation. (...) On the opposite side of a member state's argument that 'my people have spoken'—when national elections have taken place—there is always the counterargument for the will of the people of any other member state, as expressed or is about to be expressed through elections. Moreover, this is how we are seeking, supposedly, for the people of Europe, the European demos"*.[5] So, we live both in an age of negotiation and in an age of political volatility. This is a particularly challenging environment for national politics, where national politicians think "I want to find a space where I can decide without negotiating anything" (the issue of sovereignty becomes increasingly important[6]) and at the same time they should be able to participate in a negotiation with other elected governments throughout Europe. Furthermore, there is not always a political grand bargain able to cover all issues, because countries negotiate on different dossiers.

Let us try to consider democracy and transparency in this environment. What is transparency in a negotiation, in the age of social media? During the July 2015 negotiations on Greece, the Slovak Minister of Finance and Deputy Prime Minister,

[5] Venizelos (2016), pp. 12–13. On the idea of Europe-negotiation, see also Aresu (2015).

[6] Including misunderstandings between "declared sovereignty" and "real sovereignty". See Stephens (2016), at http://www.ft.com/cms/s/2/26b6a12c-daf2-11e5-a72f-1e7744c66818.html?ftcamp=social/free_to_read/brexit_sovereignty_comment/awareness/editorial&segid=0100320#axzz41gTZU3RK.

Peter Kažimír, tweeted: "Following latest developments, listening to #Greece govt officials one can wonder how quickly can caterpillar turn into butterfly #Eurozone" (10 July 2015). This outraged the Greek government, among others and, of course, when you have a public debate on the future of the EMU split between insulting a Member State and exposing a coup d'état, finding a modus vivendi is quite difficult. I think we should be able to think about transparency in a different way, particularly on the relationship between Member States and the European Commission and on relevant issues for a EU-wide public debate.

In this respect, the Italian case could be of some interest. Take the 2015 Budget Law. The Italian Ministry of Economy and Finance sent Italy's Draft Budgetary Plan to the European Commission on 15 October 2014. In a 22 October letter, Vice-President Katainen wrote Minister Padoan, emphasizing the sensitive issue of debt. In his reply, Minister Padoan conceded a series of additional measures, but he also emphasized the "growth-friendly fiscal adjustment" strategy of the government, where the budget supports the structural reform process. Structural reforms were at the core of other official communications and they played a crucial role on the EC's Communication on flexibility of 13 January 2015.[7] Reforms are not just numbers: they require more political awareness and more political accountability than the simple respect of rules. Structural reforms are about changing a system through political decision-making: they are part of the political debate, they are discussed (and, of course, criticized) within parties, in Parliament and in the media. Of course, we often talk about technical issues, but they also have to do with the state of democracy in Europe. It is difficult to imagine that the vast majority of citizens will get passionate about the output gap, but even on this issue Italy's action, starting from Minister Padoan's letter of October 22nd to Vice President Jyrki Katainen, has been key to gain support from other finance ministers throughout the euro area (Lavia, Lithuania, Luxembourg, Portugal, Slovenia, Slovakia, Spain).

On February 22, 2016, the Italian government presented an official contribution to the European debate, the document "A Shared European Policy Strategy for Growth, Jobs, and Stability".[8] The aim of the Italian government, building on previous proposals advanced by Minister Padoan,[9] was to assess the challenges and opportunities for the European project (including "*new formidable systemic challenges represented by the influx of migrants and asylum seekers*") in a comprehensive way, putting also more emphasis on tools such as a common unemployment benefit and a mutualized funding mechanism to finance a shared management of the EU external frontiers. The document also calls for a "*politically endowed*" Eurozone Finance Minister to manage these functions, with an adequate Eurozone

[7]Making the best use of the flexibility within the existing rules of the stability and growth pact, 13/1/2015, available at http://ec.europa.eu/economy_finance/economic_governance/sgp/pdf/2015-01-13_communication_sgp_flexibility_guidelines_en.pdf.

[8]http://www.governo.it/sites/governo.it/files/ASharedPolicyStrategy_20160222.pdf.

[9]See for instance Padoan (2015), at http://www.mef.gov.it/inevidenza/documenti/Luxembourg_lecture_int.pdf.

budget. In a nutshell, Italy tried to offer a policy agenda for the medium-term, but also concrete proposals to be discussed in the short term. I believe more of these contributions need to be at the common table, in order to foster transparency and democracy in Europe. We should not think of these documents as "weapons" against one government or the other: they should rather be "confidence building measures" because, in a crisis of confidence, it is key to have a debate about real issues and not a debate about mutual prejudices.

Our age of negotiation and political volatility can avoid chaos only if we have a frank assessment of how national sovereignty changes, too. Italy recently had a debate on national interest and assertiveness at the EU level, trying to reassess its self-made theory of external constraint ("vincolo esterno").[10] In 1998, Alberto Predieri[11] analyzed the changing role of the State in Europe and in Italy through four keywords: *losing, transfering, negotiating, networking*.

First, losing is not disappearing. If the rumours on the death of the State are premature (yes, they are), the answer in our system cannot be autarchy. If we pursue the illusion of autarchy, we are bound to face harsher conditionality.

Second, the State transfers, which is different from losing, because it is a transition to another settlement that we need to manage, in which you have to be a real player. In order to do so, you have to negotiate.

Third, when we consider Europe as a negotiation, it means that your reputation matters, your credibility matters, your system of alliances matters, your hierarchy of interests matters.

Fourth, you will be a real player in this negotiation through networking. Networking is proving, in policy and politics, the coordination between national interests and the global context. Of course, cohesion is strictly related with this this process: consider for instance the relevance of public administration and State capacity at all levels in order to make cohesion work, and more generally to make "national-European" policies work. A proper "Investment Union" requires the capacity to present, implement and deliver projects: this is the challenge of the so-called Juncker Plan and of future projects on migration. No, it is not simply about pouring more money into them, considering that, as Nino Andreatta said, *"La Pira's multipliers of bread and fish actually don't multiply anything anymore"*.[12] The key challenge concerns new networks of public policy. Other examples of the new "network" of responsibilities within the euro area are supervision between the ECB and national central banks, the role of national courts in the EU system and—in the present and in the future—shared institutions for defense, science and research (for instance, a European DARPA).

---

[10]See Dyson and Featherstone (1996), pp. 272–299; Aresu (2016), at http://www.ilfoglio.it/economia/2016/01/26/il-vincolo-esterno-come-unico-argine-al-peggio-degli-italiani-produce-deresponsabilizzazione___1-v-137469-rubriche_c532.htm.

[11]Predieri (1998).

[12]"Andreatta politico", *La Rivista dell'AREL*, 3-2015/1-2016: 70.

"You don't fall in love with an internal market", Jacques Delors famously said.[13] But to foster democracy, transparency and accountability we should fall in love, at least a little bit, with the four-legged process described by Predieri. It could be more satisfactory than shouting "Give us back our sovereignty" or whispering "Crises are opportunities". Therefore, our task is to imagine "Italy in, with and for Europe", to imagine our countries in, with, and for Europe and talk frankly, honestly, but also passionately about this process, following Helmut Schmidt's lead in his 2011 speech at the SPD party conference in Berlin.[14] In this task, we need the contribution of the various institutions of European democracy (such as universities, research centers, Parliaments and political parties), starting from the euro area. Without it, I am sure Europe's Groundhog Day will go on indefinitely.

References

Aresu A (2012) Volatile ma pianificata: il paradosso della politica europea. Limesonline, 5/6/2012

Aresu A (2015) L'Italia si salva se si sveglia dal sonno post-sovranista. Limes 7/2015

Aresu A (2016) Il vincolo interno come unico argine al peggio degli italiani? Produce deresponsabilizzazione. Il Foglio, 26/1/2016

Dyson K, Featherstone K (1996) Italy and EMU as a 'Vincolo Esterno': empowering the technocrats, transforming the state. S Eur Soc Polit 1(2):272–299

Grewal DS (2010) The return of the state. Harv Int Rev 31:38–43

Lamy P (2015) After Paris November 13: more geopolitics than geoeconomics. Lecture at Scuola di Politiche, Rome, 25/11/2015

Padoan PC (2015) Making progress in economic and monetary union. University of Luxembourg, 6/10/2015

Predieri A (1998) Euro. Poliarchie democratiche e mercati monetari. Giappichelli, Torino

Rodrik D (2012) Who needs the nation state? Association of American Geographers, 25/02/2012

Stephens P (2016) Boris Johnson is wrong. Parliament has the ultimate authority. Financial Times, 25/2/2016

Tsoukalis L (2014) The unhappy state of the union. Policy Network, 21/3/2014, p 17

Venizelos E (2016) State Transformation and the European Integration Project. Lessons from the financial crisis and the Greek paradigm. CEPS No. 130/February 2016, pp 12–13

[13] See Lamy (2015), available at http://www.scuoladipolitiche.eu/after-paris-november-13-more-geopolitics-than-geoeconomics/.

[14] See H. Schmidt, "Germany in and with Europe", Friedrich Ebert Stiftung, at http://library.fes.de/pdf-files/id/ipa/08888.pdf.

FSC www.fsc.org

MIX
Papier aus verantwortungsvollen Quellen
Paper from responsible sources
FSC® C105338

If you have any concerns about our products,
you can contact us on
ProductSafety@springernature.com

In case Publisher is established outside the EU,
the EU authorized representative is:
Springer Nature Customer Service Center GmbH
Europaplatz 3, 69115 Heidelberg, Germany

Printed by Libri Plureos GmbH
in Hamburg, Germany